DAILY LIGHT
on the
DAILY PATH

Compiled by the
Samuel
BAGSTER
family

WHITAKER
HOUSE

DAILY LIGHT ON THE DAILY PATH

ISBN-13: 978-0-88368-556-3
ISBN-10: 0-88368-556-6
Printed in the United States of America
© 1999 by Whitaker House

Whitaker House
1030 Hunt Valley Circle
New Kensington, PA 15068
www.whitakerhouse.com

Library of Congress Cataloging-in-Publication Data

Bible. English. New King James. Selections. 1999.
    Daily light on the daily path / prepared by Jonathan Bagster and other members of his family.
        p.   cm.
    ISBN 0-88368-556-6
    1. Devotional calendars. I. Bagster, Jonathan, 1813–1872. II. Title.
BS390.B2   1999
242'.2—dc21
                                99-34809

4 5 6 7 8 9 10 11 12 **w** 17 16 15 14 13 12 11

Introduction

Daily Light on the Daily Path is one of the most beloved classic devotionals of all time. It was prepared by Jonathan Bagster and other members of his family, who were descendants of noted London bookseller Samuel Bagster. The patriarch of the family, Samuel Bagster established a strong tradition of daily family Bible reading and meditation on the Scriptures. His descendants drew from the well of this heritage as they compiled this devotional for the benefit of other believers. A timeless volume, *Daily Light on the Daily Path* is the fruit of the devotions of this devout Christian family.

One of the unique features of this devotional is the order and presentation of the Scripture verses. Each reading is designed around a central biblical theme and includes verses specifically chosen to give you insight into the theme as you read, meditate on, and apply the Scriptures to your life. Sometimes this means that a later verse of a chapter will precede an earlier verse of the same chapter. This is intentional; the verses have been arranged in this way in order to bring out the progression of thought and the themes that the Bagsters wanted to emphasize.

A helpful feature of this new edition of *Daily Light on the Daily Path* is that the Scripture citations follow immediately after each verse or verses, for easy reference, instead of being listed at the bottom of the page. The Scriptures have also been put into the *New King James Version* for clarity for today's reader. The theme Scripture for each reading is in italics at the beginning of the reading, and the verses that follow it relate to this general theme.

Daily Light on the Daily Path can be used year after year. Since the Scriptures are always fresh, and our life circumstances are always changing, you will continually gain new insights, and the breadth of your understanding of the Scriptures will deepen each year as you read the daily selections.

This devotional is also ideal for meditating on the Scriptures. Psalm 1:2 shows us how we are to relate to the Word of God in our everyday lives: *"His delight is in the law of the LORD, and in His law he meditates day and night."* Joshua 1:8 reinforces this theme:

This Book of the Law shall not depart from your mouth, but you shall meditate in it day and night, that you may observe to do according to all that is written in it. For then you will make your way prosperous, and then you will have good success.

Meditating on the Word of God—deeply pondering its meaning over a period of time and absorbing its truths into one's inner being—has almost become a lost art in our day. We often read a portion of Scripture, answer a few questions about it, and move on to something else. We may read a longer passage in context or just read unconnected verses in a haphazard way. In *Daily Light on the Daily Path*, each Scripture was chosen with great care by the Bagster family to give the greatest spiritual insight and to inspire the greatest devotion to God. As you read the selections, you will see connections between Scriptures and themes from various books of the Bible, both Old Testament and New. This will help you to reflect on biblical truths in the context of the entire Scriptures and to see associations you may not have noticed before. A deeper and broader scope of the Scriptures will open up to you. Through the juxtaposition of the verses, you will see the Bible's themes, promises, and purposes as a whole and not as isolated pieces. You will see the nature of God, His great love for mankind, His unfolding plan for humanity, His way of salvation, and our future hope, with new and enriching insights. Most of all, you will reach out to God in true worship and gratitude as you are refreshed and taught by His Word.

May you be blessed daily as the Word of God permeates and transforms your life, bringing salvation, faith, hope, love, healing, wisdom, and an ever-deepening personal knowledge of God the Father and our Savior Jesus Christ through the ministry of the Holy Spirit.

JANUARY

January 1

Morning Reading

One thing I do, forgetting those things which are behind...I press toward the goal for the prize of the upward call of God in Christ Jesus.
PHILIPPIANS 3:13–14

Father, I desire that they also whom You gave Me may be with Me where I am, that they may behold My glory which You have given Me. JOHN 17:24 • I know whom I have believed and am persuaded that He is able to keep what I have committed to Him until that Day. 2 TIMOTHY 1:12 • He who has begun a good work in you will complete it until the day of Jesus Christ. PHILIPPIANS 1:6 •

Do you not know that those who run in a race all run, but one receives the prize? Run in such a way that you may obtain it. And everyone who competes for the prize is temperate in all things. Now they do it to obtain a perishable crown, but we for an imperishable crown. 1 CORINTHIANS 9:24–25 • Therefore we also, since we are surrounded by so great a cloud of witnesses, let us lay aside every weight, and the sin which so easily ensnares us, and let us run with endurance the race that is set before us, looking unto Jesus. HEBREWS 12:1–2 •

Evening Reading

The Lord, He is the one who goes before you.
He will be with you, He will not leave you nor forsake you.
DEUTERONOMY 31:8

If Your Presence does not go with us, do not bring us up from here. EXODUS 33:15 • O LORD, I know the way of man is not in himself; it is not in man who walks to direct his own steps. JEREMIAH 10:23 •

The steps of a good man are ordered by the LORD, and He delights in his way. Though he fall, he shall not be utterly cast down; for the LORD upholds him with His hand. PSALM 37:23–24 •

I am continually with You; You hold me by my right hand. You will guide me with Your counsel, and afterward receive me to glory. PSALM 73:23–24 • For I am persuaded that neither death nor life, nor angels nor principalities nor powers, nor things present nor things to come, nor height nor depth, nor any other created thing, shall be able to separate us from the love of God which is in Christ Jesus our Lord. ROMANS 8:38–39 •

January 2

Morning Reading

Sing to the Lord a new song.
ISAIAH 42:10

Sing aloud to God our strength; make a joyful shout to the God of Jacob. Raise a song and strike the timbrel, the pleasant harp with the lute. PSALM 81:1–2 • He has put a new song in my mouth; praise to our God; many will see it and fear, and will trust in the LORD. PSALM 40:3 •

Be strong and of good courage; do not be afraid, nor be dismayed, for the LORD your God is with you wherever you go. JOSHUA 1:9 • The joy of the LORD is your strength. NEHEMIAH 8:10 • Paul...thanked God and took courage. ACTS 28:15 •

Knowing the time, that now it is high time to awake out of sleep; for now our salvation is nearer than when we first believed. The night is far spent, the day is at hand. Therefore let us cast off the works of darkness, and let us put on the armor of light. Let us walk properly, as in the day, not in revelry and drunkenness, not in lewdness and lust, not in strife and envy. But put on the Lord Jesus Christ, and make no provision for the flesh, to fulfill its lusts. ROMANS 13:11–14 •

Evening Reading

Let my prayer be set before You as incense,
the lifting up of my hands as the evening sacrifice.
PSALM 141:2

You shall make an altar to burn incense on....And you shall put it before the veil that is before the ark of the Testimony, before the mercy seat that is over the Testimony, where I will meet with you. Aaron shall burn on it sweet incense every morning....And when Aaron lights the lamps at twilight, he shall burn incense on it, a perpetual incense before the LORD throughout your generations. EXODUS 30:1, 6–8 •

[Jesus] is also able to save to the uttermost those who come to God through Him, since He always lives to make intercession for them. HEBREWS 7:25 • The smoke of the incense, with the prayers of the saints, ascended before God from the angel's hand. REVELATION 8:4 •

You also, as living stones, are being built up a spiritual house, a holy priesthood, to offer up spiritual sacrifices acceptable to God through Jesus Christ. 1 PETER 2:5 •

Pray without ceasing. 1 THESSALONIANS 5:17 •

January 3

Morning Reading

He led them forth by the right way.
PSALM 107:7

He found [Jacob] in a desert land and in the wasteland, a howling wilderness; He encircled him, He instructed him, He kept him as the apple of His eye. As an eagle stirs up its nest, hovers over its young, spreading out its wings, taking them up, carrying them on its wings, so the LORD alone led him. DEUTERONOMY 32:10–12 • Even to your old age, I am He, and even to gray hairs I will carry you! I have made, and I will bear; even I will carry, and will deliver you. ISAIAH 46:4 •

He restores my soul; He leads me in the paths of righteousness for His name's sake. Yea, though I walk through the valley of the shadow of death, I will fear no evil; for You are with me; Your rod and Your staff, they comfort me. PSALM 23:3–4 •

The LORD will guide you continually, and satisfy your soul in drought, and strengthen your bones; you shall be like a watered garden, and like a spring of water, whose waters do not fail. ISAIAH 58:11 & For this is God, our God forever and ever; He will be our guide even to death. PSALM 48:14 • Who teaches like Him? JOB 36:22 •

Evening Reading

[Jesus asked,] *"What do you want Me to do for you?"*
He said, "Lord, that I may receive my sight."
LUKE 18:41

Open my eyes, that I may see wondrous things from Your law. PSALM 119:18 •

And He opened their understanding, that they might comprehend the Scriptures. LUKE 24:45 • The Helper, the Holy Spirit, whom the Father will send in My name, He will teach you all things. JOHN 14:26 • Every good gift and every perfect gift is from above, and comes down from the Father of lights. JAMES 1:17 •

[May] the God of our Lord Jesus Christ, the Father of glory...give to you the spirit of wisdom and revelation in the knowledge of Him, the eyes of your understanding being enlightened; that you may know what is the hope of His calling, what are the riches of the glory of His inheritance in the saints, and what is the exceeding greatness of His power toward us who believe, according to the working of His mighty power. EPHESIANS 1:17–19 •

January 4

Morning Reading

For as yet you have not come to the rest and the inheritance which the
Lord your God is giving you.
DEUTERONOMY 12:9

This is not your rest. MICAH 2:10 • There remains therefore a rest for the people of God. HEBREWS 4:9 • This hope we have as an anchor of the soul, both sure and steadfast, and which enters the Presence behind the veil, where the forerunner has entered for us, even Jesus. HEBREWS 6:19–20 •

In My Father's house are many mansions; if it were not so, I would have told you. I go to prepare a place for you. And if I go and prepare a place for you, I will come again and receive you to Myself; that where I am, there you may be also. JOHN 14:2–3 • With Christ, which is far better. PHILIPPIANS 1:23 •

God will wipe away every tear from their eyes; there shall be no more death, nor sorrow, nor crying. There shall be no more pain, for the former things have passed away. REVELATION 21:4 • There the wicked cease from troubling, and there the weary are at rest. JOB 3:17 •

Lay up for yourselves treasures in heaven,...for where your treasure is, there your heart will be also. MATTHEW 6:20–21 • Set your mind on things above, not on things on the earth. COLOSSIANS 3:2 •

Evening Reading

Death, where is your sting?
O Hades, where is your victory?
1 CORINTHIANS 15:55

The sting of death is sin. 1 CORINTHIANS 15:56 • But now, once at the end of the ages, He has appeared to put away sin by the sacrifice of Himself. And as it is appointed for men to die once, but after this the judgment, so Christ was offered once to bear the sins of many. To those who eagerly wait for Him He will appear a second time, apart from sin, for salvation. HEBREWS 9:26–28 •

Inasmuch then as the children have partaken of flesh and blood, He Himself likewise shared in the same, that through death He might destroy him who had the power of death, that is, the devil, and release those who through fear of death were all their lifetime subject to bondage. HEBREWS 2:14–15 •

I am already being poured out as a drink offering, and the time of my departure is at hand. I have fought the good fight, I have finished the race, I have kept the faith. Finally, there is laid up for me the crown of righteousness. 2 TIMOTHY 4:6–8 •

January 5

Morning Reading

For we who have believed do enter that rest.
HEBREWS 4:3

They weary themselves to commit iniquity. JEREMIAH 9:5 10 • I see another law in my members, warring against the law of my mind, and bringing me into captivity to the law of sin which is in my members. O wretched man that I am! Who will deliver me from this body of death? ROMANS 7:23–24 •

Come to Me, all you who labor and are heavy laden, and I will give you rest. MATTHEW 11:28 • Having been justified by faith, we have peace with God through our Lord Jesus Christ, through whom also we have access by faith into this grace in which we stand, and rejoice in hope of the glory of God. ROMANS 5:1–2 •

For he who has entered His rest has himself also ceased from his works. HEBREWS 4:10 • Not having my own righteousness, which is from the law, but that which is through faith in Christ, the righteousness which is from God by faith. PHILIPPIANS 3:9 • This is the rest with which you may cause the weary to rest....This is the refreshing. ISAIAH 28:12 •

Evening Reading

Set a guard, O Lord, over my mouth;
keep watch over the door of my lips.
PSALM 141:3

If You, LORD, should mark iniquities, O Lord, who could stand? PSALM 130:3 • They rebelled against His Spirit, so that [Moses] spoke rashly with his lips. PSALM 106:33 •

Not what goes into the mouth defiles a man; but what comes out of the mouth, this defiles a man. MATTHEW 15:11 •

A whisperer separates the best of friends. PROVERBS 16:28 • There is one who speaks like the piercings of a sword, but the tongue of the wise promotes health. The truthful lip shall be established forever, but a lying tongue is but for a moment. PROVERBS 12:18–19 • No man can tame the tongue. It is an unruly evil, full of deadly poison. JAMES 3:8 • Out of the same mouth proceed blessing and cursing. My brethren, these things ought not to be so. JAMES 3:10 •

Put off all these: anger, wrath, malice, blasphemy, filthy language out of your mouth. Do not lie to one another, since you have put off the old man with his deeds. COLOSSIANS 3:8–9 • This is the will of God, [even] your sanctification. 1 THESSALONIANS 4:3 • In their mouth was found no deceit. REVELATION 14:5 •

January 6

Let the beauty of the Lord our God be upon us,
and establish the work of our hands.
PSALM 90:17

"Your fame went out among the nations because of your beauty, for it was perfect through My splendor which I had bestowed on you," says the Lord GOD. EZEKIEL 16:14 • We all, with unveiled face, beholding as in a mirror the glory of the Lord, are being transformed into the same image from glory to glory, just as by the Spirit of the Lord. 2 CORINTHIANS 3:18 • The Spirit of glory and of God rests upon you. 1 PETER 4:14 •

Blessed is every one who fears the LORD, who walks in His ways. When you eat the labor of your hands, you shall be happy, and it shall be well with you. PSALM 128:1–2 • Commit your works to the LORD, and your thoughts will be established. PROVERBS 16:3 •

Work out your own salvation with fear and trembling; for it is God who works in you both to will and to do for His good pleasure. PHILIPPIANS 2:12–13 • May our Lord Jesus Christ Himself, and our God and Father, who has loved us and given us everlasting consolation and good hope by grace, comfort your hearts and establish you in every good word and work. 2 THESSALONIANS 2:16–17 •

Evening Reading

The apostles gathered to Jesus and told Him all things,
both what they had done and what they had taught.
MARK 6:30

There is a friend who sticks closer than a brother. PROVERBS 18:24 • The LORD spoke to Moses face to face, as a man speaks to his friend. EXODUS 33:11 • You are My friends if you do whatever I command you. No longer do I call you servants, for a servant does not know what his master is doing; but I have called you friends, for all things that I heard from My Father I have made known to you. JOHN 15:14–15 •

When you have done all those things which you are commanded, say, "We are unprofitable servants. We have done what was our duty to do." LUKE 17:10 •

You did not receive the spirit of bondage again to fear, but you received the Spirit of adoption by whom we cry out, "Abba, Father." ROMANS 8:15 •

By prayer and supplication, with thanksgiving, let your requests be made known to God. PHILIPPIANS 4:6 • The prayer of the upright is His delight. PROVERBS 15:8 •

January 7

Morning Reading

Remember me, my God, for good.
NEHEMIAH 5:19

Thus says the LORD: "I remember you, the kindness of your youth, the love of your betrothal, when you went after Me in the wilderness." JEREMIAH 2:2 • I will remember My covenant with you in the days of your youth, and I will establish an everlasting covenant with you. EZEKIEL 16:60 • I will visit you and perform My good word toward you....For I know the thoughts that I think toward you, says the LORD, thoughts of peace and not of evil, to give you a future and a hope. JEREMIAH 29:10–11 •

As the heavens are higher than the earth, so are My ways higher than your ways, and My thoughts than your thoughts. ISAIAH 55:9 • I would seek God, and to God I would commit my cause; who does great things, and unsearchable, marvelous things without number. JOB 5:8–9 • Many, O LORD my God, are Your wonderful works which You have done; and Your thoughts toward us cannot be recounted to You in order; if I would declare and speak of them, they are more than can be numbered. PSALM 40:5 •

Evening Reading

I will not leave you nor forsake you.
JOSHUA 1:5

Not a word failed of any good thing which the LORD had spoken to the house of Israel. All came to pass. JOSHUA 21:45 • God is not a man, that He should lie, nor a son of man, that He should repent. Has He said, and will He not do? Or has He spoken, and will He not make it good? NUMBERS 23:19 •

The LORD your God, He is God, the faithful God who keeps covenant and mercy for a thousand generations with those who love Him and keep His commandments. DEUTERONOMY 7:9 • He will ever be mindful of His covenant. PSALM 111:5 •

Can a woman forget her nursing child, and not have compassion on the son of her womb? Surely they may forget, yet I will not forget you. See, I have inscribed you on the palms of My hands; your walls are continually before Me. ISAIAH 49:15–16 •

The LORD your God in your midst, the Mighty One, will save; He will rejoice over you with gladness, He will quiet you with His love, He will rejoice over you with singing. ZEPHANIAH 3:17 •

Daily Light on the Daily Path

January 8

Morning Reading

Those who know Your name will put their trust in You; for You, LORD, have not forsaken those who seek You.
PSALM 9:10

The name of the LORD is a strong tower; the righteous run to it and are safe. PROVERBS 18:10 • I will trust and not be afraid; "for YAH, the LORD, is my strength and song; He also has become my salvation." ISAIAH 12:2 •

I have been young, and now am old; yet I have not seen the righteous forsaken, nor his descendants begging bread....For the LORD loves justice, and does not forsake His saints; they are preserved forever, but the descendants of the wicked shall be cut off. PSALM 37:25, 28 • The LORD will not forsake His people, for His great name's sake, because it has pleased the LORD to make you His people. 1 SAMUEL 12:22 • Who delivered us from so great a death, and does deliver us; in whom we trust that He will still deliver us. 2 CORINTHIANS 1:10 •

Be content with such things as you have. For He Himself has said, "I will never leave you nor forsake you." So we may boldly say: "The LORD is my helper; I will not fear. What can man do to me?" HEBREWS 13:5–6 •

Evening Reading

They are without fault before the throne of God.
REVELATION 14:5

The iniquity of Israel shall be sought, but there shall be none; and the sins of Judah, but they shall not be found; for I will pardon those whom I preserve. JEREMIAH 50:20 • Who is a God like You, pardoning iniquity and passing over the transgression of the remnant of His heritage? He does not retain His anger forever, because He delights in mercy. He will again have compassion on us, and will subdue our iniquities. You will cast all our sins into the depths of the sea. MICAH 7:18–19 •

He has made us accepted in the Beloved. EPHESIANS 1:6 • To present you holy, and blameless, and above reproach in His sight. COLOSSIANS 1:22 •

Now to Him who is able to keep you from stumbling, and to present you faultless before the presence of His glory with exceeding joy, to God our Savior, who alone is wise, be glory and majesty, dominion and power, both now and forever. Amen. JUDE 24–25 •

January 9

Morning Reading

You have given a banner to those who fear You,
that it may be displayed because of the truth.
PSALM 60:4

The-LORD-Is-My-Banner. EXODUS 17:15 • When the enemy comes in like a flood, the Spirit of the LORD will lift up a standard against him. ISAIAH 59:19 •

We will rejoice in your salvation, and in the name of our God we will set up our banners! PSALM 20:5 • The LORD has revealed our righteousness. Come and let us declare in Zion the work of the LORD our God. JEREMIAH 51:10 • We are more than conquerors through Him who loved us. ROMANS 8:37 • Thanks be to God, who gives us the victory through our Lord Jesus Christ. 1 CORINTHIANS 15:57 • The captain of their salvation. HEBREWS 2:10 •

My brethren, be strong in the Lord and in the power of His might. EPHESIANS 6:10 • Valiant for the truth. JEREMIAH 9:3 • Fight the Lord's battles. 1 SAMUEL 18:17 • "Be strong, all you people of the land," says the LORD, "and work....Do not fear!" HAGGAI 2:4–5 • Lift up your eyes and look at the fields, for they are already white for harvest! JOHN 4:35 • Yet a little while, and He who is coming will come and will not tarry. HEBREWS 10:37 •

Evening Reading

One thing is needed.
LUKE 10:42

There are many who say, "Who will show us any good?" LORD, lift up the light of Your countenance upon us. You have put gladness in my heart, more than in the season that their grain and wine increased. PSALM 4:6–7 •

As the deer pants for the water brooks, so pants my soul for You, O God. My soul thirsts for God, for the living God. PSALM 42:1–2 • O God, You are my God; early will I seek You; my soul thirsts for You; my flesh longs for You in a dry and thirsty land where there is no water. PSALM 63:1 •

I am the bread of life. He who comes to Me shall never hunger, and he who believes in Me shall never thirst. JOHN 6:35 • Lord, give us this bread always. JOHN 6:34 • Mary...sat at Jesus' feet and heard His word. LUKE 10:39 • One thing I have desired of the LORD, that will I seek: that I may dwell in the house of the LORD all the days of my life, to behold the beauty of the LORD, and to inquire in His temple. PSALM 27:4 •

January 10

Morning Reading

May your whole spirit, soul, and body be preserved blameless at the coming of our Lord Jesus Christ.
1 THESSALONIANS 5:23

Christ also loved the church and gave Himself for her...that He might present her to Himself a glorious church, not having spot or wrinkle or any such thing, but that she should be holy and without blemish. EPHESIANS 5:25, 27 • Him we preach, warning every man and teaching every man in all wisdom, that we may present every man perfect in Christ Jesus. COLOSSIANS 1:28 •

The peace of God...surpasses all understanding. PHILIPPIANS 4:7 • Let the peace of God rule in your hearts, to which also you were called in one body. COLOSSIANS 3:15 •

May our Lord Jesus Christ Himself, and our God and Father, who has loved us and given us everlasting consolation and good hope by grace, comfort your hearts and establish you in every good word and work. 2 THESSALONIANS 2:16–17 • Who will also confirm you to the end, that you may be blameless in the day of our Lord Jesus Christ. 1 CORINTHIANS 1:8 •

Evening Reading

Will God indeed dwell with men on the earth?
2 CHRONICLES 6:18

Let them make Me a sanctuary, that I may dwell among them. EXODUS 25:8 • I will meet with the children of Israel, and the tabernacle shall be sanctified by My glory....I will dwell among the children of Israel and will be their God. EXODUS 29:43, 45 •

You have ascended on high, You have led captivity captive; You have received gifts among men, even from the rebellious, that the LORD God might dwell there. PSALM 68:18 •

You are the temple of the living God. As God has said: "I will dwell in them and walk among them. I will be their God, and they shall be My people." 2 CORINTHIANS 6:16 • Your body is the temple of the Holy Spirit who is in you. 1 CORINTHIANS 6:19 • You also are being built together for a dwelling place of God in the Spirit. EPHESIANS 2:22 •

The nations also will know that I, the LORD, sanctify Israel, when My sanctuary is in their midst forevermore. EZEKIEL 37:28 •

January 11

Morning Reading

Praise is awaiting You, O God, in Zion.
PSALM 65:1

For us there is one God, the Father, of whom are all things, and we for Him; and one Lord Jesus Christ, through whom are all things, and through whom we live. 1 CORINTHIANS 8:6 • All should honor the Son just as they honor the Father. He who does not honor the Son does not honor the Father who sent Him. JOHN 5:23 • Therefore by Him let us continually offer the sacrifice of praise to God, that is, the fruit of our lips, giving thanks to His name. HEBREWS 13:15 • Whoever offers praise glorifies Me; and to him who orders his conduct aright I will show the salvation of God. PSALM 50:23 •

I looked, and behold, a great multitude which no one could number, of all nations, tribes, peoples, and tongues, standing before the throne and before the Lamb, clothed with white robes, with palm branches in their hands, and crying out with a loud voice, saying, "Salvation belongs to our God who sits on the throne, and to the Lamb!" REVELATION 7:9–10 • "Amen! Blessing and glory and wisdom, thanksgiving and honor and power and might, be to our God forever and ever. Amen." REVELATION 7:12 •

Evening Reading

Who redeems your life from destruction.
PSALM 103:4

Their Redeemer is strong; the LORD of hosts is His name. JEREMIAH 50:34 • I will ransom them from the power of the grave; I will redeem them from death. O Death, I will be your plagues! O Grave, I will be your destruction! HOSEA 13:14 •

Inasmuch then as the children have partaken of flesh and blood, He Himself likewise shared in the same, that through death He might destroy him who had the power of death, that is, the devil, and release those who through fear of death were all their lifetime subject to bondage. HEBREWS 2:14–15 •

He who believes in the Son has everlasting life; and he who does not believe the Son shall not see life, but the wrath of God abides on him. JOHN 3:36 •

For you died, and your life is hidden with Christ in God. When Christ who is our life appears, then you also will appear with Him in glory. COLOSSIANS 3:3–4 • When He comes, in that Day, to be glorified in His saints and to be admired among all those who believe, because our testimony among you was believed. 2 THESSALONIANS 1:10 •

January 12

Morning Reading

To God our Savior, who alone is wise.
JUDE 25

You are in Christ Jesus, who became for us wisdom from God; and righteousness and sanctification and redemption. 1 CORINTHIANS 1:30 • Can you search out the deep things of God? Can you find out the limits of the Almighty? They are higher than heaven; what can you do? Deeper than Sheol; what can you know? JOB 11:7–8 •

But we speak the wisdom of God in a mystery, the hidden wisdom which God ordained before the ages for our glory. 1 CORINTHIANS 2:7 • The mystery, which from the beginning of the ages has been hidden in God who created all things through Jesus Christ; to the intent that now the manifold wisdom of God might be made known by the church to the principalities and powers in the heavenly places. EPHESIANS 3:9–10 •

If any of you lacks wisdom, let him ask of God, who gives to all liberally and without reproach, and it will be given to him. JAMES 1:5 • The wisdom that is from above is first pure, then peaceable, gentle, willing to yield, full of mercy and good fruits, without partiality and without hypocrisy. JAMES 3:17 •

Evening Reading

When shall I arise, and the night be ended?
JOB 7:4

[Someone] calls,..."Watchman, what of the night?" The watchman said, "The morning comes." ISAIAH 21:11–12 •

Yet a little while, and He who is coming will come and will not tarry. HEBREWS 10:37 • He shall be like the light of the morning when the sun rises, a morning without clouds. 2 SAMUEL 23:4 •

I go to prepare a place for you. And if I go and prepare a place for you, I will come again and receive you to Myself; that where I am, there you may be also....Let not your heart be troubled, neither let it be afraid. You have heard Me say to you, "I am going away and coming back to you." JOHN 14:2–3, 27–28 •

Let all Your enemies perish, O LORD! But let those who love Him be like the sun when it comes out in full strength. JUDGES 5:31 • You are all sons of light and sons of the day. We are not of the night nor of darkness. 1 THESSALONIANS 5:5 •

There shall be no night there. REVELATION 21:25 •

January 13

Morning Reading

You will keep him in perfect peace, whose mind is stayed on You,
because he trusts in You.
ISAIAH 26:3

Cast your burden on the Lord, and He shall sustain you; He shall never permit the righteous to be moved. PSALM 55:22 • I will trust and not be afraid; "for Yah, the Lord, is my strength and song; He also has become my salvation." ISAIAH 12:2 •

Why are you fearful, O you of little faith? MATTHEW 8:26 • Be anxious for nothing, but in everything by prayer and supplication, with thanksgiving, let your requests be made known to God; and the peace of God, which surpasses all understanding, will guard your hearts and minds through Christ Jesus. PHILIPPIANS 4:6–7 • In quietness and confidence shall be your strength. ISAIAH 30:15 •

The effect of righteousness [will be] quietness and assurance forever. ISAIAH 32:17 • Peace I leave with you, My peace I give to you; not as the world gives do I give to you. Let not your heart be troubled, neither let it be afraid. JOHN 14:27 • Peace from Him who is and who was and who is to come. REVELATION 1:4 •

Evening Reading

Do not let the sun go down on your wrath.
EPHESIANS 4:26

If your brother sins against you, go and tell him his fault between you and him alone. If he hears you, you have gained your brother. MATTHEW 18:15 • Peter came to Him and said, "Lord, how often shall my brother sin against me, and I forgive him? Up to seven times?" Jesus said to him, "I do not say to you, up to seven times, but up to seventy times seven." MATTHEW 18:21–22 • Whenever you stand praying, if you have anything against anyone, forgive him, that your Father in heaven may also forgive you your trespasses. MARK 11:25 •

Therefore, as the elect of God, holy and beloved, put on tender mercies, kindness, humility, meekness, longsuffering; bearing with one another, and forgiving one another, if anyone has a complaint against another; even as Christ forgave you, so you also must do. COLOSSIANS 3:12–13 • Be kind to one another, tenderhearted, forgiving one another, just as God in Christ forgave you. EPHESIANS 4:32 •

And the apostles said to the Lord, "Increase our faith." LUKE 17:5 •

January 14

Morning Reading

My Father is greater than I.
JOHN 14:28

When you pray, say: Our Father in heaven. LUKE 11:2 • My Father and your Father,...My God and your God. JOHN 20:17 •

As the Father gave Me commandment, so I do. JOHN 14:31 • The words that I speak to you I do not speak on My own authority; but the Father who dwells in Me does the works. JOHN 14:10 •

The Father loves the Son, and has given all things into His hand. JOHN 3:35 • You have given Him authority over all flesh, that He should give eternal life to as many as You have given Him. JOHN 17:2 •

Philip said to Him, "Lord, show us the Father, and it is sufficient for us." Jesus said to him, "Have I been with you so long, and yet you have not known Me, Philip? He who has seen Me has seen the Father; so how can you say, 'Show us the Father'? Do you not believe that I am in the Father, and the Father in Me?" JOHN 14:8–10 • I and My Father are one. JOHN 10:30 • As the Father loved Me, I also have loved you; abide in My love. If you keep My commandments, you will abide in My love, just as I have kept My Father's commandments and abide in His love. JOHN 15:9–10 •

Evening Reading

He shall bruise your head, and you shall bruise His heel.
GENESIS 3:15

His visage was marred more than any man, and His form more than the sons of men. ISAIAH 52:14 • He was wounded for our transgressions, He was bruised for our iniquities; the chastisement for our peace was upon Him, and by His stripes we are healed. ISAIAH 53:5 •

[Jesus said to the Jewish leaders,] "This is your hour, and the power of darkness." LUKE 22:53 • Jesus answered [Pilate], "You could have no power at all against Me unless it had been given you from above. JOHN 19:11 •

The Son of God was manifested, that He might destroy the works of the devil. 1 JOHN 3:8 • He...cast out many demons; and He did not allow the demons to speak, because they knew Him. MARK 1:34 •

All authority has been given to Me in heaven and on earth. MATTHEW 28:18 • In My name they will cast out demons. MARK 16:17 •

The God of peace will crush Satan under your feet shortly. ROMANS 16:20 •

January 15

Morning Reading

My soul clings to the dust; revive me according to Your word.
PSALM 119:25

If then you were raised with Christ, seek those things which are above, where Christ is, sitting at the right hand of God. Set your mind on things above, not on things on the earth. For...your life is hidden with Christ in God. COLOSSIANS 3:1–3 • Our citizenship is in heaven, from which we also eagerly wait for the Savior, the Lord Jesus Christ, who will transform our lowly body that it may be conformed to His glorious body, according to the working by which He is able even to subdue all things to Himself. PHILIPPIANS 3:20–21 •

The flesh lusts against the Spirit, and the Spirit against the flesh; and these are contrary to one another, so that you do not do the things that you wish. GALATIANS 5:17 • Brethren, we are debtors; not to the flesh, to live according to the flesh. For if you live according to the flesh you will die; but if by the Spirit you put to death the deeds of the body, you will live. ROMANS 8:12–13 • Beloved, I beg you as sojourners and pilgrims, abstain from fleshly lusts which war against the soul. 1 PETER 2:11 •

Evening Reading

A measure of faith.
ROMANS 12:3

Receive one who is weak in the faith. ROMANS 14:1 • Strengthened in faith, giving glory to God. ROMANS 4:20 •

O you of little faith, why did you doubt? MATTHEW 14:31 • Great is your faith! Let it be to you as you desire. MATTHEW 15:28 •

Jesus said to [the blind men], "Do you believe that I am able to do this?" They said to Him, "Yes, Lord." Then He touched their eyes, saying, "According to your faith let it be to you." MATTHEW 9:28–29 •

Increase our faith. LUKE 17:5 • Building yourselves up on your most holy faith. JUDE 20 • Rooted and built up in Him and established in the faith. COLOSSIANS 2:7 • He who establishes us with you in Christ...is God. 2 CORINTHIANS 1:21 • May the God of all grace,...after you have suffered a while, perfect, establish, strengthen, and settle you. 1 PETER 5:10 •

We then who are strong ought to bear with the scruples of the weak, and not to please ourselves. ROMANS 15:1 • Let us not judge one another anymore, but rather resolve this, not to put a stumbling block or a cause to fall in our brother's way. ROMANS 14:13 •

January 16

Morning Reading

It pleased the Father that in Him all the fullness should dwell.
COLOSSIANS 1:19

The Father loves the Son, and has given all things into His hand. JOHN 3:35 • God also has highly exalted Him and given Him the name which is above every name, that at the name of Jesus every knee should bow, of those in heaven, and of those on earth, and of those under the earth, and that every tongue should confess that Jesus Christ is Lord, to the glory of God the Father. PHILIPPIANS 2:9–11 • Far above all principality and power and might and dominion, and every name that is named, not only in this age but also in that which is to come. EPHESIANS 1:21 • By Him all things were created that are in heaven and that are on earth, visible and invisible, whether thrones or dominions or principalities or powers. All things were created through Him and for Him. COLOSSIANS 1:16 •

Christ died and rose and lived again, that He might be Lord of both the dead and the living. ROMANS 14:9 • And you are complete in Him, who is the head of all principality and power. COLOSSIANS 2:10 • Of His fullness we have all received, and grace for grace. JOHN 1:16 •

Evening Reading

Write the things which you have seen, and the things which are, and the things which will take place after this.
REVELATION 1:19

Holy men of God spoke as they were moved by the Holy Spirit. 2 PETER 1:21 • That which we have seen and heard we declare to you, that you also may have fellowship with us; and truly our fellowship is with the Father and with His Son Jesus Christ. 1 JOHN 1:3 •

[Jesus said to his disciples,] "Behold My hands and My feet, that it is I Myself. Handle Me and see, for a spirit does not have flesh and bones as you see I have." When He had said this, He showed them His hands and His feet. LUKE 24:39–40 • He who has seen has testified, and his testimony is true; and he knows that he is telling the truth, so that you may believe. JOHN 19:35 •

We did not follow cunningly devised fables when we made known to you the power and coming of our Lord Jesus Christ, but were eyewitnesses of His majesty. 2 PETER 1:16 • That your faith should not be in the wisdom of men but in the power of God. 1 CORINTHIANS 2:5 •

January 17

Morning Reading

You have lovingly delivered my soul from the pit of corruption.
ISAIAH 38:17

God has sent His only begotten Son into the world, that we might live through Him. In this is love, not that we loved God, but that He loved us and sent His Son to be the propitiation for our sins. 1 JOHN 4:9–10 •

Who is a God like You, pardoning iniquity and passing over the transgression of the remnant of His heritage? He does not retain His anger forever, because He delights in mercy. He will again have compassion on us, and will subdue our iniquities. You will cast all our sins into the depths of the sea. MICAH 7:18–19 • O LORD my God, I cried out to You, and You healed me. O LORD, You brought my soul up from the grave; You have kept me alive, that I should not go down to the pit. PSALM 30:2–3 • When my soul fainted within me, I remembered the LORD; and my prayer went up to You, into Your holy temple. JONAH 2:7 • I waited patiently for the LORD; and He inclined to me, and heard my cry. He also brought me up out of a horrible pit, out of the miry clay, and set my feet upon a rock. PSALM 40:1–2 •

Evening Reading

The things which are.
REVELATION 1:19

For now we see in a mirror, dimly. 1 CORINTHIANS 13:12 • But now we do not yet see all things put under him. HEBREWS 2:8 •

We have the prophetic word confirmed, which you do well to heed as a light that shines in a dark place, until the day dawns and the morning star rises in your hearts. 2 PETER 1:19 • Your word is a lamp to my feet and a light to my path. PSALM 119:105 •

Beloved, remember the words which were spoken before by the apostles of our Lord Jesus Christ: how they told you that there would be mockers in the last time who would walk according to their own ungodly lusts. JUDE 17–18 • The Spirit expressly says that in latter times some will depart from the faith, giving heed to deceiving spirits and doctrines of demons. 1 TIMOTHY 4:1 •

Little children, it is the last hour. 1 JOHN 2:18 • The night is far spent, the day is at hand. Therefore let us cast off the works of darkness, and let us put on the armor of light. ROMANS 13:12 •

January 18

Morning Reading

Him who was to come.
ROMANS 5:14

Jesus...was made a little lower than the angels, for the suffering of death,...that He, by the grace of God, might taste death for everyone. HEBREWS 2:9 • One died for all. 2 CORINTHIANS 5:14 • As by one man's disobedience many were made sinners, so also by one Man's obedience many will be made righteous. ROMANS 5:19 •

It is written, "The first man Adam became a living being." The last Adam became a life-giving spirit. However, the spiritual is not first, but the natural, and afterward the spiritual. 1 CORINTHIANS 15:45–46 • God said, "Let Us make man in Our image, according to Our likeness...." So God created man in His own image; in the image of God He created him. GENESIS 1:26–27 • God...has in these last days spoken to us by His Son,... the brightness of His glory and the express image of His person. HEBREWS 1:1–3 • You have given Him authority over all flesh. JOHN 17:2 •

The first man was of the earth, made of dust; the second Man is the Lord from heaven. As was the man of dust, so also are those who are made of dust; and as is the heavenly Man, so also are those who are heavenly. 1 CORINTHIANS 15:47–48 •

Evening Reading

The things which will take place after this.
REVELATION 1:19

It is written: "Eye has not seen, nor ear heard, nor have entered into the heart of man the things which God has prepared for those who love Him." But God has revealed them to us through His Spirit. 1 CORINTHIANS 2:9–10 • The Spirit of truth...will tell you things to come. JOHN 16:13 •

Behold, He is coming with clouds, and every eye will see Him, even they who pierced Him. And all the tribes of the earth will mourn because of Him. Even so, Amen. REVELATION 1:7 •

I do not want you to be ignorant, brethren, concerning those who have fallen asleep, lest you sorrow as others who have no hope. For if we believe that Jesus died and rose again, even so God will bring with Him those who sleep in Jesus....For the Lord Himself will descend from heaven with a shout, with the voice of an archangel, and with the trumpet of God. And the dead in Christ will rise first. Then we who are alive and remain shall be caught up together with them in the clouds to meet the Lord in the air. And thus we shall always be with the Lord. 1 THESSALONIANS 4:13–14, 16–17 •

January 19

Morning Reading

Serving the Lord with all humility.
ACTS 20:19

Whoever desires to become great among you, let him be your servant. And whoever desires to be first among you, let him be your slave; just as the Son of Man did not come to be served, but to serve, and to give His life a ransom for many. MATTHEW 20:26–28 •

If anyone thinks himself to be something, when he is nothing, he deceives himself. GALATIANS 6:3 • For I say, through the grace given to me, to everyone who is among you, not to think of himself more highly than he ought to think, but to think soberly, as God has dealt to each one a measure of faith. ROMANS 12:3 • When you have done all those things which you are commanded, say, "We are unprofitable servants. We have done what was our duty to do." LUKE 17:10 •

Our boasting is this: the testimony of our conscience that we conducted ourselves in the world in simplicity and godly sincerity, not with fleshly wisdom but by the grace of God. 2 CORINTHIANS 1:12 • But we have this treasure in earthen vessels, that the excellence of the power may be of God and not of us. 2 CORINTHIANS 4:7 •

Evening Reading

We have turned, every one, to his own way.
ISAIAH 53:6

Noah...planted a vineyard. Then he drank of the wine and was drunk. GENESIS 9:20–21 • [Abram] said to Sarai his wife, "...Please say you are my sister, that it may be well with me for your sake." GENESIS 12:11, 13 • Isaac said to Jacob,..."Are you really my son Esau?" He said, "I am." GENESIS 27:21, 24 • [Moses] spoke rashly with his lips. PSALM 106:33 • Then the men of Israel took some of their provisions; but they did not ask counsel of the LORD. So Joshua made peace with them. JOSHUA 9:14–15 • David did what was right in the eyes of the LORD, and had not turned aside from anything that He commanded him all the days of his life, except in the matter of Uriah the Hittite. 1 KINGS 15:5 •

All these...obtained a good testimony through faith. HEBREWS 11:39 • Being justified freely by His grace through the redemption that is in Christ Jesus. ROMANS 3:24 • The LORD has laid on Him the iniquity of us all. ISAIAH 53:6 •

"Not for your sake do I do this," says the Lord GOD, "let it be known to you. Be ashamed and confounded for your own ways." EZEKIEL 36:32 •

January 20

Morning Reading

His name will be called Wonderful.
ISAIAH 9:6

The Word became flesh and dwelt among us, and we beheld His glory, the glory as of the only begotten of the Father, full of grace and truth. JOHN 1:14 • You have magnified Your word above all Your name. PSALM 138:2 •

They shall call His name Immanuel, which is translated, "God with us." MATTHEW 1:23 • And you shall call His name JESUS, for He will save His people from their sins. MATTHEW 1:21 • That all should honor the Son just as they honor the Father. JOHN 5:23 • God also has highly exalted Him and given Him the name which is above every name. PHILIPPIANS 2:9 • Far above all principality and power and might and dominion, and every name that is named, not only in this age but also in that which is to come. And He put all things under His feet. EPHESIANS 1:21–22 • He had a name written that no one knew except Himself REVELATION 19:12 • KING OF KINGS AND LORD OF LORDS. REVELATION 19:16 •

As for the Almighty, we cannot find Him [out]. JOB 37:23 • What is His name, and what is His Son's name, if you know? PROVERBS 30:4 •

Evening Reading

The Lord's portion is His people.
DEUTERONOMY 32:9

And you are Christ's, and Christ is God's. 1 CORINTHIANS 3:23 • I am my beloved's, and his desire is toward me. SONG OF SONGS 7:10 • I am his. SONG OF SONGS 2:16 • The Son of God...loved me and gave Himself for me. GALATIANS 2:20 •

You are not your own....You were bought at a price; therefore glorify God in your body and in your spirit, which are God's. 1 CORINTHIANS 6:19–20 • The LORD has taken you and brought you out of the iron furnace, out of Egypt, to be His people, an inheritance, as you are this day. DEUTERONOMY 4:20 •

You are God's field, you are God's building. 1 CORINTHIANS 3:9 • Christ [is faithful] as a Son over His own house, whose house we are if we hold fast the confidence and the rejoicing of the hope firm to the end. HEBREWS 3:6 • A spiritual house, a holy priesthood. 1 PETER 2:5 •

"They shall be Mine," says the LORD of hosts, "on the day that I make them My jewels." MALACHI 3:17 • All Mine are Yours, and Yours are Mine, and I am glorified in them. JOHN 17:10 • The glory of His inheritance in the saints. EPHESIANS 1:18 •

January 21

Morning Reading

Every branch that bears fruit He prunes,
that it may bear more fruit.
JOHN 15:2

He is like a refiner's fire and like launderer's soap. He will sit as a refiner and a purifier of silver; He will purify the sons of Levi, and purge them as gold and silver, that they may offer to the LORD an offering in righteousness. MALACHI 3:2–3 •

We also glory in tribulations, knowing that tribulation produces perseverance; and perseverance, character; and character, hope. Now hope does not disappoint, because the love of God has been poured out in our hearts by the Holy Spirit who was given to us. ROMANS 5:3–5 • If you endure chastening, God deals with you as with sons; for what son is there whom a father does not chasten? But if you are without chastening, of which all have become partakers, then you are illegitimate and not sons....Now no chastening seems to be joyful for the present, but painful; nevertheless, afterward it yields the peaceable fruit of righteousness to those who have been trained by it. Therefore strengthen the hands which hang down, and the feeble knees. HEBREWS 12:7–8, 11–12 •

Evening Reading

Now we call the proud blessed.
MALACHI 3:15

Thus says the High and Lofty One who inhabits eternity, whose name is Holy: "I dwell in the high and holy place, with him who has a contrite and humble spirit, to revive the spirit of the humble, and to revive the heart of the contrite ones." ISAIAH 57:15 •

Better to be of a humble spirit with the lowly, than to divide the spoil with the proud. PROVERBS 16:19 • Blessed are the poor in spirit, for theirs is the kingdom of heaven. MATTHEW 5:3 •

These six things the LORD hates, yes, seven are an abomination to Him: a proud look.... PROVERBS 6:16–17 • Everyone proud in heart is an abomination to the LORD. PROVERBS 16:5 •

Search me, O God, and know my heart; try me, and know my anxieties; and see if there is any wicked way in me, and lead me in the way everlasting. PSALM 139:23–24 •

Grace to you and peace from God our Father and the Lord Jesus Christ. I thank my God upon every remembrance of you. PHILIPPIANS 1:2–3 • Blessed are the meek, for they shall inherit the earth. MATTHEW 5:5 •

Morning Reading

This is God, our God forever and ever;
He will be our guide even to death.
PSALM 48:14

O LORD, You are my God. I will exalt You, I will praise Your name, for You have done wonderful things; Your counsels of old are faithfulness and truth. ISAIAH 25:1 • O LORD, You are the portion of my inheritance and my cup. PSALM 16:5 •

He leads me in the paths of righteousness for His name's sake. Yea, though I walk through the valley of the shadow of death, I will fear no evil; for You are with me; Your rod and Your staff, they comfort me. PSALM 23:3–4 • You hold me by my right hand. You will guide me with Your counsel, and afterward receive me to glory. Whom have I in heaven but You? And there is none upon earth that I desire besides You. My flesh and my heart fail; but God is the strength of my heart and my portion forever. PSALM 73:23–26 • Our heart shall rejoice in Him, because we have trusted in His holy name. PSALM 33:21 • The LORD will perfect that which concerns me; Your mercy, O LORD, endures forever; do not forsake the works of Your hands. PSALM 138:8 •

Evening Reading

In the multitude of my anxieties within me,
Your comforts delight my soul.
PSALM 94:19

When my heart is overwhelmed; lead me to the rock that is higher than I. PSALM 61:2 •

O LORD, I am oppressed; undertake for me! ISAIAH 38:14 • Cast your burden on the LORD, and He shall sustain you. PSALM 55:22 •

I am a little child; I do not know how to go out or come in. 1 KINGS 3:7 • If any of you lacks wisdom, let him ask of God...and it will be given to him. JAMES 1:5 •

Who is sufficient for these things? 2 CORINTHIANS 2:16 • I know that in me (that is, in my flesh) nothing good dwells. ROMANS 7:18 • My grace is sufficient for you, for My strength is made perfect in weakness. 2 CORINTHIANS 12:9 •

Son, be of good cheer; your sins are forgiven you. MATTHEW 9:2 • Be of good cheer, daughter; your faith has made you well. MATTHEW 9:22 •

My soul shall be satisfied as with marrow and fatness....When I remember You on my bed, I meditate on You in the night watches. PSALM 63:5–6 •

January 23

Morning Reading

Hope does not disappoint.
ROMANS 5:5

I am the LORD....They shall not be ashamed who wait for Me. ISAIAH 49:23 • Blessed is the man who trusts in the LORD, and whose hope is the LORD. JEREMIAH 17:7 • You will keep him in perfect peace, whose mind is stayed on You, because he trusts in You. Trust in the LORD forever, for in YAH, the LORD, is everlasting strength. ISAIAH 26:3–4 • My soul, wait silently for God alone, for my expectation is from Him. He only is my rock and my salvation; He is my defense; I shall not be moved. PSALM 62:5–6 • I am not ashamed, for I know whom I have believed. 2 TIMOTHY 1:12 •

God, determining to show more abundantly to the heirs of promise the immutability of His counsel, confirmed it by an oath, that by two immutable things, in which it is impossible for God to lie, we might have strong consolation, who have fled for refuge to lay hold of the hope set before us. This hope we have as an anchor of the soul, both sure and steadfast, and which enters the Presence behind the veil, where the forerunner has entered for us, even Jesus. HEBREWS 6:17–20 •

Evening Reading

The offense of the cross.
GALATIANS 5:11

If anyone desires to come after Me, let him deny himself, and take up his cross, and follow Me. MATTHEW 16:24 •

Do you not know that friendship with the world is enmity with God? Whoever therefore wants to be a friend of the world makes himself an enemy of God. JAMES 4:4 • We must through many tribulations enter the kingdom of God. ACTS 14:22 •

Whoever believes on Him will not be put to shame. ROMANS 9:33 • Therefore, to you who believe, He is precious; but to those who are disobedient, "The stone which the builders rejected has become the chief cornerstone," and "A stone of stumbling and a rock of offense." 1 PETER 2:7–8 •

God forbid that I should boast except in the cross of our Lord Jesus Christ, by whom the world has been crucified to me, and I to the world. GALATIANS 6:14 • I have been crucified with Christ. GALATIANS 2:20 • Those who are Christ's have crucified the flesh with its passions and desires. GALATIANS 5:24 • If we endure, we shall also reign with Him. If we deny Him, He also will deny us. 2 TIMOTHY 2:12 •

January 24

Morning Reading

The Lord is at hand.
PHILIPPIANS 4:5

The Lord Himself will descend from heaven with a shout, with the voice of an archangel, and with the trumpet of God. And the dead in Christ will rise first. Then we who are alive and remain shall be caught up together with them in the clouds to meet the Lord in the air. And thus we shall always be with the Lord. Therefore comfort one another with these words. 1 THESSALONIANS 4:16–18 • He who testifies to these things says, "Surely I am coming quickly." Amen. Even so, come, Lord Jesus! REVELATION 22:20 •

Therefore, beloved, looking forward to these things, be diligent to be found by Him in peace, without spot and blameless. 2 PETER 3:14 • Abstain from every form of evil. Now may the God of peace Himself sanctify you completely; and may your whole spirit, soul, and body be preserved blameless at the coming of our Lord Jesus Christ. He who calls you is faithful, who also will do it. 1 THESSALONIANS 5:22–24 •

Be patient. Establish your hearts, for the coming of the Lord is at hand. JAMES 5:8 •

Evening Reading

The choice vine.
GENESIS 49:11

My Well-beloved has a vineyard on a very fruitful hill. He dug it up and cleared out its stones, and planted it with the choicest vine....So He expected it to bring forth good grapes, but it brought forth wild grapes. ISAIAH 5:1–2 • Yet I had planted you a noble vine, a seed of highest quality. How then have you turned before Me into the degenerate plant of an alien vine? JEREMIAH 2:21 •

Now the works of the flesh are evident, which are: adultery, fornication, uncleanness, lewdness,...envy, murders, drunkenness, revelries, and the like....But the fruit of the Spirit is love, joy, peace, longsuffering, kindness, goodness, faithfulness, gentleness, self-control. GALATIANS 5:19, 21–23 •

I am the true vine, and My Father is the vinedresser. Every branch in Me that does not bear fruit He takes away; and every branch that bears fruit He prunes, that it may bear more fruit. JOHN 15:1–2 • Abide in Me, and I in you....By this My Father is glorified, that you bear much fruit; so you will be My disciples. JOHN 15:4, 8 •

January 25

Morning Reading

The righteousness of God, through faith in Jesus Christ,
to all and on all who believe.
ROMANS 3:22

He made Him who knew no sin to be sin for us, that we might become the righteousness of God in Him. 2 CORINTHIANS 5:21 • Christ has redeemed us from the curse of the law, having become a curse for us. GALATIANS 3:13 • You are in Christ Jesus, who became for us wisdom from God; and righteousness and sanctification and redemption. 1 CORINTHIANS 1:30 • Not by works of righteousness which we have done, but according to His mercy He saved us, through the washing of regeneration and renewing of the Holy Spirit, whom He poured out on us abundantly through Jesus Christ our Savior. TITUS 3:5–6 •

I also count all things loss for the excellence of the knowledge of Christ Jesus my Lord, for whom I have suffered the loss of all things, and count them as rubbish, that I may gain Christ and be found in Him, not having my own righteousness, which is from the law, but that which is through faith in Christ, the righteousness which is from God by faith. PHILIPPIANS 3:8–9 •

Evening Reading

The Spirit of adoption by whom we cry out, "Abba, Father."
ROMANS 8:15

Jesus...lifted up His eyes to heaven, and said: "Father...Holy Father... O righteous Father!" JOHN 17:1, 11, 25 • He said, "Abba, Father." MARK 14:36 • Because you are sons, God has sent forth the Spirit of His Son into your hearts, crying out, "Abba, Father!" GALATIANS 4:6 • For through Him we both have access by one Spirit to the Father. Now, therefore, you are no longer strangers and foreigners, but fellow citizens with the saints and members of the household of God. EPHESIANS 2:18–19 •

Doubtless You are our Father....You, O LORD, are our Father; our Redeemer from Everlasting is Your name. ISAIAH 63:16 •

[The Prodigal Son said,] "I will arise and go to my father, and will say to him, 'Father, I have sinned against heaven and before you, and I am no longer worthy to be called your son. Make me like one of your hired servants.'" And he arose and came to his father. But when he was still a great way off, his father saw him and had compassion, and ran and fell on his neck and kissed him. LUKE 15:18–20 •

Therefore be imitators of God as dear children. EPHESIANS 5:1 •

January 26

Morning Reading

Therefore let us go forth to Him, outside the camp, bearing His
reproach. For here we have no continuing city,
but we seek the one to come.
HEBREWS 13:13–14

Beloved, do not think it strange concerning the fiery trial which is to try you, as though some strange thing happened to you; but rejoice to the extent that you partake of Christ's sufferings, that when His glory is revealed, you may also be glad with exceeding joy. 1 PETER 4:12–13 • As you are partakers of the sufferings, so also you will partake of the consolation. 2 CORINTHIANS 1:7 •

If you are reproached for the name of Christ, blessed are you, for the Spirit of glory and of God rests upon you. On their part He is blasphemed, but on your part He is glorified. 1 PETER 4:14 •

They departed from the presence of the council, rejoicing that they were counted worthy to suffer shame for His name. ACTS 5:41 • Choosing rather to suffer affliction with the people of God than to enjoy the passing pleasures of sin, esteeming the reproach of Christ greater riches than the treasures in Egypt; for he looked to the reward. HEBREWS 11:25–26 •

Evening Reading

The Lord Jesus Christ...will transform our lowly body that it may be
conformed to His glorious body.
PHILIPPIANS 3:20–21

On the likeness of the throne was a likeness with the appearance of a man high above it. Also from the appearance of His waist and upward I saw, as it were, the color of amber with the appearance of fire all around within it; and from the appearance of His waist and downward I saw, as it were, the appearance of fire with brightness all around. Like the appearance of a rainbow in a cloud on a rainy day, so was the appearance of the brightness all around it. This was the appearance of the likeness of the glory of the LORD. EZEKIEL 1:26–28 •

We all, with unveiled face, beholding as in a mirror the glory of the Lord, are being transformed into the same image from glory to glory, just as by the Spirit of the Lord. 2 CORINTHIANS 3:18 • It has not yet been revealed what we shall be, but we know that when He is revealed, we shall be like Him, for we shall see Him as He is. 1 JOHN 3:2 •

They shall neither hunger anymore nor thirst anymore. REVELATION 7:16 • They sing the song of Moses, the servant of God, and the song of the Lamb. REVELATION 15:3 •

January 27

Morning Reading

You know that He was manifested to take away our sins,
and in Him there is no sin.
1 JOHN 3:5

God...has in these last days spoken to us by His Son, whom He has appointed heir of all things, through whom also He made the worlds; who being the brightness of His glory and the express image of His person, and upholding all things by the word of His power, when He had by Himself purged our sins, sat down at the right hand of the Majesty on high. HEBREWS 1:1–3 • He made Him who knew no sin to be sin for us, that we might become the righteousness of God in Him. 2 CORINTHIANS 5:21 •

Conduct yourselves throughout the time of your stay here in fear; knowing that you were not redeemed with corruptible things, like silver or gold, from your aimless conduct received by tradition from your fathers, but with the precious blood of Christ, as of a lamb without blemish and without spot. He indeed was foreordained before the foundation of the world, but was manifest in these last times for you. 1 PETER 1:17–20 • The love of Christ compels us, because we judge thus: that if One died for all, then all died; and He died for all, that those who live should live no longer for themselves, but for Him who died for them and rose again. 2 CORINTHIANS 5:14–15 •

Evening Reading

I have set before you life and death,
blessing and cursing; therefore choose life.
DEUTERONOMY 30:19

"I have no pleasure in the death of one who dies," says the Lord GOD. "Therefore turn and live!" EZEKIEL 18:32 •

If I had not come and spoken to them, they would have no sin, but now they have no excuse for their sin. JOHN 15:22 •

That servant who knew his master's will, and did not prepare himself or do according to his will, shall be beaten with many stripes. LUKE 12:47 •

The wages of sin is death, but the gift of God is eternal life in Christ Jesus our Lord. ROMANS 6:23 • He who believes in the Son has everlasting life; and he who does not believe the Son shall not see life, but the wrath of God abides on him. JOHN 3:36 • Do you not know that to whom you present yourselves slaves to obey, you are that one's slaves whom you obey, whether of sin leading to death, or of obedience leading to righteousness? ROMANS 6:16 •

If anyone serves Me, let him follow Me; and where I am, there My servant will be also. If anyone serves Me, him My Father will honor. JOHN 12:26 •

January 28

Morning Reading

As your days, so shall your strength be.
DEUTERONOMY 33:25

When they arrest you and deliver you up, do not worry beforehand, or premeditate what you will speak. But whatever is given you in that hour, speak that; for it is not you who speak, but the Holy Spirit. MARK 13:11 • Do not worry about tomorrow, for tomorrow will worry about its own things. Sufficient for the day is its own trouble. MATTHEW 6:34 •

The God of Israel is He who gives strength and power to His people. Blessed be God! PSALM 68:35 • He gives power to the weak, and to those who have no might He increases strength. ISAIAH 40:29 •

And [the Lord Jesus] said to me, "My grace is sufficient for you, for My strength is made perfect in weakness." Therefore most gladly I will rather boast in my infirmities, that the power of Christ may rest upon me. Therefore I take pleasure in infirmities, in reproaches, in needs, in persecutions, in distresses, for Christ's sake. For when I am weak, then I am strong. 2 CORINTHIANS 12:9–10 • I can do all things through Christ who strengthens me. PHILIPPIANS 4:13 • O my soul, march on in strength! JUDGES 5:21 •

Evening Reading

Awake, O north wind, and...blow upon my garden,
that its spices may flow out.
SONG OF SONGS 4:16

Now no chastening seems to be joyful for the present, but painful; nevertheless, afterward it yields the peaceable fruit of righteousness to those who have been trained by it. HEBREWS 12:11 • The fruit of the Spirit. GALATIANS 5:22 •

He removes it by His rough wind in the day of the east wind. ISAIAH 27:8 •

As a father pities his children, so the LORD pities those who fear Him. PSALM 103:13 •

Even though our outward man is perishing, yet the inward man is being renewed day by day. For our light affliction, which is but for a moment, is working for us a far more exceeding and eternal weight of glory, while we do not look at the things which are seen, but at the things which are not seen. 2 CORINTHIANS 4:16–18 •

Though [Jesus] was a Son, yet He learned obedience by the things which He suffered. HEBREWS 5:8 • [He] was in all points tempted as we are, yet without sin. HEBREWS 4:15 •

January 29

Morning Reading

You-Are-the-God-Who-Sees.
Genesis 16:13

O Lord, You have searched me and known me. You know my sitting down and my rising up; You understand my thought afar off. You comprehend my path and my lying down, and are acquainted with all my ways. For there is not a word on my tongue, but behold, O Lord, You know it altogether....Such knowledge is too wonderful for me; it is high, I cannot attain it. Psalm 139:1–4, 6 •

The eyes of the Lord are in every place, keeping watch on the evil and the good. Proverbs 15:3 • The ways of man are before the eyes of the Lord, and He ponders all his paths. Proverbs 5:21 • God knows your hearts. For what is highly esteemed among men is an abomination in the sight of God. Luke 16:15 • The eyes of the Lord run to and fro throughout the whole earth, to show Himself strong on behalf of those whose heart is loyal to Him. 2 Chronicles 16:9 •

Jesus...knew all men, and had no need that anyone should testify of man, for He knew what was in man. John 2:24–25 • Lord, You know all things; You know that I love You. John 21:17 •

Evening Reading

I will praise You, O Lord my God, with all my heart,
and I will glorify Your name forevermore.
Psalm 86:12

Whoever offers praise glorifies Me. Psalm 50:23 • It is good to give thanks to the Lord, and to sing praises to Your name, O Most High; to declare Your lovingkindness in the morning, and Your faithfulness every night. Psalm 92:1–2 •

Let everything that has breath praise the Lord. Psalm 150:6 •

I beseech you therefore, brethren, by the mercies of God, that you present your bodies a living sacrifice, holy, acceptable to God, which is your reasonable service. Romans 12:1 • Jesus also, that He might sanctify the people with His own blood, suffered outside the gate....Therefore by Him let us continually offer the sacrifice of praise to God, that is, the fruit of our lips, giving thanks to His name. Hebrews 13:12, 15 • Giving thanks always for all things to God the Father in the name of our Lord Jesus Christ. Ephesians 5:20 •

Worthy is the Lamb who was slain to receive power and riches and wisdom, and strength and honor and glory and blessing! Revelation 5:12 •

January 30

Morning Reading

Let us run with endurance the race that is set before us, looking unto Jesus, the author and finisher of our faith.
HEBREWS 12:1–2

Then He said to them all, "If anyone desires to come after Me, let him deny himself, and take up his cross daily, and follow Me. LUKE 9:23 • Whoever of you does not forsake all that he has cannot be My disciple. LUKE 14:33 • Therefore let us cast off the works of darkness. ROMANS 13:12 •

Everyone who competes for the prize is temperate in all things. Now they do it to obtain a perishable crown, but we for an imperishable crown. Therefore I run thus: not with uncertainty. Thus I fight: not as one who beats the air. But I discipline my body and bring it into subjection, lest, when I have preached to others, I myself should become disqualified. 1 CORINTHIANS 9:25–27 • Brethren, I do not count myself to have apprehended; but one thing I do, forgetting those things which are behind and reaching forward to those things which are ahead, I press toward the goal for the prize of the upward call of God in Christ Jesus. PHILIPPIANS 3:13–14 • Let us know, let us pursue the knowledge of the LORD. HOSEA 6:3 •

Evening Reading

It is good for a man to bear the yoke in his youth.
LAMENTATIONS 3:27

Train up a child in the way he should go, and when he is old he will not depart from it. PROVERBS 22:6 •

We have had human fathers who corrected us, and we paid them respect. Shall we not much more readily be in subjection to the Father of spirits and live? For they indeed for a few days chastened us as seemed best to them, but He for our profit, that we may be partakers of His holiness. HEBREWS 12:9–10 •

Before I was afflicted I went astray, but now I keep Your word. PSALM 119:67 • It is good for me that I have been afflicted, that I may learn Your statutes. PSALM 119:71 •

I know the thoughts that I think toward you, says the LORD, thoughts of peace and not of evil, to give you a future and a hope. JEREMIAH 29:11 • Therefore humble yourselves under the mighty hand of God, that He may exalt you in due time. 1 PETER 5:6 •

January 31

Morning Reading

If you do not drive out the inhabitants of the land from before you, then it shall be that those whom you let remain shall be irritants in your eyes and thorns in your sides, and they shall harass you in the land where you dwell.
NUMBERS 33:55

Fight the good fight of faith. 1 TIMOTHY 6:12 • The weapons of our warfare are not carnal but mighty in God for pulling down strongholds, casting down arguments and...bringing every thought into captivity to the obedience of Christ. 2 CORINTHIANS 10:4–5 •

Brethren, we are debtors; not to the flesh, to live according to the flesh. For if you live according to the flesh you will die; but if by the Spirit you put to death the deeds of the body, you will live. ROMANS 8:12–13 •

The flesh lusts against the Spirit, and the Spirit against the flesh; and these are contrary to one another, so that you do not do the things that you wish. GALATIANS 5:17 • I see another law in my members, warring against the law of my mind, and bringing me into captivity to the law of sin which is in my members. ROMANS 7:23 • We are more than conquerors through Him who loved us. ROMANS 8:37 •

Evening Reading

If a man sins against the LORD, who will intercede for him?
1 SAMUEL 2:25

If anyone sins, we have an Advocate with the Father, Jesus Christ the righteous. And He Himself is the propitiation for our sins, and not for ours only but also for the whole world. 1 JOHN 2:1–2 • Whom God set forth as a propitiation by His blood, through faith, to demonstrate His righteousness, because in His forbearance God had passed over the sins that were previously committed, to demonstrate at the present time His righteousness, that He might be just and the justifier of the one who has faith in Jesus. ROMANS 3:25–26 •

He is gracious to [man], and says, "Deliver him from going down to the Pit; I have found a ransom." JOB 33:24 •

What then shall we say to these things? If God is for us, who can be against us?...Who shall bring a charge against God's elect? It is God who justifies. Who is he who condemns? It is Christ who died, and furthermore is also risen, who is even at the right hand of God, who also makes intercession for us. ROMANS 8:31, 33–34 •

FEBRUARY

February 1

Morning Reading

Whom having not seen you love.
1 PETER 1:8

We walk by faith, not by sight. 2 CORINTHIANS 5:7 • We love Him because He first loved us. 1 JOHN 4:19 • We have known and believed the love that God has for us. God is love, and he who abides in love abides in God, and God in him. 1 JOHN 4:16 • In Him you also trusted, after you heard the word of truth, the gospel of your salvation; in whom also, having believed, you were sealed with the Holy Spirit of promise. EPHESIANS 1:13 • God willed to make known what are the riches of the glory of this mystery among the Gentiles: which is Christ in you, the hope of glory. COLOSSIANS 1:27 •

If someone says, "I love God," and hates his brother, he is a liar; for he who does not love his brother whom he has seen, how can he love God whom he has not seen? 1 JOHN 4:20 •

Jesus said to him, "Thomas, because you have seen Me, you have believed. Blessed are those who have not seen and yet have believed." JOHN 20:29 • Blessed are all those who put their trust in Him. PSALM 2:12 •

Evening Reading

The Lord Our Righteousness.
JEREMIAH 23:6

We are all like an unclean thing, and all our righteousnesses are like filthy rags. ISAIAH 64:6 •

I will go in the strength of the Lord GOD; I will make mention of Your righteousness, of Yours only. PSALM 71:16 • I will greatly rejoice in the LORD, my soul shall be joyful in my God; for He has clothed me with the garments of salvation, He has covered me with the robe of righteousness, as a bridegroom decks himself with ornaments, and as a bride adorns herself with her jewels. ISAIAH 61:10 •

Bring out the best robe and put it on him. LUKE 15:22 • To her it was granted to be arrayed in fine linen, clean and bright, for the fine linen is the righteous acts of the saints. REVELATION 19:8 •

I also count all things loss for the excellence of the knowledge of Christ Jesus my Lord...that I may gain Christ and be found in Him, not having my own righteousness, which is from the law, but that which is through faith in Christ, the righteousness which is from God by faith. PHILIPPIANS 3:8–9 •

February 2

Morning Reading

Oh, that You would...keep me from evil.
1 Chronicles 4:10

Why do you sleep? Rise and pray, lest you enter into temptation. Luke 22:46 • The spirit indeed is willing, but the flesh is weak. Matthew 26:41 •

Two things I request of You (deprive me not before I die): remove falsehood and lies far from me; give me neither poverty nor riches; feed me with the food allotted to me; lest I be full and deny You, and say, "Who is the Lord?" or lest I be poor and steal, and profane the name of my God. Proverbs 30:7–9 •

The Lord shall preserve you from all evil; He shall preserve your soul. Psalm 121:7 • I will deliver you from the hand of the wicked, and I will redeem you from the grip of the terrible. Jeremiah 15:21 • He who has been born of God keeps himself, and the wicked one does not touch him. 1 John 5:18 •

Because you have kept My command to persevere, I also will keep you from the hour of trial which shall come upon the whole world, to test those who dwell on the earth. Revelation 3:10 • The Lord knows how to deliver the godly out of temptations. 2 Peter 2:9 •

Evening Reading

One star differs from another star in glory.
1 Corinthians 15:41

On the road they had disputed among themselves who would be the greatest. And He sat down, called the twelve, and said to them, "If anyone desires to be first, he shall be last of all and servant of all." Mark 9:34–35 • Be clothed with humility, for "God resists the proud, but gives grace to the humble." Therefore humble yourselves under the mighty hand of God, that He may exalt you in due time. 1 Peter 5:5–6 •

Let this mind be in you which was also in Christ Jesus, who... made Himself of no reputation, taking the form of a bondservant, and coming in the likeness of men....Therefore God also has highly exalted Him and given Him the name which is above every name, that at the name of Jesus every knee should bow. Philippians 2:5–7, 9–10 •

Those who are wise shall shine like the brightness of the firmament, and those who turn many to righteousness like the stars forever and ever. Daniel 12:3 •

February 3

Morning Reading

"Be strong,...and work; for I am with you,"
says the LORD of hosts.
Haggai 2:4

I am the vine, you are the branches. He who abides in Me, and I in him, bears much fruit; for without Me you can do nothing. John 15:5 • I can do all things through Christ who strengthens me. Philippians 4:13 • Be strong in the Lord and in the power of His might. Ephesians 6:10 • The joy of the LORD is your strength. Nehemiah 8:10 •

Thus says the LORD of hosts: "Let your hands be strong, you who have been hearing in these days these words by the mouth of the prophets." Zechariah 8:9 • Strengthen the weak hands, and make firm the feeble knees. Say to those who are fearful-hearted, "Be strong, do not fear!" Isaiah 35:3–4 • Go in this might of yours. Judges 6:14 •

If God is for us, who can be against us? Romans 8:31 • Therefore, since we have this ministry, as we have received mercy, we do not lose heart. 2 Corinthians 4:1 •

Let us not grow weary while doing good, for in due season we shall reap if we do not lose heart. Galatians 6:9 • Thanks be to God, who gives us the victory through our Lord Jesus Christ. 1 Corinthians 15:57 •

Evening Reading

The darkness shall not hide from You.
Psalm 139:12

His eyes are on the ways of man, and He sees all his steps. There is no darkness nor shadow of death where the workers of iniquity may hide themselves. Job 34:21–22 • "Can anyone hide himself in secret places, so I shall not see him?...Do I not fill heaven and earth?" says the LORD. Jeremiah 23:24 •

You shall not be afraid of the terror by night...nor of the pestilence that walks in darkness....Because you have made the LORD, who is my refuge, even the Most High, your dwelling place, no evil shall befall you, nor shall any plague come near your dwelling. Psalm 91:5–6, 9–10 • He who keeps you will not slumber....The LORD is your keeper; the LORD is your shade at your right hand. The sun shall not strike you by day, nor the moon by night. The LORD shall preserve you from all evil. Psalm 121:3, 5–7 •

Yea, though I walk through the valley of the shadow of death, I will fear no evil; for You are with me. Psalm 23:4 •

February 4

Morning Reading

You shall not return that way again.
DEUTERONOMY 17:16

And truly if they had called to mind that country from which they had come out, they would have had opportunity to return. But now they desire a better, that is, a heavenly country. Therefore God is not ashamed to be called their God, for He has prepared a city for them. HEBREWS 11:15–16 • Choosing rather to suffer affliction with the people of God than to enjoy the passing pleasures of sin, esteeming the reproach of Christ greater riches than the treasures in Egypt; for he looked to the reward. HEBREWS 11:25–26 • [The Lord said,] "The just shall live by faith; but if anyone draws back, My soul has no pleasure in him." But we are not of those who draw back to perdition, but of those who believe to the saving of the soul. HEBREWS 10:38–39 • No one, having put his hand to the plow, and looking back, is fit for the kingdom of God. LUKE 9:62 •

God forbid that I should boast except in the cross of our Lord Jesus Christ, by whom the world has been crucified to me, and I to the world. GALATIANS 6:14 • Come out from among them and be separate, says the Lord. Do not touch what is unclean, and I will receive you. 2 CORINTHIANS 6:17 •

He who has begun a good work in you will complete it until the day of Jesus Christ. PHILIPPIANS 1:6 •

Evening Reading

They...talk of the grief of those You have wounded.
PSALM 69:26

[The Lord says,] "I was a little angry, and they helped; but with evil intent." ZECHARIAH 1:15 •

Brethren, if a man is overtaken in any trespass, you who are spiritual restore such a one in a spirit of gentleness, considering yourself lest you also be tempted. GALATIANS 6:1 •

He who turns a sinner from the error of his way will save a soul from death and cover a multitude of sins. JAMES 5:20 • Comfort the fainthearted, uphold the weak, be patient with all. 1 THESSALONIANS 5:14 •

Let us not judge one another anymore, but rather resolve this, not to put a stumbling block or a cause to fall in our brother's way. ROMANS 14:13 • We then who are strong ought to bear with the scruples of the weak, and not to please ourselves. ROMANS 15:1 •

Love...does not rejoice in iniquity, but rejoices in the truth. 1 CORINTHIANS 13:4, 6 • Let him who thinks he stands take heed lest he fall. 1 CORINTHIANS 10:12 •

February 5

Morning Reading

I have come that they may have life,
and that they may have it more abundantly.
JOHN 10:10

[God said,] "In the day that you eat of [the tree of the knowledge of good and evil] you shall surely die." GENESIS 2:17 • [Eve] took of its fruit and ate. She also gave to her husband with her, and he ate. GENESIS 3:6 •

The wages of sin is death, but the gift of God is eternal life in Christ Jesus our Lord. ROMANS 6:23 • If by the one man's offense death reigned through the one, much more those who receive abundance of grace and of the gift of righteousness will reign in life through the One, Jesus Christ. ROMANS 5:17 • For since by man came death, by Man also came the resurrection of the dead. For as in Adam all die, even so in Christ all shall be made alive. 1 CORINTHIANS 15:21–22 • Our Savior Jesus Christ...has abolished death and brought life and immortality to light through the gospel. 2 TIMOTHY 1:10 •

God has given us eternal life, and this life is in His Son. He who has the Son has life; he who does not have the Son of God does not have life. 1 JOHN 5:11–12 • For God did not send His Son into the world to condemn the world, but that the world through Him might be saved. JOHN 3:17 •

Evening Reading

The judgment seat.
2 CORINTHIANS 5:10

We know that the judgment of God is according to truth. ROMANS 2:2 • When the Son of Man comes in His glory, and all the holy angels with Him, then He will sit on the throne of His glory. All the nations will be gathered before Him, and He will separate them one from another, as a shepherd divides his sheep from the goats. MATTHEW 25:31–32 •

Then the righteous will shine forth as the sun in the kingdom of their Father. MATTHEW 13:43 • Who shall bring a charge against God's elect? It is God who justifies. Who is he who condemns? It is Christ who died, and furthermore is also risen, who is even at the right hand of God, who also makes intercession for us. ROMANS 8:33–34 • There is therefore now no condemnation to those who are in Christ Jesus. ROMANS 8:1 •

We are chastened by the Lord, that we may not be condemned with the world. 1 CORINTHIANS 11:32 •

February 6

Morning Reading

The grace of our Lord was exceedingly abundant,
with faith and love which are in Christ Jesus.
1 TIMOTHY 1:14

You know the grace of our Lord Jesus Christ, that though He was rich, yet for your sakes He became poor, that you through His poverty might become rich. 2 CORINTHIANS 8:9 • Where sin abounded, grace abounded much more. ROMANS 5:20 •

That in the ages to come He might show the exceeding riches of His grace in His kindness toward us in Christ Jesus. For by grace you have been saved through faith, and that not of yourselves; it is the gift of God, not of works, lest anyone should boast. EPHESIANS 2:7–9 • Knowing that a man is not justified by the works of the law but by faith in Jesus Christ, even we have believed in Christ Jesus, that we might be justified by faith in Christ and not by the works of the law; for by the works of the law no flesh shall be justified. GALATIANS 2:16 • According to His mercy He saved us, through the washing of regeneration and renewing of the Holy Spirit, whom He poured out on us abundantly through Jesus Christ our Savior. TITUS 3:5–6 •

Evening Reading

I am...the Bright and Morning Star.
REVELATION 22:16

A Star shall come out of Jacob. NUMBERS 24:17 •

The night is far spent, the day is at hand. Therefore let us cast off the works of darkness, and let us put on the armor of light. ROMANS 13:12 • Until the day breaks and the shadows flee away, turn, my beloved, and be like a gazelle or a young stag upon the mountains of Bether. SONG OF SONGS 2:17 •

[Someone] calls,..."Watchman, what of the night? Watchman, what of the night?" The watchman said, "The morning comes, and also the night. If you will inquire, inquire; return! Come back!" ISAIAH 21:11–12 •

I am the light of the world. JOHN 8:12 • I will give him the morning star. REVELATION 2:28 •

Take heed, watch and pray; for you do not know when the time is. [The Son of Man] is like a man going to a far country, who left his house and gave authority to his servants, and to each his work, and commanded the doorkeeper to watch. Watch therefore,...lest, coming suddenly, he find you sleeping. And what I say to you, I say to all: Watch! MARK 13:33–37 •

February 7

Morning Reading

When you have eaten and are full, then you shall bless the LORD your God for the good land which He has given you.
DEUTERONOMY 8:10

Beware that you do not forget the LORD your God. DEUTERONOMY 8:11 • One of [the lepers], when he saw that he was healed, returned, and with a loud voice glorified God, and fell down on his face at His feet, giving Him thanks. And he was a Samaritan. So Jesus answered and said, "Were there not ten cleansed? But where are the nine? Were there not any found who returned to give glory to God except this foreigner?" LUKE 17:15–18 •

For every creature of God is good, and nothing is to be refused if it is received with thanksgiving; for it is sanctified by the word of God and prayer. 1 TIMOTHY 4:4–5 • He who eats, eats to the Lord, for he gives God thanks. ROMANS 14:6 • The blessing of the LORD makes one rich, and He adds no sorrow with it. PROVERBS 10:22 •

Bless the LORD, O my soul; and all that is within me, bless His holy name! Bless the LORD, O my soul,...who forgives all your iniquities,... who crowns you with lovingkindness and tender mercies. PSALM 103:1–4 •

Evening Reading

[Jesus] was moved with compassion for them.
MATTHEW 14:14

Jesus Christ is the same yesterday, today, and forever. HEBREWS 13:8 • We do not have a High Priest who cannot sympathize with our weaknesses, but was in all points tempted as we are, yet without sin. HEBREWS 4:15 • He can have compassion on those who are ignorant and going astray. HEBREWS 5:2 • He came and found them sleeping, and said to Peter, "Simon, are you sleeping? Could you not watch one hour? Watch and pray, lest you enter into temptation. The spirit indeed is willing, but the flesh is weak." MARK 14:37–38 •

As a father pities his children, so the LORD pities those who fear Him. For He knows our frame; He remembers that we are dust. PSALM 103:13–14 •

You, O Lord, are a God full of compassion, and gracious, longsuffering and abundant in mercy and truth. Oh, turn to me, and have mercy on me! Give Your strength to Your servant, and save the son of Your maidservant. PSALM 86:15–16 •

February 8

Morning Reading

No longer do I call you servants, for a servant does not know what his master is doing; but I have called you friends.
JOHN 15:15

The LORD said, "Shall I hide from Abraham what I am doing?" GENESIS 18:17 • It has been given to you to know the mysteries of the kingdom of heaven. MATTHEW 13:11 • God has revealed them to us through His Spirit. For the Spirit searches all things, yes, the deep things of God. 1 CORINTHIANS 2:10 • The hidden wisdom which God ordained before the ages for our glory. 1 CORINTHIANS 2:7 •

Blessed is the man You choose, and cause to approach You, that he may dwell in Your courts. We shall be satisfied with the goodness of Your house, of Your holy temple. PSALM 65:4 • The secret of the LORD is with those who fear Him, and He will show them His covenant. PSALM 25:14 • I have given to them the words which You have given Me; and they have received them, and have known surely that I came forth from You; and they have believed that You sent Me. JOHN 17:8 •

You are My friends if you do whatever I command you. JOHN 15:14 •

Evening Reading

You shall call your walls Salvation, and your gates Praise.
ISAIAH 60:18

The wall of the city had twelve foundations, and on them were the names of the twelve apostles of the Lamb. REVELATION 21:14 •

You are no longer strangers and foreigners, but fellow citizens with the saints and members of the household of God, having been built on the foundation of the apostles and prophets, Jesus Christ Himself being the chief cornerstone, in whom the whole building, being joined together, grows into a holy temple in the Lord, in whom you also are being built together for a dwelling place of God in the Spirit. EPHESIANS 2:19–22 • If indeed you have tasted that the Lord is gracious. Coming to Him as to a living stone, rejected indeed by men, but chosen by God and precious, you also, as living stones, are being built up a spiritual house, a holy priesthood, to offer up spiritual sacrifices acceptable to God through Jesus Christ. 1 PETER 2:3–5 •

Praise is awaiting You, O God, in Zion. PSALM 65:1 •

February 9

Morning Reading

Now he is comforted.
LUKE 16:25

Your sun shall no longer go down, nor shall your moon withdraw itself; for the LORD will be your everlasting light, and the days of your mourning shall be ended. ISAIAH 60:20 • He will swallow up death forever, and the Lord GOD will wipe away tears from all faces; the rebuke of His people He will take away from all the earth. ISAIAH 25:8 • These are the ones who come out of the great tribulation, and washed their robes and made them white in the blood of the Lamb. Therefore they are before the throne of God, and serve Him day and night in His temple. And He who sits on the throne will dwell among them. They shall neither hunger anymore nor thirst anymore; the sun shall not strike them, nor any heat; for the Lamb who is in the midst of the throne will shepherd them and lead them to living fountains of waters. REVELATION 7:14–17 • And God will wipe away every tear from their eyes; there shall be no more death, nor sorrow, nor crying. There shall be no more pain, for the former things have passed away. REVELATION 21:4 •

Evening Reading

The night is coming when no one can work.
JOHN 9:4

Blessed are the dead who die in the Lord from now on. "Yes," says the Spirit, "that they may rest from their labors, and their works follow them." REVELATION 14:13 • There the wicked cease from troubling, and there the weary are at rest. JOB 3:17 • Samuel said to Saul, "Why have you disturbed me by bringing me up?" 1 SAMUEL 28:15 •

Whatever your hand finds to do, do it with your might; for there is no work or device or knowledge or wisdom in the grave where you are going. ECCLESIASTES 9:10 • The dead do not praise the LORD, nor any who go down into silence. PSALM 115:17 •

For I am already being poured out as a drink offering, and the time of my departure is at hand. I have fought the good fight, I have finished the race, I have kept the faith. Finally, there is laid up for me the crown of righteousness, which the Lord, the righteous Judge, will give to me on that Day. 2 TIMOTHY 4:6–8 •

There remains therefore a rest for the people of God. For he who has entered His rest has himself also ceased from his works as God did from His. HEBREWS 4:9–10 •

February 10

Morning Reading

The lamp of the body is the eye. Therefore, when your eye is good, your
whole body also is full of light.
LUKE 11:34

The natural man does not receive the things of the Spirit of God, for they are foolishness to him; nor can he know them, because they are spiritually discerned. 1 CORINTHIANS 2:14 • Open my eyes, that I may see wondrous things from Your law. PSALM 119:18 •

I am the light of the world. He who follows Me shall not walk in darkness, but have the light of life. JOHN 8:12 • We all, with unveiled face, beholding as in a mirror the glory of the Lord, are being transformed into the same image from glory to glory, just as by the Spirit of the Lord. 2 CORINTHIANS 3:18 • God who commanded light to shine out of darkness...has shone in our hearts to give the light of the knowledge of the glory of God in the face of Jesus Christ. 2 CORINTHIANS 4:6 •

[May] the God of our Lord Jesus Christ, the Father of glory...give to you the spirit of wisdom and revelation in the knowledge of Him,...that you may know what is the hope of His calling, what are the riches of the glory of His inheritance in the saints. EPHESIANS 1:17–18 •

Evening Reading

He struck the rock, so that the waters gushed out,
and the streams overflowed.
PSALM 78:20

All our fathers were under the cloud, all passed through the sea, all were baptized into Moses in the cloud and in the sea, all ate the same spiritual food, and all drank the same spiritual drink. For they drank of that spiritual Rock that followed them, and that Rock was Christ. 1 CORINTHIANS 10:1–4 • One of the soldiers pierced His side with a spear, and immediately blood and water came out. JOHN 19:34 • He was wounded for our transgressions, He was bruised for our iniquities; the chastisement for our peace was upon Him, and by His stripes we are healed. ISAIAH 53:5 •

You are not willing to come to Me that you may have life. JOHN 5:40 • My people have committed two evils: they have forsaken Me, the fountain of living waters, and hewn themselves cisterns; broken cisterns that can hold no water. JEREMIAH 2:13 •

Jesus stood and cried out, saying, "If anyone thirsts, let him come to Me and drink." JOHN 7:37 • Whoever desires, let him take the water of life freely. REVELATION 22:17 •

Morning Reading

Those who feared the LORD spoke to one another, and the LORD listened and heard them; so a book of remembrance was written before Him for those who fear the LORD and who meditate on His name.
MALACHI 3:16

So it was, while they conversed and reasoned, that Jesus Himself drew near and went with them. LUKE 24:15 • Where two or three are gathered together in My name, I am there in the midst of them. MATTHEW 18:20 • My fellow workers, whose names are in the Book of Life. PHILIPPIANS 4:3 •

Let the word of Christ dwell in you richly in all wisdom, teaching and admonishing one another in psalms and hymns and spiritual songs, singing with grace in your hearts to the Lord. COLOSSIANS 3:16 • Exhort one another daily, while it is called "Today," lest any of you be hardened through the deceitfulness of sin. HEBREWS 3:13 •

For every idle word men may speak, they will give account of it in the day of judgment. For by your words you will be justified, and by your words you will be condemned. MATTHEW 12:36–37 • Behold, it is written before Me: I will not keep silence, but will repay; even repay into their bosom. ISAIAH 65:6 •

Evening Reading

The trees of the LORD are full of sap.
PSALM 104:16

I will be like the dew to Israel; he shall grow like the lily, and lengthen his roots like Lebanon. His branches shall spread; his beauty shall be like an olive tree, and his fragrance like Lebanon. HOSEA 14:5–6 • Blessed is the man who trusts in the LORD, and whose hope is the LORD. For he shall be like a tree planted by the waters, which spreads out its roots by the river, and will not fear when heat comes; but its leaf will be green, and will not be anxious in the year of drought, nor will cease from yielding fruit. JEREMIAH 17:7–8 •

I, the LORD, have brought down the high tree and exalted the low tree, dried up the green tree and made the dry tree flourish. EZEKIEL 17:24 •

The righteous shall flourish like a palm tree, he shall grow like a cedar in Lebanon. Those who are planted in the house of the LORD shall flourish in the courts of our God. They shall still bear fruit in old age; they shall be fresh and flourishing. PSALM 92:12–14 •

February 12

Morning Reading

"They shall be Mine," says the LORD of hosts,
"on the day that I make them My jewels."
MALACHI 3:17

I have manifested Your name to the men whom You have given Me out of the world. They were Yours, You gave them to Me, and they have kept Your word....I pray for them. I do not pray for the world but for those whom You have given Me, for they are Yours. And all Mine are Yours, and Yours are Mine, and I am glorified in them....Father, I desire that they also whom You gave Me may be with Me where I am, that they may behold My glory which You have given Me; for You loved Me before the foundation of the world. JOHN 17:6, 9–10, 24 •

I will come again and receive you to Myself. JOHN 14:3 • When He comes, in that Day, to be glorified in His saints and to be admired among all those who believe. 2 THESSALONIANS 1:10 • We who are alive and remain shall be caught up together with them in the clouds to meet the Lord in the air. And thus we shall always be with the Lord. 1 THESSALONIANS 4:17 • You shall also be a crown of glory in the hand of the LORD, and a royal diadem in the hand of your God. ISAIAH 62:3 •

Evening Reading

Please, show me Your glory.
EXODUS 33:18

God who commanded light to shine out of darkness...has shone in our hearts to give the light of the knowledge of the glory of God in the face of Jesus Christ. 2 CORINTHIANS 4:6 • The Word became flesh and dwelt among us, and we beheld His glory, the glory as of the only begotten of the Father, full of grace and truth. JOHN 1:14 • No one has seen God at any time. The only begotten Son, who is in the bosom of the Father, IIe has declared Him. JOHN 1:18 •

My soul thirsts for God, for the living God. When shall I come and appear before God? PSALM 42:2 • When You said, "Seek My face," my heart said to You, "Your face, LORD, I will seek." PSALM 27:8 •

We all, with unveiled face, beholding as in a mirror the glory of the Lord, are being transformed into the same image from glory to glory, just as by the Spirit of the Lord. 2 CORINTHIANS 3:18 • Father, I desire that they also whom You gave Me may be with Me where I am, that they may behold My glory which You have given Me; for You loved Me before the foundation of the world. JOHN 17:24 •

February 13

Morning Reading

On the likeness of the throne was a likeness with the appearance of a man high above it.
EZEKIEL 1:26

The Man Christ Jesus. 1 TIMOTHY 2:5 • Coming in the likeness of men...found in appearance as a man. PHILIPPIANS 2:7–8 • Inasmuch then as the children have partaken of flesh and blood, He Himself likewise shared in the same, that through death He might destroy him who had the power of death, that is, the devil. HEBREWS 2:14 •

I am He who lives, and was dead, and behold, I am alive forevermore. REVELATION 1:18 • Christ, having been raised from the dead, dies no more. Death no longer has dominion over Him. For the death that He died, He died to sin once for all; but the life that He lives, He lives to God. ROMANS 6:9–10 • What then if you should see the Son of Man ascend where He was before? JOHN 6:62 • He raised Him from the dead and seated Him at His right hand in the heavenly places. EPHESIANS 1:20 • For in Him dwells all the fullness of the Godhead bodily. COLOSSIANS 2:9 •

Though He was crucified in weakness, yet He lives by the power of God. For we also are weak in Him, but we shall live with Him by the power of God. 2 CORINTHIANS 13:4 •

Evening Reading

Your word has given me life.
PSALM 119:50

It is written, "The first man Adam became a living being." The last Adam became a life-giving spirit. 1 CORINTHIANS 15:45 •

As the Father has life in Himself, so He has granted the Son to have life in Himself. JOHN 5:26 • I am the resurrection and the life. He who believes in Me, though he may die, he shall live. And whoever lives and believes in Me shall never die. JOHN 11:25–26 •

In Him was life, and the life was the light of men. JOHN 1:4 • But as many as received Him, to them He gave the right to become children of God, to those who believe in His name: who were born, not of blood, nor of the will of the flesh, nor of the will of man, but of God. JOHN 1:12–13 •

It is the Spirit who gives life; the flesh profits nothing. The words that I speak to you are spirit, and they are life. JOHN 6:63 • The word of God is living and powerful, and sharper than any two-edged sword, piercing even to the division of soul and spirit, and of joints and marrow, and is a discerner of the thoughts and intents of the heart. HEBREWS 4:12 •

February 14

Morning Reading

*Permit it to be so now, for thus it is fitting for us
to fulfill all righteousness.*
MATTHEW 3:15

I delight to do Your will, O my God, and Your law is within my heart. PSALM 40:8 •

Do not think that I came to destroy the Law or the Prophets. I did not come to destroy but to fulfill. For assuredly, I say to you, till heaven and earth pass away, one jot or one tittle will by no means pass from the law till all is fulfilled. MATTHEW 5:17–18 • The LORD is well pleased for His righteousness' sake; He will exalt the law and make it honorable. ISAIAH 42:21 • Unless your righteousness exceeds the righteousness of the scribes and Pharisees, you will by no means enter the kingdom of heaven. MATTHEW 5:20 •

What the law could not do in that it was weak through the flesh, God did by sending His own Son in the likeness of sinful flesh, on account of sin: He condemned sin in the flesh, that the righteous requirement of the law might be fulfilled in us who do not walk according to the flesh but according to the Spirit. ROMANS 8:3–4 • Christ is the end of the law for righteousness to everyone who believes. ROMANS 10:4 •

Evening Reading

I am your portion and your inheritance.
NUMBERS 18:20

Whom have I in heaven but You? And there is none upon earth that I desire besides You. My flesh and my heart fail; but God is the strength of my heart and my portion forever. PSALM 73:25–26 • O LORD, You are the portion of my inheritance and my cup; You maintain my lot. The lines have fallen to me in pleasant places; yes, I have a good inheritance. PSALM 16:5–6 •

"The LORD is my portion," says my soul, "therefore I hope in Him!" LAMENTATIONS 3:24 •

Your testimonies I have taken as a heritage forever, for they are the rejoicing of my heart. PSALM 119:111 •

O God, You are my God; early will I seek You; my soul thirsts for You; my flesh longs for You in a dry and thirsty land where there is no water. PSALM 63:1 • Because You have been my help, therefore in the shadow of Your wings I will rejoice. PSALM 63:7 •

My beloved is mine, and I am his. SONG OF SONGS 2:16 •

February 15

Morning Reading

Who can say, "I have made my heart clean"?
PROVERBS 20:9

The LORD looks down from heaven upon the children of men, to see if there are any who understand, who seek God. They have all turned aside, they have together become corrupt; there is none who does good, no, not one. PSALM 14:2–3 • So then, those who are in the flesh cannot please God. ROMANS 8:8 •

To will is present with me, but how to perform what is good I do not find. For the good that I will to do, I do not do; but the evil I will not to do, that I practice. ROMANS 7:18–19 • We are all like an unclean thing, and all our righteousnesses are like filthy rags; we all fade as a leaf, and our iniquities, like the wind, have taken us away. ISAIAH 64:6 •

The Scripture has confined all under sin, that the promise by faith in Jesus Christ might be given to those who believe. GALATIANS 3:22 • God was in Christ reconciling the world to Himself, not imputing their trespasses to them. 2 CORINTHIANS 5:19 •

If we say that we have no sin, we deceive ourselves, and the truth is not in us. If we confess our sins, He is faithful and just to forgive us our sins and to cleanse us from all unrighteousness. 1 JOHN 1:8–9 •

Evening Reading

The floods lift up their waves.
PSALM 93:3

The LORD on high is mightier than the noise of many waters, than the mighty waves of the sea. PSALM 93:4 • O LORD God of hosts, who is mighty like You, O LORD? Your faithfulness also surrounds You. You rule the raging of the sea; when its waves rise, You still them. PSALM 89:8–9 •

"Do you not fear Me?" says the LORD. "Will you not tremble at My presence, who have placed the sand as the bound of the sea, by a perpetual decree, that it cannot pass beyond it?" JEREMIAH 5:22 •

When you pass through the waters, I will be with you; and through the rivers, they shall not overflow you. ISAIAH 43:2 •

[Peter] walked on the water to go to Jesus. But when he saw that the wind was boisterous, he was afraid; and beginning to sink he cried out, saying, "Lord, save me!" And immediately Jesus stretched out His hand and caught him, and said to him, "O you of little faith, why did you doubt?" MATTHEW 14:29–31 •

Whenever I am afraid, I will trust in You. PSALM 56:3 •

February 16

Morning Reading

Your name is ointment poured forth.
Song of Songs 1:3

Christ also has loved us and given Himself for us, an offering and a sacrifice to God for a sweet-smelling aroma. Ephesians 5:2 • Therefore, to you who believe, He is precious. 1 Peter 2:7 • God also has highly exalted Him and given Him the name which is above every name, that at the name of Jesus every knee should bow. Philippians 2:9–10 • In Him dwells all the fullness of the Godhead bodily. Colossians 2:9 •

If you love Me, keep My commandments. John 14:15 • The love of God has been poured out in our hearts by the Holy Spirit who was given to us. Romans 5:5 • The house was filled with the fragrance of the oil. John 12:3 • They realized that they had been with Jesus. Acts 4:13 •

O Lord, our Lord, how excellent is Your name in all the earth, who have set Your glory above the heavens! Psalm 8:1 • Immanuel,…"God with us." Matthew 1:23 • His name will be called Wonderful, Counselor, Mighty God, Everlasting Father, Prince of Peace. Isaiah 9:6 • The name of the Lord is a strong tower; the righteous run to it and are safe. Proverbs 18:10 •

Evening Reading

For we who are in this tent groan, being burdened.
2 Corinthians 5:4

Lord, all my desire is before You; and my sighing is not hidden from You. Psalm 38:9 • My iniquities have gone over my head; like a heavy burden they are too heavy for me. Psalm 38:4 • O wretched man that I am! Who will deliver me from this body of death? Romans 7:24 •

The whole creation groans and labors with birth pangs together until now. Not only that, but we also who have the firstfruits of the Spirit, even we ourselves groan within ourselves, eagerly waiting for the adoption, the redemption of our body. Romans 8:22–23 • Now for a little while, if need be, you have been grieved by various trials. 1 Peter 1:6 •

Shortly I must put off my tent. 2 Peter 1:14 • For this corruptible must put on incorruption, and this mortal must put on immortality. So when this corruptible has put on incorruption, and this mortal has put on immortality, then shall be brought to pass the saying that is written: "Death is swallowed up in victory." 1 Corinthians 15:53–54 •

February 17

Morning Reading

The whole bull he shall carry outside the camp to a clean place, where the ashes are poured out, and burn it on wood with fire.
LEVITICUS 4:12

They took Jesus and led Him away. And He, bearing His cross, went out to a place called the Place of a Skull, which is called in Hebrew, Golgotha, where they crucified Him. JOHN 19:16–18 • The bodies of those animals, whose blood is brought into the sanctuary by the high priest for sin, are burned outside the camp. Therefore Jesus also, that He might sanctify the people with His own blood, suffered outside the gate. Therefore let us go forth to Him, outside the camp, bearing His reproach. HEBREWS 13:11–13 • The fellowship of His sufferings. PHILIPPIANS 3:10 •

Rejoice to the extent that you partake of Christ's sufferings, that when His glory is revealed, you may also be glad with exceeding joy. 1 PETER 4:13 • Our light affliction, which is but for a moment, is working for us a far more exceeding and eternal weight of glory. 2 CORINTHIANS 4:17 •

Evening Reading

God created man in His own image.
GENESIS 1:27

Since we are the offspring of God, we ought not to think that the Divine Nature is like gold or silver or stone, something shaped by art and man's devising. ACTS 17:29 •

God, who is rich in mercy, because of His great love with which He loved us, even when we were dead in trespasses, made us alive together with Christ. EPHESIANS 2:4–5 • We are His workmanship, created in Christ Jesus for good works, which God prepared beforehand that we should walk in them. EPHESIANS 2:10 • For whom He foreknew, He also predestined to be conformed to the image of His Son, that He might be the firstborn among many brethren. ROMANS 8:29 •

We know that when He is revealed, we shall be like Him, for we shall see Him as He is. 1 JOHN 3:2 • I shall be satisfied when I awake in Your likeness. PSALM 17:15 •

He who overcomes shall inherit all things, and I will be his God and he shall be My son. REVELATION 21:7 • If children, then heirs; heirs of God and joint heirs with Christ, if indeed we suffer with Him, that we may also be glorified together. ROMANS 8:17 •

February 18

Morning Reading

You are my hope in the day of doom.
JEREMIAH 17:17

There are many who say, "Who will show us any good?" LORD, lift up the light of Your countenance upon us. PSALM 4:6 • I will sing of Your power; yes, I will sing aloud of Your mercy in the morning; for You have been my defense and refuge in the day of my trouble. PSALM 59:16 •

In my prosperity I said, "I shall never be moved."...I cried out to You, O LORD; and to the LORD I made supplication: "What profit is there in my blood, when I go down to the pit? Will the dust praise You? Will it declare Your truth? Hear, O LORD, and have mercy on me; LORD, be my helper!" PSALM 30:6, 8–10 •

"For a mere moment I have forsaken you, but with great mercies I will gather you. With a little wrath I hid My face from you for a moment; but with everlasting kindness I will have mercy on you," says the LORD, your Redeemer. ISAIAH 54:7–8 • Sorrow will be turned into joy. JOHN 16:20 • Weeping may endure for a night, but joy comes in the morning. PSALM 30:5 •

Evening Reading

Adam...begot a son in his own likeness.
GENESIS 5:3

Who can bring a clean thing out of an unclean? JOB 14:4 • Behold, I was brought forth in iniquity, and in sin my mother conceived me. PSALM 51:5 •

You...were dead in trespasses and sins,...by nature children of wrath, just as the others. EPHESIANS 2:1, 3 • I am carnal, sold under sin. For what I am doing, I do not understand. For what I will to do, that I do not practice; but what I hate, that I do. ROMANS 7:14–15 • For I know that in me (that is, in my flesh) nothing good dwells. ROMANS 7:18 •

Through one man sin entered the world....By one man's disobedience many were made sinners. ROMANS 5:12, 19 • If by the one man's offense many died, much more the grace of God and the gift by the grace of the one Man, Jesus Christ, abounded to many. ROMANS 5:15 •

The law of the Spirit of life in Christ Jesus has made me free from the law of sin and death. ROMANS 8:2 •

Thanks be to God, who gives us the victory through our Lord Jesus Christ. 1 CORINTHIANS 15:57 •

 *February 19*

Morning Reading

The LORD gives wisdom; from His mouth come
knowledge and understanding.
PROVERBS 2:6

Trust in the LORD with all your heart, and lean not on your own understanding. PROVERBS 3:5 • If any of you lacks wisdom, let him ask of God, who gives to all liberally and without reproach, and it will be given to him. JAMES 1:5 • The foolishness of God is wiser than men, and the weakness of God is stronger than men....God has chosen the foolish things of the world to put to shame the wise,...that no flesh should glory in His presence. 1 CORINTHIANS 1:25, 27, 29 •

The entrance of Your words gives light; it gives understanding to the simple. PSALM 119:130 • Your word I have hidden in my heart, that I might not sin against You! PSALM 119:11 •

All bore witness to Him, and marveled at the gracious words which proceeded out of His mouth. LUKE 4:22 • The officers answered, "No man ever spoke like this Man!" JOHN 7:46 • Of Him you are in Christ Jesus, who became for us wisdom from God; and righteousness and sanctification and redemption. 1 CORINTHIANS 1:30 •

Evening Reading

The year of My redeemed has come.
ISAIAH 63:4

You shall consecrate the fiftieth year, and proclaim liberty throughout all the land to all its inhabitants. It shall be a Jubilee for you; and each of you shall return to his possession, and...to his family. LEVITICUS 25:10 •

Your dead shall live; together with my dead body they shall arise. Awake and sing, you who dwell in dust; for your dew is like the dew of herbs, and the earth shall cast out the dead. ISAIAH 26:19 •

The Lord Himself will descend from heaven with a shout, with the voice of an archangel, and with the trumpet of God. And the dead in Christ will rise first. Then we who are alive and remain shall be caught up together with them in the clouds to meet the Lord in the air. And thus we shall always be with the Lord. 1 THESSALONIANS 4:16–17 •

I will ransom them from the power of the grave; I will redeem them from death. O Death, I will be your plagues! O Grave, I will be your destruction! HOSEA 13:14 •

Their Redeemer is strong; the LORD of hosts is His name. JEREMIAH 50:34 •

February 20

Morning Reading

He shall see the labor of His soul, and be satisfied.
ISAIAH 53:11

[Jesus] said, "It is finished!" And bowing His head, He gave up His spirit. JOHN 19:30 • He made Him who knew no sin to be sin for us, that we might become the righteousness of God in Him. 2 CORINTHIANS 5:21 •

This people I have formed for Myself; they shall declare My praise. ISAIAH 43:21 • To the intent that now the manifold wisdom of God might be made known by the church to the principalities and powers in the heavenly places, according to the eternal purpose which He accomplished in Christ Jesus our Lord. EPHESIANS 3:10–11 • That in the ages to come He might show the exceeding riches of His grace in His kindness toward us in Christ Jesus. EPHESIANS 2:7 •

After you heard the word of truth, the gospel of your salvation; in whom also, having believed, you were sealed with the Holy Spirit of promise, who is the guarantee of our inheritance until the redemption of the purchased possession, to the praise of His glory. EPHESIANS 1:13–14 • You are a chosen generation, a royal priesthood, a holy nation, His own special people, that you may proclaim the praises of Him who called you out of darkness into His marvelous light. 1 PETER 2:9 •

Evening Reading

The day of trial in the wilderness.
HEBREWS 3:8

Let no one say when he is tempted, "I am tempted by God"; for God cannot be tempted by evil, nor does He Himself tempt anyone. But each one is tempted when he is drawn away by his own desires and enticed. Then, when desire has conceived, it gives birth to sin; and sin, when it is full-grown, brings forth death. JAMES 1:13–15 •

[The children of Israel] lusted exceedingly in the wilderness, and tested God in the desert. PSALM 106:14 •

Jesus, being filled with the Holy Spirit,...was led by the Spirit into the wilderness, being tempted for forty days by the devil. And in those days He ate nothing, and afterward, when they had ended, He was hungry. And the devil said to Him, "If You are the Son of God, command this stone to become bread." LUKE 4:1–3 •

For in that He Himself has suffered, being tempted, He is able to aid those who are tempted. HEBREWS 2:18 • And the Lord said, "Simon, Simon! Indeed, Satan has asked for you, that he may sift you as wheat. But I have prayed for you, that your faith should not fail." LUKE 22:31–32 •

February 21

Morning Reading

I am the LORD who sanctifies you.
LEVITICUS 20:8

I am the LORD your God, who has separated you from the peoples....And you shall be holy to Me, for I the LORD am holy, and have separated you from the peoples, that you should be Mine. LEVITICUS 20:24, 26 •

Sanctified by God the Father. JUDE 1 • Sanctify them by Your truth. Your word is truth. JOHN 17:17 • May the God of peace Himself sanctify you completely; and may your whole spirit, soul, and body be preserved blameless at the coming of our Lord Jesus Christ. 1 THESSALONIANS 5:23 •

Jesus also, that He might sanctify the people with His own blood, suffered outside the gate. HEBREWS 13:12 • Our great God and Savior Jesus Christ...gave Himself for us, that He might redeem us from every lawless deed and purify for Himself His own special people, zealous for good works. TITUS 2:13–14 • Both He who sanctifies and those who are being sanctified are all of one, for which reason He is not ashamed to call them brethren. HEBREWS 2:11 • For their sakes I sanctify Myself, that they also may be sanctified by the truth. JOHN 17:19 • In sanctification of the Spirit, for obedience and sprinkling of the blood of Jesus Christ: grace to you and peace be multiplied. 1 PETER 1:2 •

Evening Reading

Light is sown for the righteous, and gladness
for the upright in heart.
PSALM 97:11

Those who sow in tears shall reap in joy. He who continually goes forth weeping, bearing seed for sowing, shall doubtless come again with rejoicing, bringing his sheaves with him. PSALM 126:5–6 •

And what you sow, you do not sow that body that shall be. 1 CORINTHIANS 15:37 •

Blessed be the God and Father of our Lord Jesus Christ, who according to His abundant mercy has begotten us again to a living hope through the resurrection of Jesus Christ from the dead....In this you greatly rejoice, though now for a little while, if need be, you have been grieved by various trials, that the genuineness of your faith, being much more precious than gold that perishes, though it is tested by fire, may be found to praise, honor, and glory at the revelation of Jesus Christ. 1 PETER 1:3, 6–7 •

February 22

Morning Reading

Who is the man that fears the LORD?
Him shall He teach in the way He chooses.
PSALM 25:12

The lamp of the body is the eye. If therefore your eye is good, your whole body will be full of light. MATTHEW 6:22 •

Your word is a lamp to my feet and a light to my path. PSALM 119:105 • Your ears shall hear a word behind you, saying, "This is the way, walk in it," whenever you turn to the right hand or whenever you turn to the left. ISAIAH 30:21 • I will instruct you and teach you in the way you should go; I will guide you with My eye. Do not be like the horse or like the mule, which have no understanding, which must be harnessed with bit and bridle, else they will not come near you. Many sorrows shall be to the wicked; but he who trusts in the LORD, mercy shall surround him. Be glad in the LORD and rejoice, you righteous; and shout for joy, all you upright in heart! PSALM 32:8–11 •

O LORD, I know the way of man is not in himself; it is not in man who walks to direct his own steps. JEREMIAH 10:23 •

Evening Reading

When you lie down, you will not be afraid;
yes, you will lie down and your sleep will be sweet.
PROVERBS 3:24

A great windstorm arose, and the waves beat into the boat, so that it was already filling. But He was in the stern, asleep on a pillow. MARK 4:37–38 •

Be anxious for nothing, but in everything by prayer and supplication, with thanksgiving, let your requests be made known to God; and the peace of God, which surpasses all understanding, will guard your hearts and minds through Christ Jesus. PHILIPPIANS 4:6–7 •

I will both lie down in peace, and sleep; for You alone, O LORD, make me dwell in safety. PSALM 4:8 • He gives His beloved sleep. PSALM 127:2 •

They stoned Stephen as he was calling on God and saying, "Lord Jesus, receive my spirit." Then he knelt down and cried out with a loud voice, "Lord, do not charge them with this sin." And when he had said this, he fell asleep. ACTS 7:59–60 • Absent from the body...present with the Lord. 2 CORINTHIANS 5:8 •

February 23

The blood of sprinkling that speaks
better things than that of Abel.
HEBREWS 12:24

Behold! The Lamb of God who takes away the sin of the world! JOHN 1:29 • The Lamb slain from the foundation of the world. REVELATION 13:8 • It is not possible that the blood of bulls and goats could take away sins. Therefore, when He came into the world, He said: "Sacrifice and offering You did not desire, but a body You have prepared for Me." HEBREWS 10:4–5 • By that will we have been sanctified through the offering of the body of Jesus Christ once for all. HEBREWS 10:10 •

Abel also brought of the firstborn of his flock and of their fat. And the LORD respected Abel and his offering. GENESIS 4:4 • Christ also has loved us and given Himself for us, an offering and a sacrifice to God for a sweet-smelling aroma. EPHESIANS 5:2 •

Let us draw near with a true heart in full assurance of faith, having our hearts sprinkled from an evil conscience and our bodies washed with pure water. HEBREWS 10:22 • Having boldness to enter the Holiest by the blood of Jesus. HEBREWS 10:19 •

Evening Reading

Who knows the power of Your anger?
PSALM 90:11

From the sixth hour until the ninth hour there was darkness over all the land. And about the ninth hour Jesus cried out with a loud voice, saying, "Eli, Eli, lama sabachthani?" that is, "My God, My God, why have You forsaken Me?" MATTHEW 27:45–46 • The LORD has laid on Him the iniquity of us all. ISAIAH 53:6 •

There is therefore now no condemnation to those who are in Christ Jesus. ROMANS 8:1 • Having been justified by faith, we have peace with God through our Lord Jesus Christ. ROMANS 5:1 • Christ has redeemed us from the curse of the law, having become a curse for us. GALATIANS 3:13 •

God has sent His only begotten Son into the world, that we might live through Him. In this is love, not that we loved God, but that He loved us and sent His Son to be the propitiation for our sins. 1 JOHN 4:9–10 • That He might be just and the justifier of the one who has faith in Jesus. ROMANS 3:26 •

February 24

Morning Reading

Thus says the Lord God: *"I will also let the house of Israel
inquire of Me to do this for them."*
EZEKIEL 36:37

You do not have because you do not ask. JAMES 4:2 • Ask, and it will be given to you; seek, and you will find; knock, and it will be opened to you. For everyone who asks receives, and he who seeks finds, and to him who knocks it will be opened. MATTHEW 7:7–8 • This is the confidence that we have in Him, that if we ask anything according to His will, He hears us. And if we know that He hears us, whatever we ask, we know that we have the petitions that we have asked of Him. 1 JOHN 5:14–15 • If any of you lacks wisdom, let him ask of God, who gives to all liberally and without reproach, and it will be given to him. JAMES 1:5 • I am the LORD your God, who brought you out of the land of Egypt; open your mouth wide, and I will fill it. PSALM 81:10 • Men always ought to pray and not lose heart. LUKE 18:1 •

The eyes of the LORD are on the righteous, and His ears are open to their cry....The righteous cry out, and the LORD hears, and delivers them out of all their troubles. PSALM 34:15, 17 • You will ask in My name, and I do not say to you that I shall pray the Father for you; for the Father Himself loves you, because you have loved Me. JOHN 16:26–27 • Ask, and you will receive, that your joy may be full. JOHN 16:24 •

Evening Reading

Shall we indeed accept good from God, and...not...adversity?
JOB 2:10

I know, O LORD, that Your judgments are right, and that in faithfulness You have afflicted me. PSALM 119:75 • O LORD, You are our Father; we are the clay, and You our potter; and all we are the work of Your hand. ISAIAH 64:8 • It is the LORD. Let Him do what seems good to Him. 1 SAMUEL 3:18 • Righteous are You, O LORD, when I plead with You; yet let me talk with You about Your judgments. JEREMIAH 12:1 •

He will sit as a refiner and a purifier of silver. MALACHI 3:3 • Whom the LORD loves He chastens, and scourges every son whom He receives. HEBREWS 12:6 • It is enough for a disciple that he be like his teacher, and a servant like his master. If they have called the master of the house Beelzebub, how much more will they call those of his household! MATTHEW 10:25 • Though He was a Son, yet He learned obedience by the things which He suffered. HEBREWS 5:8 •

But rejoice to the extent that you partake of Christ's sufferings, that when His glory is revealed, you may also be glad with exceeding joy. 1 PETER 4:13 • These are the ones who come out of the great tribulation, and washed their robes and made them white in the blood of the Lamb. REVELATION 7:14 •

February 25

Morning Reading

Resist the devil and he will flee from you.
JAMES 4:7

When the enemy comes in like a flood, the Spirit of the LORD will lift up a standard against him. ISAIAH 59:19 • Then Jesus said to him, "Away with you, Satan! For it is written, 'You shall worship the LORD your God, and Him only you shall serve.'" Then the devil left Him, and behold, angels came and ministered to Him. MATTHEW 4:10–11 •

Be strong in the Lord and in the power of His might. Put on the whole armor of God, that you may be able to stand against the wiles of the devil. EPHESIANS 6:10–11 • And have no fellowship with the unfruitful works of darkness, but rather expose them. EPHESIANS 5:11 • Lest Satan should take advantage of us; for we are not ignorant of his devices. 2 CORINTHIANS 2:11 • Be sober, be vigilant; because your adversary the devil walks about like a roaring lion, seeking whom he may devour. Resist him, steadfast in the faith, knowing that the same sufferings are experienced by your brotherhood in the world. 1 PETER 5:8–9 • This is the victory that has overcome the world; [even] our faith. 1 JOHN 5:4 •

Who shall bring a charge against God's elect? It is God who justifies. ROMANS 8:33 •

Evening Reading

Oh, that I knew where I might find Him!
JOB 23:3

Who among you fears the LORD? Who obeys the voice of His Servant? Who walks in darkness and has no light? Let him trust in the name of the LORD and rely upon his God. ISAIAH 50:10 •

You will seek Me and find Me, when you search for Me with all your heart. JEREMIAH 29:13 • Seek, and you will find; knock, and it will be opened to you. For everyone who asks receives, and he who seeks finds, and to him who knocks it will be opened. LUKE 11:9–10 •

Truly our fellowship is with the Father and with His Son Jesus Christ. 1 JOHN 1:3 • Now in Christ Jesus you who once were far off have been brought near by the blood of Christ....For through Him we both have access by one Spirit to the Father. EPHESIANS 2:13, 18 •

If we say that we have fellowship with Him, and walk in darkness, we lie and do not practice the truth. 1 JOHN 1:6 •

Lo, I am with you always. MATTHEW 28:20 • I will never leave you nor forsake you. HEBREWS 13:5 • [The Helper] dwells with you and will be in you. JOHN 14:17 •

February 26

Morning Reading

Let us search out and examine our ways,
and turn back to the LORD.
LAMENTATIONS 3:40

Examine me, O LORD, and prove me; try my mind and my heart. PSALM 26:2 • Behold, You desire truth in the inward parts, and in the hidden part You will make me to know wisdom. PSALM 51:6 • I thought about my ways, and turned my feet to Your testimonies. I made haste, and did not delay to keep Your commandments. PSALM 119:59–60 • Let a man examine himself, and so let him eat of the bread and drink of the cup. 1 CORINTHIANS 11:28 •

If we confess our sins, He is faithful and just to forgive us our sins and to cleanse us from all unrighteousness. 1 JOHN 1:9 • We have an Advocate with the Father, Jesus Christ the righteous. 1 JOHN 2:1 • Therefore, brethren, having boldness to enter the Holiest by the blood of Jesus, by a new and living way which He consecrated for us, through the veil, that is, His flesh, and having a High Priest over the house of God, let us draw near with a true heart in full assurance of faith, having our hearts sprinkled from an evil conscience and our bodies washed with pure water. HEBREWS 10:19–22 •

Evening Reading

There was a rainbow around the throne,
in appearance like an emerald.
REVELATION 4:3

And God said: "This is the sign of the covenant which I make between Me and you, and every living creature that is with you, for perpetual generations: I set My rainbow in the cloud....The rainbow shall be in the cloud, and I will look on it to remember the everlasting covenant between God and every living creature of all flesh that is on the earth." GENESIS 9:12–13, 16 • An everlasting covenant, ordered in all things and secure. 2 SAMUEL 23:5 • That by two immutable things, in which it is impossible for God to lie, we might have strong consolation, who have fled for refuge to lay hold of the hope set before us. HEBREWS 6:18 •

We declare to you glad tidings; that promise which was made to the fathers. God has fulfilled this for us their children, in that He has raised up Jesus. ACTS 13:32–33 •

Jesus Christ is the same yesterday, today, and forever. HEBREWS 13:8 •

February 27

Morning Reading

Reckon yourselves to be dead indeed to sin,
but alive to God in Christ Jesus our Lord.
ROMANS 6:11

He who hears My word and believes in Him who sent Me has everlasting life, and shall not come into judgment, but has passed from death into life. JOHN 5:24 • For I through the law died to the law that I might live to God. I have been crucified with Christ; it is no longer I who live, but Christ lives in me; and the life which I now live in the flesh I live by faith in the Son of God, who loved me and gave Himself for me. GALATIANS 2:19–20 •

Because I live, you will live also. JOHN 14:19 • I give them eternal life, and they shall never perish; neither shall anyone snatch them out of My hand. My Father, who has given them to Me, is greater than all; and no one is able to snatch them out of My Father's hand. I and My Father are one. JOHN 10:28–30 •

If then you were raised with Christ, seek those things which are above, where Christ is, sitting at the right hand of God....For you died, and your life is hidden with Christ in God. COLOSSIANS 3:1, 3 •

Evening Reading

God...gives to all liberally and without reproach.
JAMES 1:5

[Jesus] said to her, "Woman, where are those accusers of yours? Has no one condemned you?" She said, "No one, Lord." And Jesus said to her, "Neither do I condemn you; go and sin no more." JOHN 8:10–11 •

The grace of God and the gift by the grace of the one Man, Jesus Christ, abounded to many....The free gift which came from many offenses resulted in justification. ROMANS 5:15–16 •

God, who is rich in mercy, because of His great love with which He loved us, even when we were dead in trespasses, made us alive together with Christ (by grace you have been saved), and raised us up together, and made us sit together in the heavenly places in Christ Jesus, that in the ages to come He might show the exceeding riches of His grace in His kindness toward us in Christ Jesus. EPHESIANS 2:4–7 •

He who did not spare His own Son, but delivered Him up for us all, how shall He not with Him also freely give us all things? ROMANS 8:32 •

February 28

Morning Reading

*God so loved the world that He gave His only begotten Son,
that whoever believes in Him should not perish
but have everlasting life.*
JOHN 3:16

God...has reconciled us to Himself through Jesus Christ, and has given us the ministry of reconciliation, that is, that God was in Christ reconciling the world to Himself, not imputing their trespasses to them, and has committed to us the word of reconciliation. Now then, we are ambassadors for Christ, as though God were pleading through us: we implore you on Christ's behalf, be reconciled to God. For He made Him who knew no sin to be sin for us, that we might become the righteousness of God in Him. 2 CORINTHIANS 5:18–21 • God is love. In this the love of God was manifested toward us, that God has sent His only begotten Son into the world, that we might live through Him. In this is love, not that we loved God, but that He loved us and sent His Son to be the propitiation for our sins. Beloved, if God so loved us, we also ought to love one another. 1 JOHN 4:8–11 •

Evening Reading

The spirit of a man is the lamp of the LORD.
PROVERBS 20:27

[Jesus] said to them, "He who is without sin among you, let him throw a stone at her first."...Then those who heard it, being convicted by their conscience, went out one by one, beginning with the oldest even to the last. JOHN 8:7, 9 •

And [God] said, "Who told you that you were naked? Have you eaten from the tree of which I commanded you that you should not eat?" GENESIS 3:11 •

Therefore, to him who knows to do good and does not do it, to him it is sin. JAMES 4:17 • If our heart condemns us, God is greater than our heart, and knows all things. Beloved, if our heart does not condemn us, we have confidence toward God. 1 JOHN 3:20–21 •

All things indeed are pure, but it is evil for the man who eats with offense....Happy is he who does not condemn himself in what he approves. ROMANS 14:20, 22 •

Search me, O God, and know my heart; try me, and know my anxieties; and see if there is any wicked way in me, and lead me in the way everlasting. PSALM 139:23–24 •

February 29

Morning Reading

*Do not boast about tomorrow, for you do not know
what a day may bring forth.*
PROVERBS 27:1

Behold, now is the accepted time; behold, now is the day of salvation. 2 CORINTHIANS 6:2 • A little while longer the light is with you. Walk while you have the light, lest darkness overtake you; he who walks in darkness does not know where he is going. While you have the light, believe in the light, that you may become sons of light. JOHN 12:35–36 •

Whatever your hand finds to do, do it with your might; for there is no work or device or knowledge or wisdom in the grave where you are going. ECCLESIASTES 9:10 •

And I will say to my soul, "Soul, you have many goods laid up for many years; take your ease; eat, drink, and be merry." But God said to him, "Fool! This night your soul will be required of you; then whose will those things be which you have provided?" So is he who lays up treasure for himself, and is not rich toward God. LUKE 12:19–21 •

What is your life? It is even a vapor that appears for a little time and then vanishes away. JAMES 4:14 • The world is passing away, and the lust of it; but he who does the will of God abides forever. 1 JOHN 2:17 •

Evening Reading

You are the same, and Your years will have no end.
PSALM 102:27

Before the mountains were brought forth, or ever You had formed the earth and the world, even from everlasting to everlasting, You are God. PSALM 90:2 •

I am the LORD, I do not change; therefore you are not consumed, O sons of Jacob. MALACHI 3:6 • The same yesterday, today, and forever. HEBREWS 13:8 •

Every good gift and every perfect gift is from above, and comes down from the Father of lights, with whom there is no variation or shadow of turning. JAMES 1:17 • For the gifts and the calling of God are irrevocable. ROMANS 11:29 •

God is not a man, that He should lie, nor a son of man, that He should repent. NUMBERS 23:19 • Through the Lord's mercies we are not consumed, because His compassions fail not. LAMENTATIONS 3:22 •

But He, because He continues forever, has an unchangeable priesthood. Therefore He is also able to save to the uttermost those who come to God through Him, since He always lives to make intercession for them. HEBREWS 7:24–25 • Do not be afraid; I am the First and the Last. REVELATION 1:17 •

 MARCH

March 1

Morning Reading

The fruit of the Spirit is love.
GALATIANS 5:22

God is love, and he who abides in love abides in God, and God in him. 1 JOHN 4:16 • The love of God has been poured out in our hearts by the Holy Spirit who was given to us. ROMANS 5:5 • To you who believe, He is precious. 1 PETER 2:7 • We love Him because He first loved us. 1 JOHN 4:19 • The love of Christ compels us, because we judge thus: that if One died for all, then all died; and He died for all, that those who live should live no longer for themselves, but for Him who died for them and rose again. 2 CORINTHIANS 5:14–15 •

You yourselves are taught by God to love one another. 1 THESSALONIANS 4:9 • This is My commandment, that you love one another as I have loved you. JOHN 15:12 • And above all things have fervent love for one another, for "love will cover a multitude of sins." 1 PETER 4:8 • Walk in love, as Christ also has loved us and given Himself for us, an offering and a sacrifice to God for a sweet-smelling aroma. EPHESIANS 5:2 •

Evening Reading

The-LORD-Is-My-Banner.
EXODUS 17:15

If God is for us, who can be against us? ROMANS 8:31 • The LORD is on my side; I will not fear. What can man do to me? PSALM 118:6 •

You have given a banner to those who fear You. PSALM 60:4 •

The LORD is my light and my salvation; whom shall I fear? The LORD is the strength of my life; of whom shall I be afraid?...Though an army may encamp against me, my heart shall not fear; though war should rise against me, in this I will be confident. PSALM 27:1, 3 •

Look, God Himself is with us as our head. 2 CHRONICLES 13:12 • The LORD of hosts is with us; the God of Jacob is our refuge. PSALM 46:7 •

These will make war with the Lamb, and the Lamb will overcome them. REVELATION 17:14 •

Why do the nations rage, and the people plot a vain thing?...He who sits in the heavens shall laugh; the LORD shall hold them in derision. PSALM 2:1, 4 • Take counsel together, but it will come to nothing; speak the word, but it will not stand, for God is with us. ISAIAH 8:10 •

Morning Reading

God has caused me to be fruitful in the land of my affliction.
GENESIS 41:52

Blessed be the God and Father of our Lord Jesus Christ, the Father of mercies and God of all comfort, who comforts us in all our tribulation, that we may be able to comfort those who are in any trouble, with the comfort with which we ourselves are comforted by God. For as the sufferings of Christ abound in us, so our consolation also abounds through Christ. 2 CORINTHIANS 1:3–5 •

Now for a little while, if need be, you have been grieved by various trials, that the genuineness of your faith, being much more precious than gold that perishes, though it is tested by fire, may be found to praise, honor, and glory at the revelation of Jesus Christ. 1 PETER 1:6–7 • The Lord stood with me and strengthened me, so that the message might be preached fully through me, and that all the Gentiles might hear. And I was delivered out of the mouth of the lion. 2 TIMOTHY 4:17 •

Let those who suffer according to the will of God commit their souls to Him in doing good, as to a faithful Creator. 1 PETER 4:19 •

Evening Reading

There remains therefore a rest for the people of God.
HEBREWS 4:9

There the wicked cease from troubling, and there the weary are at rest. There the prisoners rest together; they do not hear the voice of the oppressor. JOB 3:17–18 •

Blessed are the dead who die in the Lord from now on....They... rest from their labors, and their works follow them. REVELATION 14:13 •

[Jesus] said to them, "Our friend Lazarus sleeps."...Jesus spoke of his death, but they thought that He was speaking about taking rest in sleep. JOHN 11:11, 13 •

We who are in this tent groan, being burdened. 2 CORINTHIANS 5:4 •

We also who have the firstfruits of the Spirit, even we ourselves groan within ourselves, eagerly waiting for the adoption, the redemption of our body. For we were saved in this hope, but hope that is seen is not hope; for why does one still hope for what he sees? But if we hope for what we do not see, we eagerly wait for it with perseverance. ROMANS 8:23–25 •

March 3

Morning Reading

Trust in the LORD with all your heart, and lean not on your own understanding; in all your ways acknowledge Him, and He shall direct your paths.
PROVERBS 3:5–6

Trust in Him at all times, you people; pour out your heart before Him; God is a refuge for us. PSALM 62:8 •

I will instruct you and teach you in the way you should go; I will guide you with My eye. Do not be like the horse or like the mule, which have no understanding, which must be harnessed with bit and bridle, else they will not come near you. Many sorrows shall be to the wicked; but he who trusts in the LORD, mercy shall surround him. PSALM 32:8–10 • Your ears shall hear a word behind you, saying, "This is the way, walk in it," whenever you turn to the right hand or whenever you turn to the left. ISAIAH 30:21 •

Then [Moses] said to Him, "If Your Presence does not go with us, do not bring us up from here. For how then will it be known that Your people and I have found grace in Your sight, except You go with us? So we shall be separate, Your people and I, from all the people who are upon the face of the earth." EXODUS 33:15–16 •

Evening Reading

I press toward the goal for the prize of the upward call of God in Christ Jesus.
PHILIPPIANS 3:14

You will have treasure in heaven;...come, follow Me. MATTHEW 19:21 • I am...your exceedingly great reward. GENESIS 15:1 •

Well done, good and faithful servant; you were faithful over a few things, I will make you ruler over many things. Enter into the joy of your lord. MATTHEW 25:21 • They shall reign forever and ever. REVELATION 22:5 •

You will receive the crown of glory that does not fade away. 1 PETER 5:4 • The crown of life. JAMES 1:12 • The crown of righteousness. 2 TIMOTHY 4:8 • An imperishable crown. 1 CORINTHIANS 9:25 •

Father, I desire that they also whom You gave Me may be with Me where I am, that they may behold My glory which You have given Me. JOHN 17:24 • Thus we shall always be with the Lord. 1 THESSALONIANS 4:17 •

I consider that the sufferings of this present time are not worthy to be compared with the glory which shall be revealed in us. ROMANS 8:18 •

March 4

Morning Reading

Set your mind on things above, not on things on the earth.
COLOSSIANS 3:2

Do not love the world or the things in the world. If anyone loves the world, the love of the Father is not in him. 1 JOHN 2:15 • Do not lay up for yourselves treasures on earth, where moth and rust destroy and where thieves break in and steal; but lay up for yourselves treasures in heaven, where neither moth nor rust destroys and where thieves do not break in and steal. For where your treasure is, there your heart will be also. MATTHEW 6:19–21 •

For we walk by faith, not by sight. 2 CORINTHIANS 5:7 • We do not lose heart. Even though our outward man is perishing, yet the inward man is being renewed day by day. For our light affliction, which is but for a moment, is working for us a far more exceeding and eternal weight of glory, while we do not look at the things which are seen, but at the things which are not seen. For the things which are seen are temporary, but the things which are not seen are eternal. 2 CORINTHIANS 4:16–18 • To an inheritance incorruptible and undefiled and that does not fade away, reserved in heaven for you. 1 PETER 1:4 •

Evening Reading

He bowed his shoulder to bear a burden.
GENESIS 49:15

My brethren, take the prophets, who spoke in the name of the Lord, as an example of suffering and patience. JAMES 5:10 • Now all these things happened to them as examples, and they were written for our admonition, upon whom the ends of the ages have come. 1 CORINTHIANS 10:11 •

Shall we indeed accept good from God, and shall we not accept adversity? JOB 2:10 • Aaron held his peace. LEVITICUS 10:3 • It is the LORD. Let Him do what seems good to Him. 1 SAMUEL 3:18 •

Cast your burden on the LORD, and He shall sustain you. PSALM 55:22 • Surely He has borne our griefs and carried our sorrows. ISAIAH 53:4 •

Come to Me, all you who labor and are heavy laden, and I will give you rest. Take My yoke upon you and learn from Me, for I am gentle and lowly in heart, and you will find rest for your souls. For My yoke is easy and My burden is light. MATTHEW 11:28–30 •

March 5

Morning Reading

O LORD, I am oppressed; undertake for me!
ISAIAH 38:14

Unto You I lift up my eyes, O You who dwell in the heavens. Behold, as the eyes of servants look to the hand of their masters, as the eyes of a maid to the hand of her mistress, so our eyes look to the LORD our God. PSALM 123:1–2 • Hear my cry, O God; attend to my prayer. From the end of the earth I will cry to You, when my heart is overwhelmed; lead me to the rock that is higher than I. For You have been a shelter for me, a strong tower from the enemy. I will abide in Your tabernacle forever; I will trust in the shelter of Your wings. PSALM 61:1–4 • You have been a strength to the poor, a strength to the needy in his distress, a refuge from the storm. ISAIAH 25:4 •

Christ also suffered for us, leaving us an example, that you should follow His steps: "Who committed no sin, nor was deceit found in His mouth"; who, when He was reviled, did not revile in return; when He suffered, He did not threaten, but committed Himself to Him who judges righteously. 1 PETER 2:21–23 •

Evening Reading

Fight the good fight of faith.
1 TIMOTHY 6:12

We were troubled on every side. Outside were conflicts, inside were fears. 2 CORINTHIANS 7:5 • Do not fear, for those who are with us are more than those who are with them. 2 KINGS 6:16 • Be strong in the Lord and in the power of His might. EPHESIANS 6:10 •

Then David said to the Philistine, "You come to me with a sword, with a spear, and with a javelin. But I come to you in the name of the LORD of hosts, the God of the armies of Israel, whom you have defied." 1 SAMUEL 17:45 • God is my strength and power....He teaches my hands to make war, so that my arms can bend a bow of bronze. 2 SAMUEL 22:33, 35 • Our sufficiency is from God. 2 CORINTHIANS 3:5 •

The angel of the LORD encamps all around those who fear Him, and delivers them. PSALM 34:7 • Behold, the mountain was full of horses and chariots of fire all around Elisha. 2 KINGS 6:17 •

Time would fail me to tell of Gideon and Barak and Samson and Jephthah, also of David and Samuel and the prophets: who through faith subdued kingdoms, worked righteousness, obtained promises, stopped the mouths of lions, quenched the violence of fire, escaped the edge of the sword, out of weakness were made strong, became valiant in battle, turned to flight the armies of the aliens. HEBREWS 11:32–34 •

March 6

Morning Reading

He...preserves the way of His saints.
PROVERBS 2:8

The LORD your God...went in the way before you to search out a place for you to pitch your tents, to show you the way you should go, in the fire by night and in the cloud by day. DEUTERONOMY 1:32–33 • As an eagle stirs up its nest, hovers over its young, spreading out its wings, taking them up, carrying them on its wings, so the LORD alone led him, and there was no foreign god with him. DEUTERONOMY 32:11–12 • The steps of a good man are ordered by the LORD, and He delights in his way. Though he fall, he shall not be utterly cast down; for the LORD upholds him with His hand. PSALM 37:23–24 • Many are the afflictions of the righteous, but the LORD delivers him out of them all. PSALM 34:19 • For the LORD knows the way of the righteous, but the way of the ungodly shall perish. PSALM 1:6 • We know that all things work together for good to those who love God, to those who are the called according to His purpose. ROMANS 8:28 • With him is an arm of flesh; but with us is the LORD our God, to help us and to fight our battles. 2 CHRONICLES 32:8 •

The LORD your God in your midst, the Mighty One, will save; He will rejoice over you with gladness. ZEPHANIAH 3:17 •

Evening Reading

My God, My God, why have You forsaken Me?
MATTHEW 27:46

He was wounded for our transgressions, He was bruised for our iniquities; the chastisement for our peace was upon Him,...and the LORD has laid on Him the iniquity of us all. ISAIAH 53:5–6 • For the transgressions of My people He was stricken....Yet it pleased the LORD to bruise Him; He has put Him to grief. ISAIAH 53:8, 10 •

Jesus our Lord...was delivered up because of our offenses. ROMANS 4:24–25 • Christ also suffered once for sins, the just for the unjust, that He might bring us to God. 1 PETER 3:18 • Who Himself bore our sins in His own body on the tree, that we, having died to sins, might live for righteousness; by whose stripes you were healed. 1 PETER 2:24 •

He made Him who knew no sin to be sin for us, that we might become the righteousness of God in Him. 2 CORINTHIANS 5:21 •

Christ has redeemed us from the curse of the law, having become a curse for us. GALATIANS 3:13 •

March 7

Morning Reading

Your Maker is your husband, the LORD of hosts is His name.
ISAIAH 54:5

This is a great mystery, but I speak concerning Christ and the church. EPHESIANS 5:32 •

You shall no longer be termed Forsaken,...but you shall be called Hephzibah, and your land Beulah; for the LORD delights in you, and your land shall be married....And as the bridegroom rejoices over the bride, so shall your God rejoice over you. ISAIAH 62:4–5 • He has sent Me...to comfort all who mourn, to console those who mourn in Zion, to give them beauty for ashes, the oil of joy for mourning, the garment of praise for the spirit of heaviness. ISAIAH 61:1–3 •

I will greatly rejoice in the LORD, my soul shall be joyful in my God; for He has clothed me with the garments of salvation...as a bridegroom decks himself with ornaments, and as a bride adorns herself with her jewels. ISAIAH 61:10 •

I will betroth you to Me forever; yes, I will betroth you to Me in righteousness and justice, in lovingkindness and mercy. HOSEA 2:19 •

Who shall separate us from the love of Christ? ROMANS 8:35 •

Evening Reading

My times are in Your hand.
PSALM 31:15

All His saints are in Your hand. DEUTERONOMY 33:3 • The word of the LORD came to [Elijah], saying, "Get away from here and turn eastward, and hide by the Brook Cherith, which flows into the Jordan. And it will be that you shall drink from the brook, and I have commanded the ravens to feed you there."...Then the word of the LORD came to him, saying, "Arise, go to Zarephath, which belongs to Sidon, and dwell there. See, I have commanded a widow there to provide for you." 1 KINGS 17:2–4, 8–9 •

Do not worry about your life, what you will eat or what you will drink; nor about your body, what you will put on....For your heavenly Father knows that you need all these things. MATTHEW 6:25, 32 •

Trust in the LORD with all your heart, and lean not on your own understanding; in all your ways acknowledge Him, and He shall direct your paths. PROVERBS 3:5–6 • Casting all your care upon Him, for He cares for you. 1 PETER 5:7 •

March 8

Morning Reading

You have cast all my sins behind Your back.
ISAIAH 38:17

Who is a God like You, pardoning iniquity and passing over the transgression of the remnant of His heritage? He does not retain His anger forever, because He delights in mercy. He will again have compassion on us, and will subdue our iniquities. You will cast all our sins into the depths of the sea. MICAH 7:18–19 •

"For a mere moment I have forsaken you, but with great mercies I will gather you. With a little wrath I hid My face from you for a moment; but with everlasting kindness I will have mercy on you," says the LORD, your Redeemer. ISAIAH 54:7–8 • I will forgive their iniquity, and their sin I will remember no more. JEREMIAH 31:34 •

Blessed is he whose transgression is forgiven, whose sin is covered. Blessed is the man to whom the LORD does not impute iniquity, and in whose spirit there is no deceit. PSALM 32:1–2 • The blood of Jesus Christ His Son cleanses us from all sin. 1 JOHN 1:7 •

Evening Reading

I know whom I have believed and am persuaded that He is able.
2 TIMOTHY 1:12

Able to do exceedingly abundantly above all that we ask or think. EPHESIANS 3:20 •

Able to make all grace abound toward you, that you, always having all sufficiency in all things, may have an abundance for every good work. 2 CORINTHIANS 9:8 •

Able to aid those who are tempted. HEBREWS 2:18 •

Able to save to the uttermost those who come to God through Him, since He always lives to make intercession for them. HEBREWS 7:25 •

Able to keep you from stumbling, and to present you faultless before the presence of His glory with exceeding joy. JUDE 24 •

Able to keep what I have committed to Him until that Day. 2 TIMOTHY 1:12 •

[Christ] will transform our lowly body that it may be conformed to His glorious body, according to the working by which He is able even to subdue all things to Himself. PHILIPPIANS 3:21 •

Jesus said to [the blind men], "Do you believe that I am able to do this?...According to your faith let it be to you." MATTHEW 9:28–29 •

March 9

Morning Reading

Trust in...the living God, who gives us richly all things to enjoy.
1 TIMOTHY 6:17

Beware that you do not forget the LORD your God by not keeping His commandments, His judgments, and His statutes which I command you today, lest—when you have eaten and are full, and have built beautiful houses and dwell in them...your heart is lifted up, and you forget the LORD your God...for it is He who gives you power to get wealth. DEUTERONOMY 8:11–12, 14, 18 •

Unless the LORD builds the house, they labor in vain who build it; unless the LORD guards the city, the watchman stays awake in vain. It is vain for you to rise up early, to sit up late, to eat the bread of sorrows; for so He gives His beloved sleep. PSALM 127:1–2 • They did not gain possession of the land by their own sword, nor did their own arm save them; but it was Your right hand, Your arm, and the light of Your countenance, because You favored them. PSALM 44:3 • There are many who say, "Who will show us any good?" LORD, lift up the light of Your countenance upon us. PSALM 4:6 •

Evening Reading

They sang as it were a new song.
REVELATION 14:3

A new and living way which He consecrated for us. HEBREWS 10:20 • Not by works of righteousness which we have done, but according to His mercy He saved us, through the washing of regeneration and renewing of the Holy Spirit, whom He poured out on us abundantly through Jesus Christ our Savior. TITUS 3:5–6 • By grace you have been saved through faith, and that not of yourselves; it is the gift of God, not of works, lest anyone should boast. EPHESIANS 2:8–9 •

Not unto us, O LORD, not unto us, but to Your name give glory. PSALM 115:1 • To Him who loved us and washed us from our sins in His own blood, and has made us kings and priests to His God and Father, to Him be glory and dominion forever and ever. Amen. REVELATION 1:5–6 • They sang a new song, saying: "...You were slain, and have redeemed us to God by Your blood out of every tribe and tongue and people and nation." REVELATION 5:9 • I looked, and behold, a great multitude which no one could number,...crying out with a loud voice, saying, "Salvation belongs to our God who sits on the throne, and to the Lamb!" REVELATION 7:9–10 •

Daily Light on the Daily Path

March 10

Morning Reading

The-Lord-Will-Provide.
GENESIS 22:14

God will provide for Himself the lamb for a burnt offering. GENESIS 22:8 •

Behold, the Lord's hand is not shortened, that it cannot save; nor His ear heavy, that it cannot hear. ISAIAH 59:1 • The Deliverer will come out of Zion, and He will turn away ungodliness from Jacob. ROMANS 11:26 •

Happy is he who has the God of Jacob for his help, whose hope is in the LORD his God. PSALM 146:5 • Behold, the eye of the LORD is on those who fear Him, on those who hope in His mercy, to deliver their soul from death, and to keep them alive in famine. PSALM 33:18–19 •

My God shall supply all your need according to His riches in glory by Christ Jesus. PHILIPPIANS 4:19 • He Himself has said, "I will never leave you nor forsake you." So we may boldly say: "The LORD is my helper; I will not fear. What can man do to me?" HEBREWS 13:5–6 • The LORD is my strength and my shield; my heart trusted in Him, and I am helped; therefore my heart greatly rejoices, and with my song I will praise Him. PSALM 28:7 •

Evening Reading

He feeds his flock among the lilies.
SONG OF SONGS 2:16

Where two or three are gathered together in My name, I am there in the midst of them. MATTHEW 18:20 • If anyone loves Me, he will keep My word; and My Father will love him, and We will come to him and make Our home with him. JOHN 14:23 •

If you keep My commandments, you will abide in My love, just as I have kept My Father's commandments and abide in His love. JOHN 15:10 •

Let my beloved come to his garden and eat its pleasant fruits. SONG OF SONGS 4:16 • I have come to my garden, my sister, my spouse; I have gathered my myrrh with my spice; I have eaten my honeycomb with my honey. SONG OF SONGS 5:1 • The fruit of the Spirit is love, joy, peace, longsuffering, kindness, goodness, faithfulness, gentleness, self-control. GALATIANS 5:22–23 •

By this My Father is glorified, that you bear much fruit; so you will be My disciples. JOHN 15:8 • Every branch in Me that does not bear fruit He takes away; and every branch that bears fruit He prunes, that it may bear more fruit. JOHN 15:2 • Being filled with the fruits of righteousness which are by Jesus Christ, to the glory and praise of God. PHILIPPIANS 1:11 •

March 11

Morning Reading

The LORD bless you and keep you.
NUMBERS 6:24

The blessing of the LORD makes one rich, and He adds no sorrow with it. PROVERBS 10:22 • You, O LORD, will bless the righteous; with favor You will surround him as with a shield. PSALM 5:12 •

He will not allow your foot to be moved; He who keeps you will not slumber. Behold, He who keeps Israel shall neither slumber nor sleep. The LORD is your keeper; the LORD is your shade at your right hand....The LORD shall preserve you from all evil; He shall preserve your soul. The LORD shall preserve your going out and your coming in from this time forth, and even forevermore. PSALM 121:3–5, 7–8 • I, the LORD, keep it, I water it every moment; lest any hurt it, I keep it night and day. ISAIAH 27:3 •

Holy Father, keep through Your name those whom You have given Me, that they may be one as We are. While I was with them in the world, I kept them in Your name. Those whom You gave Me I have kept. JOHN 17:11–12 •

The Lord will deliver me from every evil work and preserve me for His heavenly kingdom. To Him be glory forever and ever. Amen! 2 TIMOTHY 4:18 •

Evening Reading

Jesus wept.
JOHN 11:35

A Man of sorrows and acquainted with grief. ISAIAH 53:3 • We do not have a High Priest who cannot sympathize with our weaknesses. HEBREWS 4:15 • It was fitting for Him, for whom are all things and by whom are all things, in bringing many sons to glory, to make the captain of their salvation perfect through sufferings. HEBREWS 2:10 • Though He was a Son, yet He learned obedience by the things which He suffered. HEBREWS 5:8 •

I was not rebellious, nor did I turn away. I gave My back to those who struck Me, and My cheeks to those who plucked out the beard; I did not hide My face from shame and spitting. ISAIAH 50:5–6 •

See how He loved him! JOHN 11:36 • For indeed [Jesus] does not give aid to angels, but He does give aid to the seed of Abraham. Therefore, in all things He had to be made like His brethren, that He might be a merciful and faithful High Priest in things pertaining to God, to make propitiation for the sins of the people. HEBREWS 2:16–17 •

March 12

Morning Reading

*The LORD make His face shine upon you, and be gracious to you; the
LORD lift up His countenance upon you, and give you peace.*
NUMBERS 6:25–26

No one has seen God at any time. The only begotten Son, who
is in the bosom of the Father, He has declared Him. JOHN 1:18 • The
brightness of His glory and the express image of His person. HEBREWS
1:3 • Whose minds the god of this age has blinded, who do not believe,
lest the light of the gospel of the glory of Christ, who is the image of
God, should shine on them. 2 CORINTHIANS 4:4 •

Make Your face shine upon Your servant; save me for Your mercies' sake. Do not let me be ashamed, O LORD, for I have called upon
You. PSALM 31:16–17 • LORD, by Your favor You have made my mountain
stand strong; You hid Your face, and I was troubled. PSALM 30:7 • Blessed
are the people who know the joyful sound! They walk, O LORD, in the
light of Your countenance. PSALM 89:15 •

The LORD will give strength to His people; the LORD will bless His
people with peace. PSALM 29:11 •

Jesus spoke to them, saying, "Be of good cheer! It is I; do not be
afraid." MATTHEW 14:27 •

Evening Reading

Things that are pleasing in His sight.
1 JOHN 3:22

Without faith it is impossible to please Him. HEBREWS 11:6 • So then,
those who are in the flesh cannot please God. ROMANS 8:8 • The LORD takes
pleasure in His people. PSALM 149:4 •

For this is commendable, if because of conscience toward God one
endures grief, suffering wrongfully....When you do good and suffer, if
you take it patiently, this is commendable before God. 1 PETER 2:19–20 •
The incorruptible beauty of a gentle and quiet spirit...is very precious
in the sight of God. 1 PETER 3:4 •

Whoever offers praise glorifies Me; and to him who orders his
conduct aright I will show the salvation of God. PSALM 50:23 • I will praise
the name of God with a song, and will magnify Him with thanksgiving.
This also shall please the LORD better than an ox or bull, which has
horns and hooves. PSALM 69:30–31 •

I beseech you therefore, brethren, by the mercies of God, that you
present your bodies a living sacrifice, holy, acceptable to God, which is
your reasonable service. ROMANS 12:1 •

March 13

Morning Reading

For there is one God and one Mediator between God and men, the Man Christ Jesus.
1 TIMOTHY 2:5

Inasmuch then as the children have partaken of flesh and blood, He Himself likewise shared in the same. HEBREWS 2:14 •

Look to Me, and be saved, all you ends of the earth! For I am God, and there is no other. ISAIAH 45:22 •

We have an Advocate with the Father, Jesus Christ the righteous. 1 JOHN 2:1 • In Christ Jesus you who once were far off have been brought near by the blood of Christ. For He Himself is our peace. EPHESIANS 2:13–14 • With His own blood He entered the Most Holy Place once for all, having obtained eternal redemption [for us]. HEBREWS 9:12 • For this reason He is the Mediator of the new covenant, by means of death, for the redemption of the transgressions under the first covenant, that those who are called may receive the promise of the eternal inheritance. HEBREWS 9:15 • Therefore He is also able to save to the uttermost those who come to God through Him, since He always lives to make intercession for them. HEBREWS 7:25 •

Evening Reading

O my God, my soul is cast down within me.
PSALM 42:6

You will keep him in perfect peace, whose mind is stayed on You, because he trusts in You. Trust in the LORD forever, for in YAH, the LORD, is everlasting strength. ISAIAH 26:3–4 •

Cast your burden on the LORD, and He shall sustain you. PSALM 55:22 • For He has not despised nor abhorred the affliction of the afflicted; nor has He hidden His face from Him; but when He cried to Him, He heard. PSALM 22:24 • Is anyone among you suffering? Let him pray. JAMES 5:13 •

Let not your heart be troubled, neither let it be afraid. JOHN 14:27 • Do not worry about your life, what you will eat or what you will drink; nor about your body, what you will put on. Is not life more than food and the body more than clothing? Look at the birds of the air, for they neither sow nor reap nor gather into barns; yet your heavenly Father feeds them. Are you not of more value than they? MATTHEW 6:25–26 • Do not be unbelieving, but believing. JOHN 20:27 • Lo, I am with you always. MATTHEW 28:20 •

March 14

Morning Reading

Adorn the doctrine of God our Savior in all things.
TITUS 2:10

Let your conduct be worthy of the gospel of Christ. PHILIPPIANS 1:27 •
Abstain from every form of evil. 1 THESSALONIANS 5:22 • If you are reproached
for the name of Christ, blessed are you....But let none of you suffer as a
murderer, a thief, an evildoer, or as a busybody in other people's matters. 1 PETER 4:14–15 • That you may become blameless and harmless,
children of God without fault in the midst of a crooked and perverse
generation, among whom you shine as lights in the world. PHILIPPIANS
2:15 • Let your light so shine before men, that they may see your good
works and glorify your Father in heaven. MATTHEW 5:16 •

Let not mercy and truth forsake you; bind them around your
neck, write them on the tablet of your heart, and so find favor and high
esteem in the sight of God and man. PROVERBS 3:3–4 • Finally, brethren,
whatever things are true, whatever things are noble, whatever things
are just, whatever things are pure, whatever things are lovely, whatever
things are of good report, if there is any virtue and if there is anything
praiseworthy; meditate on these things. PHILIPPIANS 4:8 •

Evening Reading

The words that I speak to you are spirit, and they are life.
JOHN 6:63

Of His own will He brought us forth by the word of truth. JAMES 1:18 •
The letter kills, but the Spirit gives life. 2 CORINTHIANS 3:6 •

Christ also loved the church and gave Himself for her, that He
might sanctify and cleanse her with the washing of water by the word,
that He might present her to Himself a glorious church, not having spot
or wrinkle or any such thing. EPHESIANS 5:25–27 •

How can a young man cleanse his way? By taking heed according
to Your word. PSALM 119:9 • Your word has given me life. PSALM 119:50 • Your
word I have hidden in my heart, that I might not sin against You! PSALM
119:11 • I will not forget Your word. PSALM 119:16 • I trust in Your word. PSALM
119:42 • The law of Your mouth is better to me than thousands of coins
of gold and silver. PSALM 119:72 • I will never forget Your precepts, for by
them You have given me life. PSALM 119:93 • How sweet are Your words to
my taste, sweeter than honey to my mouth! Through Your precepts I
get understanding; therefore I hate every false way. PSALM 119:103–04 •

March 15

Morning Reading

Perfect through sufferings.
HEBREWS 2:10

Then [Jesus] said to them, "My soul is exceedingly sorrowful, even to death. Stay here and watch with Me." He went a little farther and fell on His face, and prayed, saying, "O My Father, if it is possible, let this cup pass from Me; nevertheless, not as I will, but as You will." MATTHEW 26:38–39 • And being in agony, He prayed more earnestly. Then His sweat became like great drops of blood falling down to the ground. LUKE 22:44 •

The pains of death surrounded me, and the pangs of Sheol laid hold of me; I found trouble and sorrow. PSALM 116:3 • Reproach has broken my heart, and I am full of heaviness; I looked for someone to take pity, but there was none; and for comforters, but I found none. PSALM 69:20 • Look on my right hand and see, for there is no one who acknowledges me; refuge has failed me; no one cares for my soul. PSALM 142:4 •

He is despised and rejected by men, a Man of sorrows and acquainted with grief. And we hid, as it were, our faces from Him; He was despised, and we did not esteem Him. ISAIAH 53:3 •

Evening Reading

The LORD made the heavens and the earth, the sea,
and all that is in them.
EXODUS 20:11

The heavens declare the glory of God; and the firmament shows His handiwork. PSALM 19:1 • By the word of the LORD the heavens were made, and all the host of them by the breath of His mouth....For He spoke, and it was done; He commanded, and it stood fast. PSALM 33:6, 9 • Behold, the nations are as a drop in a bucket, and are counted as the small dust on the scales; look, He lifts up the isles as a very little thing. ISAIAH 40:15 •

By faith we understand that the worlds were framed by the word of God, so that the things which are seen were not made of things which are visible. HEBREWS 11:3 •

When I consider Your heavens, the work of Your fingers, the moon and the stars, which You have ordained, what is man that You are mindful of him, and the son of man that You visit him? PSALM 8:3–4 •

March 16

Morning Reading

For what is your life? It is even a vapor that appears for a little time and then vanishes away.
JAMES 4:14

My days are swifter than a runner; they flee away, they see no good. They pass by like swift ships, like an eagle swooping on its prey. JOB 9:25–26 • You carry them away like a flood; they are like a sleep. In the morning they are like grass which grows up. In the morning it flourishes and grows up; in the evening it is cut down and withers. PSALM 90:5–6 • Man who is born of woman is of few days and full of trouble. He comes forth like a flower and fades away. JOB 14:1–2 •

The world is passing away, and the lust of it; but he who does the will of God abides forever. 1 JOHN 2:17 • [The earth and the heavens] will perish, but You will endure; yes, they will all grow old like a garment; like a cloak You will change them, and they will be changed. But You are the same, and Your years will have no end. PSALM 102:26–27 • Jesus Christ is the same yesterday, today, and forever. HEBREWS 13:8 •

Evening Reading

I will sing with the spirit, and I will also sing with the understanding.
1 CORINTHIANS 14:15

Be filled with the Spirit, speaking to one another in psalms and hymns and spiritual songs, singing and making melody in your heart to the Lord. EPHESIANS 5:18–19 • Let the word of Christ dwell in you richly in all wisdom, teaching and admonishing one another in psalms and hymns and spiritual songs, singing with grace in your hearts to the Lord. COLOSSIANS 3:16 •

My mouth shall speak the praise of the LORD, and all flesh shall bless His holy name forever and ever. PSALM 145:21 •

Praise the LORD! For it is good to sing praises to our God; for it is pleasant, and praise is beautiful. PSALM 147:1 • Sing to the LORD with thanksgiving; sing praises on the harp to our God. PSALM 147:7 •

I heard a voice from heaven, like the voice of many waters, and like the voice of loud thunder. And I heard the sound of harpists playing their harps. REVELATION 14:2 •

Morning Reading

He shall put his hand on the head of the burnt offering, and it will be accepted on his behalf to make atonement for him.
LEVITICUS 1:4

Knowing that you were not redeemed with corruptible things, like silver or gold, from your aimless conduct received by tradition from your fathers, but with the precious blood of Christ, as of a lamb without blemish and without spot. 1 PETER 1:18–19 • Who Himself bore our sins in His own body on the tree. 1 PETER 2:24 •

[God] has made us accepted in the Beloved. EPHESIANS 1:6 •

As living stones,...built up a spiritual house, a holy priesthood, to offer up spiritual sacrifices acceptable to God through Jesus Christ. 1 PETER 2:5 • I beseech you therefore, brethren, by the mercies of God, that you present your bodies a living sacrifice, holy, acceptable to God, which is your reasonable service. ROMANS 12:1 •

Now to Him who is able to keep you from stumbling, and to present you faultless before the presence of His glory with exceeding joy, to God our Savior, who alone is wise, be glory and majesty, dominion and power, both now and forever. JUDE 24–25 •

Evening Reading

In all points tempted as we are, yet without sin.
HEBREWS 4:15

For all that is in the world; the lust of the flesh, the lust of the eyes, and the pride of life; is not of the Father but is of the world. 1 JOHN 2:16 • When the woman saw that the tree was good for food [the lust of the flesh], that it was pleasant to the eyes [the lust of the eyes], and a tree desirable to make one wise [the pride of life], she took of its fruit and ate. She also gave to her husband with her, and he ate. GENESIS 3:6 •

When the tempter came to Him, he said, "If You are the Son of God, command that these stones become bread [the lust of the flesh]." But He answered and said, "It is written, 'Man shall not live by bread alone, but by every word that proceeds from the mouth of God.'"...Again, the devil took Him up on an exceedingly high mountain, and showed Him all the kingdoms of the world and their glory [the lust of the eyes and the pride of life]....Then Jesus said to him, "Away with you, Satan!" MATTHEW 4:3–4, 8, 10 •

In that He Himself has suffered, being tempted, He is able to aid those who are tempted. HEBREWS 2:18 •

Blessed is the man who endures temptation. JAMES 1:12 •

March 18

Morning Reading

My eyes fail from looking upward.
ISAIAH 38:14

Have mercy on me, O LORD, for I am weak; O LORD, heal me, for my bones are troubled. My soul also is greatly troubled; but You, O LORD; how long? Return, O LORD, deliver me! Oh, save me for Your mercies' sake! PSALM 6:2–4 • My heart is severely pained within me, and the terrors of death have fallen upon me. Fearfulness and trembling have come upon me, and horror has overwhelmed me. So I said, "Oh, that I had wings like a dove! I would fly away and be at rest." PSALM 55:4–6 •

You have need of endurance. HEBREWS 10:36 •

While they looked steadfastly toward heaven as He went up, behold, two men stood by them in white apparel, who also said, "Men of Galilee, why do you stand gazing up into heaven? This same Jesus, who was taken up from you into heaven, will so come in like manner as you saw Him go into heaven." ACTS 1:10–11 • Our citizenship is in heaven, from which we also eagerly wait for the Savior, the Lord Jesus Christ. PHILIPPIANS 3:20 • Looking for the blessed hope and glorious appearing of our great God and Savior Jesus Christ. TITUS 2:13 •

Evening Reading

They shall see His face, and His name shall be on their foreheads.
REVELATION 22:4

I am the good shepherd; and I know My sheep. JOHN 10:14 • The solid foundation of God stands, having this seal: "The Lord knows those who are His," and, "Let everyone who names the name of Christ depart from iniquity." 2 TIMOTHY 2:19 •

The LORD is good, a stronghold in the day of trouble; and He knows those who trust in Him. NAHUM 1:7 • Do not harm the earth, the sea, or the trees till we have sealed the servants of our God on their foreheads. REVELATION 7:3 •

Having believed, you were sealed with the Holy Spirit of promise, who is the guarantee of our inheritance. EPHESIANS 1:13–14 • Now He who establishes us with you in Christ and has anointed us is God, who also has sealed us and given us the Spirit in our hearts as a guarantee. 2 CORINTHIANS 1:21–22 •

I will write on him the name of My God and the name of the city of My God, the New Jerusalem, which comes down out of heaven from My God. And I will write on him My new name. REVELATION 3:12 • This is the name by which she will be called: THE LORD OUR RIGHTEOUSNESS. JEREMIAH 33:16 •

March 19

Morning Reading

God, having raised up His Servant Jesus, sent Him to bless you, in turning away every one of you from your iniquities.
Acts 3:26

Blessed be the God and Father of our Lord Jesus Christ, who according to His abundant mercy has begotten us again to a living hope through the resurrection of Jesus Christ from the dead. 1 Peter 1:3 • Saved by His life. Romans 5:10 •

Our great God and Savior Jesus Christ...gave Himself for us, that He might redeem us from every lawless deed and purify for Himself His own special people, zealous for good works. Titus 2:13–14 • As He who called you is holy, you also be holy in all your conduct, because it is written, "Be holy, for I am holy." 1 Peter 1:15–16 •

The God and Father of our Lord Jesus Christ...has blessed us with every spiritual blessing in the heavenly places in Christ. Ephesians 1:3 • In Him dwells all the fullness of the Godhead bodily; and you are complete in Him. Colossians 2:9–10 • Of His fullness we have all received, and grace for grace. John 1:16 •

He who did not spare His own Son, but delivered Him up for us all, how shall He not with Him also freely give us all things? Romans 8:32 •

Evening Reading

Strengthen me according to Your word.
Psalm 119:28

Remember the word to Your servant, upon which You have caused me to hope. Psalm 119:49 • O Lord, I am oppressed; undertake for me! Isaiah 38:14 •

Heaven and earth will pass away, but My words will by no means pass away. Luke 21:33 • You know in all your hearts and in all your souls that not one thing has failed of all the good things which the Lord your God spoke concerning you. All have come to pass for you; not one word of them has failed. Joshua 23:14 •

And he said, "...Fear not! Peace be to you; be strong, yes, be strong!" So when he spoke to me I was strengthened, and said, "Let my lord speak, for you have strengthened me." Daniel 10:19 •

"Be strong...and work; for I am with you," says the Lord of hosts. Haggai 2:4 • "Not by might nor by power, but by My Spirit," says the Lord of hosts. Zechariah 4:6 •

Be strong in the Lord and in the power of His might. Ephesians 6:10 •

March 20

Morning Reading

The entrance of Your words gives light.
PSALM 119:130

This is the message which we have heard from Him and declare to you, that God is light and in Him is no darkness at all. 1 JOHN 1:5 • God who commanded light to shine out of darkness...has shone in our hearts to give the light of the knowledge of the glory of God in the face of Jesus Christ. 2 CORINTHIANS 4:6 • The Word was God. JOHN 1:1 • In Him was life, and the life was the light of men. JOHN 1:4 • If we walk in the light as He is in the light, we have fellowship with one another, and the blood of Jesus Christ His Son cleanses us from all sin. 1 JOHN 1:7 •

Your word I have hidden in my heart, that I might not sin against You! PSALM 119:11 • You are already clean because of the word which I have spoken to you. JOHN 15:3 •

For you were once darkness, but now you are light in the Lord. Walk as children of light. EPHESIANS 5:8 • You are a chosen generation, a royal priesthood, a holy nation, His own special people, that you may proclaim the praises of Him who called you out of darkness into His marvelous light. 1 PETER 2:9 •

Evening Reading

Noah was a just man.
GENESIS 6:9

The just shall live by faith. GALATIANS 3:11 • Noah built an altar to the LORD, and took of every clean animal and of every clean bird, and offered burnt offerings on the altar. And the LORD smelled a soothing aroma. GENESIS 8:20–21 • The Lamb slain from the foundation of the world. REVELATION 13:8 •

Having been justified by faith, we have peace with God through our Lord Jesus Christ. ROMANS 5:1 •

By the deeds of the law no flesh will be justified in His sight, for by the law is the knowledge of sin. But now the righteousness of God apart from the law is revealed, being witnessed by the Law and the Prophets, even the righteousness of God, through faith in Jesus Christ, to all and on all who believe. For there is no difference. ROMANS 3:20–22 •

We also rejoice in God through our Lord Jesus Christ, through whom we have now received the reconciliation. ROMANS 5:11 • It is God who justifies. ROMANS 8:33 • Whom He predestined, these He also called; whom He called, these He also justified. ROMANS 8:30 •

March 21

Morning Reading

Be watchful, and strengthen the things which remain,
that are ready to die.
REVELATION 3:2

The end of all things is at hand; therefore be serious and watchful in your prayers. 1 PETER 4:7 • Be sober, be vigilant; because your adversary the devil walks about like a roaring lion, seeking whom he may devour. 1 PETER 5:8 • Take heed to yourself, and diligently keep yourself, lest you forget the things your eyes have seen, and lest they depart from your heart all the days of your life. DEUTERONOMY 4:9 • [The Lord said,] "The just shall live by faith; but if anyone draws back, My soul has no pleasure in him." But we are not of those who draw back to perdition, but of those who believe to the saving of the soul. HEBREWS 10:38–39 •

What I say to you, I say to all: Watch! MARK 13:37 •

Fear not, for I am with you; be not dismayed, for I am your God. I will strengthen you, yes, I will help you, I will uphold you with My righteous right hand....I, the LORD your God, will hold your right hand. ISAIAH 41:10, 13 •

Evening Reading

Has His mercy ceased forever?
PSALM 77:8

His mercy endures forever. PSALM 136:23 • The LORD is longsuffering and abundant in mercy. NUMBERS 14:18 • Who is a God like You, pardoning iniquity?...He does not retain His anger forever, because He delights in mercy. He will again have compassion on us, and will subdue our iniquities. You will cast all our sins into the depths of the sea. MICAH 7:18–19 • Not by works of righteousness which we have done, but according to His mercy He saved us. TITUS 3:5 •

Blessed be the God and Father of our Lord Jesus Christ, the Father of mercies and God of all comfort, who comforts us in all our tribulation, that we may be able to comfort those who are in any trouble, with the comfort with which we ourselves are comforted by God. 2 CORINTHIANS 1:3–4 •

That He might be a merciful and faithful High Priest in things pertaining to God, to make propitiation for the sins of the people. For in that He Himself has suffered, being tempted, He is able to aid those who are tempted. HEBREWS 2:17–18 •

March 22

Morning Reading

Lot lifted his eyes and saw all the plain of Jordan, that it was well watered everywhere (before the Lord destroyed Sodom and Gomorrah) like the garden of the Lord....Then Lot chose for himself all the plain of Jordan.
GENESIS 13:10–11

Righteous Lot,...that righteous man. 2 PETER 2:7–8 •

Do not be deceived, God is not mocked; for whatever a man sows, that he will also reap. GALATIANS 6:7 • Remember Lot's wife. LUKE 17:32 •

Do not be unequally yoked together with unbelievers. For what fellowship has righteousness with lawlessness? And what communion has light with darkness? 2 CORINTHIANS 6:14 • Therefore "Come out from among them and be separate, says the Lord. Do not touch what is unclean." 2 CORINTHIANS 6:17 • Do not be partakers with them. For you were once darkness, but now you are light in the Lord. Walk as children of light,...finding out what is acceptable to the Lord. And have no fellowship with the unfruitful works of darkness, but rather expose them. EPHESIANS 5:7–8, 10–11 •

Evening Reading

It may be that the Lord will be with me, and I shall be able to drive them out as the Lord said.
JOSHUA 14:12

He Himself has said, "I will never leave you nor forsake you." So we may boldly say: "The Lord is my helper; I will not fear. What can man do to me?" HEBREWS 13:5–6 • I will go in the strength of the Lord God; I will make mention of Your righteousness, of Yours only. PSALM 71:16 •

The work of righteousness will be peace, and the effect of righteousness, quietness and assurance forever. ISAIAH 32:17 •

Stand therefore, having girded your waist with truth, having put on the breastplate of righteousness. EPHESIANS 6:14 • For we do not wrestle against flesh and blood, but against principalities, against powers, against the rulers of the darkness of this age, against spiritual hosts of wickedness in the heavenly places. Therefore take up the whole armor of God, that you may be able to withstand in the evil day, and having done all, to stand. EPHESIANS 6:12–13 • The Angel of the Lord appeared to [Gideon], and said to him, "The Lord is with you."...Then the Lord turned to [Gideon] and said, "Go in this might of yours." JUDGES 6:12, 14 •

March 23

Morning Reading

Holy, holy, holy, Lord God Almighty.
REVELATION 4:8

But You are holy, enthroned in the praises of Israel. PSALM 22:3 • Then [God] said, "Do not draw near this place. Take your sandals off your feet, for the place where you stand is holy ground....I am the God of your father; the God of Abraham, the God of Isaac, and the God of Jacob." And Moses hid his face, for he was afraid to look upon God. EXODUS 3:5–6 • "To whom then will you liken Me, or to whom shall I be equal?" says the Holy One. ISAIAH 40:25 • I am the LORD your God, the Holy One of Israel, your Savior.... I, even I, am the LORD, and besides Me there is no savior. ISAIAH 43:3, 11 •

As He who called you is holy, you also be holy in all your conduct, because it is written, "Be holy, for I am holy." 1 PETER 1:15–16 • Do you not know that your body is the temple of the Holy Spirit who is in you, whom you have from God, and you are not your own? 1 CORINTHIANS 6:19 • You are the temple of the living God. As God has said: "I will dwell in them and walk among them. I will be their God, and they shall be My people." 2 CORINTHIANS 6:16 • Can two walk together, unless they are agreed? AMOS 3:3 •

Evening Reading

They constrained Him, saying, "Abide with us."
LUKE 24:29

Behold, I stand at the door and knock. If anyone hears My voice and opens the door, I will come in to him and dine with him, and he with Me. REVELATION 3:20 • Tell me, O you whom I love, where you feed your flock, where you make it rest at noon. For why should I be as one who veils herself by the flocks of your companions? SONG OF SONGS 1:7 • I found the one I love. I held him and would not let him go. SONG OF SONGS 3:4 •

Let my beloved come to his garden and eat its pleasant fruits. SONG OF SONGS 4:16 • I have come to my garden. SONG OF SONGS 5:1 • I did not say to the seed of Jacob, "Seek Me in vain." ISAIAH 45:19 •

Lo, I am with you always, even to the end of the age. MATTHEW 28:20 • I will never leave you nor forsake you. HEBREWS 13:5 • Where two or three are gathered together in My name, I am there in the midst of them. MATTHEW 18:20 • The world will see Me no more, but you will see Me. JOHN 14:19 •

March 24

Morning Reading

*[Abraham] believed in the LORD, and He accounted it
to him for righteousness.*
GENESIS 15:6

He did not waver at the promise of God through unbelief, but was strengthened in faith, giving glory to God, and being fully convinced that what He had promised He was also able to perform. And therefore "it was accounted to him for righteousness." Now it was not written for his sake alone that it was imputed to him, but also for us. It shall be imputed to us who believe in Him who raised up Jesus our Lord from the dead. ROMANS 4:20–24 •

The promise that he would be the heir of the world was not to Abraham or to his seed through the law, but through the righteousness of faith. ROMANS 4:13 •

The just shall live by faith. ROMANS 1:17 • Let us hold fast the confession of our hope without wavering, for He who promised is faithful. HEBREWS 10:23 • Our God is in heaven; He does whatever He pleases. PSALM 115:3 • With God nothing will be impossible. LUKE 1:37 • Blessed is she who believed, for there will be a fulfillment of those things which were told her from the Lord. LUKE 1:45 •

Evening Reading

God...calls you into His own kingdom and glory.
1 THESSALONIANS 2:12

Jesus answered, "My kingdom is not of this world. If My kingdom were of this world, My servants would fight,...but now My kingdom is not from here." JOHN 18:36 • Waiting till His enemies are made His footstool. HEBREWS 10:13 •

The kingdoms of this world have become the kingdoms of our Lord and of His Christ, and He shall reign forever and ever! REVELATION 11:15 • [You] have made us kings and priests to our God; and we shall reign on the earth. REVELATION 5:10 • I saw thrones, and they sat on them, and judgment was committed to them....And they lived and reigned with Christ for a thousand years. REVELATION 20:4 • Then the righteous will shine forth as the sun in the kingdom of their Father. MATTHEW 13:43 • Do not fear, little flock, for it is your Father's good pleasure to give you the kingdom. LUKE 12:32 •

I bestow upon you a kingdom, just as My Father bestowed one upon Me, that you may eat and drink at My table in My kingdom, and sit on thrones judging the twelve tribes of Israel. LUKE 22:29–30 •

Your kingdom come. MATTHEW 6:10 •

March 25

Morning Reading

I will never leave you nor forsake you.
HEBREWS 13:5

So we may boldly say: "The LORD is my helper; I will not fear. What can man do to me?" HEBREWS 13:5–6 •

Behold, I am with you and will keep you wherever you go, and will bring you back to this land; for I will not leave you until I have done what I have spoken to you. GENESIS 28:15 • Be strong and of good courage, do not fear nor be afraid of them; for the LORD your God, He is the One who goes with you. He will not leave you nor forsake you. DEUTERONOMY 31:6 •

Demas has forsaken me, having loved this present world. 2 TIMOTHY 4:10 • At my first defense no one stood with me, but all forsook me. May it not be charged against them. But the Lord stood with me and strengthened me. 2 TIMOTHY 4:16–17 • When my father and my mother forsake me, then the LORD will take care of me. PSALM 27:10 •

Lo, I am with you always, even to the end of the age. MATTHEW 28:20 • I am He who lives, and was dead, and behold, I am alive forevermore. REVELATION 1:18 • I will not leave you orphans; I will come to you. JOHN 14:18 • My peace I give to you. JOHN 14:27 •

Evening Reading

Master, we have toiled all night and caught nothing; nevertheless at Your word I will let down the net.
LUKE 5:5

All authority has been given to Me in heaven and on earth. Go therefore and make disciples of all the nations, baptizing them in the name of the Father and of the Son and of the Holy Spirit....And lo, I am with you always, even to the end of the age. MATTHEW 28:18–20 •

The kingdom of heaven is like a dragnet that was cast into the sea and gathered some of every kind. MATTHEW 13:47 •

If I preach the gospel, I have nothing to boast of, for necessity is laid upon me; yes, woe is me if I do not preach the gospel! 1 CORINTHIANS 9:16 • I have become all things to all men, that I might by all means save some. 1 CORINTHIANS 9:22 •

Let us not grow weary while doing good, for in due season we shall reap if we do not lose heart. GALATIANS 6:9 • My word...shall not return to Me void, but it shall accomplish what I please. ISAIAH 55:11 • So then neither he who plants is anything, nor he who waters, but God who gives the increase. 1 CORINTHIANS 3:7 •

March 26

Morning Reading

*The kingdom of heaven is like a man traveling to a far country, who
called his own servants and delivered his goods to them...to each
according to his own ability.*
MATTHEW 25:14–15

Do you not know that to whom you present yourselves slaves to obey,
you are that one's slaves whom you obey? ROMANS 6:16 •

One and the same Spirit works all these things, distributing to
each one individually as He wills. 1 CORINTHIANS 12:11 • The manifestation
of the Spirit is given to each one for the profit of all. 1 CORINTHIANS 12:7 • As
each one has received a gift, minister it to one another, as good stewards of the manifold grace of God. 1 PETER 4:10 • It is required in stewards
that one be found faithful. 1 CORINTHIANS 4:2 • Everyone to whom much is
given, from him much will be required; and to whom much has been
committed, of him they will ask the more. LUKE 12:48 •

Who is sufficient for these things? 2 CORINTHIANS 2:16 • I can do all
things through Christ who strengthens me. PHILIPPIANS 4:13 •

Evening Reading

Distributing to the needs of the saints.
ROMANS 12:13

David said, "Is there still anyone who is left of the house of Saul,
that I may show him kindness for Jonathan's sake?" 2 SAMUEL 9:1 •

Come, you blessed of My Father, inherit the kingdom prepared
for you from the foundation of the world: for I was hungry and you
gave Me food; I was thirsty and you gave Me drink; I was a stranger
and you took Me in; I was naked and you clothed Me; I was sick and
you visited Me; I was in prison and you came to Me....Inasmuch as you
did it to one of the least of these My brethren, you did it to Me. MATTHEW
25:34–36, 40 • Whoever gives one of these little ones only a cup of cold
water in the name of a disciple, assuredly, I say to you, he shall by no
means lose his reward. MATTHEW 10:42 •

Do not forget to do good and to share, for with such sacrifices God
is well pleased. HEBREWS 13:16 • God is not unjust to forget your work and
labor of love which you have shown toward His name, in that you have
ministered to the saints, and do minister. HEBREWS 6:10 •

Morning Reading

He who sows righteousness will have a sure reward.
PROVERBS 11:18

After a long time the lord of those servants came and settled accounts with them. So he who had received five talents came and brought five other talents, saying, "Lord, you delivered to me five talents; look, I have gained five more talents besides them." His lord said to him, "Well done, good and faithful servant; you were faithful over a few things, I will make you ruler over many things. Enter into the joy of your lord." MATTHEW 25:19–21 •

We must all appear before the judgment seat of Christ, that each one may receive the things done in the body, according to what he has done, whether good or bad. 2 CORINTHIANS 5:10 •

I have fought the good fight, I have finished the race, I have kept the faith. Finally, there is laid up for me the crown of righteousness, which the Lord, the righteous Judge, will give to me on that Day, and not to me only but also to all who have loved His appearing. 2 TIMOTHY 4:7–8 •

Behold, I am coming quickly! Hold fast what you have, that no one may take your crown. REVELATION 3:11 •

Evening Reading

God is faithful.
1 CORINTHIANS 10:13

God is not a man, that He should lie, nor a son of man, that He should repent. Has He said, and will He not do? Or has He spoken, and will He not make it good? NUMBERS 23:19 • The LORD has sworn and will not relent. HEBREWS 7:21 •

God, determining to show more abundantly to the heirs of promise the immutability of His counsel, confirmed it by an oath, that by two immutable things, in which it is impossible for God to lie, we might have strong consolation, who have fled for refuge to lay hold of the hope set before us. HEBREWS 6:17–18 • Therefore let those who suffer according to the will of God commit their souls to Him in doing good, as to a faithful Creator. 1 PETER 4:19 •

I know whom I have believed and am persuaded that He is able to keep what I have committed to Him until that Day. 2 TIMOTHY 1:12 • He who calls you is faithful, who also will do it. 1 THESSALONIANS 5:24 • All the promises of God in Him are Yes, and in Him Amen, to the glory of God through us. 2 CORINTHIANS 1:20 •

March 28

Morning Reading

Be strong and of good courage.
JOSHUA 1:18

The LORD is my light and my salvation; whom shall I fear? The LORD is the strength of my life; of whom shall I be afraid? PSALM 27:1 • He gives power to the weak, and to those who have no might He increases strength. Even the youths shall faint and be weary, and the young men shall utterly fall, but those who wait on the LORD shall renew their strength; they shall mount up with wings like eagles, they shall run and not be weary, they shall walk and not faint. ISAIAH 40:29–31 • My flesh and my heart fail; but God is the strength of my heart and my portion forever. PSALM 73:26 •

If God is for us, who can be against us? ROMANS 8:31 • The LORD is on my side; I will not fear. What can man do to me? PSALM 118:6 • Through You we will push down our enemies; through Your name we will trample those who rise up against us. PSALM 44:5 • We are more than conquerors through Him who loved us. ROMANS 8:37 •

Arise and begin working, and the LORD be with you. 1 CHRONICLES 22:16 •

Evening Reading

Our friend...sleeps.
JOHN 11:11

I do not want you to be ignorant, brethren, concerning those who have fallen asleep, lest you sorrow as others who have no hope. For if we believe that Jesus died and rose again, even so God will bring with Him those who sleep in Jesus. 1 THESSALONIANS 4:13–14 •

If the dead do not rise, then Christ is not risen. And if Christ is not risen, your faith is futile; you are still in your sins! Then also those who have fallen asleep in Christ have perished....But now Christ is risen from the dead, and has become the firstfruits of those who have fallen asleep. 1 CORINTHIANS 15:16–18, 20 •

It came to pass, when all the people had completely crossed over the Jordan, that the LORD spoke to Joshua, saying: "...Take for yourselves twelve stones from here, out of the midst of the Jordan, from the place where the priests' feet stood firm....And these stones shall be for a memorial to the children of Israel forever." JOSHUA 4:1, 3, 7 • This Jesus God has raised up, of which we are all witnesses. ACTS 2:32 • Witnesses chosen before by God...who ate and drank with Him after He arose from the dead. ACTS 10: 41 •

March 29

Morning Reading

Come, you blessed of My Father, inherit the kingdom prepared for you from the foundation of the world.
MATTHEW 25:34

Do not fear, little flock, for it is your Father's good pleasure to give you the kingdom. LUKE 12:32 • Has God not chosen the poor of this world to be rich in faith and heirs of the kingdom which He promised to those who love Him? JAMES 2:5 • Heirs of God and joint heirs with Christ, if indeed we suffer with Him, that we may also be glorified together. ROMANS 8:17 •

The Father Himself loves you, because you have loved Me. JOHN 16:27 • God is not ashamed to be called their God, for He has prepared a city for them. HEBREWS 11:16 •

He who overcomes shall inherit all things, and I will be his God and he shall be My son. REVELATION 21:7 • There is laid up for me the crown of righteousness, which the Lord, the righteous Judge, will give to me on that Day, and not to me only but also to all who have loved His appearing. 2 TIMOTHY 4:8 • He who has begun a good work in you will complete it until the day of Jesus Christ. PHILIPPIANS 1:6 •

Evening Reading

Riches are not forever, nor does a crown endure to all generations.
PROVERBS 27:24

Surely every man walks about like a shadow; surely they busy themselves in vain; he heaps up riches, and does not know who will gather them. PSALM 39:6 • Set your mind on things above, not on things on the earth. COLOSSIANS 3:2 • Do not lay up for yourselves treasures on earth, where moth and rust destroy and where thieves break in and steal; but lay up for yourselves treasures in heaven, where neither moth nor rust destroys and where thieves do not break in and steal. For where your treasure is, there your heart will be also. MATTHEW 6:19–21 •

They do it to obtain a perishable crown, but we for an imperishable crown. 1 CORINTHIANS 9:25 • We do not look at the things which are seen, but at the things which are not seen. 2 CORINTHIANS 4:18 • He who sows righteousness will have a sure reward. PROVERBS 11:18 • There is laid up for me the crown of righteousness, which the Lord, the righteous Judge, will give to me on that Day, and not to me only but also to all who have loved His appearing. 2 TIMOTHY 4:8 • The crown of glory that does not fade away. 1 PETER 5:4 •

March 30

Morning Reading

Isaac went out to meditate in the field in the evening.
GENESIS 24:63

Let the words of my mouth and the meditation of my heart be acceptable in Your sight, O LORD, my strength and my Redeemer. PSALM 19:14 •

When I consider Your heavens, the work of Your fingers, the moon and the stars, which You have ordained, what is man that You are mindful of him, and the son of man that You visit him? PSALM 8:3–4 • The works of the LORD are great, studied by all who have pleasure in them. PSALM 111:2 •

Blessed is the man who walks not in the counsel of the ungodly, nor stands in the path of sinners, nor sits in the seat of the scornful; but his delight is in the law of the LORD, and in His law he meditates day and night. PSALM 1:1–2 • This Book of the Law shall not depart from your mouth, but you shall meditate in it day and night. JOSHUA 1:8 • My soul shall be satisfied as with marrow and fatness, and my mouth shall praise You with joyful lips. When I remember You on my bed, I meditate on You in the night watches. PSALM 63:5–6 •

Evening Reading

How long, O LORD? Will You forget me forever? How long will You hide Your face from me?
PSALM 13:1

Every good gift and every perfect gift is from above, and comes down from the Father of lights, with whom there is no variation or shadow of turning. JAMES 1:17 • Zion said, "The LORD has forsaken me, and my Lord has forgotten me." [The Lord says,] "Can a woman forget her nursing child, and not have compassion on the son of her womb? Surely they may forget, yet I will not forget you." ISAIAH 49:14–15 •

You will not be forgotten by Me! I have blotted out, like a thick cloud, your transgressions, and like a cloud, your sins. ISAIAH 44:21–22 •

Jesus loved Martha and her sister and Lazarus. So, when He heard that he was sick, He stayed two more days in the place where He was. JOHN 11:5–6 • A woman...cried out to Him, saying, "Have mercy on me, O Lord, Son of David! My daughter is severely demon-possessed." But He answered her not a word. MATTHEW 15:22–23 •

The genuineness of your faith, being much more precious than gold that perishes. 1 PETER 1:7 •

March 31

Morning Reading

*My God shall supply all your need according to His riches
in glory by Christ Jesus.*
PHILIPPIANS 4:19

Seek first the kingdom of God and His righteousness, and all these things shall be added to you. MATTHEW 6:33 • He who did not spare His own Son, but delivered Him up for us all, how shall He not with Him also freely give us all things? ROMANS 8:32 • For all things are yours: whether Paul or Apollos or Cephas, or the world or life or death, or things present or things to come; all are yours. And you are Christ's, and Christ is God's. 1 CORINTHIANS 3:21–23 • As having nothing, and yet possessing all things. 2 CORINTHIANS 6:10 •

The LORD is my shepherd; I shall not want. PSALM 23:1 • The LORD God is a sun and shield; the LORD will give grace and glory; no good thing will He withhold from those who walk uprightly. PSALM 84:11 • The living God...gives us richly all things to enjoy. 1 TIMOTHY 6:17 • God is able to make all grace abound toward you, that you, always having all sufficiency in all things, may have an abundance for every good work. 2 CORINTHIANS 9:8 •

Evening Reading

What fellowship has righteousness with lawlessness?
2 CORINTHIANS 6:14

Men loved darkness rather than light, because their deeds were evil. JOHN 3:19 • You are all sons of light and sons of the day. We are not of the night nor of darkness. 1 THESSALONIANS 5:5 •

Darkness has blinded his eyes. 1 JOHN 2:11 • Your word is a lamp to my feet and a light to my path. PSALM 119:105 •

The dark places of the earth are full of the haunts of cruelty. PSALM 74:20 • Love is of God; and everyone who loves is born of God and knows God. He who does not love does not know God, for God is love. 1 JOHN 4:7–8 •

The way of the wicked is like darkness; they do not know what makes them stumble. PROVERBS 4:19 • But the path of the just is like the shining sun, that shines ever brighter unto the perfect day. PROVERBS 4:18 •

I have come as a light into the world, that whoever believes in Me should not abide in darkness. JOHN 12:46 •

You were once darkness, but now you are light in the Lord. Walk as children of light. EPHESIANS 5:8 •

 APRIL

April 1

Morning Reading

The fruit of the Spirit is...joy.
GALATIANS 5:22

Joy in the Holy Spirit. ROMANS 14:17 • Joy inexpressible and full of glory. 1 PETER 1:8 •

Sorrowful, yet always rejoicing. 2 CORINTHIANS 6:10 • Exceedingly joyful in all our tribulation. 2 CORINTHIANS 7:4 • We also glory in tribulations. ROMANS 5:3 •

Jesus, the author and finisher of our faith,...for the joy that was set before Him endured the cross, despising the shame. HEBREWS 12:2 • These things I have spoken to you, that My joy may remain in you, and that your joy may be full. JOHN 15:11 • As the sufferings of Christ abound in us, so our consolation also abounds through Christ. 2 CORINTHIANS 1:5 •

Rejoice in the Lord always. Again I will say, rejoice! PHILIPPIANS 4:4 • The joy of the LORD is your strength. NEHEMIAH 8:10 •

In Your presence is fullness of joy; at Your right hand are pleasures forevermore. PSALM 16:11 • For the Lamb who is in the midst of the throne will shepherd them and lead them to living fountains of waters. And God will wipe away every tear from their eyes. REVELATION 7:17 •

Evening Reading

The-LORD-Is-Peace.
JUDGES 6:24

Behold, a son shall be born to you, who shall be a man of rest; and I will give him rest from all his enemies all around. His name shall be Solomon, for I will give peace and quietness to Israel in his days. 1 CHRONICLES 22:9 •

Indeed a greater than Solomon is here. MATTHEW 12:42 • Unto us a Child is born, unto us a Son is given; and the government will be upon His shoulder. And His name will be called Wonderful, Counselor, Mighty God, Everlasting Father, Prince of Peace. ISAIAH 9:6 • My people will dwell in a peaceful habitation, in secure dwellings, and in quiet resting places, though hail comes down on the forest, and the city is brought low in humiliation. ISAIAH 32:18–19 •

He Himself is our peace. EPHESIANS 2:14 • This One shall be peace... when the Assyrian comes into our land. MICAH 5:5 •

These will make war with the Lamb, and the Lamb will overcome them, for He is Lord of lords and King of kings. REVELATION 17:14 •

Peace I leave with you, My peace I give to you. JOHN 14:27 •

Daily Light on the Daily Path

April 2

Morning Reading

If you return to the LORD with all your hearts, then put away the foreign gods and the Ashtoreths from among you, and prepare your hearts for the LORD, and serve Him only.
1 SAMUEL 7:3

Little children, keep yourselves from idols. 1 JOHN 5:21 • Come out from among them and be separate, says the Lord. Do not touch what is unclean, and I will receive you. I will be a Father to you, and you shall be My sons and daughters, says the LORD Almighty. 2 CORINTHIANS 6:17–18 • You cannot serve God and mammon. MATTHEW 6:24 •

You shall worship no other god, for the LORD, whose name is Jealous, is a jealous God. EXODUS 34:14 • Serve Him with a loyal heart and with a willing mind; for the LORD searches all hearts and understands all the intent of the thoughts. 1 CHRONICLES 28:9 •

Behold, You desire truth in the inward parts, and in the hidden part You will make me to know wisdom. PSALM 51:6 • Man looks at the outward appearance, but the LORD looks at the heart. 1 SAMUEL 16:7 • Beloved, if our heart does not condemn us, we have confidence toward God. 1 JOHN 3:21 •

Evening Reading

When the Son of Man comes, will He really find faith on the earth?
LUKE 18:8

He came to His own, and His own did not receive Him. JOHN 1:11 • The Spirit expressly says that in latter times some will depart from the faith. 1 TIMOTHY 4:1 •

Preach the word! Be ready in season and out of season. Convince, rebuke, exhort, with all longsuffering and teaching. For the time will come when they will not endure sound doctrine, but according to their own desires, because they have itching ears, they will heap up for themselves teachers; and they will turn their ears away from the truth, and be turned aside to fables. 2 TIMOTHY 4:2–4 •

Of that day and hour no one knows, not even the angels in heaven, nor the Son, but only the Father. Take heed, watch and pray; for you do not know when the time is. MARK 13:32–33 • Blessed are those servants whom the master, when he comes, will find watching. LUKE 12:37 • Looking for the blessed hope and glorious appearing of our great God and Savior Jesus Christ. TITUS 2:13 •

April 3

Morning Reading

Beloved, do not forget this one thing, that with the Lord one day is as a thousand years, and a thousand years as one day. The Lord is not slack concerning His promise, as some count slackness.
2 Peter 3:8–9

"My thoughts are not your thoughts, nor are your ways My ways," says the Lord. "For as the heavens are higher than the earth, so are My ways higher than your ways, and My thoughts than your thoughts. For as the rain comes down, and the snow from heaven, and do not return there, but water the earth,...so shall My word be that goes forth from My mouth; it shall not return to Me void, but it shall accomplish what I please, and it shall prosper in the thing for which I sent it." Isaiah 55:8–11 •

God has committed them all to disobedience, that He might have mercy on all. Oh, the depth of the riches both of the wisdom and knowledge of God! How unsearchable are His judgments and His ways past finding out! Romans 11:32–33 •

Evening Reading

You were like a firebrand plucked from the burning.
Amos 4:11

The sinners in Zion are afraid; fearfulness has seized the hypocrites: "Who among us shall dwell with the devouring fire? Who among us shall dwell with everlasting burnings?" Isaiah 33:14 • We had the sentence of death in ourselves, that we should not trust in ourselves but in God who raises the dead, who delivered us from so great a death, and does deliver us; in whom we trust that He will still deliver us. 2 Corinthians 1:9–10 • The wages of sin is death, but the gift of God is eternal life in Christ Jesus our Lord. Romans 6:23 •

It is a fearful thing to fall into the hands of the living God. Hebrews 10:31 • Knowing, therefore, the terror of the Lord, we persuade men. 2 Corinthians 5:11 • Be ready in season and out of season. 2 Timothy 4:2 • Others save with fear, pulling them out of the fire. Jude 23 •

"Not by might nor by power, but by My Spirit," says the Lord of hosts. Zechariah 4:6 • Who desires all men to be saved and to come to the knowledge of the truth. 1 Timothy 2:4 •

April 4

Morning Reading

I am the First and the Last.
REVELATION 1:17

You have not come to the mountain that may be touched and that burned with fire, and to blackness and darkness and tempest....But you have come to Mount Zion,...to God the Judge of all, to the spirits of just men made perfect, to Jesus the Mediator of the new covenant. HEBREWS 12:18, 22–24 • Jesus, the author and finisher of our faith. HEBREWS 12:2 • We do not have a High Priest who cannot sympathize with our weaknesses, but was in all points tempted as we are, yet without sin. Let us therefore come boldly to the throne of grace, that we may obtain mercy and find grace to help in time of need. HEBREWS 4:15–16 •

Thus says the LORD, the King of Israel, and his Redeemer, the LORD of hosts: "I am the First and I am the Last; besides Me there is no God." ISAIAH 44:6 • Mighty God, Everlasting Father, Prince of Peace. ISAIAH 9:6 •

Are You not from everlasting, O LORD my God, my Holy One? HABAKKUK 1:12 • Who is God, except the LORD? And who is a rock, except our God? 2 SAMUEL 22:32 •

Evening Reading

Lead me to the rock that is higher than I.
PSALM 61:2

Be anxious for nothing, but in everything by prayer and supplication, with thanksgiving, let your requests be made known to God; and the peace of God, which surpasses all understanding, will guard your hearts and minds through Christ Jesus. PHILIPPIANS 4:6–7 •

When my spirit was overwhelmed within me, then You knew my path. PSALM 142:3 • He knows the way that I take; when He has tested me, I shall come forth as gold. JOB 23:10 • LORD, You have been our dwelling place in all generations. PSALM 90:1 • You have been a strength to the poor, a strength to the needy in his distress, a refuge from the storm, a shade from the heat. ISAIAH 25:4 •

Who is a rock, except our God? PSALM 18:31 • They shall never perish; neither shall anyone snatch them out of My hand. JOHN 10:28 • Uphold me according to Your word, that I may live; and do not let me be ashamed of my hope. PSALM 119:116 • This hope we have as an anchor of the soul, both sure and steadfast, and which enters the Presence behind the veil. HEBREWS 6:19 •

April 5

Morning Reading

I will not let You go unless You bless me!
GENESIS 32:26

Let him take hold of My strength, that he may make peace with Me; and he shall make peace with Me. ISAIAH 27:5 •

O woman, great is your faith! Let it be to you as you desire. MATTHEW 15:28 • According to your faith let it be to you. MATTHEW 9:29 • Let him ask in faith, with no doubting, for he who doubts is like a wave of the sea driven and tossed by the wind. For let not that man suppose that he will receive anything from the Lord. JAMES 1:6–7 •

They drew near to the village where they were going, and He indicated that He would have gone farther. But they constrained Him, saying, "Abide with us.".…He vanished from their sight. And they said to one another, "Did not our heart burn within us while He talked with us on the road, and while He opened the Scriptures to us?" LUKE 24:28–29, 31–32 • [Moses said,] "I pray, if I have found grace in Your sight, show me now Your way, that I may know You and that I may find grace in Your sight.".…And [God] said, "My Presence will go with you, and I will give you rest." EXODUS 33:13–14 •

Evening Reading

Jesus, the author and finisher of our faith.
HEBREWS 12:2

"I am the Alpha and the Omega, the Beginning and the End," says the Lord, "who is and who was and who is to come, the Almighty." REVELATION 1:8 • Who has performed and done it, calling the generations from the beginning? "I, the LORD, am the first; and with the last I am He." ISAIAH 41:4 •

Called, sanctified by God the Father, and preserved in Jesus Christ. JUDE 1 • May the God of peace Himself sanctify you completely; and may your whole spirit, soul, and body be preserved blameless at the coming of our Lord Jesus Christ. He who calls you is faithful, who also will do it. 1 THESSALONIANS 5:23–24 • He who has begun a good work in you will complete it until the day of Jesus Christ. PHILIPPIANS 1:6 • Are you so foolish? Having begun in the Spirit, are you now being made perfect by the flesh? GALATIANS 3:3 • The LORD will perfect that which concerns me. PSALM 138:8 •

For it is God who works in you both to will and to do for His good pleasure. PHILIPPIANS 2:13 •

April 6

Morning Reading

He always lives to make intercession.
HEBREWS 7:25

Who is he who condemns? It is Christ who died,...who also makes intercession for us. ROMANS 8:34 • Christ has not entered the holy places made with hands, which are copies of the true, but into heaven itself, now to appear in the presence of God for us. HEBREWS 9:24 •

If anyone sins, we have an Advocate with the Father, Jesus Christ the righteous. 1 JOHN 2:1 • There is one God and one Mediator between God and men, the Man Christ Jesus. 1 TIMOTHY 2:5 •

Seeing then that we have a great High Priest who has passed through the heavens, Jesus the Son of God, let us hold fast our confession. For we do not have a High Priest who cannot sympathize with our weaknesses, but was in all points tempted as we are, yet without sin. Let us therefore come boldly to the throne of grace, that we may obtain mercy and find grace to help in time of need. HEBREWS 4:14–16 • Through Him we both have access by one Spirit to the Father. EPHESIANS 2:18 •

Evening Reading

Those who know Your name will put their trust in You.
PSALM 9:10

This is His name by which He will be called: THE LORD OUR RIGHTEOUSNESS. JEREMIAH 23:6 • I will go in the strength of the Lord GOD; I will make mention of Your righteousness, of Yours only. PSALM 71:16 •

His name will be called Wonderful, Counselor. ISAIAH 9:6 • O LORD, I know the way of man is not in himself; it is not in man who walks to direct his own steps. JEREMIAH 10:23 •

Mighty God, Everlasting Father. ISAIAH 9:6 • I know whom I have believed and am persuaded that He is able to keep what I have committed to Him until that Day. 2 TIMOTHY 1:12 •

Prince of Peace. ISAIAH 9:6 • He Himself is our peace. EPHESIANS 2:14 • Having been justified by faith, we have peace with God through our Lord Jesus Christ. ROMANS 5:1 •

The name of the LORD is a strong tower; the righteous run to it and are safe. PROVERBS 18:10 • Woe to those who go down to Egypt for help. ISAIAH 31:1 • Like birds flying about, so will the LORD of hosts defend Jerusalem. Defending, He will also deliver it; passing over, He will preserve it. ISAIAH 31:5 •

April 7

Morning Reading

As sorrowful, yet always rejoicing; as poor, yet making many rich; as having nothing, and yet possessing all things.
2 CORINTHIANS 6:10

We...rejoice in hope of the glory of God. And not only that, but we also glory in tribulations. ROMANS 5:2–3 • I am filled with comfort. I am exceedingly joyful in all our tribulation. 2 CORINTHIANS 7:4 • Believing, you rejoice with joy inexpressible and full of glory. 1 PETER 1:8 •

In a great trial of affliction the abundance of their joy and their deep poverty abounded in the riches of their liberality. 2 CORINTHIANS 8:2 • To me, who am less than the least of all the saints, this grace was given, that I should preach among the Gentiles the unsearchable riches of Christ, and to make all see what is the fellowship of the mystery, which from the beginning of the ages has been hidden in God who created all things through Jesus Christ. EPHESIANS 3:8–9 •

Has God not chosen the poor of this world to be rich in faith and heirs of the kingdom which He promised to those who love Him? JAMES 2:5 • God is able to make all grace abound toward you, that you, always having all sufficiency in all things, may have an abundance for every good work. 2 CORINTHIANS 9:8 •

Evening Reading

The LORD will strengthen him on his bed of illness;
you will sustain him on his sickbed.
PSALM 41:3

In all their affliction He was afflicted, and the Angel of His Presence saved them; in His love and in His pity He redeemed them; and He bore them and carried them. ISAIAH 63:9 • He whom You love is sick. JOHN 11:3 • My grace is sufficient for you, for My strength is made perfect in weakness. 2 CORINTHIANS 12:9 •

Therefore most gladly I will rather boast in my infirmities, that the power of Christ may rest upon me. 2 CORINTHIANS 12:9 • I can do all things through Christ who strengthens me. PHILIPPIANS 4:13 •

Therefore we do not lose heart. Even though our outward man is perishing, yet the inward man is being renewed day by day. 2 CORINTHIANS 4:16 •

In Him we live and move and have our being. ACTS 17:28 • He gives power to the weak, and to those who have no might He increases strength. Even the youths shall faint and be weary, and the young men shall utterly fall, but those who wait on the LORD shall renew their strength. ISAIAH 40:29–31 • The eternal God is your refuge, and underneath are the everlasting arms. DEUTERONOMY 33:27 •

April 8

Morning Reading

You were enriched in everything by Him.
1 CORINTHIANS 1:5

When we were still without strength, in due time Christ died for the ungodly. ROMANS 5:6 • He who did not spare His own Son, but delivered Him up for us all, how shall He not with Him also freely give us all things? ROMANS 8:32 •

In Him dwells all the fullness of the Godhead bodily; and you are complete in Him, who is the head of all principality and power. COLOSSIANS 2:9–10 •

Abide in Me, and I in you. As the branch cannot bear fruit of itself, unless it abides in the vine, neither can you, unless you abide in Me. I am the vine, you are the branches. He who abides in Me, and I in him, bears much fruit; for without Me you can do nothing. JOHN 15:4–5 • To will is present with me, but how to perform what is good I do not find. ROMANS 7:18 • To each one of us grace was given according to the measure of Christ's gift. EPHESIANS 4:7 •

If you abide in Me, and My words abide in you, you will ask what you desire, and it shall be done for you. JOHN 15:7 • Let the word of Christ dwell in you richly in all wisdom. COLOSSIANS 3:16 •

Evening Reading

They shall see His face.
REVELATION 22:4

[Moses] said, "Please, show me Your glory."...But [God] said, "You cannot see My face; for no man shall see Me, and live." EXODUS 33:18, 20 • No one has seen God at any time. The only begotten Son, who is in the bosom of the Father, He has declared Him. JOHN 1:18 •

Every eye will see Him, even they who pierced Him. And all the tribes of the earth will mourn because of Him. REVELATION 1:7 • I see Him, but not now; I behold Him, but not near. NUMBERS 24:17 •

For I know that my Redeemer lives, and He shall stand at last on the earth; and after my skin is destroyed, this I know, that in my flesh I shall see God. JOB 19:25–26 • I will see Your face in righteousness; I shall be satisfied when I awake in Your likeness. PSALM 17:15 • We shall be like Him, for we shall see Him as He is. 1 JOHN 3:2 • The Lord Himself will descend from heaven....And the dead in Christ will rise first. Then we who are alive and remain shall be caught up together with them in the clouds to meet the Lord in the air. And thus we shall always be with the Lord. 1 THESSALONIANS 4:16–17 •

April 9

Morning Reading

Fear not, for I have redeemed you.
ISAIAH 43:1

Do not fear, for you will not be ashamed; neither be disgraced, for you will not be put to shame; for you will forget the shame of your youth, and will not remember the reproach of your widowhood anymore. For your Maker is your husband, the LORD of hosts is His name; and your Redeemer is the Holy One of Israel. ISAIAH 54:4–5 • I have blotted out, like a thick cloud, your transgressions, and like a cloud, your sins. Return to Me, for I have redeemed you. ISAIAH 44:22 • With the precious blood of Christ, as of a lamb without blemish and without spot. 1 PETER 1:19 •

Their Redeemer is strong; the LORD of hosts is His name. He will thoroughly plead their case. JEREMIAH 50:34 • My Father, who has given them to Me, is greater than all; and no one is able to snatch them out of My Father's hand. JOHN 10:29 •

Grace to you and peace from God the Father and our Lord Jesus Christ, who gave Himself for our sins, that He might deliver us from this present evil age, according to the will of our God and Father, to whom be glory forever and ever. Amen. GALATIANS 1:3–5 •

Evening Reading

*I will mention the lovingkindnesses of the LORD
and the praises of the LORD, according to all that
the LORD has bestowed on us.*
ISAIAH 63:7

He also brought me up out of a horrible pit, out of the miry clay, and set my feet upon a rock, and established my steps. PSALM 40:2 • The Son of God...loved me and gave Himself for me. GALATIANS 2:20 • He who did not spare His own Son, but delivered Him up for us all, how shall He not with Him also freely give us all things? ROMANS 8:32 • God demonstrates His own love toward us, in that while we were still sinners, Christ died for us. ROMANS 5:8 •

[God] also has sealed us and given us the Spirit in our hearts as a guarantee. 2 CORINTHIANS 1:22 • Who is the guarantee of our inheritance until the redemption of the purchased possession, to the praise of His glory. EPHESIANS 1:14 •

God, who is rich in mercy, because of His great love with which He loved us, even when we were dead in trespasses, made us alive together with Christ (by grace you have been saved), and raised us up together, and made us sit together in the heavenly places in Christ Jesus. EPHESIANS 2:4–6 •

April 10

Morning Reading

I am dark, but lovely.
Song of Songs 1:5

Behold, I was brought forth in iniquity, and in sin my mother conceived me. Psalm 51:5 • "Your fame went out among the nations because of your beauty, for it was perfect through My splendor which I had bestowed on you," says the Lord God. Ezekiel 16:14 •

I am a sinful man, O Lord! Luke 5:8 • Behold, you are fair, my love! Behold, you are fair! Song of Songs 4:1 •

I abhor myself, and repent in dust and ashes. Job 42:6 • You are all fair, my love, and there is no spot in you. Song of Songs 4:7 •

Evil is present with me, the one who wills to do good. Romans 7:21 • Be of good cheer; your sins are forgiven you. Matthew 9:2 •

I know that in me (that is, in my flesh) nothing good dwells. Romans 7:18 • You are complete in Him. Colossians 2:10 • Perfect in Christ Jesus. Colossians 1:28 •

You were washed,...you were sanctified,...you were justified in the name of the Lord Jesus and by the Spirit of our God. 1 Corinthians 6:11 • That you may proclaim the praises of Him who called you out of darkness into His marvelous light. 1 Peter 2:9 •

Evening Reading

All who desire to live godly in Christ Jesus will suffer persecution.
2 Timothy 3:12

I have come to "set a man against his father, a daughter against her mother, and a daughter-in-law against her mother-in-law"; and "a man's enemies will be those of his own household." Matthew 10:35–36 • Whoever therefore wants to be a friend of the world makes himself an enemy of God. James 4:4 • Do not love the world or the things in the world. If anyone loves the world, the love of the Father is not in him. For all that is in the world; the lust of the flesh, the lust of the eyes, and the pride of life; is not of the Father but is of the world. 1 John 2:15–16 •

If the world hates you, you know that it hated Me before it hated you. If you were of the world, the world would love its own. Yet because you are not of the world, but I chose you out of the world, therefore the world hates you. Remember the word that I said to you, "A servant is not greater than his master." John 15:18–20 • I have given them Your word; and the world has hated them because they are not of the world, just as I am not of the world. John 17:14 •

April 11

Morning Reading

In the multitude of words sin is not lacking,
but he who restrains his lips is wise.
PROVERBS 10:19

My beloved brethren, let every man be swift to hear, slow to speak, slow to wrath. JAMES 1:19 • He who is slow to anger is better than the mighty, and he who rules his spirit than he who takes a city. PROVERBS 16:32 • We all stumble in many things. If anyone does not stumble in word, he is a perfect man, able also to bridle the whole body. JAMES 3:2 • By your words you will be justified, and by your words you will be condemned. MATTHEW 12:37 • Set a guard, O Lord, over my mouth; keep watch over the door of my lips. PSALM 141:3 •

For to this you were called, because Christ also suffered for us, leaving us an example, that you should follow His steps: "Who committed no sin, nor was deceit found in His mouth"; who, when He was reviled, did not revile in return; when He suffered, He did not threaten, but committed Himself to Him who judges righteously. 1 PETER 2:21–23 • Consider Him who endured such hostility from sinners against Himself, lest you become weary and discouraged in your souls. HEBREWS 12:3 •

In their mouth was found no deceit, for they are without fault before the throne of God. REVELATION 14:5 •

Evening Reading

Teach me Your way, O LORD.
PSALM 27:11

I will instruct you and teach you in the way you should go; I will guide you with My eye. PSALM 32:8 • Good and upright is the LORD; therefore He teaches sinners in the way. The humble He guides in justice, and the humble He teaches His way. PSALM 25:8–9 •

I am the door. If anyone enters by Me, he will be saved, and will go in and out and find pasture. JOHN 10:9 •

Jesus said to him, "I am the way, the truth, and the life. No one comes to the Father except through Me." JOHN 14:6 • Having boldness to enter the Holiest by the blood of Jesus, by a new and living way which He consecrated for us, through the veil, that is, His flesh, and having a High Priest over the house of God, let us draw near with a true heart in full assurance of faith. HEBREWS 10:19–22 •

Let us know, let us pursue the knowledge of the LORD. HOSEA 6:3 • All the paths of the LORD are mercy and truth, to such as keep His covenant and His testimonies. PSALM 25:10 •

April 12

Morning Reading

What the law could not do in that it was weak through the flesh, God did by sending His own Son in the likeness of sinful flesh, on account of sin: He condemned sin in the flesh.
ROMANS 8:3

The law, having a shadow of the good things to come, and not the very image of the things, can never with these same sacrifices, which they offer continually year by year, make those who approach perfect. For then would they not have ceased to be offered? HEBREWS 10:1–2 • By Him everyone who believes is justified from all things from which you could not be justified by the law of Moses. ACTS 13:39 •

Inasmuch then as the children have partaken of flesh and blood, He Himself likewise shared in the same, that through death He might destroy him who had the power of death, that is, the devil, and release those who through fear of death were all their lifetime subject to bondage. For indeed He does not give aid to angels, but He does give aid to the seed of Abraham. Therefore, in all things He had to be made like His brethren. HEBREWS 2:14–17 •

Evening Reading

All have sinned and fall short of the glory of God.
ROMANS 3:23

There is none righteous, no, not one....There is none who does good, no, not one. ROMANS 3:10, 12 • There is not a just man on earth who does good and does not sin. ECCLESIASTES 7:20 • How can he be pure who is born of a woman? JOB 25:4 •

Therefore, since a promise remains of entering His rest, let us fear lest any of you seem to have come short of it. HEBREWS 4:1 •

I acknowledge my transgressions, and my sin is always before me....Behold, I was brought forth in iniquity, and in sin my mother conceived me. PSALM 51:3, 5 •

The LORD also has put away your sin; you shall not die. 2 SAMUEL 12:13 • Whom He justified, these He also glorified. ROMANS 8:30 • We all, with unveiled face, beholding as in a mirror the glory of the Lord, are being transformed into the same image from glory to glory, just as by the Spirit of the Lord. 2 CORINTHIANS 3:18 • If indeed you continue in the faith, grounded and steadfast, and are not moved away from the hope of the gospel. COLOSSIANS 1:23 •

Walk worthy of God who calls you into His own kingdom and glory. 1 THESSALONIANS 2:12 •

April 13

Honor the LORD with your possessions,
and with the firstfruits of all your increase.
PROVERBS 3:9

He who sows sparingly will also reap sparingly, and he who sows bountifully will also reap bountifully. 2 CORINTHIANS 9:6 • On the first day of the week let each one of you lay something aside, storing up as he may prosper. 1 CORINTHIANS 16:2 •

God is not unjust to forget your work and labor of love which you have shown toward His name, in that you have ministered to the saints, and do minister. HEBREWS 6:10 •

I beseech you therefore, brethren, by the mercies of God, that you present your bodies a living sacrifice, holy, acceptable to God, which is your reasonable service. ROMANS 12:1 • The love of Christ compels us, because we judge thus: that if One died for all, then all died; and He died for all, that those who live should live no longer for themselves, but for Him who died for them and rose again. 2 CORINTHIANS 5:14–15 • Therefore, whether you eat or drink, or whatever you do, do all to the glory of God. 1 CORINTHIANS 10:31 •

Evening Reading

There shall be no night there.
REVELATION 21:25

The LORD will be to you an everlasting light, and your God your glory. ISAIAH 60:19 • The city had no need of the sun or of the moon to shine in it, for the glory of God illuminated it. The Lamb is its light. REVELATION 21:23 • They need no lamp nor light of the sun, for the Lord God gives them light. REVELATION 22:5 •

You are a chosen generation, a royal priesthood, a holy nation, His own special people, that you may proclaim the praises of Him who called you out of darkness into His marvelous light. 1 PETER 2:9 • Giving thanks to the Father who has qualified us to be partakers of the inheritance of the saints in the light. He has delivered us from the power of darkness and conveyed us into the kingdom of the Son of His love. COLOSSIANS 1:12–13 • You were once darkness, but now you are light in the Lord. Walk as children of light. EPHESIANS 5:8 •

We are not of the night nor of darkness. 1 THESSALONIANS 5:5 •

The path of the just is like the shining sun, that shines ever brighter unto the perfect day. PROVERBS 4:18 •

April 14

Morning Reading

My soul shall be satisfied as with marrow and fatness, and my mouth shall praise You with joyful lips. When I remember You on my bed, I meditate on You in the night watches.
PSALM 63:5–6

How precious also are Your thoughts to me, O God! How great is the sum of them! PSALM 139:17 • How sweet are Your words to my taste, sweeter than honey to my mouth! PSALM 119:103 • Let him kiss me with the kisses of his mouth; for your love is better than wine. SONG OF SONGS 1:2 •

Whom have I in heaven but You? And there is none upon earth that I desire besides You. PSALM 73:25 • You are fairer than the sons of men. PSALM 45:2 •

Like an apple tree among the trees of the woods, so is my beloved among the sons. I sat down in his shade with great delight, and his fruit was sweet to my taste. He brought me to the banqueting house, and his banner over me was love. SONG OF SONGS 2:3–4 • His countenance is like Lebanon, excellent as the cedars. His mouth is most sweet, yes, he is altogether lovely. This is my beloved, and this is my friend! SONG OF SONGS 5:15–16 •

Evening Reading

Restore to me the joy of Your salvation.
PSALM 51:12

I have seen his ways, and will heal him; I will also lead him, and restore comforts to him and to his mourners. ISAIAH 57:18 •

"Come now, and let us reason together," says the LORD, "though your sins are like scarlet, they shall be as white as snow; though they are red like crimson, they shall be as wool." ISAIAH 1:18 • "Return, you backsliding children, and I will heal your backslidings." "Indeed we do come to You, for You are the LORD our God." JEREMIAH 3:22 • I will hear what God the LORD will speak, for He will speak peace to His people and to His saints; but let them not turn back to folly. PSALM 85:8 •

Bless the LORD, O my soul, and forget not all His benefits: who forgives all your iniquities, who heals all your diseases. PSALM 103:2–3 • He restores my soul. PSALM 23:3 • O LORD, I will praise You; though You were angry with me, Your anger is turned away, and You comfort me. ISAIAH 12:1 •

Hold me up, and I shall be safe. PSALM 119:117 •

I, even I, am He who blots out your transgressions for My own sake; and I will not remember your sins. ISAIAH 43:25 •

April 15

Morning Reading

Their Redeemer is strong.
JEREMIAH 50:34

I know your manifold transgressions and your mighty sins. AMOS 5:12 •

I have given help to one who is mighty. PSALM 89:19 • Your Savior, and your Redeemer, the Mighty One of Jacob. ISAIAH 49:26 • Mighty to save. ISAIAH 63:1 • Able to keep you from stumbling. JUDE 24 • Where sin abounded, grace abounded much more. ROMANS 5:20 •

He who believes in Him is not condemned; but he who does not believe is condemned already, because he has not believed in the name of the only begotten Son of God. JOHN 3:18 • He is also able to save to the uttermost those who come to God through Him, since He always lives to make intercession for them. HEBREWS 7:25 •

Is My hand shortened at all that it cannot redeem? ISAIAH 50:2 •

Who shall separate us from the love of Christ?...I am persuaded that neither death nor life, nor angels nor principalities nor powers, nor things present nor things to come, nor height nor depth, nor any other created thing, shall be able to separate us from the love of God which is in Christ Jesus our Lord. ROMANS 8:35, 38–39 •

Evening Reading

Do you seek great things for yourself? Do not seek them.
JEREMIAH 45:5

Take My yoke upon you and learn from Me, for I am gentle and lowly in heart, and you will find rest for your souls. MATTHEW 11:29 • Let this mind be in you which was also in Christ Jesus, who, being in the form of God, did not consider it robbery to be equal with God, but made Himself of no reputation, taking the form of a bondservant, and coming in the likeness of men. And being found in appearance as a man, He humbled Himself and became obedient to the point of death, even the death of the cross. PHILIPPIANS 2:5–8 •

He who does not take his cross and follow after Me is not worthy of Me. MATTHEW 10:38 • Christ also suffered for us, leaving us an example, that you should follow His steps. 1 PETER 2:21 •

Godliness with contentment is great gain. For we brought nothing into this world, and it is certain we can carry nothing out. And having food and clothing, with these we shall be content. 1 TIMOTHY 6:6–8 •

I have learned in whatever state I am, to be content. PHILIPPIANS 4:11 •

Daily Light on the Daily Path

April 16

Morning Reading

I said in my haste, "I am cut off from before Your eyes";
nevertheless You heard the voice of my supplications
when I cried out to You.
PSALM 31:22

I sink in deep mire, where there is no standing; I have come into deep waters, where the floods overflow me. PSALM 69:2 • The waters flowed over my head; I said, "I am cut off!" I called on Your name, O LORD, from the lowest pit. You have heard my voice: "Do not hide Your ear from my sighing, from my cry for help." You drew near on the day I called on You, and said, "Do not fear!" LAMENTATIONS 3:54–57 •

Will the Lord cast off forever? And will He be favorable no more? Has His mercy ceased forever? Has His promise failed forevermore? Has God forgotten to be gracious? Has He in anger shut up His tender mercies?...And I said, "This is my anguish; but I will remember the years of the right hand of the Most High." I will remember the works of the LORD; surely I will remember Your wonders of old. PSALM 77:7–11 • I would have lost heart, unless I had believed that I would see the goodness of the LORD in the land of the living. PSALM 27:13 •

Evening Reading

He shall call upon Me, and I will answer him;
I will be with him in trouble; I will deliver him.
PSALM 91:15

Jabez called on the God of Israel saying, "Oh, that You would bless me indeed, and enlarge my territory, that Your hand would be with me, and that You would keep me from evil, that I may not cause pain!" So God granted him what he requested. 1 CHRONICLES 4:10 • God appeared to Solomon, and said to him, "Ask! What shall I give you?" And Solomon said to God: "...Give me wisdom and knowledge, that I may go out and come in before this people; for who can judge this great people of Yours?" 2 CHRONICLES 1:7–8, 10 • And God gave Solomon wisdom and exceedingly great understanding, and largeness of heart like the sand on the seashore. 1 KINGS 4:29 •

Asa cried out to the LORD his God, and said, "LORD, it is nothing for You to help, whether with many or with those who have no power;... O LORD, You are our God; do not let man prevail against You!" So the LORD struck the Ethiopians before Asa. 2 CHRONICLES 14:11–12 •

O You who hear prayer, to You all flesh will come. PSALM 65:2 •

April 17

Morning Reading

Whoever offers praise glorifies Me.
PSALM 50:23

Let the word of Christ dwell in you richly in all wisdom, teaching and admonishing one another in psalms and hymns and spiritual songs, singing with grace in your hearts to the Lord. And whatever you do in word or deed, do all in the name of the Lord Jesus, giving thanks to God the Father through Him. COLOSSIANS 3:16–17 • Glorify God in your body and in your spirit, which are God's. 1 CORINTHIANS 6:20 •

You are a chosen generation, a royal priesthood, a holy nation, His own special people, that you may proclaim the praises of Him who called you out of darkness into His marvelous light. 1 PETER 2:9 • You also, as living stones, are being built up a spiritual house, a holy priesthood, to offer up spiritual sacrifices acceptable to God through Jesus Christ. 1 PETER 2:5 • By Him let us continually offer the sacrifice of praise to God, that is, the fruit of our lips, giving thanks to His name. HEBREWS 13:15 •

My soul shall make its boast in the LORD; the humble shall hear of it and be glad. Oh, magnify the LORD with me, and let us exalt His name together. PSALM 34:2–3 •

Evening Reading

Draw me away! We will run after you.
SONG OF SONGS 1:4

I have loved you with an everlasting love; therefore with lovingkindness I have drawn you. JEREMIAH 31:3 • I drew them with gentle cords, with bands of love. HOSEA 11:4 • I [Jesus], if I am lifted up from the earth, will draw all peoples to Myself. JOHN 12:32 • Behold the Lamb of God! JOHN 1:36 •

As Moses lifted up the serpent in the wilderness, even so must the Son of Man be lifted up, that whoever believes in Him should not perish but have eternal life. JOHN 3:14–15 •

Whom have I in heaven but You? And there is none upon earth that I desire besides You. PSALM 73:25 • We love Him because He first loved us. 1 JOHN 4:19 •

My beloved spoke, and said to me: "Rise up, my love, my fair one, and come away. For lo, the winter is past, the rain is over and gone. The flowers appear on the earth; the time of singing has come, and the voice of the turtledove is heard in our land. The fig tree puts forth her green figs, and the vines with the tender grapes give a good smell. Rise up, my love, my fair one, and come away!" SONG OF SONGS 2:10–13 •

April 18

Morning Reading

*I will raise up for them a Prophet like you
from among their brethren.*
DEUTERONOMY 18:18

I [Moses] stood between the LORD and you at that time, to declare to you the word of the LORD; for you were afraid. DEUTERONOMY 5:5 • There is one God and one Mediator between God and men, the Man Christ Jesus. 1 TIMOTHY 2:5 •

Now the man Moses was very humble, more than all men who were on the face of the earth. NUMBERS 12:3 • Take My yoke upon you and learn from Me, for I am gentle and lowly in heart, and you will find rest for your souls. MATTHEW 11:29 • Let this mind be in you which was also in Christ Jesus, who, being in the form of God, did not consider it robbery to be equal with God, but made Himself of no reputation, taking the form of a bondservant, and coming in the likeness of men. PHILIPPIANS 2:5–7 •

Moses indeed was faithful in all His house as a servant, for a testimony of those things which would be spoken afterward, but Christ [was faithful] as a Son over His own house, whose house we are if we hold fast the confidence and the rejoicing of the hope firm to the end. HEBREWS 3:5–6 •

Evening Reading

Everlasting consolation.
2 THESSALONIANS 2:16

I will remember My covenant with you in the days of your youth, and I will establish an everlasting covenant with you. EZEKIEL 16:60 •

By one offering He has perfected forever those who are being sanctified. HEBREWS 10:14 • He is also able to save to the uttermost those who come to God through Him, since He always lives to make intercession for them. HEBREWS 7:25 • I know whom I have believed and am persuaded that He is able to keep what I have committed to Him until that Day. 2 TIMOTHY 1:12 •

The gifts and the calling of God are irrevocable. ROMANS 11:29 • Who shall separate us from the love of Christ? ROMANS 8:35 • The Lamb who is in the midst of the throne will shepherd them and lead them to living fountains of waters. And God will wipe away every tear from their eyes. REVELATION 7:17 • Thus we shall always be with the Lord. Therefore comfort one another with these words. 1 THESSALONIANS 4:17–18 •

This is not your rest. MICAH 2:10 • For here we have no continuing city, but we seek the one to come. HEBREWS 13:14 •

April 19

Morning Reading

Most assuredly, I say to you, I am the door of the sheep.
JOHN 10:7

The veil of the temple was torn in two from top to bottom. MATTHEW 27:51 • Christ also suffered once for sins, the just for the unjust, that He might bring us to God. 1 PETER 3:18 • The way into the Holiest of All was not yet made manifest while the first tabernacle was still standing. HEBREWS 9:8 •

I am the door. If anyone enters by Me, he will be saved, and will go in and out and find pasture. JOHN 10:9 •

No one comes to the Father except through Me. JOHN 14:6 • Through Him we both have access by one Spirit to the Father. Now, therefore, you are no longer strangers and foreigners, but fellow citizens with the saints and members of the household of God. EPHESIANS 2:18–19 • Therefore, brethren, [we have] boldness to enter the Holiest by the blood of Jesus, by a new and living way which He consecrated for us, through the veil, that is, His flesh. HEBREWS 10:19–20 • We have peace with God through our Lord Jesus Christ, through whom also we have access by faith into this grace in which we stand, and rejoice in hope of the glory of God. ROMANS 5:1–2 •

Evening Reading

His word was in my heart like a burning fire shut up in my bones; I was weary of holding it back, and I could not.
JEREMIAH 20:9

Necessity is laid upon me; yes, woe is me if I do not preach the gospel!...What is my reward then? That when I preach the gospel, I may present the gospel of Christ without charge, that I may not abuse my authority in the gospel. 1 CORINTHIANS 9:16, 18 • [The religious leaders] called them and commanded them not to speak at all nor teach in the name of Jesus. But Peter and John answered and said to them, "...We cannot but speak the things which we have seen and heard." ACTS 4:18–20 • The love of Christ compels us. 2 CORINTHIANS 5:14 •

[The servant said,] "I was afraid, and went and hid your talent in the ground."...But his lord answered and said to him, "You wicked and lazy servant,...you ought to have deposited my money with the bankers, and at my coming I would have received back my own with interest." MATTHEW 25:25–27 •

Go...to your friends, and tell them what great things the Lord has done for you. MARK 5:19 •

April 20

Morning Reading

None of the accursed things shall remain in your hand.
DEUTERONOMY 13:17

Come out from among them and be separate, says the Lord. Do not touch what is unclean. 2 CORINTHIANS 6:17 • Beloved, I beg you as sojourners and pilgrims, abstain from fleshly lusts which war against the soul. 1 PETER 2:11 • Hating even the garment defiled by the flesh. JUDE 23 •

Beloved, now we are children of God; and it has not yet been revealed what we shall be, but we know that when He is revealed, we shall be like Him, for we shall see Him as He is. And everyone who has this hope in Him purifies himself, just as He is pure. 1 JOHN 3:2–3 • The grace of God that brings salvation has appeared to all men, teaching us that, denying ungodliness and worldly lusts, we should live soberly, righteously, and godly in the present age, looking for the blessed hope and glorious appearing of our great God and Savior Jesus Christ, who gave Himself for us, that He might redeem us from every lawless deed and purify for Himself His own special people, zealous for good works. TITUS 2:11–14 •

Evening Reading

[Paul] said, "Who are You, Lord?"
And He said, "I am Jesus."
ACTS 26:15

It is I; do not be afraid. MATTHEW 14:27 • When you pass through the waters, I will be with you; and through the rivers, they shall not overflow you. When you walk through the fire, you shall not be burned, nor shall the flame scorch you. For I am the LORD your God,...your Savior. ISAIAH 43:2–3 •

Though I walk through the valley of the shadow of death, I will fear no evil; for You are with me; Your rod and Your staff, they comfort me. PSALM 23:4 • Immanuel..."God with us." MATTHEW 1:23 •

You shall call His name JESUS, for He will save His people from their sins. MATTHEW 1:21 • If anyone sins, we have an Advocate with the Father, Jesus Christ the righteous. 1 JOHN 2:1 • Who is he who condemns? It is Christ who died, and furthermore is also risen, who is even at the right hand of God, who also makes intercession for us. Who shall separate us from the love of Christ? Shall tribulation, or distress, or persecution, or famine, or nakedness, or peril, or sword? ROMANS 8:34–35 •

April 21

Morning Reading

Stand fast in the Lord.
PHILIPPIANS 4:1

My foot has held fast to His steps; I have kept His way and not turned aside. JOB 23:11 •

The LORD loves justice, and does not forsake His saints; they are preserved forever. PSALM 37:28 • The LORD shall preserve you from all evil; He shall preserve your soul. PSALM 121:7 •

[The Lord said,] "The just shall live by faith; but if anyone draws back, My soul has no pleasure in him." But we are not of those who draw back to perdition, but of those who believe to the saving of the soul. HEBREWS 10:38–39 • If they had been of us, they would have continued with us; but they went out that they might be made manifest, that none of them were of us. 1 JOHN 2:19 •

If you abide in My word, you are My disciples indeed. JOHN 8:31 • He who endures to the end shall be saved. MATTHEW 24:13 • Watch, stand fast in the faith, be brave, be strong. 1 CORINTHIANS 16:13 • Hold fast what you have, that no one may take your crown. REVELATION 3:11 • He who overcomes shall be clothed in white garments, and I will not blot out his name from the Book of Life. REVELATION 3:5 •

Evening Reading

Enoch walked with God.
GENESIS 5:22

Can two walk together, unless they are agreed? AMOS 3:3 •

[God has] made peace through the blood of [Jesus'] cross. And you, who once were alienated and enemies in your mind by wicked works, yet now He has reconciled in the body of His flesh through death, to present you holy, and blameless, and above reproach in His sight. COLOSSIANS 1:20–22 • In Christ Jesus you who once were far off have been brought near by the blood of Christ. EPHESIANS 2:13 •

If when we were enemies we were reconciled to God through the death of His Son, much more, having been reconciled, we shall be saved by His life. And not only that, but we also rejoice in God through our Lord Jesus Christ. ROMANS 5:10–11 •

Our fellowship is with the Father and with His Son Jesus Christ. 1 JOHN 1:3 •

The grace of the Lord Jesus Christ, and the love of God, and the communion of the Holy Spirit be with you all. Amen. 2 CORINTHIANS 13:14 •

April 22

Morning Reading

If his offering is a burnt sacrifice of the herd, let him offer a male without blemish; he shall offer it of his own free will at the door of the tabernacle of meeting before the LORD. Then he shall put his hand on the head of the burnt offering, and it will be accepted on his behalf to make atonement for him.
LEVITICUS 1:3–4

God will provide for Himself the lamb for a burnt offering. GENESIS 22:8 • Behold! The Lamb of God who takes away the sin of the world! JOHN 1:29 • We have been sanctified through the offering of the body of Jesus Christ once for all. HEBREWS 10:10 • A ransom for many. MATTHEW 20:28 •

No one takes [My life] from Me, but I lay it down of Myself. I have power to lay it down, and I have power to take it again. JOHN 10:18 • I will love them freely. HOSEA 14:4 • The Son of God...loved me and gave Himself for me. GALATIANS 2:20 •

He made Him who knew no sin to be sin for us, that we might become the righteousness of God in Him. 2 CORINTHIANS 5:21 • He has made us accepted in the Beloved. EPHESIANS 1:6 •

Evening Reading

Great is Your mercy toward me, and You have delivered my soul from the depths of Sheol.
PSALM 86:13

Fear Him who is able to destroy both soul and body in hell. MATTHEW 10:28 •

Fear not, for I have redeemed you; I have called you by your name; You are Mine. ISAIAH 43:1 • I, even I, am the LORD, and besides Me there is no savior. ISAIAH 43:11 • I, even I, am He who blots out your transgressions for My own sake; and I will not remember your sins. ISAIAH 43:25 • Those who trust in their wealth and boast in the multitude of their riches, none of them can by any means redeem his brother, nor give to God a ransom for him; for the redemption of their souls is costly. PSALM 49:6–8 • I have found a ransom. JOB 33:24 • God, who is rich in mercy, because of His great love with which He loved us, even when we were dead in trespasses, made us alive together with Christ. EPHESIANS 2:4–5 •

Nor is there salvation in any other, for there is no other name under heaven given among men by which we must be saved. ACTS 4:12 •

April 23

Morning Reading

The LORD was my support.
PSALM 18:18

Truly, in vain is salvation hoped for from the hills, and from the multitude of mountains; truly, in the LORD our God is the salvation of Israel. JEREMIAH 3:23 • The LORD is my rock and my fortress and my deliverer; my God, my strength, in whom I will trust; my shield and the horn of my salvation, my stronghold. PSALM 18:2 • Cry out and shout, O inhabitant of Zion, for great is the Holy One of Israel in your midst! ISAIAH 12:6 •

The angel of the LORD encamps all around those who fear Him, and delivers them. PSALM 34:7 • The righteous cry out, and the LORD hears, and delivers them out of all their troubles. PSALM 34:17 • The eternal God is your refuge, and underneath are the everlasting arms. DEUTERONOMY 33:27 • So we may boldly say: "The LORD is my helper; I will not fear. What can man do to me?" HEBREWS 13:6 • For who is God, except the LORD? And who is a rock, except our God? It is God who arms me with strength, and makes my way perfect. PSALM 18:31–32 •

By the grace of God I am what I am. 1 CORINTHIANS 15:10 •

Evening Reading

All we like sheep have gone astray.
ISAIAH 53:6

If we say that we have no sin, we deceive ourselves, and the truth is not in us. 1 JOHN 1:8 • There is none righteous, no, not one; there is none who understands; there is none who seeks after God. They have all turned aside; they have together become unprofitable. ROMANS 3:10–12 •

You were like sheep going astray, but have now returned to the Shepherd and Overseer of your souls. 1 PETER 2:25 • I have gone astray like a lost sheep; seek Your servant, for I do not forget Your commandments. PSALM 119:176 •

He restores my soul; He leads me in the paths of righteousness for His name's sake. PSALM 23:3 • My sheep hear My voice, and I know them, and they follow Me. And I give them eternal life, and they shall never perish; neither shall anyone snatch them out of My hand. JOHN 10:27–28 •

What man of you, having a hundred sheep, if he loses one of them, does not leave the ninety-nine in the wilderness, and go after the one which is lost until he finds it? LUKE 15:4 •

April 24

Morning Reading

The LORD visited Sarah as He had said,
and the LORD did for Sarah as He had spoken.
GENESIS 21:1

Trust in Him at all times, you people; pour out your heart before Him; God is a refuge for us. PSALM 62:8 • David strengthened himself in the LORD his God. 1 SAMUEL 30:6 • God will surely visit you, and bring you out of this land to the land of which He swore to Abraham, to Isaac, and to Jacob. GENESIS 50:24 • Then the LORD said to [Moses], "... I have surely seen the oppression of my people who are in Egypt; I have heard their groaning and have come down to deliver them."...He brought them out, after he had shown wonders and signs in the land of Egypt, and in the Red Sea, and in the wilderness forty years. ACTS 7:33–34, 36 • Not a word failed of any good thing which the LORD had spoken to the house of Israel. All came to pass. JOSHUA 21:45 •

He who promised is faithful. HEBREWS 10:23 • Has He said, and will He not do? Or has He spoken, and will He not make it good? NUMBERS 23:19 • Heaven and earth will pass away, but My words will by no means pass away. MATTHEW 24:35 • The grass withers, the flower fades, but the word of our God stands forever. ISAIAH 40:8 •

Evening Reading

The eyes of all look expectantly to You.
PSALM 145:15

He gives to all life, breath, and all things. ACTS 17:25 • The LORD is good to all, and His tender mercies are over all His works. PSALM 145:9 • Look at the birds of the air, for they neither sow nor reap nor gather into barns; yet your heavenly Father feeds them. MATTHEW 6:26 •

The same Lord over all is rich to all who call upon Him. ROMANS 10:12 •

I will lift up my eyes to the hills; from whence comes my help? PSALM 121:1 • Behold, as the eyes of servants look to the hand of their masters, as the eyes of a maid to the hand of her mistress, so our eyes look to the LORD our God. PSALM 123:2 •

The LORD is a God of justice. ISAIAH 30:18 • And it will be said in that day: "Behold, this is our God; we have waited for Him, and He will save us. This is the LORD; we have waited for Him; we will be glad and rejoice in His salvation." ISAIAH 25:9 • If we hope for what we do not see, we eagerly wait for it with perseverance. ROMANS 8:25 •

April 25

Morning Reading

You shall call His name JESUS,
for He will save His people from their sins.
MATTHEW 1:21

You know that He was manifested to take away our sins. 1 JOHN 3:5 • That we, having died to sins, might live for righteousness. 1 PETER 2:24 • He is also able to save to the uttermost those who come to God through Him. HEBREWS 7:25 •

He was wounded for our transgressions, He was bruised for our iniquities; the chastisement for our peace was upon Him, and by His stripes we are healed....The LORD has laid on Him the iniquity of us all. ISAIAH 53:5–6 • Thus it was necessary for the Christ to suffer...that repentance and remission of sins should be preached in His name to all nations. LUKE 24:46–47 • He has appeared to put away sin by the sacrifice of Himself. HEBREWS 9:26 •

Him God has exalted to His right hand to be Prince and Savior, to give repentance. ACTS 5:31 • Through this Man is preached to you the forgiveness of sins; and by Him everyone who believes is justified from all things from which you could not be justified by the law of Moses. ACTS 13:38–39 • Your sins are forgiven you for His name's sake. 1 JOHN 2:12 •

Evening Reading

Our Lord Jesus Christ,...though He was rich,...became poor, that you
through His poverty might become rich.
2 CORINTHIANS 8:9

It pleased the Father that in Him all the fullness should dwell. COLOSSIANS 1:19 • [Jesus,] being the brightness of His glory and the express image of His person, and upholding all things by the word of His power, when He had by Himself purged our sins, sat down at the right hand of the Majesty on high, having become so much better than the angels, as He has by inheritance obtained a more excellent name than they. HEBREWS 1:3–4 • Who, being in the form of God, did not consider it robbery to be equal with God, but made Himself of no reputation. PHILIPPIANS 2:6–7 •

Foxes have holes and birds of the air have nests, but the Son of Man has nowhere to lay His head. MATTHEW 8:20 •

All things are yours: whether Paul or Apollos or Cephas, or the world or life or death, or things present or things to come; all are yours. And you are Christ's, and Christ is God's. 1 CORINTHIANS 3:21–23 •

April 26

Morning Reading

His left hand is under my head, and his right hand embraces me.
SONG OF SONGS 2:6

Underneath are the everlasting arms. DEUTERONOMY 33:27 • When [Peter] saw that the wind was boisterous, he was afraid; and beginning to sink he cried out, saying, "Lord, save me!" And immediately Jesus stretched out His hand and caught him, and said to him, "O you of little faith, why did you doubt?" MATTHEW 14:30–31 • The steps of a good man are ordered by the LORD, and He delights in his way. Though he fall, he shall not be utterly cast down; for the LORD upholds him with His hand. PSALM 37:23–24 •

The beloved of the LORD shall dwell in safety by Him, who shelters him all the day long; and he shall dwell between His shoulders. DEUTERONOMY 33:12 • Casting all your care upon Him, for He cares for you. 1 PETER 5:7 • He who touches you touches the apple of His eye. ZECHARIAH 2:8 •

They shall never perish; neither shall anyone snatch them out of My hand. My Father, who has given them to Me, is greater than all. JOHN 10:28–29 •

Evening Reading

Who is she who looks forth as the morning, fair as the moon, clear as the sun, awesome as an army with banners?
SONG OF SONGS 6:10

The church of God which He purchased with His own blood. ACTS 20:28 •

Christ also loved the church and gave Himself for her, that He might sanctify and cleanse her with the washing of water by the word, that He might present her to Himself a glorious church, not having spot or wrinkle or any such thing, but that she should be holy and without blemish. EPHESIANS 5:25–27 •

A great sign appeared in heaven: a woman clothed with the sun. REVELATION 12:1 • [The voice, as it were, of a great multitude said,] "The marriage of the Lamb has come, and His wife has made herself ready." And to her it was granted to be arrayed in fine linen, clean and bright, for the fine linen is the righteous acts of the saints. REVELATION 19:7–8 • The righteousness of God, through faith in Jesus Christ, to all and on all who believe. ROMANS 3:22 •

The glory which You gave Me I have given them. JOHN 17:22 •

April 27

Morning Reading

Brethren, the time is short.
1 CORINTHIANS 7:29

Man who is born of woman is of few days and full of trouble. He comes forth like a flower and fades away; he flees like a shadow and does not continue. JOB 14:1–2 • The world is passing away, and the lust of it; but he who does the will of God abides forever. 1 JOHN 2:17 • As in Adam all die, even so in Christ all shall be made alive. 1 CORINTHIANS 15:22 • Death is swallowed up in victory. 1 CORINTHIANS 15:54 • If we live, we live to the Lord; and if we die, we die to the Lord. Therefore, whether we live or die, we are the Lord's. ROMANS 14:8 • To live is Christ, and to die is gain. PHILIPPIANS 1:21 •

Do not cast away your confidence, which has great reward. For you have need of endurance, so that after you have done the will of God, you may receive the promise: "For yet a little while, and He who is coming will come and will not tarry." HEBREWS 10:35–37 • The night is far spent, the day is at hand. Therefore let us cast off the works of darkness, and let us put on the armor of light. ROMANS 13:12 • The end of all things is at hand; therefore be serious and watchful in your prayers. 1 PETER 4:7 •

Evening Reading

A new name.
REVELATION 2:17

The disciples were first called Christians in Antioch. ACTS 11:26 • Let everyone who names the name of Christ depart from iniquity. 2 TIMOTHY 2:19 • Those who are Christ's have crucified the flesh with its passions and desires. GALATIANS 5:24 • You were bought at a price; therefore glorify God in your body and in your spirit, which are God's. 1 CORINTHIANS 6:20 •

God forbid that I should boast except in the cross of our Lord Jesus Christ, by whom the world has been crucified to me, and I to the world. For in Christ Jesus neither circumcision nor uncircumcision avails anything, but a new creation. GALATIANS 6:14–15 •

Be imitators of God as dear children. And walk in love, as Christ also has loved us and given Himself for us, an offering and a sacrifice to God for a sweet-smelling aroma. But fornication and all uncleanness or covetousness, let it not even be named among you, as is fitting for saints....Now you are light in the Lord. Walk as children of light. EPHESIANS 5:1–3, 8 •

April 28

Morning Reading

Behold! The Lamb of God!
JOHN 1:29

It is not possible that the blood of bulls and goats could take away sins. Therefore, when He came into the world, He said: "Sacrifice and offering You did not desire, but a body You have prepared for Me. In burnt offerings and sacrifices for sin You had no pleasure. Then I said, 'Behold, I have come; in the volume of the book it is written of Me; to do Your will, O God.'" HEBREWS 10:4–7 • He was oppressed and He was afflicted, yet He opened not His mouth; He was led as a lamb to the slaughter, and as a sheep before its shearers is silent, so He opened not His mouth. ISAIAH 53:7 •

Knowing that you were not redeemed with corruptible things, like silver or gold,...but with the precious blood of Christ, as of a lamb without blemish and without spot...manifest in these last times for you who through Him believe in God,...so that your faith and hope are in God. 1 PETER 1:18–21 •

Worthy is the Lamb who was slain to receive power and riches and wisdom, and strength and honor and glory and blessing! REVELATION 5:12 •

Evening Reading

I will hope continually, and will praise You yet more and more.
PSALM 71:14

Not that I have already attained, or am already perfected. PHILIPPIANS 3:12 • Therefore, leaving the discussion of the elementary principles of Christ, let us go on to perfection, not laying again the foundation of repentance from dead works and of faith toward God. HEBREWS 6:1 • The path of the just is like the shining sun, that shines ever brighter unto the perfect day. PROVERBS 4:18 •

I love the LORD, because He has heard My voice and my supplications. Because He has inclined His ear to me, therefore I will call upon Him as long as I live. PSALM 116:1–2 • I will bless the LORD at all times; His praise shall continually be in my mouth. PSALM 34:1 •

Praise is awaiting You, O God, in Zion. PSALM 65:1 • [The four living creatures] do not rest day or night, saying: "Holy, holy, holy, Lord God Almighty!" REVELATION 4:8 • Whoever offers praise glorifies Me. PSALM 50:23 • Rejoice always, pray without ceasing, in everything give thanks; for this is the will of God in Christ Jesus for you. 1 THESSALONIANS 5:16–18 • Rejoice in the Lord always. Again I will say, rejoice! PHILIPPIANS 4:4 •

April 29

Morning Reading

Consider what great things He has done for you.
1 Samuel 12:24

You shall remember that the Lord your God led you all the way these forty years in the wilderness, to humble you and test you, to know what was in your heart, whether you would keep His commandments or not. Deuteronomy 8:2 • You should know in your heart that as a man chastens his son, so the Lord your God chastens you. Deuteronomy 8:5 •

I know, O Lord, that Your judgments are right, and that in faithfulness You have afflicted me. Psalm 119:75 • It is good for me that I have been afflicted, that I may learn Your statutes. Psalm 119:71 • Before I was afflicted I went astray, but now I keep Your word. Psalm 119:67 • The Lord has chastened me severely, but He has not given me over to death. Psalm 118:18 • He has not dealt with us according to our sins, nor punished us according to our iniquities. For as the heavens are high above the earth, so great is His mercy toward those who fear Him....For He knows our frame; He remembers that we are dust. Psalm 103:10–11, 14 •

Evening Reading

Looking for the blessed hope and glorious appearing
of our great God and Savior Jesus Christ.
Titus 2:13

This hope we have as an anchor of the soul, both sure and steadfast, and which enters the Presence behind the veil, where the forerunner has entered for us, even Jesus. Hebrews 6:19–20 • Whom heaven must receive until the times of restoration of all things. Acts 3:21 • When He comes, in that Day, to be glorified in His saints and to be admired among all those who believe. 2 Thessalonians 1:10 •

The whole creation groans and labors with birth pangs together until now. Not only that, but we also who have the firstfruits of the Spirit, even we ourselves groan within ourselves, eagerly waiting for the adoption, the redemption of our body. Romans 8:22–23 • Beloved, now we are children of God; and it has not yet been revealed what we shall be, but we know that when He is revealed, we shall be like Him, for we shall see Him as He is. 1 John 3:2 • When Christ who is our life appears, then you also will appear with Him in glory. Colossians 3:4 •

He who testifies to these things says, "Surely I am coming quickly." Amen. Even so, come, Lord Jesus! Revelation 22:20 •

April 30

Morning Reading

Whoever keeps His word, truly the love of God is perfected in him. By this we know that we are in Him.
1 JOHN 2:5

May the God of peace who brought up our Lord Jesus from the dead, that great Shepherd of the sheep, through the blood of the everlasting covenant, make you complete in every good work to do His will, working in you what is well pleasing in His sight, through Jesus Christ, to whom be glory forever and ever. Amen. HEBREWS 13:20–21 •

By this we know that we know Him, if we keep His commandments. 1 JOHN 2:3 • If anyone loves Me, he will keep My word; and My Father will love him, and We will come to him and make Our home with him. JOHN 14:23 • Whoever abides in Him does not sin. Whoever sins has neither seen Him nor known Him. Little children, let no one deceive you. He who practices righteousness is righteous, just as He is righteous. 1 JOHN 3:6–7 • Love has been perfected among us in this: that we may have boldness in the day of judgment; because as He is, so are we in this world. 1 JOHN 4:17 •

Evening Reading

He who is slow to wrath has great understanding.
PROVERBS 14:29

The LORD passed before [Moses] and proclaimed, "The LORD, the LORD God, merciful and gracious, longsuffering." EXODUS 34:6 • The Lord is not slack concerning His promise, as some count slackness, but is longsuffering toward us, not willing that any should perish but that all should come to repentance. 2 PETER 3:9 •

Be imitators of God as dear children. And walk in love. EPHESIANS 5:1–2 • The fruit of the Spirit is love, joy, peace, longsuffering, kindness, goodness, faithfulness, gentleness, self-control. Against such there is no law. GALATIANS 5:22–23 • This is commendable, if because of conscience toward God one endures grief, suffering wrongfully. For what credit is it if, when you are beaten for your faults, you take it patiently? But when you do good and suffer, if you take it patiently, this is commendable before God. For to this you were called, because Christ also suffered for us, leaving us an example, that you should follow His steps:... who, when He was reviled, did not revile in return; when He suffered, He did not threaten, but committed Himself to Him who judges righteously. 1 PETER 2:19–21, 23 •

Be angry, and do not sin. EPHESIANS 4:26 •

 MAY

May 1

Morning Reading

The fruit of the Spirit is...peace.
GALATIANS 5:22

To be spiritually minded is life and peace. ROMANS 8:6 •
God has called us to peace. 1 CORINTHIANS 7:15 • Peace I leave with you, My peace I give to you; not as the world gives do I give to you. Let not your heart be troubled, neither let it be afraid. JOHN 14:27 • May the God of hope fill you with all joy and peace in believing, that you may abound in hope by the power of the Holy Spirit. ROMANS 15:13 •

I know whom I have believed and am persuaded that He is able to keep what I have committed to Him until that Day. 2 TIMOTHY 1:12 • You will keep him in perfect peace, whose mind is stayed on You, because he trusts in You. ISAIAH 26:3 •

The work of righteousness will be peace, and the effect of righteousness, quietness and assurance forever. My people will dwell in a peaceful habitation, in secure dwellings, and in quiet resting places. ISAIAH 32:17–18 • Whoever listens to me will dwell safely, and will be secure, without fear of evil. PROVERBS 1:33 •

Great peace have those who love Your law. PSALM 119:165 •

Evening Reading

THE LORD IS THERE.
EZEKIEL 48:35

Behold, the tabernacle of God is with men, and He will dwell with them, and they shall be His people. God Himself will be with them and be their God. REVELATION 21:3 •

I saw no temple,...for the Lord God Almighty and the Lamb are its temple. The city had no need of the sun or of the moon to shine in it, for the glory of God illuminated it. The Lamb is its light. REVELATION 21:22–23 •

I shall be satisfied when I awake in Your likeness. PSALM 17:15 • Whom have I in heaven but You? And there is none upon earth that I desire besides You. PSALM 73:25 •

Judah shall abide forever, and Jerusalem from generation to generation. For I will acquit them of the guilt of bloodshed, whom I had not acquitted; for the LORD dwells in Zion. JOEL 3:20–21 • "Sing and rejoice, O daughter of Zion! For behold, I am coming and I will dwell in your midst," says the LORD. ZECHARIAH 2:10 • There shall be no more curse, but the throne of God and of the Lamb shall be in it, and His servants shall serve Him. REVELATION 22:3 •

May 2

Morning Reading

Surely the LORD is in this place, and I did not know it.
GENESIS 28:16

Where two or three are gathered together in My name, I am there in the midst of them. MATTHEW 18:20 • Lo, I am with you always, even to the end of the age. MATTHEW 28:20 • My Presence will go with you, and I will give you rest. EXODUS 33:14 •

Where can I go from Your Spirit? Or where can I flee from Your presence? If I ascend into heaven, You are there; if I make my bed in hell, behold, You are there. PSALM 139:7–8 • "Am I a God near at hand," says the LORD, "and not a God afar off? Can anyone hide himself in secret places, so I shall not see him?" says the LORD; "do I not fill heaven and earth?" says the LORD. JEREMIAH 23:23–24 •

Behold, heaven and the heaven of heavens cannot contain You. How much less this temple which I have built! 1 KINGS 8:27 • Thus says the High and Lofty One who inhabits eternity, whose name is Holy: "I dwell in the high and holy place, with him who has a contrite and humble spirit, to revive the spirit of the humble, and to revive the heart of the contrite ones." ISAIAH 57:15 • You are the temple of the living God. As God has said: "I will dwell in them and walk among them. I will be their God, and they shall be My people." 2 CORINTHIANS 6:16 •

Evening Reading

Keep yourselves from idols.
1 JOHN 5:21

My son, give me your heart. PROVERBS 23:26 • Set your mind on things above, not on things on the earth. COLOSSIANS 3:2 •

Son of man, these men have set up their idols in their hearts, and put before them that which causes them to stumble into iniquity. Should I let Myself be inquired of at all by them? EZEKIEL 14:3 • Put to death your members which are on the earth: fornication, uncleanness, passion, evil desire, and covetousness, which is idolatry. COLOSSIANS 3:5 • Those who desire to be rich fall into temptation and a snare, and into many foolish and harmful lusts which drown men in destruction and perdition. For the love of money is a root of all kinds of evil, for which some have strayed from the faith in their greediness, and pierced themselves through with many sorrows. But you, O man of God, flee these things. 1 TIMOTHY 6:9–11 •

If riches increase, do not set your heart on them. PSALM 62:10 • My fruit is better than gold, yes, than fine gold, and my revenue than choice silver. PROVERBS 8:19 •

Where your treasure is, there your heart will be also. MATTHEW 6:21 • The LORD looks at the heart. 1 SAMUEL 16:7 •

May 3

Morning Reading

Be perfect, just as your Father in heaven is perfect.
Matthew 5:48

I am Almighty God; walk before Me and be blameless. Genesis 17:1 • You shall be holy to Me, for I the Lord am holy, and have separated you from the peoples, that you should be Mine. Leviticus 20:26 •

You were bought at a price; therefore glorify God in your body and in your spirit, which are God's. 1 Corinthians 6:20 •

You are complete in Him, who is the head of all principality and power. Colossians 2:10 • Who gave Himself for us, that He might redeem us from every lawless deed. Titus 2:14 • Be diligent to be found by Him in peace, without spot and blameless. 2 Peter 3:14 •

Blessed are the undefiled in the way, who walk in the law of the Lord! Psalm 119:1 • He who looks into the perfect law of liberty and continues in it, and is not a forgetful hearer but a doer of the work, this one will be blessed in what he does. James 1:25 • Search me, O God, and know my heart; try me, and know my anxieties; and see if there is any wicked way in me, and lead me in the way everlasting. Psalm 139:23–24 •

Evening Reading

Perfecting holiness in the fear of God.
2 Corinthians 7:1

Beloved, let us cleanse ourselves from all filthiness of the flesh and spirit. 2 Corinthians 7:1 •

Behold, You desire truth in the inward parts, and in the hidden part You will make me to know wisdom. Psalm 51:6 • Teaching us that, denying ungodliness and worldly lusts, we should live soberly, righteously, and godly in the present age. Titus 2:12 • Let your light so shine before men, that they may see your good works and glorify your Father in heaven. Matthew 5:16 • Not that I have already attained, or am already perfected. Philippians 3:12 •

Everyone who has this hope in Him purifies himself, just as He is pure. 1 John 3:3 •

Now He who has prepared us for this very thing is God, who also has given us the Spirit as a guarantee. 2 Corinthians 5:5 • For the equipping of the saints for the work of ministry, for the edifying of the body of Christ, till we all come to the unity of the faith and of the knowledge of the Son of God, to a perfect man, to the measure of the stature of the fullness of Christ. Ephesians 4:12–13 •

May 4

Morning Reading

Behold, the Lord's hand is not shortened, that it cannot save; nor His ear heavy, that it cannot hear.
ISAIAH 59:1

In the day when I cried out, You answered me, and made me bold with strength in my soul. PSALM 138:3 • While I [Daniel] was speaking in prayer, the man Gabriel, whom I had seen in the vision at the beginning, being caused to fly swiftly, reached me about the time of the evening offering. DANIEL 9:21 •

Do not hide Your face from me; do not turn Your servant away in anger; You have been my help; do not leave me nor forsake me, O God of my salvation. PSALM 27:9 • O LORD, do not be far from Me; O My Strength, hasten to help Me! PSALM 22:19 •

Ah, Lord GOD! Behold, You have made the heavens and the earth by Your great power and outstretched arm. There is nothing too hard for You. JEREMIAH 32:17 • Who delivered us from so great a death, and does deliver us; in whom we trust that He will still deliver us. 2 CORINTHIANS 1:10 • Shall God not avenge His own elect who cry out day and night to Him, though He bears long with them? I tell you that He will avenge them speedily. LUKE 18:7–8 •

Evening Reading

I have glorified You on the earth.
JOHN 17:4

My food is to do the will of Him who sent Me, and to finish His work. JOHN 4:34 • I must work the works of Him who sent Me while it is day; the night is coming when no one can work. JOHN 9:4 •

[Jesus said,] "Did you not know that I must be about My Father's business?" But they did not understand the statement which He spoke to them. LUKE 2:49–50 • This sickness is not unto death, but for the glory of God, that the Son of God may be glorified through it. JOHN 11:4 • Did I not say to you that if you would believe you would see the glory of God? JOHN 11:40 •

Jesus increased in wisdom and stature, and in favor with God and men. LUKE 2:52 • You are My beloved Son; in You I am well pleased. LUKE 3:22 • All bore witness to Him, and marveled at the gracious words which proceeded out of His mouth. LUKE 4:22 •

You are worthy to take the scroll, and to open its seals; for You were slain, and have redeemed us to God by Your blood out of every tribe and tongue and people and nation, and have made us kings and priests to our God; and we shall reign on the earth. REVELATION 5:9–10 •

May 5

Morning Reading

Therefore do not worry, saying, "What shall we eat?" or "What shall we drink?" or "What shall we wear?" For after all these things the Gentiles seek. For your heavenly Father knows that you need all these things.
MATTHEW 6:31–32

Oh, fear the LORD, you His saints! There is no want to those who fear Him. The young lions lack and suffer hunger; but those who seek the LORD shall not lack any good thing. PSALM 34:9–10 • No good thing will He withhold from those who walk uprightly. O LORD of hosts, blessed is the man who trusts in You! PSALM 84:11–12 •

But I want you to be without care. 1 CORINTHIANS 7:32 • Be anxious for nothing, but in everything by prayer and supplication, with thanksgiving, let your requests be made known to God. PHILIPPIANS 4:6 •

Are not two sparrows sold for a copper coin? And not one of them falls to the ground apart from your Father's will. But the very hairs of your head are all numbered. Do not fear therefore; you are of more value than many sparrows. MATTHEW 10:29–31 • Why are you so fearful? How is it that you have no faith? MARK 4:40 • Have faith in God. MARK 11:22 •

Evening Reading

He spread a cloud for a covering, and fire to give light in the night.
PSALM 105:39

As a father pities his children, so the LORD pities those who fear Him. For He knows our frame; He remembers that we are dust. PSALM 103:13–14 •

The sun shall not strike you by day, nor the moon by night. PSALM 121:6 • There will be a tabernacle for shade in the daytime from the heat, for a place of refuge, and for a shelter from storm and rain. ISAIAH 4:6 •

The LORD is your keeper; the LORD is your shade at your right hand.... The LORD shall preserve your going out and your coming in from this time forth, and even forevermore. PSALM 121:5, 8 • The LORD went before them by day in a pillar of cloud to lead the way, and by night in a pillar of fire to give them light, so as to go by day and night. He did not take away the pillar of cloud by day or the pillar of fire by night from before the people. EXODUS 13:21–22 •

Jesus Christ is the same yesterday, today, and forever. HEBREWS 13:8 •

May 6

Morning Reading

Mercy and truth have met together;
righteousness and peace have kissed.
PSALM 85:10

A just God and a Savior. ISAIAH 45:21 •
The Lord is well pleased for His righteousness' sake; He will exalt the law and make it honorable. ISAIAH 42:21 •

God was in Christ reconciling the world to Himself, not imputing their trespasses to them. 2 CORINTHIANS 5:19 • Whom God set forth as a propitiation by His blood, through faith, to demonstrate His righteousness, because in His forbearance God had passed over the sins that were previously committed, to demonstrate at the present time His righteousness, that He might be just and the justifier of the one who has faith in Jesus. ROMANS 3:25–26 • He was wounded for our transgressions, He was bruised for our iniquities; the chastisement for our peace was upon Him, and by His stripes we are healed. ISAIAH 53:5 • Who shall bring a charge against God's elect? It is God who justifies. ROMANS 8:33 • To him who does not work but believes on Him who justifies the ungodly, his faith is accounted for righteousness. ROMANS 4:5 •

Evening Reading

How are the dead raised up?
And with what body do they come?
1 CORINTHIANS 15:35

Beloved, now we are children of God; and it has not yet been revealed what we shall be, but we know that when He is revealed, we shall be like Him, for we shall see Him as He is. 1 JOHN 3:2 • And as we have borne the image of the man of dust, we shall also bear the image of the heavenly Man. 1 CORINTHIANS 15:49 •

The Savior, the Lord Jesus Christ,...will transform our lowly body that it may be conformed to His glorious body, according to the working by which He is able even to subdue all things to Himself. PHILIPPIANS 3:20–21 •

Jesus Himself stood in the midst of them, and said to them, "Peace to you." But they were terrified and frightened, and supposed they had seen a spirit. LUKE 24:36–37 • He was seen by Cephas, then by the twelve. After that He was seen by over five hundred brethren at once. 1 CORINTHIANS 15:5–6 •

If the Spirit of Him who raised Jesus from the dead dwells in you, He who raised Christ from the dead will also give life to your mortal bodies through His Spirit who dwells in you. ROMANS 8:11 •

May 7

Morning Reading

You will hear of wars and rumors of wars.
See that you are not troubled.
MATTHEW 24:6

God is our refuge and strength, a very present help in trouble. Therefore we will not fear, even though the earth be removed, and though the mountains be carried into the midst of the sea; though its waters roar and be troubled, though the mountains shake with its swelling. PSALM 46:1–3 • Come, my people, enter your chambers, and shut your doors behind you; hide yourself, as it were, for a little moment, until the indignation is past. For behold, the LORD comes out of His place to punish the inhabitants of the earth for their iniquity. ISAIAH 26:20–21 • In the shadow of Your wings I will make my refuge, until these calamities have passed by. PSALM 57:1 • Your life is hidden with Christ in God. COLOSSIANS 3:3 •

He will not be afraid of evil tidings; his heart is steadfast, trusting in the LORD. PSALM 112:7 •

These things I have spoken to you, that in Me you may have peace. In the world you will have tribulation; but be of good cheer, I have overcome the world. JOHN 16:33 •

Evening Reading

They persecute the ones You have struck.
PSALM 69:26

It is impossible that no offenses should come, but woe to him through whom they do come! LUKE 17:1 • [Jesus], being delivered by the determined purpose and foreknowledge of God, you have taken by lawless hands, have crucified, and put to death. ACTS 2:23 • Then they spat in His face and beat Him; and others struck Him with the palms of their hands, saying, "Prophesy to us, Christ! Who is the one who struck You?" MATTHEW 26:67–68 • Likewise the chief priests also, mocking with the scribes and elders, said, "He saved others; Himself He cannot save. If He is the King of Israel, let Him now come down from the cross." MATTHEW 27:41–42 • Truly against Your holy Servant Jesus, whom You anointed, both Herod and Pontius Pilate, with the Gentiles and the people of Israel, were gathered together to do whatever Your hand and Your purpose determined before to be done. ACTS 4:27–28 •

Surely He has borne our griefs and carried our sorrows; yet we esteemed Him stricken, smitten by God, and afflicted. ISAIAH 53:4 •

May 8

Morning Reading

It pleased the LORD to bruise Him; He has put Him to grief.
ISAIAH 53:10

[Jesus said,] "Now My soul is troubled, and what shall I say? 'Father, save Me from this hour'? But for this purpose I came to this hour. Father, glorify Your name." Then a voice came from heaven, saying, "I have both glorified it and will glorify it again." JOHN 12:27–28 • [Jesus prayed,] "Father, if it is Your will, take this cup away from Me; nevertheless not My will, but Yours, be done." Then an angel appeared to Him from heaven, strengthening Him. LUKE 22:42–43 •

Being found in appearance as a man, He humbled Himself and became obedient to the point of death, even the death of the cross. PHILIPPIANS 2:8 • Therefore My Father loves Me, because I lay down My life that I may take it again. JOHN 10:17 • For I have come down from heaven, not to do My own will, but the will of Him who sent Me. JOHN 6:38 • Shall I not drink the cup which My Father has given Me? JOHN 18:11 •

The Father has not left Me alone, for I always do those things that please Him. JOHN 8:29 • My beloved Son, in whom I am well pleased. MATTHEW 3:17 • My Elect One in whom My soul delights! ISAIAH 42:1 •

Evening Reading

You who make mention of the LORD, do not keep silent.
ISAIAH 62:6

[Jesus has] made us kings and priests to our God. REVELATION 5:10 • The sons of Aaron, the priests, shall blow the trumpets; and these shall be to you as an ordinance forever throughout your generations. When you go to war in your land against the enemy who oppresses you, then you shall sound an alarm with the trumpets, and you will be remembered before the LORD your God, and you will be saved from your enemies. NUMBERS 10:8–9 •

I did not say to the seed of Jacob, "Seek Me in vain." ISAIAH 45:19 • Their voice was heard; and their prayer came up to His holy dwelling place, to heaven. 2 CHRONICLES 30:27 • The eyes of the LORD are on the righteous, and His ears are open to their cry. PSALM 34:15 • Pray for one another, that you may be healed. The effective, fervent prayer of a righteous man avails much. JAMES 5:16 •

Come, Lord Jesus! REVELATION 22:20 • Do not delay, O my God. PSALM 40:17 • Looking for and hastening the coming of the day of God. 2 PETER 3:12 •

Daily Light on the Daily Path

May 9

Morning Reading

Faith is the substance of things hoped for,
the evidence of things not seen.
HEBREWS 11:1

If in this life only we have hope in Christ, we are of all men the most pitiable. 1 CORINTHIANS 15:19 •

Eye has not seen, nor ear heard, nor have entered into the heart of man the things which God has prepared for those who love Him. 1 CORINTHIANS 2:9 • Having believed, you were sealed with the Holy Spirit of promise, who is the guarantee of our inheritance until the redemption of the purchased possession. EPHESIANS 1:13–14 •

Jesus said to him, "Thomas, because you have seen Me, you have believed. Blessed are those who have not seen and yet have believed." JOHN 20:29 • Whom having not seen you love. Though now you do not see Him, yet believing, you rejoice with joy inexpressible and full of glory, receiving the end of your faith; the salvation of your souls. 1 PETER 1:8–9 •

We walk by faith, not by sight. 2 CORINTHIANS 5:7 • Therefore do not cast away your confidence, which has great reward. HEBREWS 10:35 •

Evening Reading

It is I; do not be afraid.
JOHN 6:20

When I saw Him, I fell at His feet as dead. But He laid His right hand on me, saying to me, "Do not be afraid; I am the First and the Last. I am He who lives, and was dead, and behold, I am alive forevermore. Amen. And I have the keys of Hades and of Death." REVELATION 1:17–18 • I, even I, am He who blots out your transgressions for My own sake; and I will not remember your sins. ISAIAH 43:25 •

I [Isaiah] said: "Woe is me, for I am undone!...My eyes have seen the King, the LORD of hosts." Then one of the seraphim flew to me, having in his hand a live coal which he had taken with the tongs from the altar. And he touched my mouth with it, and said: "Behold, this has touched your lips; your iniquity is taken away, and your sin purged." ISAIAH 6:5–7 • I have blotted out, like a thick cloud, your transgressions, and like a cloud, your sins. Return to Me, for I have redeemed you. ISAIAH 44:22 •

If anyone sins, we have an Advocate with the Father, Jesus Christ the righteous. 1 JOHN 2:1 •

May 10

For this purpose the Son of God was manifested,
that He might destroy the works of the devil.
1 JOHN 3:8

We do not wrestle against flesh and blood, but against principalities, against powers, against the rulers of the darkness of this age, against spiritual hosts of wickedness in the heavenly places. EPHESIANS 6:12 • Inasmuch then as the children have partaken of flesh and blood, He Himself likewise shared in the same, that through death He might destroy him who had the power of death, that is, the devil. HEBREWS 2:14 • Having disarmed principalities and powers, He made a public spectacle of them, triumphing over them. COLOSSIANS 2:15 • I heard a loud voice saying in heaven, "Now salvation, and strength, and the kingdom of our God, and the power of His Christ have come, for the accuser of our brethren, who accused them before our God day and night, has been cast down. And they overcame him by the blood of the Lamb and by the word of their testimony, and they did not love their lives to the death." REVELATION 12:10–11 •

Thanks be to God, who gives us the victory through our Lord Jesus Christ. 1 CORINTHIANS 15:57 •

Evening Reading

Vanity of vanities, all is vanity.
ECCLESIASTES 1:2

We finish our years like a sigh. The days of our lives are seventy years; and if by reason of strength they are eighty years, yet their boast is only labor and sorrow; for it is soon cut off, and we fly away. PSALM 90:9–10 •

If in this life only we have hope in Christ, we are of all men the most pitiable. 1 CORINTHIANS 15:19 • Here we have no continuing city, but we seek the one to come. HEBREWS 13:14 • I am the LORD, I do not change. MALACHI 3:6 • Our citizenship is in heaven, from which we also eagerly wait for the Savior, the Lord Jesus Christ, who will transform our lowly body that it may be conformed to His glorious body, according to the working by which He is able even to subdue all things to Himself. PHILIPPIANS 3:20–21 • The creation was subjected to futility, not willingly, but because of Him who subjected it in hope. ROMANS 8:20 •

Jesus Christ is the same yesterday, today, and forever. HEBREWS 13:8 • Holy, holy, holy, Lord God Almighty, who was and is and is to come! REVELATION 4:8 •

May 11

Morning Reading

Awake to righteousness, and do not sin.
1 CORINTHIANS 15:34

You are all sons of light and sons of the day. We are not of the night nor of darkness. Therefore let us not sleep, as others do, but let us watch and be sober. 1 THESSALONIANS 5:5–6 •

It is high time to awake out of sleep; for now our salvation is nearer than when we first believed. The night is far spent, the day is at hand. Therefore let us cast off the works of darkness, and let us put on the armor of light. ROMANS 13:11–12 • Therefore take up the whole armor of God, that you may be able to withstand in the evil day, and having done all, to stand. EPHESIANS 6:13 • Cast away from you all the transgressions which you have committed, and get yourselves a new heart and a new spirit. EZEKIEL 18:31 • Lay aside all filthiness and overflow of wickedness, and receive with meekness the implanted word, which is able to save your souls. JAMES 1:21 • Little children, abide in Him, that when He appears, we may have confidence and not be ashamed before Him at His coming. If you know that He is righteous, you know that everyone who practices righteousness is born of Him. 1 JOHN 2:28–29 •

Evening Reading

My sheep hear My voice.
JOHN 10:27

Behold, I stand at the door and knock. If anyone hears My voice and opens the door, I will come in to him and dine with him, and he with Me. REVELATION 3:20 •

I sleep, but my heart is awake; it is the voice of my beloved! He knocks, saying, "Open for me, my sister, my love, my dove, my perfect one; for my head is covered with dew, my locks with the drops of the night." I have taken off my robe; how can I put it on again? I have washed my feet; how can I defile them? My beloved put his hand by the latch of the door....I opened for my beloved, but my beloved had turned away and was gone. My heart leaped up when he spoke. I sought him, but I could not find him; I called him, but he gave me no answer. SONG OF SONGS 5:2–4, 6 •

Speak, for Your servant hears. 1 SAMUEL 3:10 • When Jesus came to the place, He looked up and saw him, and said to him, "Zacchaeus, make haste and come down, for today I must stay at your house." So he made haste and came down, and received Him joyfully. LUKE 19:5–6 • I will hear what God the LORD will speak, for He will speak peace to His people and to His saints; but let them not turn back to folly. PSALM 85:8 •

May 12

Beloved, let us love one another, for love is of God;
and everyone who loves is born of God and knows God.
1 JOHN 4:7

The love of God has been poured out in our hearts by the Holy Spirit who was given to us. ROMANS 5:5 • You did not receive the spirit of bondage again to fear, but you received the Spirit of adoption by whom we cry out, "Abba, Father." The Spirit Himself bears witness with our spirit that we are children of God. ROMANS 8:15–16 • He who believes in the Son of God has the witness in himself. 1 JOHN 5:10 •

In this the love of God was manifested toward us, that God has sent His only begotten Son into the world, that we might live through Him. 1 JOHN 4:9 • In Him we have redemption through His blood, the forgiveness of sins, according to the riches of His grace. EPHESIANS 1:7 • That in the ages to come He might show the exceeding riches of His grace in His kindness toward us in Christ Jesus. EPHESIANS 2:7 •

Beloved, if God so loved us, we also ought to love one another. 1 JOHN 4:11 •

Evening Reading

Reproach has broken my heart.
PSALM 69:20

Is this not the carpenter's son? MATTHEW 13:55 • Can anything good come out of Nazareth? JOHN 1:46 • Do we not say rightly that You are a Samaritan and have a demon? JOHN 8:48 • He casts out demons by the ruler of the demons. MATTHEW 9:34 • We know that this Man is a sinner. JOHN 9:24 • He deceives the people. JOHN 7:12 • This Man blasphemes! MATTHEW 9:3 • Look, a glutton and a winebibber, a friend of tax collectors and sinners! MATTHEW 11:19 •

It is enough for a disciple that he be like his teacher, and a servant like his master. If they have called the master of the house Beelzebub, how much more will they call those of his household! MATTHEW 10:25 • This is commendable, if because of conscience toward God one endures grief, suffering wrongfully....For to this you were called, because Christ also suffered for us, leaving us an example, that you should follow His steps: "Who committed no sin, nor was deceit found in His mouth"; who, when He was reviled, did not revile in return; when He suffered, He did not threaten, but committed Himself to Him who judges righteously. 1 PETER 2:19, 21–23 • If you are reproached for the name of Christ, blessed are you, for the Spirit of glory and of God rests upon you. On their part He is blasphemed, but on your part He is glorified. 1 PETER 4:14 •

May 13

Morning Reading

Pray everywhere, lifting up holy hands,
without wrath and doubting.
1 TIMOTHY 2:8

The true worshipers will worship the Father in spirit and truth; for the Father is seeking such to worship Him. God is Spirit, and those who worship Him must worship in spirit and truth. JOHN 4:23–24 • Then you shall call, and the LORD will answer; you shall cry, and He will say, "Here I am." ISAIAH 58:9 • Whenever you stand praying, if you have anything against anyone, forgive him. MARK 11:25 •

Without faith it is impossible to please Him, for he who comes to God must believe that He is, and that He is a rewarder of those who diligently seek Him. HEBREWS 11:6 • Let him ask in faith, with no doubting, for he who doubts is like a wave of the sea driven and tossed by the wind. For let not that man suppose that he will receive anything from the Lord. JAMES 1:6–7 •

If I regard iniquity in my heart, the Lord will not hear. PSALM 66:18 • My little children, these things I write to you, so that you may not sin. And if anyone sins, we have an Advocate with the Father, Jesus Christ the righteous. And He Himself is the propitiation for our sins, and not for ours only but also for the whole world. 1 JOHN 2:1–2 •

Evening Reading

My heart pants, my strength fails me.
PSALM 38:10

Hear my cry, O God; attend to my prayer. From the end of the earth I will cry to You, when my heart is overwhelmed; lead me to the rock that is higher than I. PSALM 61:1–2 •

[The Lord Jesus] said to me, "My grace is sufficient for you, for My strength is made perfect in weakness." Therefore most gladly I will rather boast in my infirmities, that the power of Christ may rest upon me....For when I am weak, then I am strong. 2 CORINTHIANS 12:9–10 •

When [Peter] saw that the wind was boisterous, he was afraid; and beginning to sink he cried out, saying, "Lord, save me!" And immediately Jesus stretched out His hand and caught him, and said to him, "O you of little faith, why did you doubt?" MATTHEW 14:30–31 • If you faint in the day of adversity, your strength is small. PROVERBS 24:10 • He gives power to the weak, and to those who have no might He increases strength. ISAIAH 40:29 • The eternal God is your refuge, and underneath are the everlasting arms. DEUTERONOMY 33:27 • Strengthened with all might, according to His glorious power, for all patience and longsuffering with joy. COLOSSIANS 1:11 •

May 14

Morning Reading

The fellowship of His sufferings.
PHILIPPIANS 3:10

It is enough for a disciple that he be like his teacher, and a servant like his master. MATTHEW 10:25 •

He is despised and rejected by men, a Man of sorrows and acquainted with grief. And we hid, as it were, our faces from Him; He was despised, and we did not esteem Him. ISAIAH 53:3 • In the world you will have tribulation. JOHN 16:33 • Because you are not of the world, but I chose you out of the world, therefore the world hates you. JOHN 15:19 •

I looked for someone to take pity, but there was none. PSALM 69:20 • At my first defense no one stood with me, but all forsook me. 2 TIMOTHY 4:16 •

Foxes have holes and birds of the air have nests, but the Son of Man has nowhere to lay His head. MATTHEW 8:20 • Here we have no continuing city, but we seek the one to come. HEBREWS 13:14 •

Let us run with endurance the race that is set before us, looking unto Jesus, the author and finisher of our faith, who for the joy that was set before Him endured the cross, despising the shame, and has sat down at the right hand of the throne of God. HEBREWS 12:1–2 •

Evening Reading

They overcame...by the blood of the Lamb.
REVELATION 12:11

Who shall bring a charge against God's elect? It is God who justifies. Who is he who condemns? It is Christ who died. ROMANS 8:33–34 • It is the blood that makes atonement for the soul. LEVITICUS 17:11 • I am the LORD. Now the blood shall be a sign for you on the houses where you are. And when I see the blood, I will pass over you. EXODUS 12:12–13 •

There is therefore now no condemnation to those who are in Christ Jesus. ROMANS 8:1 •

Then one of the elders answered, saying to me, "Who are these arrayed in white robes, and where did they come from?"...So he said to me, "These are the ones who come out of the great tribulation, and washed their robes and made them white in the blood of the Lamb." REVELATION 7:13–14 •

To Him who loved us and washed us from our sins in His own blood, and has made us kings and priests to His God and Father, to Him be glory and dominion forever and ever. Amen. REVELATION 1:5–6 •

May 15

Morning Reading

God will wipe away every tear from their eyes; there shall be no more death, nor sorrow,...for the former things have passed away.
REVELATION 21:4

He will swallow up death forever, and the Lord GOD will wipe away tears from all faces; the rebuke of His people He will take away from all the earth; for the LORD has spoken. ISAIAH 25:8 • Your sun shall no longer go down, nor shall your moon withdraw itself; for the LORD will be your everlasting light, and the days of your mourning shall be ended. ISAIAH 60:20 • The inhabitant will not say, "I am sick"; the people who dwell in it will be forgiven their iniquity. ISAIAH 33:24 • The voice of weeping shall no longer be heard in her, nor the voice of crying. ISAIAH 65:19 • Sorrow and sighing shall flee away. ISAIAH 35:10 •

I will ransom them from the power of the grave; I will redeem them from death. O Death, I will be your plagues! O Grave, I will be your destruction! HOSEA 13:14 • The last enemy that will be destroyed is death. 1 CORINTHIANS 15:26 • Then shall be brought to pass the saying that is written: "Death is swallowed up in victory." 1 CORINTHIANS 15:54 •

The things which are not seen are eternal. 2 CORINTHIANS 4:18 •

Evening Reading

[God] raised us up together...in Christ Jesus.
EPHESIANS 2:6

Do not be afraid....I am He who lives. REVELATION 1:17–18 • Father, I desire that they also whom You gave Me may be with Me where I am. JOHN 17:24 •

We are members of His body, of His flesh and of His bones. EPHESIANS 5:30 • He is the head of the body, the church, who is the beginning, the firstborn from the dead. COLOSSIANS 1:18 • You are complete in Him, who is the head. COLOSSIANS 2:10 •

Inasmuch then as the children have partaken of flesh and blood, He Himself likewise shared in the same, that through death He might destroy him who had the power of death, that is, the devil, and release those who through fear of death were all their lifetime subject to bondage. HEBREWS 2:14–15 •

This corruptible must put on incorruption, and this mortal must put on immortality. So when this corruptible has put on incorruption, and this mortal has put on immortality, then shall be brought to pass the saying that is written: "Death is swallowed up in victory." 1 CORINTHIANS 15:53–54 •

May 16

Morning Reading

A bondservant of Jesus Christ.
ROMANS 1:1

You call me Teacher and Lord, and you say well, for so I am. JOHN 13:13 • If anyone serves Me, let him follow Me; and where I am, there My servant will be also. If anyone serves Me, him My Father will honor. JOHN 12:26 • Take My yoke upon you and learn from Me, for I am gentle and lowly in heart, and you will find rest for your souls. For My yoke is easy and My burden is light. MATTHEW 11:29–30 •

But what things were gain to me, these I have counted loss for Christ. PHILIPPIANS 3:7 • Having been set free from sin, and having become slaves of God, you have your fruit to holiness, and the end, everlasting life. ROMANS 6:22 •

No longer do I call you servants, for a servant does not know what his master is doing; but I have called you friends, for all things that I heard from My Father I have made known to you. JOHN 15:15 • You are no longer a slave but a son. GALATIANS 4:7 •

Stand fast therefore in the liberty by which Christ has made us free, and do not be entangled again with a yoke of bondage....For you, brethren, have been called to liberty; only do not use liberty as an opportunity for the flesh. GALATIANS 5:1, 13 •

Evening Reading

I will bless the LORD who has given me counsel.
PSALM 16:7

His name will be called Wonderful, Counselor. ISAIAH 9:6 • Counsel is mine, and sound wisdom; I am understanding, I have strength. PROVERBS 8:14 • Your word is a lamp to my feet and a light to my path. PSALM 119:105 • Trust in the LORD with all your heart, and lean not on your own understanding; in all your ways acknowledge Him, and He shall direct your paths. PROVERBS 3:5–6 •

O LORD, I know the way of man is not in himself; it is not in man who walks to direct his own steps. JEREMIAH 10:23 • Your ears shall hear a word behind you, saying, "This is the way, walk in it," whenever you turn to the right hand or whenever you turn to the left. ISAIAH 30:21 • Commit your works to the LORD, and your thoughts will be established. PROVERBS 16:3 • He knows the way that I take. JOB 23:10 • A man's steps are of the LORD; how then can a man understand his own way? PROVERBS 20:24 •

You will guide me with Your counsel, and afterward receive me to glory. PSALM 73:24 • This is God, our God forever and ever; He will be our guide even to death. PSALM 48:14 •

May 17

Morning Reading

I am the LORD your God: walk in My statutes, keep My judgments, and do them.
EZEKIEL 20:19

As He who called you is holy, you also be holy in all your conduct. 1 PETER 1:15 • He who says he abides in Him ought himself also to walk just as He walked. 1 JOHN 2:6 • If you know that He is righteous, you know that everyone who practices righteousness is born of Him. 1 JOHN 2:29 • Circumcision is nothing and uncircumcision is nothing, but keeping the commandments of God is what matters. 1 CORINTHIANS 7:19 • Whoever shall keep the whole law, and yet stumble in one point, he is guilty of all. JAMES 2:10 •

Not that we are sufficient of ourselves to think of anything as being from ourselves, but our sufficiency is from God. 2 CORINTHIANS 3:5 • Teach me, O LORD, the way of Your statutes. PSALM 119:33 •

Work out your own salvation with fear and trembling; for it is God who works in you both to will and to do for His good pleasure. PHILIPPIANS 2:12–13 • May the God of peace...make you complete in every good work to do His will, working in you what is well pleasing in His sight, through Jesus Christ. HEBREWS 13:20–21 •

Evening Reading

I have exalted one chosen from the people.
PSALM 89:19

Indeed He does not give aid to angels, but He does give aid to the seed of Abraham. Therefore, in all things He had to be made like His brethren. HEBREWS 2:16–17 • On the likeness of the throne was a likeness with the appearance of a man high above it. EZEKIEL 1:26 • The Son of Man who is in heaven. JOHN 3:13 • Behold My hands and My feet, that it is I Myself. Handle Me and see, for a spirit does not have flesh and bones as you see I have. LUKE 24:39 •

[Christ] made Himself of no reputation, taking the form of a bondservant, and coming in the likeness of men. And being found in appearance as a man, He humbled Himself and became obedient to the point of death, even the death of the cross. Therefore God also has highly exalted Him and given Him the name which is above every name, that at the name of Jesus every knee should bow. PHILIPPIANS 2:7–10 • Be watchful, and strengthen the things which remain, that are ready to die, for I have not found your works perfect before God. REVELATION 3:2 •

May 18

Morning Reading

As the Father has life in Himself,
so He has granted the Son to have life in Himself.
JOHN 5:26

Our Savior Jesus Christ...has abolished death and brought life and immortality to light through the gospel. 2 TIMOTHY 1:10 • I am the resurrection and the life. JOHN 11:25 • Because I live, you will live also. JOHN 14:19 • We have become partakers of Christ. HEBREWS 3:14 • Partakers of the Holy Spirit. HEBREWS 6:4 • Partakers of the divine nature. 2 PETER 1:4 • It is written, "The first man Adam became a living being." The last Adam became a life-giving spirit. 1 CORINTHIANS 15:45 • Behold, I tell you a mystery: we shall not all sleep, but we shall all be changed; in a moment, in the twinkling of an eye, at the last trumpet. For the trumpet will sound, and the dead will be raised incorruptible, and we shall be changed. 1 CORINTHIANS 15:51–52 •

Holy, holy, holy, Lord God Almighty, who was and is and is to come! REVELATION 4:8 • Who lives forever and ever. REVELATION 4:9 • The blessed and only Potentate, the King of kings and Lord of lords, who alone has immortality. 1 TIMOTHY 6:15–16 • Now to the King eternal, immortal, invisible, to God who alone is wise, be honor and glory forever and ever. Amen. 1 TIMOTHY 1:17 •

Evening Reading

Let us not become conceited.
GALATIANS 5:26

Gideon said to them, "I would like to make a request of you, that each of you would give me the earrings from his plunder." For they had gold earrings, because they were Ishmaelites. So they answered, "We will gladly give them." And they spread out a garment, and each man threw into it the earrings from his plunder....Then Gideon made it into an ephod and set it up in his city, Ophrah. And all Israel played the harlot with it there. It became a snare to Gideon and to his house. JUDGES 8:24–25, 27 •

Do you seek great things for yourself? Do not seek them. JEREMIAH 45:5 • Lest I should be exalted above measure by the abundance of the revelations, a thorn in the flesh was given to me. 2 CORINTHIANS 12:7 •

Let nothing be done through selfish ambition or conceit, but in lowliness of mind let each esteem others better than himself. PHILIPPIANS 2:3 • Love suffers long and is kind; love does not envy; love does not parade itself, is not puffed up; does not behave rudely, does not seek its own. 1 CORINTHIANS 13:4–5 •

Take My yoke upon you and learn from Me. MATTHEW 11:29 •

May 19

Morning Reading

Wash me thoroughly from my iniquity.
PSALM 51:2

I will cleanse them from all their iniquity by which they have sinned against Me, and I will pardon all their iniquities by which they have sinned and by which they have transgressed against Me. JEREMIAH 33:8 • Then I will sprinkle clean water on you, and you shall be clean; I will cleanse you from all your filthiness and from all your idols. EZEKIEL 36:25 •

Unless one is born of water and the Spirit, he cannot enter the kingdom of God. JOHN 3:5 • If the blood of bulls and goats and the ashes of a heifer, sprinkling the unclean, sanctifies for the purifying of the flesh, how much more shall the blood of Christ, who through the eternal Spirit offered Himself without spot to God, cleanse your conscience from dead works to serve the living God? HEBREWS 9:13–14 •

He saved them for His name's sake, that He might make His mighty power known. PSALM 106:8 • Not unto us, O LORD, not unto us, but to Your name give glory, because of Your mercy, because of Your truth. PSALM 115:1 •

Evening Reading

Fellowship in the gospel.
PHILIPPIANS 1:5

As the body is one and has many members, but all the members of that one body, being many, are one body, so also is Christ. For by one Spirit we were all baptized into one body; whether Jews or Greeks, whether slaves or free; and have all been made to drink into one Spirit. 1 CORINTHIANS 12:12–13 •

God is faithful, by whom you were called into the fellowship of His Son, Jesus Christ our Lord. 1 CORINTHIANS 1:9 • That which we have seen and heard we declare to you, that you also may have fellowship with us; and truly our fellowship is with the Father and with His Son Jesus Christ. 1 JOHN 1:3 •

If we walk in the light as He is in the light, we have fellowship with one another, and the blood of Jesus Christ His Son cleanses us from all sin. 1 JOHN 1:7 • Jesus spoke these words,..."I do not pray for these alone, but also for those who will believe in Me through their word; that they all may be one, as You, Father, are in Me, and I in You; that they also may be one in Us, that the world may believe that You sent Me. JOHN 17:1, 20–21 •

May 20

Morning Reading

Take heed to yourself.
1 TIMOTHY 4:16

Everyone who competes for the prize is temperate in all things. Now they do it to obtain a perishable crown, but we for an imperishable crown. Therefore I run thus: not with uncertainty. Thus I fight: not as one who beats the air. But I discipline my body and bring it into subjection, lest, when I have preached to others, I myself should become disqualified. 1 CORINTHIANS 9:25–27 • Put on the whole armor of God, that you may be able to stand against the wiles of the devil. For we do not wrestle against flesh and blood, but against principalities, against powers, against the rulers of the darkness of this age, against spiritual hosts of wickedness in the heavenly places. EPHESIANS 6:11–12 •

Those who are Christ's have crucified the flesh with its passions and desires. If we live in the Spirit, let us also walk in the Spirit. GALATIANS 5:24–25 • For as many as are led by the Spirit of God, these are sons of God. ROMANS 8:14 • Meditate on these things; give yourself entirely to them, that your progress may be evident to all. 1 TIMOTHY 4:15 •

Evening Reading

Jesus said to her, "Mary!"
JOHN 20:16

Fear not, for I have redeemed you; I have called you by your name; you are Mine. ISAIAH 43:1 • The sheep hear his voice; and he calls his own sheep by name....And the sheep follow him, for they know his voice. JOHN 10:3–4 •

See, I have inscribed you on the palms of My hands; your walls are continually before Me. ISAIAH 49:16 •

The solid foundation of God stands, having this seal: "The Lord knows those who are His." 2 TIMOTHY 2:19 • We have a great High Priest who has passed through the heavens, Jesus the Son of God. HEBREWS 4:14 •

You shall take two onyx stones and engrave on them the names of the sons of Israel....So Aaron shall bear their names before the LORD on his two shoulders as a memorial....You shall make the breastplate of judgment....And you shall put settings of stones in it, four rows of stones....And the stones shall have the names of the sons of Israel....They shall be over Aaron's heart when he goes in before the LORD. EXODUS 28:9, 12, 15, 17, 21, 30 •

May 21

Morning Reading

My brethren, be strong in the Lord
and in the power of His might.
EPHESIANS 6:10

And [the Lord Jesus] said to me, "My grace is sufficient for you, for My strength is made perfect in weakness." Therefore most gladly I will rather boast in my infirmities, that the power of Christ may rest upon me. Therefore I take pleasure in infirmities, in reproaches, in needs, in persecutions, in distresses, for Christ's sake. For when I am weak, then I am strong. 2 CORINTHIANS 12:9–10 • I will go in the strength of the Lord GOD; I will make mention of Your righteousness, of Yours only. PSALM 71:16 • The gospel of Christ...is the power of God to salvation. ROMANS 1:16 •

I can do all things through Christ who strengthens me. PHILIPPIANS 4:13 • I also labor, striving according to His working which works in me mightily. COLOSSIANS 1:29 • We have this treasure in earthen vessels, that the excellence of the power may be of God and not of us. 2 CORINTHIANS 4:7 •

The joy of the LORD is your strength. NEHEMIAH 8:10 • Strengthened with all might, according to His glorious power, for all patience and longsuffering with joy. COLOSSIANS 1:11 •

Evening Reading

Jesus Christ our Lord.
1 CORINTHIANS 1:9

You shall call His name JESUS, for He will save His people from their sins. MATTHEW 1:21 • He humbled Himself and became obedient to the point of death, even the death of the cross. Therefore God also has highly exalted Him and given Him the name which is above every name, that at the name of Jesus every knee should bow, of those in heaven, and of those on earth, and of those under the earth. PHILIPPIANS 2:8–10 •

Messiah...who is called Christ. JOHN 4:25 • The LORD has anointed Me to preach good tidings to the poor; He has sent Me to heal the brokenhearted, to proclaim liberty to the captives. ISAIAH 61:1 •

The last Adam became a life-giving spirit....The first man was of the earth, made of dust; the second Man is the Lord from heaven. 1 CORINTHIANS 15:45, 47 • My Lord and my God! JOHN 20:28 • You call me Teacher and Lord, and you say well, for so I am. If I then, your Lord and Teacher, have washed your feet, you also ought to wash one another's feet. For I have given you an example, that you should do as I have done to you. JOHN 13:13–15 •

May 22

Morning Reading

Peace I leave with you, My peace I give to you;
not as the world gives do I give to you.
JOHN 14:27

The world is passing away, and the lust of it. 1 JOHN 2:17 • Surely every man walks about like a shadow; surely they busy themselves in vain; he heaps up riches, and does not know who will gather them. PSALM 39:6 • What fruit did you have then in the things of which you are now ashamed? For the end of those things is death. ROMANS 6:21 •

Jesus...said to her, "Martha, Martha, you are worried and troubled about many things. But one thing is needed, and Mary has chosen that good part, which will not be taken away from her." LUKE 10:41–42 • I want you to be without care. 1 CORINTHIANS 7:32 •

These things I have spoken to you, that in Me you may have peace. In the world you will have tribulation; but be of good cheer, I have overcome the world. JOHN 16:33 • May the Lord of peace Himself give you peace always in every way. 2 THESSALONIANS 3:16 • The LORD bless you and keep you; the LORD make His face shine upon you, and be gracious to you; the LORD lift up His countenance upon you, and give you peace. NUMBERS 6:24–26 •

Evening Reading

The Spirit also helps in our weaknesses.
ROMANS 8:26

The Helper, the Holy Spirit. JOHN 14:26 • Do you not know that your body is the temple of the Holy Spirit who is in you, whom you have from God? 1 CORINTHIANS 6:19 • It is God who works in you. PHILIPPIANS 2:13 •

We do not know what we should pray for as we ought, but the Spirit Himself makes intercession for us with groanings which cannot be uttered. Now He who searches the hearts knows what the mind of the Spirit is, because He makes intercession for the saints according to the will of God. ROMANS 8:26–27 •

He knows our frame; He remembers that we are dust. PSALM 103:14 • A bruised reed He will not break, and smoking flax He will not quench. ISAIAH 42:3 •

The spirit indeed is willing, but the flesh is weak. MATTHEW 26:41 •

The LORD is my shepherd; I shall not want. He makes me to lie down in green pastures; He leads me beside the still waters. PSALM 23:1–2 •

May 23

Morning Reading

*You shall put the two stones on the shoulders of the ephod
as memorial stones for the sons of Israel. So Aaron shall bear
their names before the LORD.*
EXODUS 28:12

[Jesus,] because He continues forever, has an unchangeable priesthood. Therefore He is also able to save to the uttermost those who come to God through Him, since He always lives to make intercession for them. HEBREWS 7:24–25 • [He] is able to keep you from stumbling, and to present you faultless before the presence of His glory with exceeding joy. JUDE 24 •

Seeing then that we have a great High Priest who has passed through the heavens, Jesus the Son of God, let us hold fast our confession. For we do not have a High Priest who cannot sympathize with our weaknesses, but was in all points tempted as we are, yet without sin. Let us therefore come boldly to the throne of grace. HEBREWS 4:14–16 •

The beloved of the LORD shall dwell in safety by Him, who shelters him all the day long; and he shall dwell between His shoulders. DEUTERONOMY 33:12 •

Evening Reading

That night the king could not sleep.
ESTHER 6:1

You hold my eyelids open. PSALM 77:4 • Who is like the LORD our God, who dwells on high, who humbles Himself to behold the things that are in the heavens and in the earth? PSALM 113:5–6 •

He does according to His will in the army of heaven and among the inhabitants of the earth. DANIEL 4:35 • Your way was in the sea, your path in the great waters, and Your footsteps were not known. PSALM 77:19 • Surely the wrath of man shall praise You; with the remainder of wrath You shall gird Yourself. PSALM 76:10 •

The eyes of the LORD run to and fro throughout the whole earth, to show Himself strong on behalf of those whose heart is loyal to Him. 2 CHRONICLES 16:9 • We know that all things work together for good to those who love God. ROMANS 8:28 •

Are not two sparrows sold for a copper coin? And not one of them falls to the ground apart from your Father's will. But the very hairs of your head are all numbered. MATTHEW 10:29–30 •

May 24

Morning Reading

*Do not grieve the Holy Spirit of God, by whom you were sealed
for the day of redemption.*
EPHESIANS 4:30

The love of the Spirit. ROMANS 15:30 • The Helper, the Holy Spirit. JOHN 14:26 • In all their affliction He was afflicted, and the Angel of His Presence saved them; in His love and in His pity He redeemed them; and He bore them and carried them all the days of old. But they rebelled and grieved His Holy Spirit; so He turned Himself against them as an enemy, and He fought against them. ISAIAH 63:9–10 •

By this we know that we abide in Him, and He in us, because He has given us of His Spirit. 1 JOHN 4:13 • Having believed, you were sealed with the Holy Spirit of promise, who is the guarantee of our inheritance until the redemption of the purchased possession. EPHESIANS 1:13–14 • I say then: Walk in the Spirit, and you shall not fulfill the lust of the flesh. For the flesh lusts against the Spirit, and the Spirit against the flesh; and these are contrary to one another, so that you do not do the things that you wish. GALATIANS 5:16–17 •

The Spirit also helps in our weaknesses. ROMANS 8:26 •

Evening Reading

*I will return again to My place till they acknowledge their
offense. Then they will seek My face.*
HOSEA 5:15

Your iniquities have separated you from your God; and your sins have hidden His face from you. ISAIAH 59:2 • My beloved had turned away and was gone....I sought him, but I could not find him; I called him, but he gave me no answer. SONG OF SONGS 5:6 • I hid and was angry, and he went on backsliding in the way of his heart. I have seen his ways, and will heal him. ISAIAH 57:17–18 • Have you not brought this on yourself, in that you have forsaken the LORD your God when He led you in the way? JEREMIAH 2:17 •

He arose and came to his father. But when he was still a great way off, his father saw him and had compassion, and ran and fell on his neck and kissed him. LUKE 15:20 • I will heal their backsliding, I will love them freely, for My anger has turned away. HOSEA 14:4 •

If we confess our sins, He is faithful and just to forgive us our sins and to cleanse us from all unrighteousness. 1 JOHN 1:9 •

May 25

Morning Reading

*How great is Your goodness, which You have laid up
for those who fear You!*
PSALM 31:19

Since the beginning of the world men have not heard nor perceived by the ear, nor has the eye seen any God besides You, who acts for the one who waits for Him. ISAIAH 64:4 • As it is written: "Eye has not seen, nor ear heard, nor have entered into the heart of man the things which God has prepared for those who love Him." But God has revealed them to us through His Spirit. 1 CORINTHIANS 2:9–10 • You will show me the path of life; in Your presence is fullness of joy; at Your right hand are pleasures forevermore. PSALM 16:11 •

How precious is Your lovingkindness, O God! Therefore the children of men put their trust under the shadow of Your wings. They are abundantly satisfied with the fullness of Your house, and You give them drink from the river of Your pleasures. For with You is the fountain of life; in Your light we see light. PSALM 36:7–9 •

Godliness is profitable for all things, having promise of the life that now is and of that which is to come. 1 TIMOTHY 4:8 •

Evening Reading

The Son of God...has eyes like a flame of fire.
REVELATION 2:18

The heart is deceitful above all things, and desperately wicked; who can know it? I, the LORD, search the heart, I test the mind, even to give every man according to his ways, according to the fruit of his doings. JEREMIAH 17:9–10 • You have set our iniquities before You, our secret sins in the light of Your countenance. PSALM 90:8 • The Lord turned and looked at Peter. And Peter remembered the word of the Lord, how He had said to him, "Before the rooster crows, you will deny Me three times." So Peter went out and wept bitterly. LUKE 22:61–62 •

Jesus did not commit Himself to them, because He knew all men, and had no need that anyone should testify of man, for He knew what was in man. JOHN 2:24–25 • He knows our frame; He remembers that we are dust. PSALM 103:14 • A bruised reed He will not break, and smoking flax He will not quench. ISAIAH 42:3 •

The Lord knows those who are His. 2 TIMOTHY 2:19 • I am the good shepherd; and I know My sheep, and am known by My own. JOHN 10:14 • My sheep hear My voice, and I know them, and they follow Me. And I give them eternal life, and they shall never perish; neither shall anyone snatch them out of My hand. JOHN 10:27–28 •

May 26

Morning Reading

Our Lord Jesus,...that great Shepherd of the sheep.
HEBREWS 13:20

The Chief Shepherd. 1 PETER 5:4 • I am the good shepherd; and I know My sheep, and am known by My own....My sheep hear My voice, and I know them, and they follow Me. And I give them eternal life, and they shall never perish; neither shall anyone snatch them out of My hand. JOHN 10:14, 27–28 •

The LORD is my shepherd; I shall not want. He makes me to lie down in green pastures; He leads me beside the still waters. He restores my soul; He leads me in the paths of righteousness for His name's sake. PSALM 23:1–3 •

All we like sheep have gone astray; we have turned, every one, to his own way; and the LORD has laid on Him the iniquity of us all. ISAIAH 53:6 • I am the good shepherd. The good shepherd gives His life for the sheep. JOHN 10:11 • I will seek what was lost and bring back what was driven away, bind up the broken and strengthen what was sick. EZEKIEL 34:16 • You were like sheep going astray, but have now returned to the Shepherd and Overseer of your souls. 1 PETER 2:25 •

Evening Reading

The city had no need of the sun or of the moon to shine in it,
for the glory of God illuminated it. The Lamb is its light.
REVELATION 21:23

Along the road I saw a light from heaven, brighter than the sun, shining around me and those who journeyed with me....So I said, "Who are You, Lord?" And He said, "I am Jesus, whom you are persecuting." ACTS 26:13, 15 • Jesus took Peter, James, and John his brother, led them up on a high mountain by themselves; and He was transfigured before them. His face shone like the sun, and His clothes became as white as the light. MATTHEW 17:1–2 • The sun shall no longer be your light by day, nor for brightness shall the moon give light to you; but the LORD will be to you an everlasting light, and your God your glory. Your sun shall no longer go down, nor shall your moon withdraw itself; for the LORD will be your everlasting light, and the days of your mourning shall be ended. ISAIAH 60:19–20 •

The God of all grace...called us to His eternal glory by Christ Jesus. 1 PETER 5:10 •

May 27

Morning Reading

The LORD is good, a stronghold in the day of trouble;
and He knows those who trust in Him.
NAHUM 1:7

Praise the Lord of hosts, for the Lord is good, for His mercy endures forever. JEREMIAH 33:11 • God is our refuge and strength, a very present help in trouble. PSALM 46:1 • I will say of the Lord, "He is my refuge and my fortress; my God, in Him I will trust." PSALM 91:2 • Who is like you, a people saved by the Lord, the shield of your help and the sword of your majesty! DEUTERONOMY 33:29 • As for God, His way is perfect; the word of the Lord is proven; He is a shield to all who trust in Him. For who is God, except the Lord? And who is a rock, except our God? 2 SAMUEL 22:31–32 •

If anyone loves God, this one is known by Him. 1 CORINTHIANS 8:3 • The solid foundation of God stands, having this seal: "The Lord knows those who are His," and, "Let everyone who names the name of Christ depart from iniquity." 2 TIMOTHY 2:19 • The Lord knows the way of the righteous, but the way of the ungodly shall perish. PSALM 1:6 • You have found grace in My sight, and I know you by name. EXODUS 33:17 •

Evening Reading

I want you to be without care.
1 CORINTHIANS 7:32

He cares for you. 1 PETER 5:7 • The eyes of the LORD run to and fro throughout the whole earth, to show Himself strong on behalf of those whose heart is loyal to Him. 2 CHRONICLES 16:9 •

Oh, taste and see that the LORD is good; blessed is the man who trusts in Him!...The young lions lack and suffer hunger; but those who seek the LORD shall not lack any good thing. PSALM 34:8, 10 • Therefore I say to you, do not worry about your life, what you will eat or what you will drink; nor about your body, what you will put on. Is not life more than food and the body more than clothing? Look at the birds of the air, for they neither sow nor reap nor gather into barns; yet your heavenly Father feeds them. Are you not of more value than they? MATTHEW 6:25–26 •

Be anxious for nothing, but in everything by prayer and supplication, with thanksgiving, let your requests be made known to God; and the peace of God, which surpasses all understanding, will guard your hearts and minds through Christ Jesus. PHILIPPIANS 4:6–7 •

May 28

Morning Reading

We...eagerly wait for the Savior.
PHILIPPIANS 3:20

The grace of God that brings salvation has appeared to all men, teaching us that, denying ungodliness and worldly lusts, we should live soberly, righteously, and godly in the present age, looking for the blessed hope and glorious appearing of our great God and Savior Jesus Christ, who gave Himself for us, that He might redeem us from every lawless deed and purify for Himself His own special people, zealous for good works. TITUS 2:11–14 • We, according to His promise, look for new heavens and a new earth in which righteousness dwells. Therefore, beloved, looking forward to these things, be diligent to be found by Him in peace, without spot and blameless. 2 PETER 3:13–14 •

Christ was offered once to bear the sins of many. To those who eagerly wait for Him He will appear a second time, apart from sin, for salvation. HEBREWS 9:28 • And it will be said in that day: "Behold, this is our God; we have waited for Him, and He will save us. This is the LORD; we have waited for Him; we will be glad and rejoice in His salvation." ISAIAH 25:9 •

Evening Reading

Run in such a way that you may obtain.
1 CORINTHIANS 9:24

The lazy man says, "There is a lion outside! I shall be slain in the streets!" PROVERBS 22:13 • Let us lay aside every weight, and the sin which so easily ensnares us, and let us run with endurance the race that is set before us, looking unto Jesus, the author and finisher of our faith. HEBREWS 12:1–2 •

Let us cleanse ourselves from all filthiness of the flesh and spirit, perfecting holiness in the fear of God. 2 CORINTHIANS 7:1 •

I press toward the goal. PHILIPPIANS 3:14 • Therefore I run thus: not with uncertainty....But I discipline my body and bring it into subjection, lest, when I have preached to others, I myself should become disqualified. 1 CORINTHIANS 9:26–27 •

The form of this world is passing away. 1 CORINTHIANS 7:31 •

Nevertheless we, according to His promise, look for new heavens and a new earth in which righteousness dwells. Therefore, beloved, looking forward to these things, be diligent. 2 PETER 3:13–14 • Gird up the loins of your mind, be sober, and rest your hope fully upon the grace that is to be brought to you at the revelation of Jesus Christ. 1 PETER 1:13 •

May 29

Morning Reading

The life of the flesh is in the blood, and I have given it to you upon the altar to make atonement for your souls; for it is the blood that makes atonement for the soul.
LEVITICUS 17:11

Behold! The Lamb of God who takes away the sin of the world! JOHN 1:29 • The blood of the Lamb. REVELATION 7:14 • The precious blood of Christ, as of a lamb without blemish and without spot. 1 PETER 1:19 • Without shedding of blood there is no remission. HEBREWS 9:22 • The blood of Jesus Christ His Son cleanses us from all sin. 1 JOHN 1:7 •

With His own blood He entered the Most Holy Place once for all, having obtained eternal redemption [for us]. HEBREWS 9:12 • Therefore, brethren, having boldness to enter the Holiest by the blood of Jesus, by a new and living way which He consecrated for us, through the veil, that is, His flesh,...let us draw near with a true heart in full assurance of faith. HEBREWS 10:19–20, 22 •

You were bought at a price; therefore glorify God in your body and in your spirit, which are God's. 1 CORINTHIANS 6:20 •

Evening Reading

Oh, that I had wings like a dove! I would fly away and be at rest.
PSALM 55:6

It happened, when the sun arose, that God prepared a vehement east wind; and the sun beat on Jonah's head, so that he grew faint. Then he wished death for himself, and said, "It is better for me to die than to live." JONAH 4:8 •

And Job spoke, and said: "...Why is light given to him who is in misery, and life to the bitter of soul, who long for death, but it does not come, and search for it more than hidden treasures?" JOB 3:2, 20–21 • Many are the afflictions of the righteous, but the Lord delivers him out of them all. PSALM 34:19 •

Now My soul is troubled, and what shall I say? "Father, save Me from this hour"? But for this purpose I came to this hour. JOHN 12:27 • In all things He had to be made like His brethren, that He might be a merciful and faithful High Priest in things pertaining to God, to make propitiation for the sins of the people. For in that He Himself has suffered, being tempted, He is able to aid those who are tempted. HEBREWS 2:17–18 •

May 30

Morning Reading

Let us therefore be diligent to enter that rest.
HEBREWS 4:11

Enter by the narrow gate; for wide is the gate and broad is the way that leads to destruction....Because narrow is the gate and difficult is the way which leads to life, and there are few who find it. MATTHEW 7:13–14 • The kingdom of heaven suffers violence, and the violent take it by force. MATTHEW 11:12 • Do not labor for the food which perishes, but for the food which endures to everlasting life, which the Son of Man will give you. JOHN 6:27 • Be even more diligent to make your call and election sure, for if you do these things you will never stumble; for so an entrance will be supplied to you abundantly into the everlasting kingdom of our Lord and Savior Jesus Christ. 2 PETER 1:10–11 • Run in such a way that you may obtain it. And everyone who competes for the prize is temperate in all things. Now they do it to obtain a perishable crown, but we for an imperishable crown. 1 CORINTHIANS 9:24–25 •

For he who has entered His rest has himself also ceased from his works as God did from His. HEBREWS 4:10 • The LORD will be to you an everlasting light, and your God your glory. ISAIAH 60:19 •

Evening Reading

You always hear Me.
JOHN 11:42

Jesus lifted up His eyes and said, "Father, I thank You that You have heard Me." JOHN 11:41 • [Jesus prayed,] "Father, glorify Your name." Then a voice came from heaven, saying, "I have both glorified it and will glorify it again." JOHN 12:28 • Behold, I have come...to do Your will, O God. HEBREWS 10:7 • Not My will, but Yours, be done. LUKE 22:42 •

As He is, so are we in this world. 1 JOHN 4:17 • This is the confidence that we have in Him, that if we ask anything according to His will, He hears us. 1 JOHN 5:14 •

Whatever we ask we receive from Him, because we keep His commandments and do those things that are pleasing in His sight. 1 JOHN 3:22 •

Without faith it is impossible to please Him, for he who comes to God must believe that He is, and that He is a rewarder of those who diligently seek Him. HEBREWS 11:6 •

He always lives to make intercession for them. HEBREWS 7:25 • We have an Advocate with the Father, Jesus Christ the righteous. 1 JOHN 2:1 •

May 31

Morning Reading

Your name shall no longer be called Jacob, but Israel; for you have struggled with God and with men, and have prevailed.
GENESIS 32:28

In his strength [Jacob] struggled with God. Yes, he struggled with the Angel and prevailed; he wept, and sought favor from Him. HOSEA 12:3–4 • [Abraham] did not waver at the promise of God through unbelief, but was strengthened in faith, giving glory to God. ROMANS 4:20 •

Jesus...said to them, "Have faith in God. For assuredly, I say to you, whoever says to this mountain, 'Be removed and be cast into the sea,' and does not doubt in his heart, but believes that those things he says will be done, he will have whatever he says. Therefore I say to you, whatever things you ask when you pray, believe that you receive them, and you will have them." MARK 11:22–24 • If you can believe, all things are possible to him who believes. MARK 9:23 • Blessed is she who believed, for there will be a fulfillment of those things which were told her from the Lord. LUKE 1:45 •

[Lord,] increase our faith. LUKE 17:5 •

Evening Reading

Little children, abide in Him.
1 JOHN 2:28

He who doubts is like a wave of the sea driven and tossed by the wind. For let not that man suppose that he will receive anything from the Lord; he is a double-minded man, unstable in all his ways. JAMES 1:6–8 •

I marvel that you are turning away so soon from Him who called you in the grace of Christ, to a different gospel, which is not another; but there are some who trouble you and want to pervert the gospel of Christ. But even if we, or an angel from heaven, preach any other gospel to you than what we have preached to you, let him be accursed. GALATIANS 1:6–8 •

You have become estranged from Christ, you who attempt to be justified by law; you have fallen from grace....You ran well. Who hindered you from obeying the truth? GALATIANS 5:4, 7 •

As the branch cannot bear fruit of itself, unless it abides in the vine, neither can you, unless you abide in Me....If you abide in Me, and My words abide in you, you will ask what you desire, and it shall be done for you. JOHN 15:4, 7 • For all the promises of God in Him are Yes, and in Him Amen, to the glory of God through us. 2 CORINTHIANS 1:20 •

JUNE

June 1

Morning Reading

The fruit of the Spirit is...longsuffering, kindness.
GALATIANS 5:22

The LORD, the LORD God, merciful and gracious, longsuffering, and abounding in goodness and truth. EXODUS 34:6 •

Walk worthy of the calling with which you were called, with all lowliness and gentleness, with longsuffering, bearing with one another in love. EPHESIANS 4:1–2 • Be kind to one another, tenderhearted, forgiving one another, just as God in Christ forgave you. EPHESIANS 4:32 • The wisdom that is from above is first pure, then peaceable, gentle, willing to yield, full of mercy and good fruits, without partiality and without hypocrisy. JAMES 3:17 • Love suffers long and is kind. 1 CORINTHIANS 13:4 •

In due season we shall reap if we do not lose heart. GALATIANS 6:9 • Therefore be patient, brethren, until the coming of the Lord. See how the farmer waits for the precious fruit of the earth, waiting patiently for it until it receives the early and latter rain. You also be patient. Establish your hearts, for the coming of the Lord is at hand. JAMES 5:7–8 •

Evening Reading

Immanuel..."God with us."
MATTHEW 1:23

Will God indeed dwell with men on the earth? Behold, heaven and the heaven of heavens cannot contain You. 2 CHRONICLES 6:18 • The Word became flesh and dwelt among us, and we beheld His glory, the glory as of the only begotten of the Father, full of grace and truth. JOHN 1:14 • Great is the mystery of godliness: God was manifested in the flesh. 1 TIMOTHY 3:16 •

[God] has in these last days spoken to us by His Son, whom He has appointed heir of all things, through whom also He made the worlds. HEBREWS 1:2 •

The first day of the week, when the doors were shut where the disciples were assembled,...Jesus came and stood in the midst....Then the disciples were glad when they saw the Lord....And after eight days His disciples were again inside, and Thomas with them. Jesus came, the doors being shut, and stood in the midst, and said, "Peace to you!" Then He said to Thomas, "Reach your finger here, and look at My hands; and reach your hand here, and put it into My side. Do not be unbelieving, but believing." And Thomas...said to Him, "My Lord and my God!" JOHN 20:19–20, 26–28 • Unto us a Son is given....His name will be called...Mighty God. ISAIAH 9:6 •

June 2

Morning Reading

Thus you shall eat it: with a belt on your waist....So you shall eat it in haste. It is the Lord's Passover.
EXODUS 12:11

Arise and depart, for this is not your rest. MICAH 2:10 • Here we have no continuing city, but we seek the one to come. HEBREWS 13:14 • There remains therefore a rest for the people of God. HEBREWS 4:9 •

Let your waist be girded and your lamps burning; and you yourselves be like men who wait for their master, when he will return from the wedding, that when he comes and knocks they may open to him immediately. Blessed are those servants whom the master, when he comes, will find watching. LUKE 12:35–37 • Gird up the loins of your mind, be sober, and rest your hope fully upon the grace that is to be brought to you at the revelation of Jesus Christ. 1 PETER 1:13 • One thing I do, forgetting those things which are behind,...I press toward the goal for the prize of the upward call of God in Christ Jesus. Therefore let us, as many as are mature, have this mind. PHILIPPIANS 3:13–15 •

Evening Reading

LORD, You are the portion of my inheritance and my cup.
PSALM 16:5

Heirs of God and joint heirs with Christ. ROMANS 8:17 • All things are yours. 1 CORINTHIANS 3:21 • My beloved is mine. SONG OF SONGS 2:16 • The Son of God...loved me and gave Himself for me. GALATIANS 2:20 •

The LORD said to Aaron: "You shall have no inheritance in their land, nor shall you have any portion among them; I am your portion and your inheritance among the children of Israel." NUMBERS 18:20 •

Whom have I in heaven but You? And there is none upon earth that I desire besides You. My flesh and my heart fail; but God is the strength of my heart and my portion forever. PSALM 73:25–26 •

Though I walk through the valley of the shadow of death, I will fear no evil; for You are with me; Your rod and Your staff, they comfort me. PSALM 23:4 • I know whom I have believed and am persuaded that He is able to keep what I have committed to Him until that Day. 2 TIMOTHY 1:12 •

O God, You are my God; early will I seek You; my soul thirsts for You; my flesh longs for You in a dry and thirsty land. PSALM 63:1 •

June 3

Morning Reading

Watch therefore, for you know neither the day nor the hour in which the Son of Man is coming.
MATTHEW 25:13

Take heed to yourselves, lest your hearts be weighed down with carousing, drunkenness, and cares of this life, and that Day come on you unexpectedly. For it will come as a snare on all those who dwell on the face of the whole earth. Watch therefore, and pray always that you may be counted worthy to escape all these things that will come to pass, and to stand before the Son of Man. LUKE 21:34–36 •

The day of the Lord so comes as a thief in the night. For when they say, "Peace and safety!" then sudden destruction comes upon them, as labor pains upon a pregnant woman. And they shall not escape. But you, brethren, are not in darkness, so that this Day should overtake you as a thief. You are all sons of light and sons of the day. We are not of the night nor of darkness. Therefore let us not sleep, as others do, but let us watch and be sober. 1 THESSALONIANS 5:2–6 •

Evening Reading

I am Almighty God; walk before Me and be blameless.
GENESIS 17:1

Not that I have already attained, or am already perfected; but I press on, that I may lay hold of that for which Christ Jesus has also laid hold of me. Brethren, I do not count myself to have apprehended; but one thing I do, forgetting those things which are behind and reaching forward to those things which are ahead, I press toward the goal for the prize of the upward call of God in Christ Jesus. PHILIPPIANS 3:12–14 •

Enoch walked with God; and he was not, for God took him. GENESIS 5:24 •

Grow in the grace and knowledge of our Lord and Savior Jesus Christ. 2 PETER 3:18 • We all, with unveiled face, beholding as in a mirror the glory of the Lord, are being transformed into the same image from glory to glory, just as by the Spirit of the Lord. 2 CORINTHIANS 3:18 •

Jesus...lifted up His eyes to heaven, and said: "...I do not pray that You should take them out of the world, but that You should keep them from the evil one....I in them, and You in Me; that they may be made perfect in one." JOHN 17:1, 15, 23 •

June 4

Morning Reading

The glory of this latter temple shall be greater than the former....And in this place I will give peace.
HAGGAI 2:9

The house to be built for the LORD must be exceedingly magnificent, famous and glorious throughout all countries. 1 CHRONICLES 22:5 • The glory of the LORD had filled the Lord's house. 2 CHRONICLES 7:2 •

[Jesus said,] "Destroy this temple, and in three days I will raise it up."...He was speaking of the temple of His body. JOHN 2:19, 21 • What was made glorious had no glory in this respect, because of the glory that excels. 2 CORINTHIANS 3:10 • The Word became flesh and dwelt among us, and we beheld His glory, the glory as of the only begotten of the Father, full of grace and truth. JOHN 1:14 • God...has in these last days spoken to us by His Son, whom He has appointed heir of all things, through whom also He made the worlds. HEBREWS 1:1–2 •

Glory to God in the highest, and on earth peace, goodwill toward men! LUKE 2:14 • Prince of Peace. ISAIAH 9:6 • He Himself is our peace. EPHESIANS 2:14 • The peace of God, which surpasses all understanding, will guard your hearts and minds through Christ Jesus. PHILIPPIANS 4:7 •

Evening Reading

Let us put on the armor of light.
ROMANS 13:12

Put on the Lord Jesus Christ. ROMANS 13:14 • That I may gain Christ and be found in Him, not having my own righteousness, which is from the law, but that which is through faith in Christ, the righteousness which is from God by faith. PHILIPPIANS 3:8–9 • The righteousness of God, through faith in Jesus Christ, to all and on all who believe. For there is no difference. ROMANS 3:22 •

He has covered me with the robe of righteousness. ISAIAH 61:10 • I will go in the strength of the Lord GOD; I will make mention of Your righteousness, of Yours only. PSALM 71:16 •

You were once darkness, but now you are light in the Lord. Walk as children of light....And have no fellowship with the unfruitful works of darkness, but rather expose them....All things that are exposed are made manifest by the light, for whatever makes manifest is light. Therefore He says: "Awake, you who sleep, arise from the dead, and Christ will give you light." See then that you walk circumspectly, not as fools but as wise. EPHESIANS 5:8, 11, 13–15 •

June 5

Morning Reading

When you have done all those things which you are commanded, say,
"We are unprofitable servants. We have done
what was our duty to do."
LUKE 17:10

Where is boasting then? It is excluded. By what law? Of works? No, but by the law of faith. ROMANS 3:27 • What do you have that you did not receive? Now if you did indeed receive it, why do you boast as if you had not received it? 1 CORINTHIANS 4:7 • By grace you have been saved through faith, and that not of yourselves; it is the gift of God, not of works, lest anyone should boast. For we are His workmanship, created in Christ Jesus for good works, which God prepared beforehand that we should walk in them. EPHESIANS 2:8–10 •

By the grace of God I am what I am, and His grace toward me was not in vain; but I labored more abundantly than they all, yet not I, but the grace of God which was with me. 1 CORINTHIANS 15:10 • For of Him and through Him and to Him are all things. ROMANS 11:36 • All things come from You, and of Your own we have given You. 1 CHRONICLES 29:14 •

Do not enter into judgment with Your servant, for in Your sight no one living is righteous. PSALM 143:2 •

Evening Reading

He knows our frame; He remembers that we are dust.
PSALM 103:14

The LORD God formed man of the dust of the ground, and breathed into his nostrils the breath of life; and man became a living being. GENESIS 2:7 •

I will praise You, for I am fearfully and wonderfully made; marvelous are Your works, and that my soul knows very well. My frame was not hidden from You, when I was made in secret, and skillfully wrought in the lowest parts of the earth. Your eyes saw my substance, being yet unformed. And in Your book they all were written, the days fashioned for me, when as yet there were none of them. PSALM 139:14–16 •

Have we not all one Father? Has not one God created us? MALACHI 2:10 • In Him we live and move and have our being. ACTS 17:28 • As a father pities his children, so the LORD pities those who fear Him. PSALM 103:13 •

He, being full of compassion, forgave their iniquity, and did not destroy them. Yes, many a time He turned His anger away, and did not stir up all His wrath; for He remembered that they were but flesh, a breath that passes away and does not come again. PSALM 78:38–39 •

June 6

Morning Reading

He will quiet you with His love.
ZEPHANIAH 3:17

The LORD did not set His love on you nor choose you because you were more in number than any other people, for you were the least of all peoples; but because the LORD loves you. DEUTERONOMY 7:7–8 • We love Him because He first loved us. 1 JOHN 4:19 • You...He has reconciled in the body of His flesh through death, to present you holy, and blameless, and above reproach in His sight. COLOSSIANS 1:21–22 •

In this is love, not that we loved God, but that He loved us and sent His Son to be the propitiation for our sins. 1 JOHN 4:10 • God demonstrates His own love toward us, in that while we were still sinners, Christ died for us. ROMANS 5:8 •

Suddenly a voice came from heaven, saying, "This is My beloved Son, in whom I am well pleased." MATTHEW 3:17 • Therefore My Father loves Me, because I lay down My life that I may take it again. JOHN 10:17 • His Son,...who being the brightness of His glory and the express image of His person, and upholding all things by the word of His power, when He had by Himself purged our sins, sat down at the right hand of the Majesty on high. HEBREWS 1:2–3 •

Evening Reading

A new and living way.
HEBREWS 10:20

Cain went out from the presence of the LORD. GENESIS 4:16 • Your iniquities have separated you from your God; and your sins have hidden His face from you. ISAIAH 59:2 • Pursue...holiness, without which no one will see the Lord. HEBREWS 12:14 •

I am the way, the truth, and the life. No one comes to the Father except through Me. JOHN 14:6 • Our Savior Jesus Christ...has abolished death and brought life and immortality to light through the gospel. 2 TIMOTHY 1:10 •

The way into the Holiest of All was not yet made manifest while the first tabernacle was still standing. HEBREWS 9:8 • He Himself is our peace, who has made both one, and has broken down the middle wall of separation. EPHESIANS 2:14 • The veil of the temple was torn in two from top to bottom. MATTHEW 27:51 •

Narrow is the gate and difficult is the way which leads to life, and there are few who find it. MATTHEW 7:14 • You will show me the path of life; in Your presence is fullness of joy; at Your right hand are pleasures forevermore. PSALM 16:11 •

June 7

Morning Reading

Men always ought to pray and not lose heart.
LUKE 18:1

Which of you shall have a friend, and go to him at midnight and say to him, "Friend, lend me three loaves; for a friend of mine has come to me on his journey, and I have nothing to set before him"; and he will answer from within and say, "Do not trouble me; the door is now shut, and my children are with me in bed; I cannot rise and give to you"? I say to you, though he will not rise and give to him because he is his friend, yet because of his persistence he will rise and give him as many as he needs. LUKE 11:5–8 • Praying always with all prayer and supplication in the Spirit, being watchful to this end with all perseverance and supplication for all the saints. EPHESIANS 6:18 •

[Jacob] said, "I will not let You go unless You bless me!"...[The Man] said, "...You have struggled with God and with men, and have prevailed." GENESIS 32:26, 28 • Continue earnestly in prayer, being vigilant in it with thanksgiving. COLOSSIANS 4:2 •

[Jesus] went out to the mountain to pray, and continued all night in prayer to God. LUKE 6:12 •

Evening Reading

Forgive all my sins.
PSALM 25:18

"Come now, and let us reason together," says the LORD, "though your sins are like scarlet, they shall be as white as snow; though they are red like crimson, they shall be as wool." ISAIAH 1:18 •

Be of good cheer; your sins are forgiven you. MATTHEW 9:2 • I, even I, am He who blots out your transgressions for My own sake; and I will not remember your sins. ISAIAH 43:25 •

The Son of Man has power on earth to forgive sins. MATTHEW 9:6 • In Him we have redemption through His blood, the forgiveness of sins, according to the riches of His grace. EPHESIANS 1:7 • Not by works of righteousness which we have done, but according to His mercy He saved us, through the washing of regeneration and renewing of the Holy Spirit, whom He poured out on us abundantly through Jesus Christ our Savior. TITUS 3:5–6 • Having forgiven you all trespasses, having wiped out the handwriting of requirements that was against us, which was contrary to us. And He has taken it out of the way, having nailed it to the cross. COLOSSIANS 2:13–14 •

Bless the LORD, O my soul,...who forgives all your iniquities. PSALM 103:2–3 •

June 8

Morning Reading

The Lord made all he did to prosper in his hand.
GENESIS 39:3

Blessed is every one who fears the Lord, who walks in His ways. When you eat the labor of your hands, you shall be happy, and it shall be well with you. PSALM 128:1–2 • Trust in the Lord, and do good; dwell in the land, and feed on His faithfulness. Delight yourself also in the Lord, and He shall give you the desires of your heart. PSALM 37:3–4 • Have I not commanded you? Be strong and of good courage; do not be afraid, nor be dismayed, for the Lord your God is with you wherever you go. JOSHUA 1:9 •

Seek first the kingdom of God and His righteousness, and all these things shall be added to you. MATTHEW 6:33 •

As long as he sought the Lord, God made him prosper. 2 CHRONICLES 26:5 • Beware that you do not forget the Lord your God by not keeping His commandments, His judgments, and His statutes which I command you today,...[and] say in your heart, "My power and the might of my hand have gained me this wealth." DEUTERONOMY 8:11, 17 •

Is not the Lord your God with you? And has He not given you rest on every side? 1 CHRONICLES 22:18 •

Evening Reading

Why do you reason about these things in your hearts?
MARK 2:8

Not being weak in faith, [Abraham] did not consider his own body, already dead (since he was about a hundred years old), and the deadness of Sarah's womb. He did not waver at the promise of God through unbelief, but was strengthened in faith, giving glory to God. ROMANS 4:19–20 •

Which is easier, to say to the paralytic, "Your sins are forgiven you," or to say, "Arise, take up your bed and walk"? MARK 2:9 • If you can believe, all things are possible to him who believes. MARK 9:23 •

All authority has been given to Me in heaven and on earth. MATTHEW 28:18 • Why are you so fearful? How is it that you have no faith? MARK 4:40 • Look at the birds of the air....Your heavenly Father feeds them. Are you not of more value than they? MATTHEW 6:26 • Why do you reason among yourselves because you have brought no bread? Do you not... remember the five loaves of the five thousand? MATTHEW 16:8–9 •

My God shall supply all your need according to His riches in glory by Christ Jesus. PHILIPPIANS 4:19 •

June 9

Morning Reading

No man ever spoke like this Man!
JOHN 7:46

You are fairer than the sons of men; grace is poured upon Your lips; therefore God has blessed You forever. PSALM 45:2 • The Lord GOD has given Me the tongue of the learned, that I should know how to speak a word in season to him who is weary. ISAIAH 50:4 • His mouth is most sweet, yes, he is altogether lovely. This is my beloved, and this is my friend. SONG OF SONGS 5:16 •

All bore witness to Him, and marveled at the gracious words which proceeded out of His mouth. LUKE 4:22 • For He taught them as one having authority, and not as the scribes. MATTHEW 7:29 •

Let the word of Christ dwell in you richly in all wisdom. COLOSSIANS 3:16 • The sword of the Spirit...is the word of God. EPHESIANS 6:17 • The word of God is living and powerful, and sharper than any two-edged sword. HEBREWS 4:12 • The weapons of our warfare are not carnal but mighty in God for pulling down strongholds, casting down arguments and every high thing that exalts itself against the knowledge of God, bringing every thought into captivity to the obedience of Christ. 2 CORINTHIANS 10:4–5 •

Evening Reading

The triumphing of the wicked is short.
JOB 20:5

You shall bruise His heel. GENESIS 3:15 • This is your hour, and the power of darkness. LUKE 22:53 • Inasmuch then as the children have partaken of flesh and blood, He Himself likewise shared in the same, that through death He might destroy him who had the power of death, that is, the devil. HEBREWS 2:14 • Having disarmed principalities and powers, He made a public spectacle of them, triumphing over them in it. COLOSSIANS 2:15 •

Be sober, be vigilant; because your adversary the devil walks about like a roaring lion, seeking whom he may devour. Resist him, steadfast in the faith. 1 PETER 5:8–9 • Resist the devil and he will flee from you. JAMES 4:7 •

The wicked plots against the just, and gnashes at him with his teeth. The Lord laughs at him, for He sees that his day is coming. PSALM 37:12–13 • The God of peace will crush Satan under your feet shortly. ROMANS 16:20 • The devil...was cast into the lake of fire and brimstone...[to] be tormented day and night forever and ever. REVELATION 20:10 •

June 10

Morning Reading

The younger son...journeyed to a far country,
and there wasted his possessions with prodigal living.
LUKE 15:13

Such were some of you. But you were washed, but you were sanctified, but you were justified in the name of the Lord Jesus and by the Spirit of our God. 1 CORINTHIANS 6:11 • [We] were by nature children of wrath, just as the others. But God, who is rich in mercy, because of His great love with which He loved us, even when we were dead in trespasses, made us alive together with Christ (by grace you have been saved), and raised us up together, and made us sit together in the heavenly places in Christ Jesus. EPHESIANS 2:3–6 •

In this is love, not that we loved God, but that He loved us and sent His Son to be the propitiation for our sins. 1 JOHN 4:10 •

God demonstrates His own love toward us, in that while we were still sinners, Christ died for us....If when we were enemies we were reconciled to God through the death of His Son, much more, having been reconciled, we shall be saved by His life. ROMANS 5:8, 10 •

Evening Reading

As Christ forgave you, so you also must do.
COLOSSIANS 3:13

There was a certain creditor who had two debtors. One owed five hundred denarii, and the other fifty. And when they had nothing with which to repay, he freely forgave them both. LUKE 7:41–42 • I forgave you all that debt because you begged me. Should you not also have had compassion on your fellow servant, just as I had pity on you? MATTHEW 18:32–33 •

Whenever you stand praying, if you have anything against anyone, forgive him, that your Father in heaven may also forgive you your trespasses. But if you do not forgive, neither will your Father in heaven forgive your trespasses. MARK 11:25–26 • Therefore, as the elect of God, holy and beloved, put on tender mercies, kindness, humility, meekness, longsuffering; bearing with one another, and forgiving one another, if anyone has a complaint against another. COLOSSIANS 3:12–13 •

Peter came to Him and said, "Lord, how often shall my brother sin against me, and I forgive him? Up to seven times?" Jesus said to him, "I do not say to you, up to seven times, but up to seventy times seven." MATTHEW 18:21–22 •

June 11

Morning Reading

He arose and came to his father. But when he was still a great way off, his father saw him and had compassion, and ran and fell on his neck and kissed him.
LUKE 15:20

The LORD is merciful and gracious, slow to anger, and abounding in mercy. He will not always strive with us, nor will He keep His anger forever. He has not dealt with us according to our sins, nor punished us according to our iniquities. For as the heavens are high above the earth, so great is His mercy toward those who fear Him; as far as the east is from the west, so far has He removed our transgressions from us. As a father pities his children, so the LORD pities those who fear Him. PSALM 103:8–13 •

You did not receive the spirit of bondage again to fear, but you received the Spirit of adoption by whom we cry out, "Abba, Father." The Spirit Himself bears witness with our spirit that we are children of God. ROMANS 8:15–16 • You who once were far off have been brought near by the blood of Christ. EPHESIANS 2:13 • Now, therefore, you are no longer strangers and foreigners, but fellow citizens with the saints and members of the household of God. EPHESIANS 2:19 •

Evening Reading

Behold, I make all things new.
REVELATION 21:5

Unless one is born again, he cannot see the kingdom of God. JOHN 3:3 • If anyone is in Christ, he is a new creation; old things have passed away; behold, all things have become new. 2 CORINTHIANS 5:17 •

I will give you a new heart and put a new spirit within you; I will take the heart of stone out of your flesh and give you a heart of flesh. EZEKIEL 36:26 • Therefore purge out the old leaven, that you may be a new lump, since you truly are unleavened. 1 CORINTHIANS 5:7 • Put on the new man which was created according to God, in true righteousness and holiness. EPHESIANS 4:24 •

You shall be called by a new name, which the mouth of the LORD will name. ISAIAH 62:2 •

Behold, I create new heavens and a new earth; and the former shall not be remembered or come to mind. ISAIAH 65:17 • Therefore, since all these things will be dissolved, what manner of persons ought you to be in holy conduct and godliness? 2 PETER 3:11 •

June 12

Morning Reading

*Everything that can endure fire, you shall put through the fire,
and it shall be clean.*
NUMBERS 31:23

The Lord your God is testing you to know whether you love the Lord your God with all your heart and with all your soul. DEUTERONOMY 13:3 • He will sit as a refiner and a purifier of silver; He will purify the sons of Levi, and purge them as gold and silver, that they may offer to the Lord an offering in righteousness. MALACHI 3:3 • Each one's work will become clear; for the Day will declare it, because it will be revealed by fire; and the fire will test each one's work, of what sort it is. 1 CORINTHIANS 3:13 •

I will turn My hand [upon] you, and thoroughly purge away your dross, and take away all your alloy. ISAIAH 1:25 • I will refine them and try them. JEREMIAH 9:7 •

You, O God, have tested us; You have refined us as silver is refined.... You have caused men to ride over our heads; we went through fire and through water; but You brought us out to rich fulfillment. PSALM 66:10, 12 •

When you pass through the waters, I will be with you; and through the rivers, they shall not overflow you. ISAIAH 43:2 •

Evening Reading

That we, having died to sins, might live for righteousness.
1 PETER 2:24

Put off, concerning your former conduct, the old man which grows corrupt according to the deceitful lusts, and be renewed in the spirit of your mind, and...put on the new man which was created according to God, in true righteousness and holiness. EPHESIANS 4:22–24 •

You died, and your life is hidden with Christ in God. COLOSSIANS 3:3 • As Christ was raised from the dead by the glory of the Father, even so we also should walk in newness of life....Knowing this, that our old man was crucified with Him, that the body of sin might be done away with, that we should no longer be slaves of sin. For he who has died has been freed from sin....Likewise you also, reckon yourselves to be dead indeed to sin, but alive to God in Christ Jesus our Lord. Therefore do not let sin reign in your mortal body, that you should obey it in its lusts. And do not present your members as instruments of unrighteousness to sin, but present yourselves to God as being alive from the dead, and your members as instruments of righteousness to God. ROMANS 6:4, 6–7, 11–13 •

June 13

Morning Reading

Abide in Me, and I in you.
JOHN 15:4

I have been crucified with Christ; it is no longer I who live, but Christ lives in me; and the life which I now live in the flesh I live by faith in the Son of God, who loved me and gave Himself for me. GALATIANS 2:20 •

I know that in me (that is, in my flesh) nothing good dwells; for to will is present with me, but how to perform what is good I do not find.... O wretched man that I am! Who will deliver me from this body of death? I thank God; through Jesus Christ our Lord! ROMANS 7:18, 24–25 • If Christ is in you, the body is dead because of sin, but the Spirit is life because of righteousness. ROMANS 8:10 • If indeed you continue in the faith, grounded and steadfast, and are not moved away from the hope of the gospel which you heard. COLOSSIANS 1:23 •

Little children, abide in Him, that when He appears, we may have confidence and not be ashamed before Him at His coming. 1 JOHN 2:28 • He who says he abides in Him ought himself also to walk just as He walked. 1 JOHN 2:6 •

Evening Reading

Do you believe in the Son of God?
JOHN 9:35

He answered and said, "Who is He, Lord, that I may believe in Him?" JOHN 9:36 •

The brightness of His glory and the express image of His person. HEBREWS 1:3 • The blessed and only Potentate, the King of kings and Lord of lords, who alone has immortality, dwelling in unapproachable light, whom no man has seen or can see, to whom be honor and everlasting power. Amen. 1 TIMOTHY 6:15–16 • "I am the Alpha and the Omega, the Beginning and the End," says the Lord, "who is and who was and who is to come, the Almighty." REVELATION 1:8 •

Lord, I believe! JOHN 9:38 • I know whom I have believed and am persuaded that He is able to keep what I have committed to Him until that Day. 2 TIMOTHY 1:12 •

Behold, I lay in Zion a chief cornerstone, elect, precious, and he who believes on Him will by no means be put to shame. Therefore, to you who believe, He is precious. 1 PETER 2:6–7 •

June 14

Morning Reading

As the sufferings of Christ abound in us,
so our consolation also abounds through Christ.
2 CORINTHIANS 1:5

The fellowship of His sufferings. PHILIPPIANS 3:10 • Rejoice to the extent that you partake of Christ's sufferings, that when His glory is revealed, you may also be glad with exceeding joy. 1 PETER 4:13 • If we died with Him, we shall also live with Him. 2 TIMOTHY 2:11 • If children, then heirs; heirs of God and joint heirs with Christ, if indeed we suffer with Him, that we may also be glorified together. ROMANS 8:17 •

God, determining to show more abundantly to the heirs of promise the immutability of His counsel, confirmed it by an oath, that by two immutable things, in which it is impossible for God to lie, we might have strong consolation, who have fled for refuge to lay hold of the hope set before us. HEBREWS 6:17–18 • May our Lord Jesus Christ Himself, and our God and Father, who has loved us and given us everlasting consolation and good hope by grace, comfort your hearts and establish you in every good word and work. 2 THESSALONIANS 2:16–17 •

Evening Reading

Martha, Martha, you are worried and troubled about many things.
LUKE 10:41

Consider the ravens, for they neither sow nor reap....Consider the lilies, how they grow: they neither toil nor spin....Do not seek what you should eat or what you should drink, nor have an anxious mind....Your Father knows that you need these things. LUKE 12:24, 27, 29–30 •

Having food and clothing, with these we shall be content. But those who desire to be rich fall into temptation and a snare, and into many foolish and harmful lusts which drown men in destruction and perdition. For the love of money is a root of all kinds of evil, for which some have strayed from the faith in their greediness, and pierced themselves through with many sorrows. 1 TIMOTHY 6:8–10 •

The cares of this world, the deceitfulness of riches, and the desires for other things entering in choke the word, and it becomes unfruitful. MARK 4:19 •

Let us lay aside every weight, and the sin which so easily ensnares us, and let us run with endurance the race that is set before us. HEBREWS 12:1 •

June 15

Morning Reading

The secret things belong to the LORD our God, but those things which
are revealed belong to us.
DEUTERONOMY 29:29

Lord, my heart is not haughty, nor my eyes lofty. Neither do I concern myself with great matters, nor with things too profound for me. Surely I have calmed and quieted my soul, like a weaned child with his mother; like a weaned child is my soul within me. PSALM 131:1–2 •

The secret of the Lord is with those who fear Him, and He will show them His covenant. PSALM 25:14 • There is a God in heaven who reveals secrets. DANIEL 2:28 • Indeed these are the mere edges of His ways, and how small a whisper we hear of Him! JOB 26:14 •

No longer do I call you servants, for a servant does not know what his master is doing; but I have called you friends, for all things that I heard from My Father I have made known to you. JOHN 15:15 • If you love Me, keep My commandments. And I will pray the Father, and He will give you another Helper, that He may abide with you forever; the Spirit of truth. JOHN 14:15–17 •

Evening Reading

The Spirit...makes intercession for the saints
according to the will of God.
ROMANS 8:27

Most assuredly, I say to you, whatever you ask the Father in My name He will give you. Until now you have asked nothing in My name. Ask, and you will receive, that your joy may be full. JOHN 16:23–24 • Praying always with all prayer and supplication in the Spirit. EPHESIANS 6:18 •

This is the confidence that we have in Him, that if we ask anything according to His will, He hears us. And if we know that He hears us, whatever we ask, we know that we have the petitions that we have asked of Him. 1 JOHN 5:14–15 • This is the will of God, [even] your sanctification. 1 THESSALONIANS 4:3 •

God did not call us to uncleanness, but in holiness....[He] has also given us His Holy Spirit. 1 THESSALONIANS 4:7–8 •

Rejoice always, pray without ceasing, in everything give thanks; for this is the will of God in Christ Jesus for you. Do not quench the Spirit. 1 THESSALONIANS 5:16–19 •

June 16

Morning Reading

*See then that you walk circumspectly, not as fools but as wise,
redeeming the time, because the days are evil.*
EPHESIANS 5:15–16

Take careful heed to do the commandment and the law which
Moses the servant of the LORD commanded you, to love the LORD your
God, to walk in all His ways, to keep His commandments, to hold fast
to Him, and to serve Him with all your heart and with all your soul.
JOSHUA 22:5 • Walk in wisdom toward those who are outside, redeeming
the time. Let your speech always be with grace, seasoned with salt,
that you may know how you ought to answer each one. COLOSSIANS 4:5–6 •
Abstain from every form of evil. 1 THESSALONIANS 5:22 •

While the bridegroom was delayed, they all slumbered and slept.
And at midnight a cry was heard: "Behold, the bridegroom is coming;
go out to meet him!"...Watch therefore, for you know neither the day
nor the hour in which the Son of Man is coming. MATTHEW 25:5–6, 13 •

Brethren, be even more diligent to make your call and election sure,
for if you do these things you will never stumble. 2 PETER 1:10 • Blessed are
those servants whom the master, when he comes, will find watching. LUKE
12:37 •

Evening Reading

Hold fast what you have, that no one may take your crown.
REVELATION 3:11

If only I may touch His garment, I shall be made well. MATTHEW 9:21 •
A leper came and worshiped Him, saying, "Lord, if You are willing, You
can make me clean." Then Jesus put out His hand and touched him,
saying, "I am willing; be cleansed." MATTHEW 8:2–3 • Faith as a mustard
seed. MATTHEW 17:20 •

Do not cast away your confidence, which has great reward. HEBREWS
10:35 • Work out your own salvation with fear and trembling; for it is
God who works in you both to will and to do for His good pleasure.
PHILIPPIANS 2:12–13 •

First the blade, then the head, after that the full grain in the head.
MARK 4:28 • Let us know, let us pursue the knowledge of the LORD. HOSEA 6:3
• The kingdom of heaven suffers violence, and the violent take it by force.
MATTHEW 11:12 • Run in such a way that you may obtain. 1 CORINTHIANS 9:24 •

I have fought the good fight, I have finished the race, I have kept the
faith. Finally, there is laid up for me the crown of righteousness, which the
Lord, the righteous Judge, will give to me on that Day. 2 TIMOTHY 4:7–8 •

June 17

Morning Reading

In everything by prayer and supplication, with thanksgiving,
let your requests be made known to God.
PHILIPPIANS 4:6

I love the LORD, because He has heard my voice and my supplications. Because He has inclined His ear to me, therefore I will call upon Him as long as I live. PSALM 116:1–2 •

When you pray, do not use vain repetitions as the heathen do. For they think that they will be heard for their many words. MATTHEW 6:7 • The Spirit also helps in our weaknesses. For we do not know what we should pray for as we ought, but the Spirit Himself makes intercession for us with groanings which cannot be uttered. ROMANS 8:26 •

I desire therefore that the men pray everywhere, lifting up holy hands, without wrath and doubting. 1 TIMOTHY 2:8 • Praying always with all prayer and supplication in the Spirit, being watchful to this end with all perseverance and supplication for all the saints. EPHESIANS 6:18 •

Again I say to you that if two of you agree on earth concerning anything that they ask, it will be done for them by My Father in heaven. MATTHEW 18:19 •

Evening Reading

All Your works shall praise You, O LORD,
and Your saints shall bless You.
PSALM 145:10

Bless the LORD, O my soul; and all that is within me, bless His holy name! Bless the LORD, O my soul, and forget not all His benefits. PSALM 103:1–2 • I will bless the LORD at all times; His praise shall continually be in my mouth. PSALM 34:1 • Every day I will bless You, and I will praise Your name forever and ever. PSALM 145:2 •

Because Your lovingkindness is better than life, my lips shall praise You. Thus I will bless You while I live; I will lift up my hands in Your name. My soul shall be satisfied as with marrow and fatness, and my mouth shall praise You with joyful lips. PSALM 63:3–5 •

My soul magnifies the Lord, and my spirit has rejoiced in God my Savior. LUKE 1:46–47 •

You are worthy, O Lord, to receive glory and honor and power; for You created all things, and by Your will they exist and were created. REVELATION 4:11 •

June 18

Morning Reading

You shall put the mercy seat on top of the ark,...
and there I will meet with you.
EXODUS 25:21–22

The way into the Holiest of All was not yet made manifest. HEBREWS 9:8 • Jesus cried out again with a loud voice, and yielded up His spirit. Then, behold, the veil of the temple was torn in two from top to bottom. MATTHEW 27:50–51 •

Brethren, having boldness to enter the Holiest by the blood of Jesus, by a new and living way which He consecrated for us, through the veil, that is, His flesh,...let us draw near with a true heart in full assurance of faith, having our hearts sprinkled from an evil conscience and our bodies washed with pure water. HEBREWS 10:19–20, 22 • Let us therefore come boldly to the throne of grace, that we may obtain mercy and find grace to help in time of need. HEBREWS 4:16 •

Being justified freely by His grace through the redemption that is in Christ Jesus, whom God set forth as a propitiation [mercy seat] by His blood, through faith, to demonstrate His righteousness, because in His forbearance God had passed over the sins that were previously committed. ROMANS 3:24–25 • Through Him we both have access by one Spirit to the Father. EPHESIANS 2:18 •

Evening Reading

Faith as a mustard seed.
MATTHEW 17:20

Barak said to [Deborah], "If you will go with me, then I will go; but if you will not go with me, I will not go!"...So on that day God subdued Jabin king of Canaan in the presence of the children of Israel. JUDGES 4:8, 23 • Gideon...did as the LORD had said to him. But because he feared his father's household and the men of the city too much to do it by day, he did it by night....Gideon said to God, "If You will save Israel by my hand as You have said,...let me test, I pray."...And God did so that night. JUDGES 6:27, 36, 39–40 •

You have a little strength, have kept My word, and have not denied My name. REVELATION 3:8 • Who has despised the day of small things? ZECHARIAH 4:10 •

We are bound to thank God always for you, brethren, as it is fitting, because your faith grows exceedingly. 2 THESSALONIANS 1:3 • [Lord,] increase our faith. LUKE 17:5 • I will be like the dew to Israel; he shall grow like the lily, and lengthen his roots like Lebanon. His branches shall spread; his beauty shall be like an olive tree, and his fragrance like Lebanon. HOSEA 14:5–6 •

June 19

Morning Reading

Pursue...holiness, without which no one will see the Lord.
HEBREWS 12:14

Unless one is born again, he cannot see the kingdom of God. JOHN 3:3 • There shall by no means enter it anything that defiles. REVELATION 21:27 • There is no spot in you. SONG OF SONGS 4:7 •

You shall be holy, for I the LORD your God am holy. LEVITICUS 19:2 • [Be] obedient children, not conforming yourselves to the former lusts, as in your ignorance; but as He who called you is holy, you also be holy in all your conduct, because it is written, "Be holy, for I am holy." And if you call on the Father, who without partiality judges according to each one's work, conduct yourselves throughout the time of your stay here in fear. 1 PETER 1:14–17 • Put off, concerning your former conduct, the old man which grows corrupt according to the deceitful lusts, and be renewed in the spirit of your mind, and...put on the new man which was created according to God, in true righteousness and holiness. EPHESIANS 4:22–24 • He chose us in Him before the foundation of the world, that we should be holy and without blame before Him in love. EPHESIANS 1:4 •

Evening Reading

Gold refined in the fire.
REVELATION 3:18

There is no one who has left house or brothers or sisters or father or mother or wife or children or lands, for My sake and the gospel's, who shall not receive a hundredfold now in this time; houses and brothers and sisters and mothers and children and lands, with persecutions; and in the age to come, eternal life. MARK 10:29–30 •

Beloved, do not think it strange concerning the fiery trial which is to try you, as though some strange thing happened to you. 1 PETER 4:12 • Now for a little while, if need be, you have been grieved by various trials, that the genuineness of your faith, being much more precious than gold that perishes, though it is tested by fire, may be found to praise, honor, and glory at the revelation of Jesus Christ. 1 PETER 1:6–7 •

May the God of all grace, who called us to His eternal glory by Christ Jesus, after you have suffered a while, perfect, establish, strengthen, and settle you. 1 PETER 5:10 • In the world you will have tribulation; but be of good cheer, I have overcome the world. JOHN 16:33 •

June 20

Morning Reading

Take this child away and nurse him for me,
and I will give you your wages.
EXODUS 2:9

Go into the vineyard, and whatever is right I will give you. MATTHEW 20:4 • Whoever gives you a cup of water to drink in My name, because you belong to Christ, assuredly, I say to you, he will by no means lose his reward. MARK 9:41 • The generous soul will be made rich, and he who waters will also be watered himself. PROVERBS 11:25 • God is not unjust to forget your work and labor of love...in that you have ministered to the saints, and do minister. HEBREWS 6:10 •

Each one will receive his own reward according to his own labor. 1 CORINTHIANS 3:8 •

Then the righteous will answer Him, saying, "Lord, when did we see You hungry and feed You, or thirsty and give You drink? When did we see You a stranger and take You in, or naked and clothe You?"...And the King will answer and say to them, "Assuredly, I say to you, inasmuch as you did it to one of the least of these My brethren, you did it to Me." MATTHEW 25:37–38, 40 • Come, you blessed of My Father, inherit the kingdom prepared for you from the foundation of the world. MATTHEW 25:34 •

Evening Reading

You comprehend my path and my lying down.
PSALM 139:3

Jacob awoke from his sleep and said, "Surely the LORD is in this place, and I did not know it." And he was afraid and said, "How awesome is this place! This is none other than the house of God, and this is the gate of heaven!" GENESIS 28:16–17 •

The eyes of the LORD run to and fro throughout the whole earth, to show Himself strong on behalf of those whose heart is loyal to Him. 2 CHRONICLES 16:9 •

I will both lie down in peace, and sleep; for You alone, O LORD, make me dwell in safety. PSALM 4:8 •

Because you have made the LORD, who is my refuge, even the Most High, your dwelling place, no evil shall befall you, nor shall any plague come near your dwelling; for He shall give His angels charge over you, to keep you in all your ways. PSALM 91:9–11 • When you lie down, you will not be afraid; yes, you will lie down and your sleep will be sweet. PROVERBS 3:24 • He gives His beloved sleep. PSALM 127:2 •

June 21

Morning Reading

Christ also suffered for us, leaving us an example,
that you should follow His steps.
1 PETER 2:21

Even the Son of Man did not come to be served, but to serve, and to give His life a ransom for many. MARK 10:45 • Whoever of you desires to be first shall be slave of all. MARK 10:44 •

Jesus of Nazareth...went about doing good. ACTS 10:38 • Bear one another's burdens, and so fulfill the law of Christ. GALATIANS 6:2 •

The meekness and gentleness of Christ. 2 CORINTHIANS 10:1 • In lowliness of mind let each esteem others better than himself. PHILIPPIANS 2:3 •

Father, forgive them, for they do not know what they do. LUKE 23:34 • Be kind to one another, tenderhearted, forgiving one another, just as God in Christ forgave you. EPHESIANS 4:32 •

He who says he abides in Him ought himself also to walk just as He walked. 1 JOHN 2:6 • Looking unto Jesus, the author and finisher of our faith, who for the joy that was set before Him endured the cross, despising the shame, and has sat down at the right hand of the throne of God. HEBREWS 12:2 •

Evening Reading

I sought him, but I could not find him;
I called him, but he gave me no answer.
SONG OF SONGS 5:6

[Joshua said,] "O Lord, what shall I say when Israel turns its back before its enemies?"...So the LORD said to Joshua: "Get up! Why do you lie thus on your face? Israel has sinned,...for they have even taken some of the accursed things,...and they have also put it among their own stuff." JOSHUA 7:8, 10–11 •

Behold, the Lord's hand is not shortened, that it cannot save; nor His ear heavy, that it cannot hear. But your iniquities have separated you from your God; and your sins have hidden His face from you, so that He will not hear. ISAIAH 59:1–2 •

If I regard iniquity in my heart, the Lord will not hear. PSALM 66:18 •

Beloved, if our heart does not condemn us, we have confidence toward God. And whatever we ask we receive from Him, because we keep His commandments and do those things that are pleasing in His sight. 1 JOHN 3:21–22 •

June 22

Morning Reading

You died, and your life is hidden with Christ in God.
COLOSSIANS 3:3

How shall we who died to sin live any longer in it? ROMANS 6:2 • I have been crucified with Christ; it is no longer I who live, but Christ lives in me; and the life which I now live in the flesh I live by faith in the Son of God, who loved me and gave Himself for me. GALATIANS 2:20 • He died for all, that those who live should live no longer for themselves, but for Him who died for them and rose again....Therefore, if anyone is in Christ, he is a new creation; old things have passed away; behold, all things have become new. 2 CORINTHIANS 5:15, 17 •

We are in Him who is true, in His Son Jesus Christ. 1 JOHN 5:20 • As You, Father, are in Me, and I in You; that they also may be one in Us. JOHN 17:21 • You are the body of Christ, and members individually. 1 CORINTHIANS 12:27 • Because I live, you will live also. JOHN 14:19 •

To him who overcomes I will give some of the hidden manna to eat. And I will give him a white stone, and on the stone a new name written which no one knows except him who receives it. REVELATION 2:17 •

Evening Reading

See how He loved him!
JOHN 11:36

He died for all. 2 CORINTHIANS 5:15 • Greater love has no one than this, than to lay down one's life for his friends. JOHN 15:13 •

He always lives to make intercession for them. HEBREWS 7:25 • I go to prepare a place for you. JOHN 14:2 •

I will come again and receive you to Myself; that where I am, there you may be also. JOHN 14:3 • Father, I desire that they also whom You gave Me may be with Me where I am. JOHN 17:24 • Having loved His own who were in the world, He loved them to the end. JOHN 13:1 •

We love Him because He first loved us. 1 JOHN 4:19 • The love of Christ compels us, because we judge thus: that if One died for all, then all died; and He died for all, that those who live should live no longer for themselves, but for Him who died for them and rose again. 2 CORINTHIANS 5:14–15 •

If you keep My commandments, you will abide in My love, just as I have kept My Father's commandments and abide in His love. JOHN 15:10 •

June 23

Morning Reading

I will pray the Father, and He will give you
another Helper,...the Spirit of truth.
JOHN 14:16–17

It is to your advantage that I go away; for if I do not go away, the Helper will not come to you; but if I depart, I will send Him to you. JOHN 16:7 •

The Spirit Himself bears witness with our spirit that we are children of God. ROMANS 8:16 • For you did not receive the spirit of bondage again to fear, but you received the Spirit of adoption by whom we cry out, "Abba, Father." ROMANS 8:15 • The Spirit also helps in our weaknesses. For we do not know what we should pray for as we ought, but the Spirit Himself makes intercession for us with groanings which cannot be uttered. ROMANS 8:26 •

May the God of hope fill you with all joy and peace in believing, that you may abound in hope by the power of the Holy Spirit. ROMANS 15:13 • Now hope does not disappoint, because the love of God has been poured out in our hearts by the Holy Spirit who was given to us. ROMANS 5:5 •

By this we know that we abide in Him, and He in us, because He has given us of His Spirit. 1 JOHN 4:13 •

Evening Reading

Shall I not seek security for you, that it may be well with you?
RUTH 3:1

There remains therefore a rest for the people of God. HEBREWS 4:9 • My people will dwell in a peaceful habitation, in secure dwellings, and in quiet resting places. ISAIAH 32:18 • There the wicked cease from troubling, and there the weary are at rest. JOB 3:17 • They...rest from their labors. REVELATION 14:13 •

The forerunner has entered for us, even Jesus, having become High Priest forever according to the order of Melchizedek. HEBREWS 6:20 •

Come to Me, all you who labor and are heavy laden, and I will give you rest. Take My yoke upon you and learn from Me, for I am gentle and lowly in heart, and you will find rest for your souls. For My yoke is easy and My burden is light. MATTHEW 11:28–30 • In returning and rest you shall be saved; in quietness and confidence shall be your strength. ISAIAH 30:15 •

The LORD is my shepherd; I shall not want. He makes me to lie down in green pastures; He leads me beside the still waters. PSALM 23:1–2 •

 # June 24

Morning Reading

*The ark of the covenant of the LORD went before them...to search
out a resting place for them.*
NUMBERS 10:33

My times are in Your hand. PSALM 31:15 • He will choose our inheritance for us. PSALM 47:4 • Lead me, O LORD, in Your righteousness....Make Your way straight before my face. PSALM 5:8 •

Commit your way to the LORD, trust also in Him, and He shall bring it to pass. PSALM 37:5 • In all your ways acknowledge Him, and He shall direct your paths. PROVERBS 3:6 • Your ears shall hear a word behind you, saying, "This is the way, walk in it," whenever you turn to the right hand or whenever you turn to the left. ISAIAH 30:21 •

The LORD is my shepherd; I shall not want. He makes me to lie down in green pastures; He leads me beside the still waters. PSALM 23:1–2 • As a father pities his children, so the LORD pities those who fear Him. For He knows our frame; He remembers that we are dust. PSALM 103:13–14 • Your heavenly Father knows that you need all these things. MATTHEW 6:32 • Casting all your care upon Him, for He cares for you. 1 PETER 5:7 •

Evening Reading

*They said to Him, "Rabbi,...where are You
staying?" He said to them, "Come and see."*
JOHN 1:38–39

In My Father's house are many mansions; if it were not so, I would have told you. I go to prepare a place for you. And if I go and prepare a place for you, I will come again and receive you to Myself; that where I am, there you may be also. JOHN 14:2–3 • To him who overcomes I will grant to sit with Me on My throne. REVELATION 3:21 •

Thus says the High and Lofty One who inhabits eternity, whose name is Holy: "I dwell in the high and holy place, with him who has a contrite and humble spirit, to revive the spirit of the humble, and to revive the heart of the contrite ones." ISAIAH 57:15 •

Behold, I stand at the door and knock. If anyone hears My voice and opens the door, I will come in to him and dine with him, and he with Me. REVELATION 3:20 •

Lo, I am with you always, even to the end of the age. MATTHEW 28:20 • How precious is Your lovingkindness, O God! Therefore the children of men put their trust under the shadow of Your wings. PSALM 36:7 •

June 25

Morning Reading

When He is revealed, we shall be like Him,
for we shall see Him as He is.
1 JOHN 3:2

As many as received Him, to them He gave the right to become children of God, to those who believe in His name. JOHN 1:12 • By which have been given to us exceedingly great and precious promises, that through these you may be partakers of the divine nature, having escaped the corruption that is in the world through lust. 2 PETER 1:4 •

Since the beginning of the world men have not heard nor perceived by the ear, nor has the eye seen any God besides You, who acts for the one who waits for Him. ISAIAH 64:4 •

Now we see in a mirror, dimly, but then face to face. Now I know in part, but then I shall know just as I also am known. 1 CORINTHIANS 13:12 • [Christ] will transform our lowly body that it may be conformed to His glorious body, according to the working by which He is able even to subdue all things to Himself. PHILIPPIANS 3:21 • As for me, I will see Your face in righteousness; I shall be satisfied when I awake in Your likeness. PSALM 17:15 •

Evening Reading

"The Man who is My Companion," says the LORD of hosts.
ZECHARIAH 13:7

In Him dwells all the fullness of the Godhead bodily. COLOSSIANS 2:9 • I have given help to one who is mighty; I have exalted one chosen from the people. PSALM 89:19 • I have trodden the winepress alone, and from the peoples no one was with Me. ISAIAH 63:3 •

Great is the mystery of godliness: God was manifested in the flesh. 1 TIMOTHY 3:16 • Unto us a Child is born, unto us a Son is given; and the government will be upon His shoulder. And His name will be called Wonderful, Counselor, Mighty God, Everlasting Father, Prince of Peace. ISAIAH 9:6 •

[Jesus,] being the brightness of His glory and the express image of His person, and upholding all things by the word of His power, when He had by Himself purged our sins, sat down at the right hand of the Majesty on high. HEBREWS 1:3 • To the Son He says: "Your throne, O God, is forever and ever." HEBREWS 1:8 •

Let all the angels of God worship Him. HEBREWS 1:6 •

KING OF KINGS AND LORD OF LORDS. REVELATION 19:16 •

June 26

Morning Reading

Jabez called on the God of Israel saying, "Oh, that You would bless me indeed,...and that You would keep me from evil!"...So God granted him what he requested.
1 Chronicles 4:10

The blessing of the Lord makes one rich, and He adds no sorrow with it. Proverbs 10:22 • When He gives quietness, who then can make trouble? And when He hides His face, who then can see Him? Job 34:29 •

Salvation belongs to the Lord. Your blessing is upon Your people. Psalm 3:8 • Oh, how great is Your goodness, which You have laid up for those who fear You, which You have prepared for those who trust in You in the presence of the sons of men! Psalm 31:19 • I do not pray that You should take them out of the world, but that You should keep them from the evil one. John 17:15 •

Ask, and it will be given to you; seek, and you will find; knock, and it will be opened to you. For everyone who asks receives, and he who seeks finds, and to him who knocks it will be opened. Matthew 7:7–8 • The Lord redeems the soul of His servants, and none of those who trust in Him shall be condemned. Psalm 34:22 •

Evening Reading

It is a night of solemn observance to the Lord for bringing them out of the land of Egypt.
Exodus 12:42

The Lord Jesus on the same night in which He was betrayed took bread; and when He had given thanks, He broke it and said, "Take, eat; this is My body which is broken for you; do this in remembrance of Me." In the same manner He also took the cup after supper, saying, "This cup is the new covenant in My blood. This do, as often as you drink it, in remembrance of Me." 1 Corinthians 11:23–25 •

[Jesus] knelt down and prayed....And being in agony, He prayed more earnestly. Then His sweat became like great drops of blood falling down to the ground. Luke 22:41, 44 •

It was the Preparation Day of the Passover, and about the sixth hour....They took Jesus and led Him away...to a place called the Place of a Skull, which is called in Hebrew, Golgotha, where they crucified Him. John 19:14, 16–18 •

Christ, our Passover, was sacrificed for us. Therefore let us keep the feast. 1 Corinthians 5:7–8 •

June 27

Morning Reading

Who is able to stand?
REVELATION 6:17

Who can endure the day of His coming? And who can stand when He appears? For He is like a refiner's fire and like launderer's soap. MALACHI 3:2 •

I looked, and behold, a great multitude which no one could number, of all nations, tribes, peoples, and tongues, standing before the throne and before the Lamb, clothed with white robes, with palm branches in their hands....These are the ones who come out of the great tribulation, and washed their robes and made them white in the blood of the Lamb....They shall neither hunger anymore nor thirst anymore; the sun shall not strike them, nor any heat; for the Lamb who is in the midst of the throne will shepherd them and lead them to living fountains of waters. And God will wipe away every tear from their eyes. REVELATION 7:9, 14, 16–17 •

There is therefore now no condemnation to those who are in Christ Jesus, who do not walk according to the flesh, but according to the Spirit. ROMANS 8:1 • Stand fast therefore in the liberty by which Christ has made us free. GALATIANS 5:1 •

Evening Reading

Do not enter into judgment with Your servant,
for in Your sight no one living is righteous.
PSALM 143:2

"Come now, and let us reason together," says the LORD, "though your sins are like scarlet, they shall be as white as snow; though they are red like crimson, they shall be as wool." ISAIAH 1:18 •

Let him take hold of My strength, that he may make peace with Me; and he shall make peace with Me. ISAIAH 27:5 • Now acquaint yourself with Him, and be at peace. JOB 22:21 •

Having been justified by faith, we have peace with God through our Lord Jesus Christ. ROMANS 5:1 • A man is not justified by the works of the law but by faith in Jesus Christ. GALATIANS 2:16 • By the deeds of the law no flesh will be justified in His sight. ROMANS 3:20 •

By Him everyone who believes is justified from all things from which you could not be justified by the law of Moses. ACTS 13:39 •

Thanks be to God, who gives us the victory through our Lord Jesus Christ. 1 CORINTHIANS 15:57 •

June 28

Morning Reading

I know that my Redeemer lives.
Job 19:25

If when we were enemies we were reconciled to God through the death of His Son, much more, having been reconciled, we shall be saved by His life. Romans 5:10 • But He, because He continues forever, has an unchangeable priesthood. Therefore He is also able to save to the uttermost those who come to God through Him, since He always lives to make intercession for them. Hebrews 7:24–25 •

Because I live, you will live also. John 14:19 • If in this life only we have hope in Christ, we are of all men the most pitiable. But now Christ is risen from the dead, and has become the firstfruits of those who have fallen asleep. 1 Corinthians 15:19–20 •

"The Redeemer will come to Zion, and to those who turn from transgression in Jacob," says the Lord. Isaiah 59:20 • We have redemption through His blood, the forgiveness of sins, according to the riches of His grace. Ephesians 1:7 • You were not redeemed with corruptible things, like silver or gold, from your aimless conduct received by tradition from your fathers, but with the precious blood of Christ, as of a lamb without blemish and without spot. 1 Peter 1:18–19 •

Evening Reading

The Spirit expressly says that in latter times some will depart from the faith, giving heed to deceiving spirits.
1 Timothy 4:1

Therefore take heed how you hear. Luke 8:18 • Let the word of Christ dwell in you richly in all wisdom. Colossians 3:16 • Above all, taking the shield of faith with which you will be able to quench all the fiery darts of the wicked one. Ephesians 6:16 •

Great peace have those who love Your law, and nothing causes them to stumble. Psalm 119:165 • How sweet are Your words to my taste, sweeter than honey to my mouth! Through Your precepts I get understanding; therefore I hate every false way. Psalm 119:103–04 •

Your word is a lamp to my feet and a light to my path. Psalm 119:105 • I have more understanding than all my teachers, for Your testimonies are my meditation. Psalm 119:99 •

Satan himself transforms himself into an angel of light. 2 Corinthians 11:14 • But even if we, or an angel from heaven, preach any other gospel to you than what we have preached to you, let him be accursed. Galatians 1:8 •

June 29

Morning Reading

His commandments are not burdensome.
1 JOHN 5:3

This is the will of Him who sent Me, that everyone who sees the Son and believes in Him may have everlasting life. JOHN 6:40 • Whatever we ask we receive from Him, because we keep His commandments and do those things that are pleasing in His sight. 1 JOHN 3:22 •

My yoke is easy and My burden is light. MATTHEW 11:30 • If you love Me, keep My commandments....He who has My commandments and keeps them, it is he who loves Me. And he who loves Me will be loved by My Father, and I will love him and manifest Myself to him. JOHN 14:15, 21 •

Happy is the man who finds wisdom, and the man who gains under-standing....Her ways are ways of pleasantness, and all her paths are peace. PROVERBS 3:13, 17 • Great peace have those who love Your law, and nothing causes them to stumble. PSALM 119:165 • I delight in the law of God according to the inward man. ROMANS 7:22 •

This is His commandment: that we should believe on the name of His Son Jesus Christ and love one another. 1 JOHN 3:23 • Love does no harm to a neighbor; therefore love is the fulfillment of the law. ROMANS 13:10 •

Evening Reading

Do not remember the sins of my youth, nor my transgressions.
PSALM 25:7

I have blotted out, like a thick cloud, your transgressions, and like a cloud, your sins. ISAIAH 44:22 • I, even I, am He who blots out your trans-gressions for My own sake; and I will not remember your sins. ISAIAH 43:25 • "Come now, and let us reason together," says the LORD, "though your sins are like scarlet, they shall be as white as snow; though they are red like crimson, they shall be as wool." ISAIAH 1:18 • Their sin I will remember no more. JEREMIAH 31:34 • You will cast all our sins into the depths of the sea. MICAH 7:19 •

You have lovingly delivered my soul from the pit of corruption, for You have cast all my sins behind Your back. ISAIAH 38:17 • Who is a God like You, pardoning iniquity?...He does not retain His anger forever, because He delights in mercy. MICAH 7:18 • To Him who loved us and washed us from our sins in His own blood. REVELATION 1:5 •

June 30

Morning Reading

As many as I love, I rebuke and chasten.
REVELATION 3:19

My son, do not despise the chastening of the LORD, nor be discouraged when you are rebuked by Him; for whom the LORD loves He chastens, and scourges every son whom He receives. HEBREWS 12:5–6 • For whom the LORD loves He corrects, just as a father the son in whom he delights. PROVERBS 3:12 • He bruises, but He binds up; He wounds, but His hands make whole. JOB 5:18 • Therefore humble yourselves under the mighty hand of God, that He may exalt you in due time. 1 PETER 5:6 • I have tested you in the furnace of affliction. ISAIAH 48:10 •

He does not afflict willingly, nor grieve the children of men. LAMENTATIONS 3:33 • He has not dealt with us according to our sins, nor punished us according to our iniquities. For as the heavens are high above the earth, so great is His mercy toward those who fear Him; as far as the east is from the west, so far has He removed our transgressions from us. As a father pities his children, so the LORD pities those who fear Him. For He knows our frame; He remembers that we are dust. PSALM 103:10–14 •

Evening Reading

*God is in heaven, and you on earth;
therefore let your words be few.*
ECCLESIASTES 5:2

When you pray, do not use vain repetitions as the heathen do. For they think that they will be heard for their many words. Therefore do not be like them. For your Father knows the things you have need of before you ask Him. MATTHEW 6:7–8 •

They...called on the name of Baal from morning even till noon, saying, "O Baal, hear us!" 1 KINGS 18:26 •

Two men went up to the temple to pray, one a Pharisee and the other a tax collector. The Pharisee stood and prayed thus with himself, "God, I thank You that I am not like other men; extortioners, unjust, adulterers, or even as this tax collector."...And the tax collector, standing afar off, would not so much as raise his eyes to heaven, but beat his breast, saying, "God, be merciful to me a sinner!" I tell you, this man went down to his house justified rather than the other. LUKE 18:10–11, 13–14 •

Lord, teach us to pray. LUKE 11:1 •

JULY

July 1

Morning Reading

The fruit of the Spirit is...goodness.
GALATIANS 5:22

Be imitators of God as dear children. EPHESIANS 5:1 • Love your enemies, bless those who curse you, do good to those who hate you, and pray for those who spitefully use you and persecute you, that you may be sons of your Father in heaven; for He makes His sun rise on the evil and on the good, and sends rain on the just and on the unjust. MATTHEW 5:44–45 • Therefore be merciful, just as your Father also is merciful. LUKE 6:36 •

The fruit of the Spirit is in all goodness, righteousness, and truth. EPHESIANS 5:9 •

When the kindness and the love of God our Savior toward man appeared, not by works of righteousness which we have done, but according to His mercy He saved us, through the washing of regeneration and renewing of the Holy Spirit, whom He poured out on us abundantly through Jesus Christ our Savior. TITUS 3:4–6 • The LORD is good to all, and His tender mercies are over all His works. PSALM 145:9 • He who did not spare His own Son, but delivered Him up for us all, how shall He not with Him also freely give us all things? ROMANS 8:32 •

Evening Reading

Ebenezer...“Thus far the LORD has helped us.”
1 SAMUEL 7:12

I was brought low, and He saved me. PSALM 116:6 • Blessed be the LORD, because He has heard the voice of my supplications! The LORD is my strength and my shield; my heart trusted in Him, and I am helped; therefore my heart greatly rejoices, and with my song I will praise Him. PSALM 28:6–7 •

It is better to trust in the LORD than to put confidence in man. It is better to trust in the LORD than to put confidence in princes. PSALM 118:8–9 • Happy is he who has the God of Jacob for his help, whose hope is in the LORD his God. PSALM 146:5 • He led them forth by the right way, that they might go to a city for a dwelling place. PSALM 107:7 • Not a word failed of any good thing which the LORD had spoken to the house of Israel. All came to pass. JOSHUA 21:45 •

[Jesus] said to [His disciples], “When I sent you without money bag, knapsack, and sandals, did you lack anything?” So they said, “Nothing.” LUKE 22:35 • Because You have been my help, therefore in the shadow of Your wings I will rejoice. PSALM 63:7 •

July 2

Morning Reading

This is the ordinance of the Passover: no foreigner shall eat it.
EXODUS 12:43

We have an altar from which those who serve the tabernacle have no right to eat. HEBREWS 13:10 • Unless one is born again, he cannot see the kingdom of God. JOHN 3:3 • At that time you were without Christ, being aliens from the commonwealth of Israel and strangers from the covenants of promise, having no hope and without God in the world. But now in Christ Jesus you who once were far off have been brought near by the blood of Christ. EPHESIANS 2:12–13 •

For He Himself is our peace, who has made both one,...having abolished in His flesh the enmity, that is, the law of commandments contained in ordinances, so as to create in Himself one new man from the two, thus making peace. EPHESIANS 2:14–15 •

Now, therefore, you are no longer strangers and foreigners, but fellow citizens with the saints and members of the household of God. EPHESIANS 2:19 •

If anyone hears My voice and opens the door, I will come in to him and dine with him, and he with Me. REVELATION 3:20 •

Evening Reading

[Jesus] prayed the third time, saying the same words.
MATTHEW 26:44

[Jesus], in the days of His flesh,...offered up prayers and supplications, with vehement cries and tears to Him who was able to save Him from death. HEBREWS 5:7 •

Let us know, let us pursue the knowledge of the LORD. HOSEA 6:3 • Continuing steadfastly in prayer. ROMANS 12:12 • Praying always with all prayer and supplication in the Spirit, being watchful to this end with all perseverance and supplication. EPHESIANS 6:18 • By prayer and supplication, with thanksgiving, let your requests be made known to God; and the peace of God, which surpasses all understanding, will guard your hearts and minds through Christ Jesus. PHILIPPIANS 4:6–7 •

Nevertheless, not as I will, but as You will. MATTHEW 26:39 • This is the confidence that we have in Him, that if we ask anything according to His will, He hears us. 1 JOHN 5:14 •

Delight yourself also in the LORD, and He shall give you the desires of your heart. Commit your way to the LORD, trust also in Him, and He shall bring it to pass. PSALM 37:4–5 •

July 3

Morning Reading

If children, then heirs; heirs of God and joint heirs with Christ.
ROMANS 8:17

If you are Christ's, then you are Abraham's seed, and heirs according to the promise. GALATIANS 3:29 •

Behold what manner of love the Father has bestowed on us, that we should be called children of God! 1 JOHN 3:1 • You are no longer a slave but a son, and if a son, then an heir of God through Christ. GALATIANS 4:7 • Having predestined us to adoption as sons by Jesus Christ to Himself, according to the good pleasure of His will. EPHESIANS 1:5 •

Father, I desire that they also whom You gave Me may be with Me where I am, that they may behold My glory which You have given Me. JOHN 17:24 •

He who overcomes, and keeps My works until the end, to him I will give power over the nations. REVELATION 2:26 • To him who overcomes I will grant to sit with Me on My throne, as I also overcame and sat down with My Father on His throne. REVELATION 3:21 •

Evening Reading

The things which are despised God has chosen.
1 CORINTHIANS 1:28

Look, are not all these who speak Galileans? ACTS 2:7 •

Jesus...saw two brothers...casting a net into the sea; for they were fishermen. Then He said to them, "Follow Me." MATTHEW 4:18–19 • Now when they saw the boldness of Peter and John, and perceived that they were uneducated and untrained men, they marveled. And they realized that they had been with Jesus. ACTS 4:13 •

My speech and my preaching were not with persuasive words of human wisdom, but in demonstration of the Spirit and of power, that your faith should not be in the wisdom of men but in the power of God. 1 CORINTHIANS 2:4–5 •

You did not choose Me, but I chose you and appointed you that you should go and bear fruit. JOHN 15:16 • I am the vine, you are the branches. He who abides in Me, and I in him, bears much fruit; for without Me you can do nothing. JOHN 15:5 • We have this treasure in earthen vessels, that the excellence of the power may be of God and not of us. 2 CORINTHIANS 4:7 •

July 4

Morning Reading

Leaning on Jesus' bosom.
JOHN 13:23

As one whom his mother comforts, so I will comfort you. ISAIAH 66:13 • They brought little children to Him, that He might touch them; but the disciples rebuked those who brought them....[But] He took them up in His arms, put His hands on them, and blessed them. MARK 10:13, 16 • Jesus called His disciples to Himself and said, "I have compassion on the multitude, because they have now continued with Me three days and have nothing to eat. And I do not want to send them away hungry, lest they faint on the way." MATTHEW 15:32 • We do not have a High Priest who cannot sympathize with our weaknesses, but was in all points tempted as we are, yet without sin. HEBREWS 4:15 • In His love and in His pity He redeemed them. ISAIAH 63:9 •

I will not leave you orphans; I will come to you. JOHN 14:18 • Can a woman forget her nursing child, and not have compassion on the son of her womb? Surely they may forget, yet I will not forget you. ISAIAH 49:15 •

The Lamb who is in the midst of the throne will shepherd them and lead them to living fountains of waters. And God will wipe away every tear from their eyes. REVELATION 7:17 •

Evening Reading

Jesus Christ the righteous....The propitiation for our sins.
1 JOHN 2:1–2

The faces of the cherubim shall be toward the mercy seat. You shall put the mercy seat on top of the ark, and in the ark you shall put the Testimony that I will give you. And there I will meet with you, and I will speak with you from above the mercy seat. EXODUS 25:20–22 •

Surely His salvation is near to those who fear Him....Mercy and truth have met together; righteousness and peace have kissed. PSALM 85:9–10 •

If You, LORD, should mark iniquities, O Lord, who could stand? But there is forgiveness with You, that You may be feared. PSALM 130:3–4 • O Israel, hope in the LORD; for with the LORD there is mercy, and with Him is abundant redemption. And He shall redeem Israel from all his iniquities. PSALM 130:7–8 • All have sinned and fall short of the glory of God, being justified freely by His grace through the redemption that is in Christ Jesus, whom God set forth as a propitiation by His blood, through faith, to demonstrate His righteousness, because in His forbearance God had passed over the sins that were previously committed. ROMANS 3:23–25 •

July 5

Morning Reading

We have known and believed the love
that God has for us.
1 JOHN 4:16

God, who is rich in mercy, because of His great love with which He loved us, even when we were dead in trespasses, made us alive together with Christ (by grace you have been saved), and raised us up together, and made us sit together in the heavenly places in Christ Jesus, that in the ages to come He might show the exceeding riches of His grace in His kindness toward us in Christ Jesus. EPHESIANS 2:4–7 •

God so loved the world that He gave His only begotten Son, that whoever believes in Him should not perish but have everlasting life. JOHN 3:16 • He who did not spare His own Son, but delivered Him up for us all, how shall He not with Him also freely give us all things? ROMANS 8:32 • The Lord is good to all, and His tender mercies are over all His works. PSALM 145:9 •

We love Him because He first loved us. 1 JOHN 4:19 •

Blessed is she who believed, for there will be a fulfillment of those things which were told her from the Lord. LUKE 1:45 •

Evening Reading

Do not set your mind on high things,
but associate with the humble.
ROMANS 12:16

My brethren, do not hold the faith of our Lord Jesus Christ, the Lord of glory, with partiality. JAMES 2:1 • Has God not chosen the poor of this world to be rich in faith and heirs of the kingdom which He promised to those who love Him? JAMES 2:5 •

Let no one seek his own, but each one the other's well-being. 1 CORINTHIANS 10:24 • Having food and clothing, with these we shall be content. But those who desire to be rich fall into temptation and a snare, and into many foolish and harmful lusts which drown men in destruction and perdition. 1 TIMOTHY 6:8–9 •

God has chosen the foolish things of the world to put to shame the wise, and God has chosen the weak things of the world to put to shame the things which are mighty; and the base things of the world and the things which are despised God has chosen, and the things which are not, to bring to nothing the things that are, that no flesh should glory in His presence. 1 CORINTHIANS 1:27–29 •

LORD, my heart is not haughty, nor my eyes lofty. PSALM 131:1 •

July 6

Morning Reading

Let your speech always be with grace.
Colossians 4:6

A word fitly spoken is like apples of gold in settings of silver. Like an earring of gold and an ornament of fine gold is a wise rebuker to an obedient ear. Proverbs 25:11–12 • Let no corrupt word proceed out of your mouth, but what is good for necessary edification, that it may impart grace to the hearers. Ephesians 4:29 • A good man out of the good treasure of his heart brings forth good things, and an evil man out of the evil treasure brings forth evil things. Matthew 12:35 • By your words you will be justified. Matthew 12:37 • The tongue of the wise promotes health. Proverbs 12:18 •

Those who feared the LORD spoke to one another, and the LORD listened and heard them; so a book of remembrance was written before Him for those who fear the LORD and who meditate on His name. Malachi 3:16 •

If you take out the precious from the vile, you shall be as My mouth. Jeremiah 15:19 • But as you abound in everything; in faith, in speech, in knowledge, in all diligence, and in your love...see that you abound in this grace also. 2 Corinthians 8:7 •

Evening Reading

Your lovingkindness is before my eyes.
Psalm 26:3

The LORD is gracious and full of compassion, slow to anger and great in mercy. Psalm 145:8 • That you may be sons of your Father in heaven; for He makes His sun rise on the evil and on the good, and sends rain on the just and on the unjust. Matthew 5:45 •

Be imitators of God as dear children. And walk in love, as Christ also has loved us and given Himself for us, an offering and a sacrifice to God for a sweet-smelling aroma. Ephesians 5:1–2 • Be kind to one another, tenderhearted, forgiving one another, just as God in Christ forgave you. Ephesians 4:32 • Since you have purified your souls in obeying the truth through the Spirit in sincere love of the brethren, love one another fervently with a pure heart. 1 Peter 1:22 • The love of Christ compels us. 2 Corinthians 5:14 •

Love your enemies, do good, and lend, hoping for nothing in return; and your reward will be great, and you will be sons of the Most High. For He is kind to the unthankful and evil. Therefore be merciful, just as your Father also is merciful. Luke 6:35–36 •

July 7

Morning Reading

*Then Jesus was led up by the Spirit into the wilderness
to be tempted by the devil.*
MATTHEW 4:1

In the days of His flesh, when He had offered up prayers and supplications, with vehement cries and tears to Him who was able to save Him from death, and was heard because of His godly fear, though He was a Son, yet He learned obedience by the things which He suffered. And having been perfected, He became the author of eternal salvation to all who obey Him. HEBREWS 5:7–9 • We do not have a High Priest who cannot sympathize with our weaknesses, but was in all points tempted as we are, yet without sin. HEBREWS 4:15 •

No temptation has overtaken you except such as is common to man; but God is faithful, who will not allow you to be tempted beyond what you are able, but with the temptation will also make the way of escape, that you may be able to bear it. 1 CORINTHIANS 10:13 • My grace is sufficient for you, for My strength is made perfect in weakness. 2 CORINTHIANS 12:9 •

Evening Reading

*The Son of Man did not come to be served, but to serve,
and to give His life a ransom for many.*
MATTHEW 20:28

If the blood of bulls and goats and the ashes of a heifer, sprinkling the unclean, sanctifies for the purifying of the flesh, how much more shall the blood of Christ, who through the eternal Spirit offered Himself without spot to God, cleanse your conscience from dead works to serve the living God? HEBREWS 9:13–14 •

He was led as a lamb to the slaughter. ISAIAH 53:7 • I lay down My life for the sheep....No one takes it from Me, but I lay it down of Myself. I have power to lay it down, and I have power to take it again. JOHN 10:15, 18 •

The life of the flesh is in the blood, and I have given it to you upon the altar to make atonement for your souls; for it is the blood that makes atonement for the soul. LEVITICUS 17:11 • Without shedding of blood there is no remission. HEBREWS 9:22 •

While we were still sinners, Christ died for us. Much more then, having now been justified by His blood, we shall be saved from wrath through Him. ROMANS 5:8–9 •

July 8

Morning Reading

If we confess our sins, He is faithful and just to forgive us our sins and to cleanse us from all unrighteousness.
1 John 1:9

I acknowledge my transgressions, and my sin is always before me. Against You, You only, have I sinned, and done this evil in Your sight. Psalm 51:3–4 •

And [the Prodigal Son] arose and came to his father. But when he was still a great way off, his father saw him and had compassion, and ran and fell on his neck and kissed him. Luke 15:20 • I have blotted out, like a thick cloud, your transgressions, and like a cloud, your sins. Return to Me, for I have redeemed you. Isaiah 44:22 • Your sins are forgiven you for His name's sake. 1 John 2:12 • God in Christ forgave you. Ephesians 4:32 • That He might be just and the justifier of the one who has faith in Jesus. Romans 3:26 •

Then I will sprinkle clean water on you, and you shall be clean. Ezekiel 36:25 • They shall walk with Me in white, for they are worthy. Revelation 3:4 •

This is He who came by water and blood; Jesus Christ; not only by water, but by water and blood. 1 John 5:6 •

Evening Reading

Shall the throne of iniquity...have fellowship with You?
Psalm 94:20

Truly our fellowship is with the Father and with His Son Jesus Christ. 1 John 1:3 • Beloved, now we are children of God; and it has not yet been revealed what we shall be, but we know that when He is revealed, we shall be like Him, for we shall see Him as He is. And everyone who has this hope in Him purifies himself, just as He is pure. 1 John 3:2–3 •

The ruler of this world is coming, and he has nothing in Me. John 14:30 • A High Priest...holy, harmless, undefiled. Hebrews 7:26 •

We do not wrestle against flesh and blood, but against principalities, against powers, against the rulers of the darkness of this age, against spiritual hosts of wickedness in the heavenly places. Ephesians 6:12 • The prince of the power of the air, the spirit who now works in the sons of disobedience. Ephesians 2:2 •

Whoever is born of God does not sin; but he who has been born of God keeps himself, and the wicked one does not touch him. We know that we are of God, and the whole world lies under the sway of the wicked one. 1 John 5:18–19 •

July 9

Morning Reading

I have removed your iniquity from you,
and I will clothe you with rich robes.
ZECHARIAH 3:4

Blessed is he whose transgression is forgiven, whose sin is covered. PSALM 32:1 • We are all like an unclean thing. ISAIAH 64:6 • I know that in me (that is, in my flesh) nothing good dwells; for to will is present with me, but how to perform what is good I do not find. ROMANS 7:18 •

As many of you as were baptized into Christ have put on Christ. GALATIANS 3:27 • You have put off the old man with his deeds, and have put on the new man who is renewed in knowledge according to the image of Him who created him. COLOSSIANS 3:9–10 • Not having my own righteousness, which is from the law, but...the righteousness which is from God by faith. PHILIPPIANS 3:9 •

Bring out the best robe and put it on him. LUKE 15:22 • The fine linen is the righteous acts of the saints. REVELATION 19:8 • I will greatly rejoice in the LORD, my soul shall be joyful in my God; for He has clothed me with the garments of salvation, He has covered me with the robe of righteousness. ISAIAH 61:10 •

Evening Reading

The Day will declare it.
1 CORINTHIANS 3:13

Judge nothing before the time, until the Lord comes, who will both bring to light the hidden things of darkness and reveal the counsels of the hearts. Then each one's praise will come from God. 1 CORINTHIANS 4:5 •

Why do you judge your brother? Or why do you show contempt for your brother? For we shall all stand before the judgment seat of Christ. ROMANS 14:10 •

So then each of us shall give account of himself to God. Therefore let us not judge one another anymore, but rather resolve this, not to put a stumbling block or a cause to fall in our brother's way. ROMANS 14:12–13 •

God will judge the secrets of men by Jesus Christ. ROMANS 2:16 • The Father judges no one, but has committed all judgment to the Son...and has given Him authority to execute judgment also, because He is the Son of Man. JOHN 5:22, 27 •

[You are] the Great, the Mighty God, whose name is the LORD of hosts. You are great in counsel and mighty in work, for Your eyes are open to all the ways of the sons of men, to give everyone according to his ways and according to the fruit of his doings. JEREMIAH 32:18–19 •

July 10

Morning Reading

A disciple is not above his teacher.
MATTHEW 10:24

You call me Teacher and Lord, and you say well, for so I am. JOHN 13:13 •

It is enough for a disciple that he be like his teacher, and a servant like his master. MATTHEW 10:25 • If they persecuted Me, they will also persecute you. If they kept My word, they will keep yours also. JOHN 15:20 • I have given them Your word; and the world has hated them because they are not of the world, just as I am not of the world. JOHN 17:14 •

Consider Him who endured such hostility from sinners against Himself, lest you become weary and discouraged in your souls. You have not yet resisted to bloodshed, striving against sin. HEBREWS 12:3–4 •

Let us lay aside every weight, and the sin which so easily ensnares us, and let us run with endurance the race that is set before us, looking unto Jesus, the author and finisher of our faith, who for the joy that was set before Him endured the cross, despising the shame, and has sat down at the right hand of the throne of God. HEBREWS 12:1–2 • Since Christ suffered for us in the flesh, arm yourselves also with the same mind. 1 PETER 4:1 •

Evening Reading

My son, give me your heart.
PROVERBS 23:26

Oh, that they had such a heart in them that they would fear Me and always keep all My commandments, that it might be well with them and with their children forever! DEUTERONOMY 5:29 •

Your heart is not right in the sight of God. ACTS 8:21 • Because the carnal mind is enmity against God; for it is not subject to the law of God, nor indeed can be. So then, those who are in the flesh cannot please God. ROMANS 8:7–8 •

They first gave themselves to the Lord. 2 CORINTHIANS 8:5 • In every work that [Hezekiah] began...to seek his God, he did it with all his heart. So he prospered. 2 CHRONICLES 31:21 •

Keep your heart with all diligence, for out of it spring the issues of life. PROVERBS 4:23 •

Whatever you do, do it heartily, as to the Lord. COLOSSIANS 3:23 • As bondservants of Christ, doing the will of God from the heart, with good-will doing service, as to the Lord, and not to men. EPHESIANS 6:6–7 •

I will run the course of Your commandments, for You shall enlarge my heart. PSALM 119:32 •

July 11

Morning Reading

I am with you to save you.
JEREMIAH 15:20

Shall the prey be taken from the mighty, or the captives of the righteous be delivered? But thus says the LORD: "Even the captives of the mighty shall be taken away, and the prey of the terrible be delivered; for I will contend with him who contends with you, and I will save your children. I will feed those who oppress you with their own flesh, and they shall be drunk with their own blood as with sweet wine. All flesh shall know that I, the LORD, am your Savior, and your Redeemer, the Mighty One of Jacob." ISAIAH 49:24–26 • Fear not, for I am with you; be not dismayed, for I am your God. I will strengthen you, yes, I will help you, I will uphold you with My righteous right hand. ISAIAH 41:10 •

We do not have a High Priest who cannot sympathize with our weaknesses, but was in all points tempted as we are, yet without sin. HEBREWS 4:15 • In that He Himself has suffered, being tempted, He is able to aid those who are tempted. HEBREWS 2:18 • The steps of a good man are ordered by the LORD, and He delights in his way. Though he fall, he shall not be utterly cast down; for the LORD upholds him with His hand. PSALM 37:23–24 •

Evening Reading

He satisfies the longing soul,
and fills the hungry soul with goodness.
PSALM 107:9

You have tasted that the Lord is gracious. 1 PETER 2:3 •

O God, You are my God; early will I seek You; my soul thirsts for You; my flesh longs for You in a dry and thirsty land where there is no water,...to see Your power and Your glory. PSALM 63:1–2 • My soul longs, yes, even faints for the courts of the LORD; my heart and my flesh cry out for the living God. PSALM 84:2 • Having a desire to depart and be with Christ, which is far better. PHILIPPIANS 1:23 •

I shall be satisfied when I awake in Your likeness. PSALM 17:15 • They shall neither hunger anymore nor thirst anymore; the sun shall not strike them, nor any heat; for the Lamb who is in the midst of the throne will shepherd them and lead them to living fountains of waters. And God will wipe away every tear from their eyes. REVELATION 7:16–17 • They are abundantly satisfied with the fullness of Your house, and You give them drink from the river of Your pleasures. PSALM 36:8 • My people shall be satisfied with My goodness, says the LORD. JEREMIAH 31:14 •

July 12

Morning Reading

My Presence will go with you, and I will give you rest.
EXODUS 33:14

Be strong and of good courage, do not fear nor be afraid of them; for the LORD your God, He is the One who goes with you. He will not leave you nor forsake you....The LORD, He is the One who goes before you. He will be with you, He will not leave you nor forsake you; do not fear nor be dismayed. DEUTERONOMY 31:6, 8 • Have I not commanded you? Be strong and of good courage; do not be afraid, nor be dismayed, for the LORD your God is with you wherever you go. JOSHUA 1:9 • In all your ways acknowledge Him, and He shall direct your paths. PROVERBS 3:6 •

[God] Himself has said, "I will never leave you nor forsake you." So we may boldly say: "The LORD is my helper; I will not fear. What can man do to me?" HEBREWS 13:5–6 • Our sufficiency is from God. 2 CORINTHIANS 3:5 •

Do not lead us into temptation. MATTHEW 6:13 • O LORD, I know the way of man is not in himself; it is not in man who walks to direct his own steps. JEREMIAH 10:23 • My times are in Your hand. PSALM 31:15 •

Evening Reading

*Let us consider one another in order to stir up
love and good works.*
HEBREWS 10:24

How forceful are right words! JOB 6:25 • I stir up your pure minds by way of reminder. 2 PETER 3:1 •

Those who feared the LORD spoke to one another, and the LORD listened and heard them; so a book of remembrance was written before Him for those who fear the LORD and who meditate on His name. MALACHI 3:16 • If two of you agree on earth concerning anything that they ask, it will be done for them by My Father in heaven. MATTHEW 18:19 •

The LORD God said, "It is not good that man should be alone." GENESIS 2:18 • Two are better than one, because they have a good reward for their labor. For if they fall, one will lift up his companion. But woe to him who is alone when he falls, for he has no one to help him up. ECCLESIASTES 4:9–10 •

Let us not...put a stumbling block or a cause to fall in our brother's way. ROMANS 14:13 • Bear one another's burdens, and so fulfill the law of Christ. GALATIANS 6:2 • Brethren, if a man is overtaken in any trespass, you who are spiritual restore such a one in a spirit of gentleness, considering yourself lest you also be tempted. GALATIANS 6:1 •

July 13

Morning Reading

I am my beloved's, and his desire is toward me.
SONG OF SONGS 7:10

I know whom I have believed and am persuaded that He is able to keep what I have committed to Him until that Day. 2 TIMOTHY 1:12 • I am persuaded that neither death nor life, nor angels nor principalities nor powers, nor things present nor things to come, nor height nor depth, nor any other created thing, shall be able to separate us from the love of God which is in Christ Jesus our Lord. ROMANS 8:38–39 • Those whom You gave Me I have kept; and none of them is lost. JOHN 17:12 •

The LORD takes pleasure in His people. PSALM 149:4 • My delight was with the sons of men. PROVERBS 8:31 • His great love with which He loved us. EPHESIANS 2:4 • Greater love has no one than this, than to lay down one's life for his friends. JOHN 15:13 •

You were bought at a price; therefore glorify God in your body and in your spirit, which are God's. 1 CORINTHIANS 6:20 • If we live, we live to the Lord; and if we die, we die to the Lord. Therefore, whether we live or die, we are the Lord's. ROMANS 14:8 •

Evening Reading

Search from the book of the LORD.
ISAIAH 34:16

Therefore you shall lay up these words of mine in your heart and in your soul, and bind them as a sign on your hand, and they shall be as frontlets between your eyes. DEUTERONOMY 11:18 • This Book of the Law shall not depart from your mouth, but you shall meditate in it day and night, that you may observe to do according to all that is written in it. For then you will make your way prosperous, and then you will have good success. JOSHUA 1:8 •

The law of his God is in his heart; none of his steps shall slide. PSALM 37:31 • By the word of Your lips, I have kept away from the paths of the destroyer. PSALM 17:4 • Your word I have hidden in my heart, that I might not sin against You! PSALM 119:11 •

We have the prophetic word confirmed, which you do well to heed as a light that shines in a dark place, until the day dawns and the morning star rises in your hearts. 2 PETER 1:19 • That we through the patience and comfort of the Scriptures might have hope. ROMANS 15:4 •

Morning Reading

Out of the abundance of the heart the mouth speaks.
MATTHEW 12:34

Let the word of Christ dwell in you richly in all wisdom. COLOSSIANS 3:16 •

Keep your heart with all diligence, for out of it spring the issues of life. PROVERBS 4:23 • Death and life are in the power of the tongue. PROVERBS 18:21 • The mouth of the righteous speaks wisdom, and his tongue talks of justice. The law of his God is in his heart; none of his steps shall slide. PSALM 37:30–31 • Let no corrupt word proceed out of your mouth, but what is good for necessary edification, that it may impart grace to the hearers. EPHESIANS 4:29 •

We cannot but speak the things which we have seen and heard. ACTS 4:20 • I believed, therefore I spoke. PSALM 116:10 •

Whoever confesses Me before men, him I will also confess before My Father who is in heaven. MATTHEW 10:32 • With the heart one believes unto righteousness, and with the mouth confession is made unto salvation. ROMANS 10:10 •

Evening Reading

I hope to see you shortly, and we shall speak face to face.
3 JOHN 14

Oh, that You would rend the heavens! That You would come down! ISAIAH 64:1 • As the deer pants for the water brooks, so pants my soul for You, O God. My soul thirsts for God, for the living God. When shall I come and appear before God? PSALM 42:1–2 • Make haste, my beloved, and be like a gazelle or a young stag on the mountains of spices. SONG OF SONGS 8:14 •

Our citizenship is in heaven, from which we also eagerly wait for the Savior, the Lord Jesus Christ. PHILIPPIANS 3:20 • Looking for the blessed hope and glorious appearing of our great God and Savior Jesus Christ. TITUS 2:13 • God our Savior and the Lord Jesus Christ, our hope. 1 TIMOTHY 1:1 • Whom having not seen you love. 1 PETER 1:8 •

He who testifies to these things says, "Surely I am coming quickly." Amen. Even so, come, Lord Jesus! REVELATION 22:20 • It will be said in that day: "Behold, this is our God; we have waited for Him, and He will save us. This is the LORD; we have waited for Him; we will be glad and rejoice in His salvation." ISAIAH 25:9 •

July 15

Morning Reading

Your will be done on earth as it is in heaven.
MATTHEW 6:10

Bless the LORD, you His angels, who excel in strength, who do His word, heeding the voice of His word. Bless the LORD, all you His hosts, you ministers of His, who do His pleasure. PSALM 103:20–21 •

I have come down from heaven, not to do My own will, but the will of Him who sent Me. JOHN 6:38 • I delight to do Your will, O my God, and Your law is within my heart. PSALM 40:8 • O My Father, if this cup cannot pass away from Me unless I drink it, Your will be done. MATTHEW 26:42 •

Not everyone who says to Me, "Lord, Lord," shall enter the kingdom of heaven, but he who does the will of My Father in heaven. MATTHEW 7:21 • Not the hearers of the law are just in the sight of God, but the doers of the law will be justified. ROMANS 2:13 • If you know these things, blessed are you if you do them. JOHN 13:17 • To him who knows to do good and does not do it, to him it is sin. JAMES 4:17 •

Do not be conformed to this world, but be transformed by the renewing of your mind, that you may prove what is that good and acceptable and perfect will of God. ROMANS 12:2 •

Evening Reading

The ear tests words as the palate tastes food.
JOB 34:3

Beloved, do not believe every spirit, but test the spirits, whether they are of God; because many false prophets have gone out into the world. 1 JOHN 4:1 • Do not judge according to appearance, but judge with righteous judgment. JOHN 7:24 • I speak as to wise men; judge for your-selves what I say. 1 CORINTHIANS 10:15 • Let the word of Christ dwell in you richly in all wisdom. COLOSSIANS 3:16 •

He who has an ear, let him hear what the Spirit says. REVELATION 2:29 • He who is spiritual judges all things. 1 CORINTHIANS 2:15 •

Take heed what you hear. MARK 4:24 • I know your works,...and that... you have tested those who say they are apostles and are not, and have found them liars. REVELATION 2:2 • Test all things; hold fast what is good. 1 THESSALONIANS 5:21 •

He calls his own sheep by name and leads them out. And when he brings out his own sheep, he goes before them; and the sheep follow him, for they know his voice. Yet they will by no means follow a stranger, but will flee from him, for they do not know the voice of strangers. JOHN 10:3–5 •

Daily Light on the Daily Path

July 16

Morning Reading

You shall be to Me a kingdom of priests and a holy nation.
EXODUS 19:6

You were slain, and have redeemed us to God by Your blood out of every tribe and tongue and people and nation, and have made us kings and priests to our God. REVELATION 5:9–10 • You are a chosen generation, a royal priesthood, a holy nation, His own special people, that you may proclaim the praises of Him who called you out of darkness into His marvelous light. 1 PETER 2:9 •

You shall be named the priests of the LORD, [men] shall call you the servants of our God. ISAIAH 61:6 • Priests of God and of Christ. REVELATION 20:6 •

Holy brethren, partakers of the heavenly calling, consider the Apostle and High Priest of our confession, Christ Jesus. HEBREWS 3:1 • Therefore by Him let us continually offer the sacrifice of praise to God, that is, the fruit of our lips, giving thanks to His name. HEBREWS 13:15 •

For we are His workmanship, created in Christ Jesus for good works, which God prepared beforehand that we should walk in them. EPHESIANS 2:10 • The temple of God is holy, which temple you are. 1 CORINTHIANS 3:17 •

Evening Reading

We made our prayer to our God, and…set a watch against them.
NEHEMIAH 4:9

Watch and pray, lest you enter into temptation. MATTHEW 26:41 • Continue earnestly in prayer, being vigilant in it with thanksgiving. COLOSSIANS 4:2 • Casting all your care upon Him, for He cares for you. Be sober, be vigilant; because your adversary the devil walks about like a roaring lion, seeking whom he may devour. Resist him, steadfast in the faith. 1 PETER 5:7–9 •

Why do you call Me "Lord, Lord," and do not do the things which I say? LUKE 6:46 • Be doers of the word, and not hearers only, deceiving yourselves. JAMES 1:22 •

Why do you cry to Me? Tell the children of Israel to go forward. EXODUS 14:15 •

Be anxious for nothing, but in everything by prayer and supplication, with thanksgiving, let your requests be made known to God; and the peace of God, which surpasses all understanding, will guard your hearts and minds through Christ Jesus. PHILIPPIANS 4:6–7 •

July 17

Morning Reading

You are a gracious and merciful God, slow to anger and
abundant in lovingkindness, One who relents from doing harm.
JONAH 4:2

Now, I pray, let the power of my LORD be great, just as You have spoken, saying, "The LORD is longsuffering and abundant in mercy, forgiving iniquity and transgression; but He by no means clears the guilty, visiting the iniquity of the fathers on the children to the third and fourth generation." NUMBERS 14:17–18 •

Oh, do not remember former iniquities against us! Let Your tender mercies come speedily to meet us, for we have been brought very low. Help us, O God of our salvation, for the glory of Your name; and deliver us, and provide atonement for our sins, for Your name's sake! PSALM 79:8–9 • O LORD, though our iniquities testify against us, do it for Your name's sake; for our backslidings are many, we have sinned against You....We acknowledge, O LORD, our wickedness and the iniquity of our fathers, for we have sinned against You. JEREMIAH 14:7, 20 •

If You, LORD, should mark iniquities, O Lord, who could stand? But there is forgiveness with You, that You may be feared. PSALM 130:3–4 •

Evening Reading

Sanctification by the Spirit and belief in the truth.
2 THESSALONIANS 2:13

Awake, O north wind, and come, O south! Blow upon my garden, that its spices may flow out. SONG OF SONGS 4:16 •

Observe this very thing, that you sorrowed in a godly manner: what diligence it produced in you, what clearing of yourselves, what indignation, what fear, what vehement desire, what zeal, what vindication! 2 CORINTHIANS 7:11 • (The fruit of the Spirit is in all goodness, righteousness, and truth), finding out what is acceptable to the Lord. EPHESIANS 5:9–10 •

The Father...will give you another Helper. JOHN 14:16 • The love of God has been poured out in our hearts by the Holy Spirit who was given to us. ROMANS 5:5 •

The fruit of the Spirit is love, joy, peace. GALATIANS 5:22 •

In a great trial of affliction the abundance of their joy and their deep poverty abounded in the riches of their liberality. 2 CORINTHIANS 8:2 •

One and the same Spirit works all these things, distributing to each one individually as He wills. 1 CORINTHIANS 12:11 •

July 18

Morning Reading

He calls his own sheep by name and leads them out.
JOHN 10:3

The solid foundation of God stands, having this seal: "The Lord knows those who are His," and, "Let everyone who names the name of Christ depart from iniquity." 2 TIMOTHY 2:19 • Many will say to Me in that day, "Lord, Lord, have we not prophesied in Your name, cast out demons in Your name, and done many wonders in Your name?" And then I will declare to them, "I never knew you; depart from Me, you who practice lawlessness!" MATTHEW 7:22–23 • The LORD knows the way of the righteous, but the way of the ungodly shall perish. PSALM 1:6 •

See, I have inscribed you on the palms of My hands; your walls are continually before Me. ISAIAH 49:16 • Set me as a seal upon your heart, as a seal upon your arm. SONG OF SONGS 8:6 • The LORD is good, a stronghold in the day of trouble; and He knows those who trust in Him. NAHUM 1:7 •

I go to prepare a place for you. And if I go and prepare a place for you, I will come again and receive you to Myself; that where I am, there you may be also. JOHN 14:2–3 •

Evening Reading

She has done what she could.
MARK 14:8

This poor widow has put in more than all. LUKE 21:3 • Whoever gives you a cup of water to drink in My name, because you belong to Christ, assuredly, I say to you, he will by no means lose his reward. MARK 9:41 • If there is first a willing mind, it is accepted according to what one has, and not according to what he does not have. 2 CORINTHIANS 8:12 •

Let us not love in word or in tongue, but in deed and in truth. 1 JOHN 3:18 • If a brother or sister is naked and destitute of daily food, and one of you says to them, "Depart in peace, be warmed and filled," but you do not give them the things which are needed for the body, what does it profit? JAMES 2:15–16 • But this I say: He who sows sparingly will also reap sparingly, and he who sows bountifully will also reap bountifully. 2 CORINTHIANS 9:6 • So let each one give as he purposes in his heart, not grudgingly or of necessity; for God loves a cheerful giver. 2 CORINTHIANS 9:7 •

So likewise you, when you have done all those things which you are commanded, say, "We are unprofitable servants. We have done what was our duty to do." LUKE 17:10 •

July 19

Morning Reading

He who is mighty has done great things for me,
and holy is His name.
Luke 1:49

Who is like You, O Lord, among the gods? Who is like You, glorious in holiness, fearful in praises, doing wonders? Exodus 15:11 • Among the gods there is none like You, O Lord; nor are there any works like Your works. Psalm 86:8 • Who shall not fear You, O Lord, and glorify Your name? For You alone are holy. Revelation 15:4 • Hallowed be Your name. Matthew 6:9 •

Blessed is the Lord God of Israel, for He has visited and redeemed His people. Luke 1:68 •

Who is this who comes from Edom, with dyed garments from Bozrah, this One who is glorious in His apparel, traveling in the greatness of His strength?; "I who speak in righteousness, mighty to save." Isaiah 63:1 • I have given help to one who is mighty; I have exalted one chosen from the people. Psalm 89:19 •

Now to Him who is able to do exceedingly abundantly above all that we ask or think, according to the power that works in us,...be glory. Ephesians 3:20–21 •

Evening Reading

The dew of Hermon.
Psalm 133:3

Mount Sion (that is, Hermon). Deuteronomy 4:48 • There the Lord commanded the blessing; life forevermore. Psalm 133:3 • I will be like the dew to Israel; he shall grow like the lily, and lengthen his roots like Lebanon. Hosea 14:5 •

Let my teaching drop as the rain, my speech distill as the dew, as raindrops on the tender herb, and as showers on the grass. Deuteronomy 32:2 • As the rain comes down, and the snow from heaven, and do not return there, but water the earth, and make it bring forth and bud, that it may give seed to the sower and bread to the eater, so shall My word be that goes forth from My mouth; it shall not return to Me void, but it shall accomplish what I please, and it shall prosper in the thing for which I sent it. Isaiah 55:10–11 •

God does not give the Spirit by measure. John 3:34 • And of His fullness we have all received, and grace for grace. John 1:16 • It is like the precious oil upon the head, running down on the beard, the beard of Aaron, running down on the edge of his garments. Psalm 133:2 •

July 20

Morning Reading

They are not of the world, just as I am not of the world.
JOHN 17:16

He is despised and rejected by men, a Man of sorrows and acquainted with grief. ISAIAH 53:3 • In the world you will have tribulation; but be of good cheer, I have overcome the world. JOHN 16:33 •

Such a High Priest was fitting for us, who is holy, harmless, unde-filed, separate from sinners. HEBREWS 7:26 • That you may become blame-less and harmless, children of God without fault in the midst of a crooked and perverse generation. PHILIPPIANS 2:15 •

Jesus of Nazareth...went about doing good and healing all who were oppressed by the devil, for God was with Him. ACTS 10:38 • Therefore, as we have opportunity, let us do good to all, especially to those who are of the household of faith. GALATIANS 6:10 •

That was the true Light which gives light to every man coming into the world. JOHN 1:9 • You are the light of the world. A city that is set on a hill cannot be hidden....Let your light so shine before men, that they may see your good works and glorify your Father in heaven. MATTHEW 5:14, 16 •

Evening Reading

He who is of a merry heart has a continual feast.
PROVERBS 15:15

The joy of the LORD is your strength. NEHEMIAH 8:10 • The kingdom of God is not eating and drinking, but righteousness and peace and joy in the Holy Spirit. ROMANS 14:17 • Be filled with the Spirit, speaking to one another in psalms and hymns and spiritual songs, singing and making melody in your heart to the Lord, giving thanks always for all things to God the Father in the name of our Lord Jesus Christ. EPHESIANS 5:18–20 •

By Him let us continually offer the sacrifice of praise to God, that is, the fruit of our lips, giving thanks to His name. HEBREWS 13:15 •

Though the fig tree may not blossom, nor fruit be on the vines; though the labor of the olive may fail, and the fields yield no food; though the flock may be cut off from the fold, and there be no herd in the stalls; yet I will rejoice in the LORD, I will joy in the God of my salva-tion. HABAKKUK 3:17–18 • Sorrowful, yet always rejoicing. 2 CORINTHIANS 6:10 • We also glory in tribulations. ROMANS 5:3 •

July 21

Morning Reading

What is the profit of circumcision?
ROMANS 3:1

Much in every way! ROMANS 3:2 • Circumcise yourselves to the LORD, and take away the foreskins of your hearts. JEREMIAH 4:4 • If their uncircumcised hearts are humbled, and they accept their guilt; then I will remember My covenant with Jacob, and My covenant with Isaac and My covenant with Abraham I will remember. LEVITICUS 26:41–42 •

Jesus Christ has become a servant to the circumcision for the truth of God, to confirm the promises made to the fathers. ROMANS 15:8 • In Him you were also circumcised with the circumcision made without hands, by putting off the body of the sins of the flesh, by the circumcision of Christ....You, being dead in your trespasses and the uncircumcision of your flesh, He has made alive together with Him, having forgiven you all trespasses. COLOSSIANS 2:11, 13 •

Put off, concerning your former conduct, the old man which grows corrupt according to the deceitful lusts, and be renewed in the spirit of your mind, and...put on the new man which was created according to God, in true righteousness and holiness. EPHESIANS 4:22–24 •

Evening Reading

The veil of the temple was torn in two from top to bottom.
MATTHEW 27:51

The Lord Jesus on the same night in which He was betrayed took bread; and when He had given thanks, He broke it and said, "Take, eat; this is My body which is broken for you; do this in remembrance of Me." 1 CORINTHIANS 11:23–24 • The bread that I shall give is My flesh, which I shall give for the life of the world. JOHN 6:51 •

[Jesus said,] "Unless you eat the flesh of the Son of Man and drink His blood, you have no life in you. Whoever eats My flesh and drinks My blood has eternal life, and I will raise him up at the last day....He who eats My flesh and drinks My blood abides in Me, and I in him. As the living Father sent Me, and I live because of the Father, so he who feeds on Me will live because of Me."...When Jesus knew in Himself that His disciples complained about this, He said to them, "Does this offend you? What then if you should see the Son of Man ascend where He was before? It is the Spirit who gives life; the flesh profits nothing." JOHN 6:53–54, 56–57, 61–63 •

Having boldness to enter the Holiest by the blood of Jesus, by a new and living way which He consecrated for us, through the veil, that is, His flesh,...let us draw near. HEBREWS 10:19–20, 22 •

July 22

Morning Reading

The death that He died, He died to sin once for all;
but the life that He lives, He lives to God.
ROMANS 6:10

He was numbered with the transgressors. ISAIAH 53:12 • Christ was offered once to bear the sins of many. HEBREWS 9:28 • Who Himself bore our sins in His own body on the tree, that we, having died to sins, might live for righteousness; by whose stripes you were healed. 1 PETER 2:24 • By one offering He has perfected forever those who are being sanctified. HEBREWS 10:14 •

But [Jesus], because He continues forever, has an unchangeable priesthood. Therefore He is also able to save to the uttermost those who come to God through Him, since He always lives to make intercession for them. HEBREWS 7:24–25 • While we were still sinners, Christ died for us. Much more then, having now been justified by His blood, we shall be saved from wrath through Him. ROMANS 5:8–9 •

Since Christ suffered for us in the flesh, arm yourselves also with the same mind, for he who has suffered in the flesh has ceased from sin, that he no longer should live the rest of his time in the flesh for the lusts of men, but for the will of God. 1 PETER 4:1–2 •

Evening Reading

Keep yourselves in the love of God.
JUDE 21

Abide in Me, and I in you. As the branch cannot bear fruit of itself, unless it abides in the vine, neither can you, unless you abide in Me. I am the vine, you are the branches. He who abides in Me, and I in him, bears much fruit; for without Me you can do nothing. JOHN 15:4–5 •

The fruit of the Spirit is love. GALATIANS 5:22 •

By this My Father is glorified, that you bear much fruit; so you will be My disciples. As the Father loved Me, I also have loved you; abide in My love. If you keep My commandments, you will abide in My love, just as I have kept My Father's commandments and abide in His love. JOHN 15:8–10 • Whoever keeps His word, truly the love of God is perfected in him. By this we know that we are in Him. 1 JOHN 2:5 •

This is My commandment, that you love one another as I have loved you. JOHN 15:12 • God demonstrates His own love toward us, in that while we were still sinners, Christ died for us. ROMANS 5:8 • God is love, and he who abides in love abides in God, and God in him. 1 JOHN 4:16 •

July 23

Morning Reading

Then comes the end.
1 CORINTHIANS 15:24

Of that day and hour no one knows, not even the angels in heaven, nor the Son, but only the Father. Take heed, watch and pray; for you do not know when the time is....And what I say to you, I say to all: Watch! MARK 13:32–33, 37 • The Lord is not slack concerning His promise, as some count slackness, but is longsuffering toward us, not willing that any should perish but that all should come to repentance. 2 PETER 3:9 • The coming of the Lord is at hand....The Judge is standing at the door! JAMES 5:8–9 • Surely I am coming quickly. REVELATION 22:20 •

Since all these things will be dissolved, what manner of persons ought you to be in holy conduct and godliness? 2 PETER 3:11 •

The end of all things is at hand; therefore be serious and watchful in your prayers. 1 PETER 4:7 • Let your waist be girded and your lamps burning; and you yourselves be like men who wait for their master, when he will return from the wedding, that when he comes and knocks they may open to him immediately. LUKE 12:35–36 •

Evening Reading

Brethren, pray for us.
1 THESSALONIANS 5:25

Is anyone among you sick? Let him call for the elders of the church, and let them pray over him, anointing him with oil in the name of the Lord. And the prayer of faith will save the sick, and the Lord will raise him up....Pray for one another, that you may be healed. The effective, fervent prayer of a righteous man avails much. Elijah was a man with a nature like ours, and he prayed earnestly that it would not rain; and it did not rain on the land for three years and six months. And he prayed again, and the heaven gave rain, and the earth produced its fruit. JAMES 5:14–18 •

Praying always with all prayer and supplication in the Spirit, being watchful to this end with all perseverance and supplication for all the saints. EPHESIANS 6:18 •

Without ceasing I make mention of you always in my prayers. ROMANS 1:9 • Always laboring fervently for you in prayers, that you may stand perfect and complete in all the will of God. COLOSSIANS 4:12 •

July 24

Morning Reading

Patient in tribulation.
ROMANS 12:12

It is the LORD. Let Him do what seems good to Him. 1 SAMUEL 3:18 • Though I were righteous, I could not answer Him; I would beg mercy of my Judge. JOB 9:15 • The LORD gave, and the LORD has taken away; blessed be the name of the LORD. JOB 1:21 • Shall we indeed accept good from God, and shall we not accept adversity? JOB 2:10 •

Jesus wept. JOHN 11:35 • A Man of sorrows and acquainted with grief....Surely He has borne our griefs and carried our sorrows. ISAIAH 53:3–4 •

Whom the LORD loves He chastens, and scourges every son whom He receives....Now no chastening seems to be joyful for the present, but painful; nevertheless, afterward it yields the peaceable fruit of righteousness to those who have been trained by it. HEBREWS 12:6, 11 • Strengthened with all might, according to His glorious power, for all patience and longsuffering with joy. COLOSSIANS 1:11 • In the world you will have tribulation; but be of good cheer, I have overcome the world. JOHN 16:33 •

Evening Reading

He did not waver at the promise of God through unbelief.
ROMANS 4:20

Have faith in God....Whoever says to this mountain, "Be removed and be cast into the sea," and does not doubt in his heart, but believes that those things he says will be done, he will have whatever he says. Therefore I say to you, whatever things you ask when you pray, believe that you receive them, and you will have them. MARK 11:22–24 • Without faith it is impossible to please Him, for he who comes to God must believe that He is, and that He is a rewarder of those who diligently seek Him. HEBREWS 11:6 •

He who had received the promises offered up his only begotten son, of whom it was said, "In Isaac your seed shall be called," concluding that God was able to raise him up, even from the dead. HEBREWS 11:17–19 • Being fully convinced that what He had promised He was also able to perform. ROMANS 4:21 •

Is anything too hard for the LORD? GENESIS 18:14 • With God all things are possible. MATTHEW 19:26 • [Lord,] increase our faith. LUKE 17:5 •

July 25

Morning Reading

We know that we have passed from death to life.
1 John 3:14

He who hears My word and believes in Him who sent Me has everlasting life, and shall not come into judgment, but has passed from death into life. John 5:24 • He who has the Son has life; he who does not have the Son of God does not have life. 1 John 5:12 •

He who establishes us with you in Christ and has anointed us is God, who also has sealed us and given us the Spirit in our hearts. 2 Corinthians 1:21–22 • By this we know that we are of the truth, and shall assure our hearts before Him....Beloved, if our heart does not condemn us, we have confidence toward God. 1 John 3:19, 21 • We know that we are of God, and the whole world lies under the sway of the wicked one. 1 John 5:19 •

You He made alive, who were dead in trespasses and sins. Ephesians 2:1 • Made...alive together with Christ. Ephesians 2:5 • He has delivered us from the power of darkness and conveyed us into the kingdom of the Son of His love. Colossians 1:13 •

Evening Reading

You will show me the path of life.
Psalm 16:11

Thus says the Lord: "Behold, I set before you the way of life and the way of death." Jeremiah 21:8 • I will teach you the good and the right way. 1 Samuel 12:23 • I am the way, the truth, and the life. No one comes to the Father except through Me. John 14:6 • Follow Me. Matthew 4:19 •

There is a way that seems right to a man, but its end is the way of death. Proverbs 14:12 • Wide is the gate and broad is the way that leads to destruction, and there are many who go in by it. Because narrow is the gate and difficult is the way which leads to life, and there are few who find it. Matthew 7:13–14 •

A highway shall be there, and a road, and it shall be called the Highway of Holiness. The unclean shall not pass over it, but it shall be for others. Whoever walks the road, although a fool, shall not go astray. Isaiah 35:8 • Let us know, let us pursue the knowledge of the Lord. Hosea 6:3 •

In My Father's house are many mansions; if it were not so, I would have told you. I go to prepare a place for you. John 14:2 •

July 26

Morning Reading

By faith Abraham obeyed when he was called to go out to the place
which he would receive as an inheritance.
HEBREWS 11:8

He will choose our inheritance for us. PSALM 47:4 • He encircled him, He instructed him, He kept him as the apple of His eye. As an eagle stirs up its nest, hovers over its young, spreading out its wings, taking them up, carrying them on its wings, so the LORD alone led him, and there was no foreign god with him. DEUTERONOMY 32:10–12 •

I am the LORD your God, who teaches you to profit, who leads you by the way you should go. ISAIAH 48:17 • Who teaches like Him? JOB 36:22 •

We walk by faith, not by sight. 2 CORINTHIANS 5:7 • Here we have no continuing city, but we seek the one to come. HEBREWS 13:14 • Beloved, I beg you as sojourners and pilgrims, abstain from fleshly lusts which war against the soul. 1 PETER 2:11 • Arise and depart, for this is not your rest; because it is defiled, it shall destroy, yes, with utter destruction. MICAH 2:10 •

Evening Reading

Give thanks at the remembrance of His holy name.
PSALM 97:12

The heavens are not pure in His sight, how much less man, who is abominable and filthy, who drinks iniquity like water! JOB 15:15–16 • The stars are not pure in His sight, how much less man, who is a maggot? JOB 25:5–6 •

Who is like You, O LORD, among the gods? Who is like You, glorious in holiness? EXODUS 15:11 • Holy, holy, holy is the LORD of hosts. ISAIAH 6:3 •

As He who called you is holy, you also be holy in all your conduct, because it is written, "Be holy, for I am holy." 1 PETER 1:15–16 • Partakers of His holiness. HEBREWS 12:10 •

The temple of God is holy, which temple you are. 1 CORINTHIANS 3:17 • What manner of persons ought you to be in holy conduct and godliness?... Without spot and blameless. 2 PETER 3:11, 14 •

Let no corrupt word proceed out of your mouth, but what is good for necessary edification, that it may impart grace to the hearers. And do not grieve the Holy Spirit of God, by whom you were sealed for the day of redemption. EPHESIANS 4:29–30 •

July 27

Morning Reading

Christ, who is the image of God.
2 CORINTHIANS 4:4

The glory of the LORD shall be revealed, and all flesh shall see it together. ISAIAH 40:5 • No one has seen God at any time. The only begotten Son, who is in the bosom of the Father, He has declared Him. JOHN 1:18 • And the Word became flesh and dwelt among us, and we beheld His glory, the glory as of the only begotten of the Father, full of grace and truth. JOHN 1:14 • He who has seen Me has seen the Father. JOHN 14:9 • The brightness of His glory and the express image of His person. HEBREWS 1:3 • God was manifested in the flesh. 1 TIMOTHY 3:16 •

In whom we have redemption through His blood, the forgiveness of sins. He is the image of the invisible God, the firstborn over all creation. COLOSSIANS 1:14–15 • Whom He foreknew, He also predestined to be conformed to the image of His Son, that He might be the firstborn among many brethren. ROMANS 8:29 •

As we have borne the image of the man of dust, we shall also bear the image of the heavenly Man. 1 CORINTHIANS 15:49 •

Evening Reading

You have armed me with strength for the battle.
PSALM 18:39

When I am weak, then I am strong. 2 CORINTHIANS 12:10 •

Asa cried out to the LORD his God, and said, "LORD, it is nothing for You to help, whether with many or with those who have no power; help us, O LORD our God, for we rest on You, and in Your name we go against this multitude. O LORD, You are our God; do not let man prevail against You!" 2 CHRONICLES 14:11 • Jehoshaphat cried out, and the LORD helped him, and God diverted them from him. 2 CHRONICLES 18:31 •

It is better to trust in the LORD than to put confidence in man. It is better to trust in the LORD than to put confidence in princes. PSALM 118:8–9 • No king is saved by the multitude of an army; a mighty man is not delivered by great strength. A horse is a vain hope for safety; neither shall it deliver any by its great strength. PSALM 33:16–17 •

We do not wrestle against flesh and blood, but against principalities, against powers, against the rulers of the darkness of this age, against spiritual hosts of wickedness in the heavenly places. Therefore take up the whole armor of God. EPHESIANS 6:12–13 •

July 28

Morning Reading

Walk in love.
EPHESIANS 5:2

A new commandment I give to you, that you love one another; as I have loved you, that you also love one another. JOHN 13:34 • Above all things have fervent love for one another, for "love will cover a multitude of sins." 1 PETER 4:8 • Love covers all sins. PROVERBS 10:12 •

Whenever you stand praying, if you have anything against anyone, forgive him, that your Father in heaven may also forgive you your trespasses. MARK 11:25 • Love your enemies, do good, and lend, hoping for nothing in return. LUKE 6:35 • Do not rejoice when your enemy falls, and do not let your heart be glad when he stumbles. PROVERBS 24:17 • Not returning evil for evil or reviling for reviling, but on the contrary blessing, knowing that you were called to this, that you may inherit a blessing. 1 PETER 3:9 • If it is possible, as much as depends on you, live peaceably with all men. ROMANS 12:18 • Be kind to one another, tenderhearted, forgiving one another, just as God in Christ forgave you. EPHESIANS 4:32 •

My little children, let us not love in word or in tongue, but in deed and in truth. 1 JOHN 3:18 •

Evening Reading

Let your requests be made known to God.
PHILIPPIANS 4:6

Abba, Father, all things are possible for You. Take this cup away from Me; nevertheless, not what I will, but what You will. MARK 14:36 • A thorn in the flesh was given to me, a messenger of Satan to buffet me, lest I be exalted above measure. Concerning this thing I pleaded with the Lord three times that it might depart from me. And He said to me, "My grace is sufficient for you, for My strength is made perfect in weakness." Therefore most gladly I will rather boast in my infirmities. 2 CORINTHIANS 12:7–9 •

I pour out my complaint before Him; I declare before Him my trouble. PSALM 142:2 • [Hannah] was in bitterness of soul, and prayed to the LORD and wept in anguish. Then she made a vow and said, "O LORD of hosts, if You will indeed look on the affliction of Your maidservant and...will give Your maidservant a male child, then I will give him to the LORD all the days of his life."...And the LORD remembered her. 1 SAMUEL 1:10–11, 19 •

We do not know what we should pray for as we ought. ROMANS 8:26 • He will choose our inheritance for us. PSALM 47:4 •

July 29

Morning Reading

Oh, that You would rend the heavens!
That You would come down!
ISAIAH 64:1

Make haste, my beloved, and be like a gazelle or a young stag on the mountains of spices. SONG OF SONGS 8:14 • We ourselves groan within ourselves, eagerly waiting for the adoption, the redemption of our body. ROMANS 8:23 • Bow down Your heavens, O LORD, and come down; touch the mountains, and they shall smoke. PSALM 144:5 •

This same Jesus, who was taken up from you into heaven, will so come in like manner as you saw Him go into heaven. ACTS 1:11 • To those who eagerly wait for Him He will appear a second time, apart from sin, for salvation. HEBREWS 9:28 • It will be said in that day: "Behold, this is our God; we have waited for Him, and He will save us. This is the LORD; we have waited for Him; we will be glad and rejoice in His salvation." ISAIAH 25:9 •

He who testifies to these things says, "Surely I am coming quickly." Amen. Even so, come, Lord Jesus! REVELATION 22:20 • The blessed hope and glorious appearing of our great God and Savior Jesus Christ. TITUS 2:13 • Our citizenship is in heaven. PHILIPPIANS 3:20 •

Evening Reading

You have given me the heritage of those who fear Your name.
PSALM 61:5

"No weapon formed against you shall prosper, and every tongue which rises against you in judgment you shall condemn. This is the heritage of the servants of the LORD, and their righteousness is from Me," says the LORD. ISAIAH 54:17 •

The angel of the LORD encamps all around those who fear Him, and delivers them. Oh, taste and see that the LORD is good; blessed is the man who trusts in Him! Oh, fear the LORD, you His saints! There is no want to those who fear Him. The young lions lack and suffer hunger; but those who seek the LORD shall not lack any good thing. PSALM 34:7–10 • The lines have fallen to me in pleasant places; yes, I have a good inheritance. PSALM 16:6 •

To you who fear My name the Sun of Righteousness shall arise with healing in His wings; and you shall go out and grow fat like stall-fed calves. MALACHI 4:2 • He who did not spare His own Son, but delivered Him up for us all, how shall He not with Him also freely give us all things? ROMANS 8:32 •

July 30

Morning Reading

Seek those things which are above, where Christ is,
sitting at the right hand of God.
COLOSSIANS 3:1

Get wisdom! Get understanding! PROVERBS 4:5 • The wisdom that is from above. JAMES 3:17 • The deep says, "[Wisdom] is not in me"; and the sea says, "It is not with me." JOB 28:14 • We were buried with Him through baptism into death, that just as Christ was raised from the dead by the glory of the Father, even so we also should walk in newness of life. For if we have been united together in the likeness of His death, certainly we also shall be in the likeness of His resurrection. ROMANS 6:4–5 •

Let us lay aside every weight, and the sin which so easily ensnares us, and let us run with endurance the race that is set before us. HEBREWS 12:1 • God...made us alive together with Christ (by grace you have been saved), and raised us up together, and made us sit together in the heavenly places in Christ Jesus. EPHESIANS 2:4–6 •

Those who say such things declare plainly that they seek a homeland. HEBREWS 11:14 • Seek the LORD, all you meek of the earth, who have upheld His justice. Seek righteousness, seek humility. ZEPHANIAH 2:3 •

Evening Reading

Nicodemus (he who came to Jesus by night).
JOHN 7:50

Peter followed [Jesus] at a distance. MATTHEW 26:58 • Among the rulers many believed in Him, but because of the Pharisees they did not confess Him, lest they should be put out of the synagogue; for they loved the praise of men more than the praise of God. JOHN 12:42–43 • The fear of man brings a snare, but whoever trusts in the LORD shall be safe. PROVERBS 29:25 •

The one who comes to Me I will by no means cast out. JOHN 6:37 • A bruised reed He will not break, and smoking flax He will not quench. ISAIAH 42:3 • Faith as a mustard seed. MATTHEW 17:20 •

God has not given us a spirit of fear, but of power and of love and of a sound mind. Therefore do not be ashamed of the testimony of our Lord. 2 TIMOTHY 1:7–8 • Little children, abide in Him, that when He appears, we may have confidence and not be ashamed before Him at His coming. 1 JOHN 2:28 • Whoever confesses Me before men, him I will also confess before My Father who is in heaven. MATTHEW 10:32 •

July 31

Morning Reading

Endure hardship as a good soldier of Jesus Christ.
2 TIMOTHY 2:3

Indeed I have given him as a witness to the people, a leader and commander for the people. ISAIAH 55:4 • It was fitting for Him, for whom are all things and by whom are all things, in bringing many sons to glory, to make the captain of their salvation perfect through sufferings. HEBREWS 2:10 • We must through many tribulations enter the kingdom of God. ACTS 14:22 •

For we do not wrestle against flesh and blood, but against principalities, against powers, against the rulers of the darkness of this age, against spiritual hosts of wickedness in the heavenly places. Therefore take up the whole armor of God. EPHESIANS 6:12–13 • We do not war according to the flesh. For the weapons of our warfare are not carnal but mighty in God for pulling down strongholds. 2 CORINTHIANS 10:3–4 •

May the God of all grace, who called us to His eternal glory by Christ Jesus, after you have suffered a while, perfect, establish, strengthen, and settle you. 1 PETER 5:10 •

Evening Reading

The unity of the Spirit.
EPHESIANS 4:3

There is one body and one Spirit. EPHESIANS 4:4 • Through Him we both have access by one Spirit to the Father. Now, therefore, you are no longer strangers and foreigners, but fellow citizens with the saints and members of the household of God, having been built on the foundation of the apostles and prophets, Jesus Christ Himself being the chief cornerstone, in whom the whole building, being joined together, grows into a holy temple in the Lord, in whom you also are being built together for a dwelling place of God in the Spirit. EPHESIANS 2:18–22 •

Behold, how good and how pleasant it is for brethren to dwell together in unity! It is like the precious oil upon the head, running down on the beard, the beard of Aaron, running down on the edge of his garments. PSALM 133:1–2 •

Since you have purified your souls in obeying the truth through the Spirit in sincere love of the brethren, love one another fervently with a pure heart. 1 PETER 1:22 •

 AUGUST

August 1

Morning Reading

The fruit of the Spirit is...[faith].
GALATIANS 5:22

By grace you have been saved through faith, and that not of yourselves; it is the gift of God. EPHESIANS 2:8 • Without faith it is impossible to please Him. HEBREWS 11:6 • He who believes in Him is not condemned; but he who does not believe is condemned already, because he has not believed in the name of the only begotten Son of God. JOHN 3:18 • Lord, I believe; help my unbelief! MARK 9:24 •

Whoever keeps His word, truly the love of God is perfected in him. By this we know that we are in Him. 1 JOHN 2:5 • Faith working through love. GALATIANS 5:6 • Faith without works is dead. JAMES 2:20 •

We walk by faith, not by sight. 2 CORINTHIANS 5:7 • I have been crucified with Christ; it is no longer I who live, but Christ lives in me; and the life which I now live in the flesh I live by faith in the Son of God, who loved me and gave Himself for me. GALATIANS 2:20 • Whom having not seen you love. Though now you do not see Him, yet believing, you rejoice with joy inexpressible and full of glory, receiving the end of your faith; the salvation of your souls. 1 PETER 1:8–9 •

Evening Reading

The Lord is very compassionate and merciful.
JAMES 5:11

As a father pities his children, so the LORD pities those who fear Him. PSALM 103:13 • The LORD is gracious and full of compassion. He has given food to those who fear Him; He will ever be mindful of His covenant. PSALM 111:4–5 •

He who keeps you will not slumber. Behold, He who keeps Israel shall neither slumber nor sleep. PSALM 121:3–4 • As an eagle stirs up its nest, hovers over its young, spreading out its wings, taking them up, carrying them on its wings, so the LORD alone led him, and there was no foreign god with him. DEUTERONOMY 32:11–12 •

His compassions fail not. They are new every morning; great is Your faithfulness. LAMENTATIONS 3:22–23 •

When Jesus went out He saw a great multitude; and He was moved with compassion for them, and healed their sick. MATTHEW 14:14 • Jesus Christ is the same yesterday, today, and forever. HEBREWS 13:8 •

The very hairs of your head are all numbered. MATTHEW 10:30 • Are not two sparrows sold for a copper coin? And not one of them falls to the ground apart from your Father's will....Do not fear therefore; you are of more value than many sparrows. MATTHEW 10:29, 31 •

August 2

Morning Reading

The Lamb slain from the foundation of the world.
REVELATION 13:8

Your lamb shall be without blemish, a male of the first year....Then the whole assembly of the congregation of Israel shall kill it at twilight. And they shall take some of the blood and put it on the two doorposts and on the lintel of the houses where they eat it....And when I see the blood, I will pass over you. EXODUS 12:5–7, 13 • The blood of sprinkling. HEBREWS 12:24 • Christ, our Passover, was sacrificed for us. 1 CORINTHIANS 5:7 • Being delivered by the determined purpose and foreknowledge of God. ACTS 2:23 • According to His own purpose and grace which was given to us in Christ Jesus before time began. 2 TIMOTHY 1:9 •

We have redemption through His blood, the forgiveness of sins. EPHESIANS 1:7 •

Therefore, since Christ suffered for us in the flesh, arm yourselves also with the same mind, for he who has suffered in the flesh has ceased from sin, that he no longer should live the rest of his time in the flesh for the lusts of men, but for the will of God. 1 PETER 4:1–2 •

Evening Reading

I have trodden the winepress alone.
ISAIAH 63:3

Who is like You, O LORD, among the gods? Who is like You, glorious in holiness, fearful in praises, doing wonders? EXODUS 15:11 • He saw that there was no man, and wondered that there was no intercessor; therefore His own arm brought salvation for Him; and His own righteousness, it sustained Him. ISAIAH 59:16 • Who Himself bore our sins in His own body on the tree. 1 PETER 2:24 • Having become a curse for us. GALATIANS 3:13 •

Oh, sing to the LORD a new song! For He has done marvelous things; His right hand and His holy arm have gained Him the victory. PSALM 98:1 • Having disarmed principalities and powers, He made a public spectacle of them, triumphing over them in it. COLOSSIANS 2:15 • He shall see the labor of His soul, and be satisfied. By His knowledge My righteous Servant shall justify many, for He shall bear their iniquities. ISAIAH 53:11 •

O my soul, march on in strength! JUDGES 5:21 • We are more than conquerors through Him who loved us. ROMANS 8:37 • They overcame...by the blood of the Lamb and by the word of their testimony. REVELATION 12:11 •

August 3

Morning Reading

His mercy is on those who fear Him.
LUKE 1:50

Oh, how great is Your goodness, which You have laid up for those who fear You, which You have prepared for those who trust in You in the presence of the sons of men! You shall hide them in the secret place of Your presence from the plots of man; You shall keep them secretly in a pavilion from the strife of tongues. PSALM 31:19–20 •

If you call on the Father, who without partiality judges according to each one's work, conduct yourselves throughout the time of your stay here in fear. 1 PETER 1:17 • The LORD is near to all who call upon Him... in truth. He will fulfill the desire of those who fear Him; He also will hear their cry and save them. PSALM 145:18–19 •

"Because your heart was tender, and you humbled yourself before the LORD...and you tore your clothes and wept before Me, I also have heard you," says the LORD. 2 KINGS 22:19 • On this one will I look: on him who is poor and of a contrite spirit, and who trembles at My word. ISAIAH 66:2 • The LORD is near to those who have a broken heart, and saves such as have a contrite spirit. PSALM 34:18 •

Evening Reading

Those who honor Me I will honor.
1 SAMUEL 2:30

Whoever confesses Me before men, him I will also confess before My Father who is in heaven. MATTHEW 10:32 • He who loves father or mother more than Me is not worthy of Me. And he who loves son or daughter more than Me is not worthy of Me. And he who does not take his cross and follow after Me is not worthy of Me. He who finds his life will lose it, and he who loses his life for My sake will find it. MATTHEW 10:37–39 •

Blessed is the man who endures temptation; for when he has been approved, he will receive the crown of life which the Lord has promised to those who love Him. JAMES 1:12 •

Do not fear any of those things which you are about to suffer....Be faithful until death, and I will give you the crown of life. REVELATION 2:10 •

Our light affliction, which is but for a moment, is working for us a far more exceeding and eternal weight of glory. 2 CORINTHIANS 4:17 • Praise, honor, and glory at the revelation of Jesus Christ. 1 PETER 1:7 •

August 4

Morning Reading

*[Jesus] said, "It is finished!" And bowing His head,
He gave up His spirit.*
JOHN 19:30

Jesus, the author and finisher of our faith. HEBREWS 12:2 • I have glorified You on the earth. I have finished the work which You have given Me to do. JOHN 17:4 • We have been sanctified through the offering of the body of Jesus Christ once for all. And every priest stands ministering daily and offering repeatedly the same sacrifices, which can never take away sins. But this Man, after He had offered one sacrifice for sins forever, sat down at the right hand of God, from that time waiting till His enemies are made His footstool. For by one offering He has perfected forever those who are being sanctified. HEBREWS 10:10–14 • Having wiped out the handwriting of requirements that was against us, which was contrary to us. And He has taken it out of the way, having nailed it to the cross. COLOSSIANS 2:14 •

Therefore My Father loves Me, because I lay down My life that I may take it again. No one takes it from Me, but I lay it down of Myself. I have power to lay it down, and I have power to take it again. JOHN 10:17–18 • Greater love has no one than this, than to lay down one's life for his friends. JOHN 15:13 •

Evening Reading

He sent from above, He took me; He drew me out of many waters.
PSALM 18:16

He also brought me up out of a horrible pit, out of the miry clay, and set my feet upon a rock, and established my steps. PSALM 40:2 • You He made alive, who were dead in trespasses and sins, in which you once walked according to the course of this world....We all once conducted ourselves in the lusts of our flesh. EPHESIANS 2:1–3 •

Hear my cry, O God; attend to my prayer. From the end of the earth I will cry to You, when my heart is overwhelmed. PSALM 61:1-2 • Out of the belly of Sheol I cried, and You heard my voice. For You cast me into the deep, into the heart of the seas, and the floods surrounded me; all Your billows and Your waves passed over me. JONAH 2:2-3 • We went through fire and through water; but You brought us out to rich fulfillment. PSALM 66:12 •

When you pass through the waters, I will be with you; and through the rivers, they shall not overflow you. ISAIAH 43:2 •

August 5

Morning Reading

Walk in newness of life.
ROMANS 6:4

As you presented your members as slaves of uncleanness, and of lawlessness leading to more lawlessness, so now present your members as slaves of righteousness for holiness. ROMANS 6:19 • I beseech you therefore, brethren, by the mercies of God, that you present your bodies a living sacrifice, holy, acceptable to God, which is your reasonable service. And do not be conformed to this world, but be transformed by the renewing of your mind. ROMANS 12:1–2 •

If anyone is in Christ, he is a new creation; old things have passed away; behold, all things have become new. 2 CORINTHIANS 5:17 • In Christ Jesus neither circumcision nor uncircumcision avails anything, but a new creation. And as many as walk according to this rule, peace and mercy be upon them. GALATIANS 6:15–16 • This I say, therefore, and testify in the Lord, that you should no longer walk as the rest of the Gentiles walk, in the futility of their mind....You have not so learned Christ, if indeed you have heard Him and have been taught by Him, as the truth is in Jesus:...that you put on the new man which was created according to God, in true righteousness and holiness. EPHESIANS 4:17, 20–21, 24 •

Evening Reading

Your will be done.
MATTHEW 26:42

O LORD, I know the way of man is not in himself; it is not in man who walks to direct his own steps. JEREMIAH 10:23 • Not as I will, but as You will. MATTHEW 26:39 • Surely I have calmed and quieted my soul, like a weaned child with his mother; like a weaned child is my soul within me. PSALM 131:2 •

We do not know what we should pray for as we ought, but the Spirit Himself makes intercession for us with groanings which cannot be uttered. Now He who searches the hearts knows what the mind of the Spirit is, because He makes intercession for the saints according to the will of God. ROMANS 8:26–27 •

You do not know what you ask. MATTHEW 20:22 • He gave them their request, but sent leanness into their soul. PSALM 106:15 • These things became our examples, to the intent that we should not lust after evil things as they also lusted. 1 CORINTHIANS 10:6 •

I want you to be without care. 1 CORINTHIANS 7:32 • You will keep him in perfect peace, whose mind is stayed on You, because he trusts in You. ISAIAH 26:3 •

August 6

Morning Reading

Whom the Lord loves He corrects.
PROVERBS 3:12

See that I, even I, am He, and there is no God besides Me; I kill and I make alive; I wound and I heal; nor is there any who can deliver from My hand. DEUTERONOMY 32:39 • I know the thoughts that I think toward you, says the LORD, thoughts of peace and not of evil, to give you a future and a hope. JEREMIAH 29:11 • "My thoughts are not your thoughts, nor are your ways My ways," says the LORD. ISAIAH 55:8 •

I will allure her, will bring her into the wilderness, and speak comfort to her. HOSEA 2:14 • As a man chastens his son, so the LORD your God chastens you. DEUTERONOMY 8:5 • Now no chastening seems to be joyful for the present, but painful; nevertheless, afterward it yields the peaceable fruit of righteousness to those who have been trained by it. HEBREWS 12:11 • Therefore humble yourselves under the mighty hand of God, that He may exalt you in due time. 1 PETER 5:6 •

I know, O LORD, that Your judgments are right, and that in faithfulness You have afflicted me. PSALM 119:75 •

Evening Reading

The earth is the Lord's, and all its fullness.
PSALM 24:1

She did not know that I gave her grain, new wine, and oil, and multiplied her silver and gold; which they prepared for Baal. Therefore I will return and take away My grain in its time and My new wine in its season, and will take back My wool and My linen. HOSEA 2:8–9 •

All things come from You, and of Your own we have given You. For we are aliens and pilgrims before You, as were all our fathers; our days on earth are as a shadow, and without hope. O LORD our God, all this abundance...is from Your hand, and is all Your own. 1 CHRONICLES 29:14–16 • Of Him and through Him and to Him are all things, to whom be glory forever. Amen. ROMANS 11:36 •

The living God...gives us richly all things to enjoy. 1 TIMOTHY 6:17 • Every creature of God is good, and nothing is to be refused if it is received with thanksgiving; for it is sanctified by the word of God and prayer. 1 TIMOTHY 4:4–5 •

My God shall supply all your need according to His riches in glory by Christ Jesus. PHILIPPIANS 4:19 •

August 7

Morning Reading

The Helper, the Holy Spirit, whom the Father will send in My name.
JOHN 14:26

If you knew the gift of God, and who it is who says to you, "Give Me a drink," you would have asked Him, and He would have given you living water. JOHN 4:10 • If you then, being evil, know how to give good gifts to your children, how much more will your heavenly Father give the Holy Spirit to those who ask Him! LUKE 11:13 • Most assuredly, I say to you, whatever you ask the Father in My name He will give you. Until now you have asked nothing in My name. Ask, and you will receive, that your joy may be full. JOHN 16:23–24 • You do not have because you do not ask. JAMES 4:2 •

When...the Spirit of truth, has come, He will guide you into all truth; for He will not speak on His own authority, but whatever He hears He will speak; and He will tell you things to come. He will glorify Me, for He will take of what is Mine and declare it to you. JOHN 16:13–14 •

They rebelled and grieved His Holy Spirit; so He turned Himself against them as an enemy, and He fought against them. ISAIAH 63:10 •

Evening Reading

What do you think about the Christ?
MATTHEW 22:42

Lift up your heads, O you gates! Lift up, you everlasting doors! And the King of glory shall come in. Who is this King of glory? The LORD of hosts, He is the King of glory. PSALM 24:9–10 • He has on His robe and on His thigh a name written: KING OF KINGS AND LORD OF LORDS. REVELATION 19:16 •

To you who believe, He is precious; but to those who are disobedient, "The stone which the builders rejected has become the chief cornerstone." 1 PETER 2:7 • Christ crucified, to the Jews a stumbling block and to the Greeks foolishness, but to those who are called, both Jews and Greeks, Christ the power of God and the wisdom of God. 1 CORINTHIANS 1:23–24 •

I also count all things loss for the excellence of the knowledge of Christ Jesus my Lord, for whom I have suffered the loss of all things, and count them as rubbish, that I may gain Christ. PHILIPPIANS 3:8 • Lord, You know all things; You know that I love You. JOHN 21:17 •

August 8

Morning Reading

The path of the just is like the shining sun,
that shines ever brighter unto the perfect day.
PROVERBS 4:18

Not that I have already attained, or am already perfected; but I press on, that I may lay hold of that for which Christ Jesus has also laid hold of me. PHILIPPIANS 3:12 • Let us know, let us pursue the knowledge of the LORD. HOSEA 6:3 •

Then the righteous will shine forth as the sun in the kingdom of their Father. MATTHEW 13:43 • We all, with unveiled face, beholding as in a mirror the glory of the Lord, are being transformed into the same image from glory to glory, just as by the Spirit of the Lord. 2 CORINTHIANS 3:18 • When that which is perfect has come, then that which is in part will be done away....For now we see in a mirror, dimly, but then face to face. Now I know in part, but then I shall know just as I also am known. 1 CORINTHIANS 13:10, 12 • Beloved, now we are children of God; and it has not yet been revealed what we shall be, but we know that when He is revealed, we shall be like Him, for we shall see Him as He is. And everyone who has this hope in Him purifies himself, just as He is pure. 1 JOHN 3:2–3 •

Evening Reading

Whoever calls on the name of the LORD shall be saved.
ROMANS 10:13

The one who comes to Me I will by no means cast out. JOHN 6:37 • [The thief on the cross] said to Jesus, "Lord, remember me when You come into Your kingdom." And Jesus said to him, "Assuredly, I say to you, today you will be with Me in Paradise." LUKE 23:42–43 • [Jesus] said, "What do you want Me to do for you?" They said to Him, "Lord, that our eyes may be opened." So Jesus had compassion and touched their eyes. And immediately their eyes received sight, and they followed Him. MATTHEW 20:32–34 •

If you then, being evil, know how to give good gifts to your children, how much more will your heavenly Father give the Holy Spirit to those who ask Him! LUKE 11:13 • I will put My Spirit within you. EZEKIEL 36:27 • Thus says the Lord GOD: "I will also let the house of Israel inquire of Me to do this for them." EZEKIEL 36:37 •

This is the confidence that we have in Him, that if we ask anything according to His will, He hears us. And if we know that He hears us, whatever we ask, we know that we have the petitions that we have asked of Him. 1 JOHN 5:14–15 •

August 9

Morning Reading

You are all fair, my love, and there is no spot in you.
SONG OF SONGS 4:7

The whole head is sick, and the whole heart faints. From the sole of the foot even to the head, there is no soundness in it, but wounds and bruises and putrefying sores; they have not been closed or bound up, or soothed with ointment. ISAIAH 1:5–6 • We are all like an unclean thing, and all our righteousnesses are like filthy rags. ISAIAH 64:6 • I know that in me (that is, in my flesh) nothing good dwells. ROMANS 7:18 •

You were washed,...you were sanctified,...you were justified in the name of the Lord Jesus and by the Spirit of our God. 1 CORINTHIANS 6:11 • The royal daughter is all glorious within. PSALM 45:13 • "Your beauty...was perfect through My splendor which I had bestowed on you," says the Lord GOD. EZEKIEL 16:14 •

Let the beauty of the LORD our God be upon us. PSALM 90:17 •

These are the ones who...washed their robes and made them white in the blood of the Lamb. REVELATION 7:14 • A glorious church, not having spot or wrinkle or any such thing, but...holy and without blemish. EPHESIANS 5:27 • You are complete in Him. COLOSSIANS 2:10 •

Evening Reading

Broken cisterns that can hold no water.
JEREMIAH 2:13

Eve...bore Cain, and said, "I have acquired a man from the LORD." GENESIS 4:1 •

[Men] said, "Come, let us build ourselves a city, and a tower whose top is in the heavens."...So the LORD scattered them. GENESIS 11:4, 8 • Lot chose for himself all the plain of Jordan. GENESIS 13:11 • It was well watered everywhere...like the garden of the LORD,...but the men of Sodom were exceedingly wicked and sinful against the LORD. GENESIS 13:10, 13 •

I set my heart to know wisdom and to know madness and folly. I perceived that this also is grasping for the wind. For in much wisdom is much grief, and he who increases knowledge increases sorrow. ECCLESIASTES 1:17–18 • I made my works great, I built myself houses, and planted myself vineyards....I also gathered for myself silver and gold.... Then I looked on all...and indeed all was vanity and grasping for the wind. ECCLESIASTES 2:4, 8, 11 •

If anyone thirsts, let him come to Me and drink. JOHN 7:37 • He satisfies the longing soul, and fills the hungry soul with goodness. PSALM 107:9 •

Set your mind on things above, not on things on the earth. COLOSSIANS 3:2 •

August 10

Morning Reading

I do not pray that You should take them out of the world,
but that You should keep them from the evil one.
JOHN 17:15

Blameless and harmless, children of God without fault in the midst of a crooked and perverse generation, among whom you shine as lights in the world. PHILIPPIANS 2:15 • You are the salt of the earth,...the light of the world....Let your light so shine before men, that they may see your good works and glorify your Father in heaven. MATTHEW 5:13–14, 16 •

I also withheld you from sinning against Me. GENESIS 20:6 •

The Lord is faithful, who will establish you and guard you from the evil one. 2 THESSALONIANS 3:3 • I did not do so, because of the fear of God. NEHEMIAH 5:15 • Who gave Himself for our sins, that He might deliver us from this present evil age, according to the will of our God and Father. GALATIANS 1:4 •

Now to Him who is able to keep you from stumbling, and to present you faultless before the presence of His glory with exceeding joy, to God our Savior, who alone is wise, be glory and majesty, dominion and power, both now and forever. Amen. JUDE 24–25 •

Evening Reading

Whoever trusts in the LORD shall be safe.
PROVERBS 29:25

The LORD is exalted, for He dwells on high. ISAIAH 33:5 • The LORD is high above all nations, His glory above the heavens....He raises the poor out of the dust, and lifts the needy out of the ash heap, that He may seat him with princes. PSALM 113:4, 7–8 •

God, who is rich in mercy, because of His great love with which He loved us, even when we were dead in trespasses, made us alive together with Christ (by grace you have been saved), and raised us up together, and made us sit together in the heavenly places in Christ Jesus. EPHESIANS 2:4–6 •

He who did not spare His own Son, but delivered Him up for us all, how shall He not with Him also freely give us all things? ROMANS 8:32 • I am persuaded that neither death nor life, nor angels nor principalities nor powers, nor things present nor things to come, nor height nor depth, nor any other created thing, shall be able to separate us from the love of God which is in Christ Jesus our Lord. ROMANS 8:38–39 •

August 11

Morning Reading

*That through death He might destroy him who
had the power of death.*
HEBREWS 2:14

Our Savior Jesus Christ...has abolished death and brought life and immortality to light through the gospel. 2 TIMOTHY 1:10 • He will swallow up death forever, and the Lord GOD will wipe away tears from all faces; the rebuke of His people He will take away from all the earth; for the LORD has spoken. ISAIAH 25:8 • So when this corruptible has put on incorruption, and this mortal has put on immortality, then shall be brought to pass the saying that is written: "Death is swallowed up in victory." "O Death, where is your sting? O Hades, where is your victory?" The sting of death is sin, and the strength of sin is the law. But thanks be to God, who gives us the victory through our Lord Jesus Christ. 1 CORINTHIANS 15:54–57 •

God has not given us a spirit of fear, but of power and of love and of a sound mind. 2 TIMOTHY 1:7 • Yea, though I walk through the valley of the shadow of death, I will fear no evil; for You are with me; Your rod and Your staff, they comfort me. PSALM 23:4 •

Evening Reading

Where is the way to the dwelling of light?
JOB 38:19

God is light and in Him is no darkness at all. 1 JOHN 1:5 • As long as I am in the world, I am the light of the world. JOHN 9:5 •

If we say that we have fellowship with Him, and walk in darkness, we lie and do not practice the truth. But if we walk in the light as He is in the light, we have fellowship with one another, and the blood of Jesus Christ His Son cleanses us from all sin. 1 JOHN 1:6–7 • The Father... has qualified us to be partakers of the inheritance of the saints in the light. He has delivered us from the power of darkness and conveyed us into the kingdom of the Son of His love, in whom we have redemption through His blood, the forgiveness of sins. COLOSSIANS 1:12–14 •

You are all sons of light and sons of the day. We are not of the night nor of darkness. 1 THESSALONIANS 5:5 • You are the light of the world. A city that is set on a hill cannot be hidden....Let your light so shine before men, that they may see your good works and glorify your Father in heaven. MATTHEW 5:14, 16 •

August 12

Morning Reading

The Lord will not cast off forever. Though He causes grief,
yet He will show compassion.
LAMENTATIONS 3:31–32

"Do not fear," says the LORD, "for I am with you;...I will not make a complete end of you. I will rightly correct you." JEREMIAH 46:28 • "For a mere moment I have forsaken you, but with great mercies I will gather you. With a little wrath I hid My face from you for a moment; but with everlasting kindness I will have mercy on you," says the LORD, your Redeemer...."For the mountains shall depart and the hills be removed, but My kindness shall not depart from you, nor shall My covenant of peace be removed," says the LORD, who has mercy on you. "O you afflicted one, tossed with tempest, and not comforted, behold, I will lay your stones with colorful gems, and lay your foundations with sapphires." ISAIAH 54:7–8, 10–11 •

I will bear the indignation of the LORD, because I have sinned against Him, until He pleads my case and executes justice for me. He will bring me forth to the light; I will see His righteousness. MICAH 7:9 •

Evening Reading

God has chosen the weak things of the world to put to shame
the things which are mighty.
1 CORINTHIANS 1:27

When the children of Israel cried out to the LORD, the LORD raised up a deliverer for them: Ehud,...a left-handed man....After him was Shamgar,...who killed six hundred men of the Philistines with an ox goad; and he also delivered Israel. JUDGES 3:15, 31 •

The LORD turned to [Gideon] and said, "Go in this might of yours.... Have I not sent you?" So he said to Him, "O my Lord, how can I save Israel? Indeed my clan is the weakest in Manasseh, and I am the least in my father's house." JUDGES 6:14–15 •

And the LORD said to Gideon, "The people who are with you are too many for Me,...lest Israel claim glory for itself against Me, saying, 'My own hand has saved me.'" JUDGES 7:2 •

"Not by might nor by power, but by My Spirit," says the LORD of hosts. ZECHARIAH 4:6 • My brethren, be strong in the Lord and in the power of His might. EPHESIANS 6:10 •

August 13

Morning Reading

He has prepared a city for them.
HEBREWS 11:16

If I go and prepare a place for you, I will come again and receive you to Myself; that where I am, there you may be also. JOHN 14:3 • An inheritance incorruptible and undefiled...that does not fade away, reserved in heaven for you. 1 PETER 1:4 • Here we have no continuing city, but we seek the one to come. HEBREWS 13:14 •

This same Jesus, who was taken up from you into heaven, will so come in like manner as you saw Him go into heaven. ACTS 1:11 • Therefore be patient, brethren, until the coming of the Lord. See how the farmer waits for the precious fruit of the earth, waiting patiently for it until it receives the early and latter rain. You also be patient. Establish your hearts, for the coming of the Lord is at hand. JAMES 5:7–8 • Yet a little while, and He who is coming will come and will not tarry. HEBREWS 10:37 •

We who are alive and remain shall be caught up together with them in the clouds to meet the Lord in the air. And thus we shall always be with the Lord. Therefore comfort one another with these words. 1 THESSALONIANS 4:17–18 •

Evening Reading

The base things of the world...God has chosen.
1 CORINTHIANS 1:28

Do not be deceived. Neither fornicators, nor idolaters, nor adulterers, nor homosexuals, nor sodomites, nor thieves, nor covetous, nor drunkards, nor revilers, nor extortioners will inherit the kingdom of God. And such were some of you. But you were washed, but you were sanctified, but you were justified in the name of the Lord Jesus and by the Spirit of our God. 1 CORINTHIANS 6:9–11 •

You He made alive, who were dead in trespasses and sins, in which you once walked according to the course of this world,...among whom also we all once conducted ourselves in the lusts of our flesh, fulfilling the desires of the flesh and of the mind. EPHESIANS 2:1–3 •

According to His mercy He saved us, through the washing of regeneration and renewing of the Holy Spirit, whom He poured out on us abundantly through Jesus Christ our Savior. TITUS 3:5–6 •

"My thoughts are not your thoughts, nor are your ways My ways," says the LORD. ISAIAH 55:8 •

August 14

Morning Reading

The joy of the LORD is your strength.
NEHEMIAH 8:10

Sing, O heavens! Be joyful, O earth! And break out in singing, O mountains! For the LORD has comforted His people, and will have mercy on His afflicted. ISAIAH 49:13 • Behold, God is my salvation, I will trust and not be afraid; "for YAH, the LORD, is my strength and song; He also has become my salvation." ISAIAH 12:2 • The LORD is my strength and my shield; my heart trusted in Him, and I am helped; therefore my heart greatly rejoices, and with my song I will praise Him. PSALM 28:7 • My soul shall be joyful in my God; for He has clothed me with the garments of salvation, He has covered me with the robe of righteousness, as a bridegroom decks himself with ornaments, and as a bride adorns herself with her jewels. ISAIAH 61:10 •

Therefore I have reason to glory in Christ Jesus in the things which pertain to God. ROMANS 15:17 • We also rejoice in God through our Lord Jesus Christ, through whom we have now received the reconciliation. ROMANS 5:11 • I will rejoice in the LORD, I will joy in the God of my salvation. HABAKKUK 3:18 •

Evening Reading

He has made with me an everlasting covenant,
ordered in all things and secure.
2 SAMUEL 23:5

I know whom I have believed and am persuaded that He is able to keep what I have committed to Him until that Day. 2 TIMOTHY 1:12 •

Blessed be the God and Father of our Lord Jesus Christ, who has blessed us with every spiritual blessing in the heavenly places in Christ, just as He chose us in Him before the foundation of the world, that we should be holy and without blame before Him in love, having predestined us to adoption as sons by Jesus Christ to Himself, according to the good pleasure of His will. EPHESIANS 1:3–5 •

We know that all things work together for good to those who love God, to those who are the called according to His purpose. For whom He foreknew, He also predestined to be conformed to the image of His Son, that He might be the firstborn among many brethren. Moreover whom He predestined, these He also called; whom He called, these He also justified; and whom He justified, these He also glorified. ROMANS 8:28–30 •

August 15

Morning Reading

May the God of peace...make you complete
in every good work to do His will.
HEBREWS 13:20–21

Become complete. Be of good comfort, be of one mind, live in peace; and the God of love and peace will be with you. 2 CORINTHIANS 13:11 •

By grace you have been saved through faith, and that not of yourselves; it is the gift of God, not of works, lest anyone should boast. EPHESIANS 2:8–9 • Every good gift and every perfect gift is from above, and comes down from the Father of lights, with whom there is no variation or shadow of turning. JAMES 1:17 •

Work out your own salvation with fear and trembling; for it is God who works in you both to will and to do for His good pleasure. PHILIPPIANS 2:12–13 • Be transformed by the renewing of your mind, that you may prove what is that good and acceptable and perfect will of God. ROMANS 12:2 • Being filled with the fruits of righteousness which are by Jesus Christ, to the glory and praise of God. PHILIPPIANS 1:11 •

Not that we are sufficient of ourselves to think of anything as being from ourselves, but our sufficiency is from God. 2 CORINTHIANS 3:5 •

Evening Reading

I will allure her, will bring her into the wilderness,
and speak comfort to her.
HOSEA 2:14

Come out from among them and be separate, says the Lord. Do not touch what is unclean, and I will receive you. I will be a Father to you, and you shall be My sons and daughters, says the LORD Almighty. 2 CORINTHIANS 6:17–18 • Therefore, having these promises, beloved, let us cleanse ourselves from all filthiness of the flesh and spirit, perfecting holiness in the fear of God. 2 CORINTHIANS 7:1 •

Jesus,...that He might sanctify the people with His own blood, suffered outside the gate. Therefore let us go forth to Him, outside the camp, bearing His reproach. HEBREWS 13:12–13 •

[Jesus] said to them, "Come aside by yourselves to a deserted place and rest a while." MARK 6:31 • The LORD is my shepherd; I shall not want. He makes me to lie down in green pastures; He leads me beside the still waters. He restores my soul; He leads me in the paths of righteousness for His name's sake. PSALM 23:1–3 •

August 16

Morning Reading

The house to be built for the LORD must be
exceedingly magnificent.
1 CHRONICLES 22:5

You also, as living stones, are being built up a spiritual house. 1 PETER 2:5 • Do you not know that you are the temple of God and that the Spirit of God dwells in you? If anyone defiles the temple of God, God will destroy him. For the temple of God is holy, which temple you are. 1 CORINTHIANS 3:16–17 • Or do you not know that your body is the temple of the Holy Spirit who is in you, whom you have from God, and you are not your own? For you were bought at a price; therefore glorify God in your body and in your spirit, which are God's. 1 CORINTHIANS 6:19–20 • What agreement has the temple of God with idols? For you are the temple of the living God. As God has said: "I will dwell in them and walk among them. I will be their God, and they shall be My people." 2 CORINTHIANS 6:16 •

[You have] been built on the foundation of the apostles and prophets, Jesus Christ Himself being the chief cornerstone, in whom the whole building, being joined together, grows into a holy temple in the Lord, in whom you also are being built together for a dwelling place of God in the Spirit. EPHESIANS 2:20–22 •

Evening Reading

He is before all things.
COLOSSIANS 1:17

The Amen,...the Beginning of the creation of God. REVELATION 3:14 • [Jesus is] the beginning, the firstborn from the dead, that in all things He may have the preeminence. COLOSSIANS 1:18 •

The LORD possessed me at the beginning of His way, before His works of old. I have been established from everlasting, from the beginning, before there was ever an earth....When He prepared the heavens, I was there, when He drew a circle on the face of the deep, when He established the clouds above, when He strengthened the fountains of the deep, when He assigned to the sea its limit, so that the waters would not transgress His command,...I was beside Him as a master craftsman; and I was daily His delight, rejoicing always before Him. PROVERBS 8:22–23, 27–30 • Indeed before the day was, I am He. ISAIAH 43:13 •

The Lamb slain from the foundation of the world. REVELATION 13:8 • Jesus, the author and finisher of our faith, who for the joy that was set before Him endured the cross, despising the shame, and has sat down at the right hand of the throne of God. HEBREWS 12:2 •

August 17

Morning Reading

Pray for one another, that you may be healed.
JAMES 5:16

Abraham answered and said, "Indeed now, I who am but dust and ashes have taken it upon myself to speak to the Lord: Suppose there were five less than the fifty righteous; would You destroy all of the city for lack of five?" So He said, "If I find there forty-five, I will not destroy it." GENESIS 18:27–28 •

Father, forgive them, for they do not know what they do. LUKE 23:34 • Pray for those who spitefully use you and persecute you. MATTHEW 5:44 •

I pray for them. I do not pray for the world but for those whom You have given Me, for they are Yours....I do not pray for these alone, but also for those who will believe in Me through their word. JOHN 17:9, 20 • Bear one another's burdens, and so fulfill the law of Christ. GALATIANS 6:2 •

The effective, fervent prayer of a righteous man avails much. Elijah was a man with a nature like ours, and he prayed earnestly that it would not rain; and it did not rain on the land for three years and six months. JAMES 5:16–17 •

Evening Reading

As for man, his days are like grass; as a flower of the field, so he flour-ishes. For the wind passes over it, and it is gone,
and its place remembers it no more.
PSALM 103:15–16

So teach us to number our days, that we may gain a heart of wisdom. PSALM 90:12 • What will it profit a man if he gains the whole world, and loses his own soul? MARK 8:36 •

Surely the people are grass. The grass withers, the flower fades, but the word of our God stands forever. ISAIAH 40:7–8 • The world is pass-ing away, and the lust of it; but he who does the will of God abides forever. 1 JOHN 2:17 •

Behold, now is the accepted time; behold, now is the day of sal-vation. 2 CORINTHIANS 6:2 • Use this world as not misusing it. For the form of this world is passing away. 1 CORINTHIANS 7:31 • Let us consider one another in order to stir up love and good works, not forsaking the assembling of ourselves together, as is the manner of some, but exhorting one another, and so much the more as you see the Day approaching. HEBREWS 10:24–25 •

August 18

Morning Reading

What god is there in heaven or on earth who can do anything like Your works and Your mighty deeds?
DEUTERONOMY 3:24

Who in the heavens can be compared to the LORD? Who among the sons of the mighty can be likened to the LORD?...O LORD God of hosts, who is mighty like You, O LORD? Your faithfulness also surrounds You. PSALM 89:6, 8 • Among the gods there is none like You, O Lord; nor are there any works like Your works. PSALM 86:8 • For Your word's sake, and according to Your own heart, You have done all these great things, to make Your servant know them. Therefore You are great, O Lord GOD. For there is none like You, nor is there any God besides You, according to all that we have heard with our ears. 2 SAMUEL 7:21–22 •

As it is written: "Eye has not seen, nor ear heard, nor have entered into the heart of man the things which God has prepared for those who love Him." But God has revealed them to us through His Spirit. 1 CORINTHIANS 2:9–10 • The secret things belong to the LORD our God, but those things which are revealed belong to us and to our children. DEUTERONOMY 29:29 •

Evening Reading

He who glories, let him glory in the LORD.
1 CORINTHIANS 1:31

Let not the wise man glory in his wisdom, let not the mighty man glory in his might, nor let the rich man glory in his riches; but let him who glories glory in this, that he understands and knows Me, that I am the LORD. JEREMIAH 9:23–24 •

I also count all things loss for the excellence of the knowledge of Christ Jesus my Lord, for whom I have suffered the loss of all things, and count them as rubbish, that I may gain Christ. PHILIPPIANS 3:8 • I am not ashamed of the gospel of Christ, for it is the power of God to salvation for everyone who believes. ROMANS 1:16 • I have reason to glory in Christ Jesus in the things which pertain to God. ROMANS 15:17 •

Whom have I in heaven but You? And there is none upon earth that I desire besides You. PSALM 73:25 • My heart rejoices in the LORD;...I rejoice in Your salvation. 1 SAMUEL 2:1 •

Not unto us, O LORD, not unto us, but to Your name give glory, because of Your mercy, because of Your truth. PSALM 115:1 •

August 19

Morning Reading

As He who called you is holy, you also be holy in all your conduct.
1 PETER 1:15

You know how we exhorted...and charged every one of you,...that you would walk worthy of God who calls you into His own kingdom and glory. 1 THESSALONIANS 2:11–12 • That you may proclaim the praises of Him who called you out of darkness into His marvelous light. 1 PETER 2:9 •

You were once darkness, but now you are light in the Lord. Walk as children of light (for the fruit of the Spirit is in all goodness, righteousness, and truth), finding out what is acceptable to the Lord. And have no fellowship with the unfruitful works of darkness, but rather expose them. EPHESIANS 5:8–11 • Being filled with the fruits of righteousness which are by Jesus Christ, to the glory and praise of God. PHILIPPIANS 1:11 •

Let your light so shine before men, that they may see your good works and glorify your Father in heaven. MATTHEW 5:16 • Therefore, whether you eat or drink, or whatever you do, do all to the glory of God. 1 CORINTHIANS 10:31 •

Evening Reading

Ask Me of things to come concerning My sons;
and concerning the work of My hands, you command Me.
ISAIAH 45:11

[The Lord says,] "I will give you a new heart and put a new spirit within you; I will take the heart of stone out of your flesh and give you a heart of flesh. I will put My Spirit within you and cause you to walk in My statutes."...Thus says the Lord GOD: "I will also let the house of Israel inquire of Me to do this for them." EZEKIEL 36:26–27, 37 •

If two of you agree on earth concerning anything that they ask, it will be done for them by My Father in heaven. For where two or three are gathered together in My name, I am there in the midst of them. MATTHEW 18:19–20 •

Have faith in God. For assuredly, I say to you, whoever says to this mountain, "Be removed and be cast into the sea," and does not doubt in his heart, but believes that those things he says will be done, he will have whatever he says. MARK 11:22–23 •

August 20

Morning Reading

God is not a man, that He should lie, nor a son of man,
that He should repent.
NUMBERS 23:19

The Father of lights, with whom there is no variation or shadow of turning. JAMES 1:17 • Jesus Christ is the same yesterday, today, and forever. HEBREWS 13:8 •

His truth shall be your shield and buckler. PSALM 91:4 •

God, determining to show more abundantly to the heirs of promise the immutability of His counsel, confirmed it by an oath, that by two immutable things, in which it is impossible for God to lie, we might have strong consolation, who have fled for refuge to lay hold of the hope set before us. HEBREWS 6:17–18 •

The faithful God who keeps covenant and mercy for a thousand generations with those who love Him and keep His commandments. DEUTERONOMY 7:9 • All the paths of the LORD are mercy and truth, to such as keep His covenant and His testimonies. PSALM 25:10 • Happy is he who has the God of Jacob for his help, whose hope is in the LORD his God, who made heaven and earth, the sea, and all that is in them; who keeps truth forever. PSALM 146:5–6 •

Evening Reading

If you faint in the day of adversity, your strength is small.
PROVERBS 24:10

He gives power to the weak, and to those who have no might He increases strength. ISAIAH 40:29 • My grace is sufficient for you, for My strength is made perfect in weakness. 2 CORINTHIANS 12:9 • He shall call upon Me, and I will answer him; I will be with him in trouble; I will deliver him and honor him. PSALM 91:15 • The eternal God is your refuge, and underneath are the everlasting arms; He will thrust out the enemy from before you. DEUTERONOMY 33:27 •

I looked for someone to take pity, but there was none; and for comforters, but I found none. PSALM 69:20 •

Every high priest taken from among men is appointed for men in things pertaining to God....He can have compassion on those who are ignorant and going astray....So also Christ...though He was a Son, yet He learned obedience by the things which He suffered. And having been perfected, He became the author of eternal salvation to all who obey Him. HEBREWS 5:1–2, 5, 8–9 • Surely He has borne our griefs and carried our sorrows. ISAIAH 53:4 •

August 21

Morning Reading

You are my portion, O LORD.
PSALM 119:57

All things are yours....And you are Christ's, and Christ is God's. 1 CORINTHIANS 3:21, 23 •

Our great God and Savior Jesus Christ...gave Himself for us. TITUS 2:13–14 • [God] gave Him to be head over all things to the church. EPHESIANS 1:22 • Christ also loved the church and gave Himself for her,... that He might present her to Himself a glorious church, not having spot or wrinkle or any such thing, but that she should be holy and without blemish. EPHESIANS 5:25, 27 •

My soul shall make its boast in the LORD. PSALM 34:2 • I will greatly rejoice in the LORD, my soul shall be joyful in my God; for He has clothed me with the garments of salvation, He has covered me with the robe of righteousness. ISAIAH 61:10 •

Whom have I in heaven but You? And there is none upon earth that I desire besides You. My flesh and my heart fail; but God is the strength of my heart and my portion forever. PSALM 73:25–26 • O my soul, you have said to the LORD, "You are my Lord, my goodness is nothing apart from You." PSALM 16:2 • O LORD, You are the portion of my inheritance and my cup; You maintain my lot. The lines have fallen to me in pleasant places; yes, I have a good inheritance. PSALM 16:5–6 •

Evening Reading

There is a way that seems right to a man,
but its end is the way of death.
PROVERBS 14:12

He who trusts in his own heart is a fool. PROVERBS 28:26 •

Your word is a lamp to my feet and a light to my path. PSALM 119:105 • Concerning the works of men, by the word of Your lips, I have kept away from the paths of the destroyer. PSALM 17:4 •

If there arises among you a prophet or a dreamer of dreams, and he gives you a sign or a wonder, and the sign or the wonder comes to pass, of which he spoke to you, saying, "Let us go after other gods"; which you have not known; "and let us serve them," you shall not listen to the words of that prophet or that dreamer of dreams, for the LORD your God is testing you to know whether you love the LORD your God with all your heart and with all your soul. You shall walk after the LORD your God and fear Him, and keep His commandments and obey His voice, and you shall serve Him and hold fast to Him. DEUTERONOMY 13:1–4 •

I will instruct you and teach you in the way you should go; I will guide you with My eye. PSALM 32:8 •

August 22

Morning Reading

None of us lives to himself, and no one dies to himself.
ROMANS 14:7

If we live, we live to the Lord; and if we die, we die to the Lord. Therefore, whether we live or die, we are the Lord's. ROMANS 14:8 • Let no one seek his own, but each one the other's well-being. 1 CORINTHIANS 10:24 • You were bought at a price; therefore glorify God in your body and in your spirit, which are God's. 1 CORINTHIANS 6:20 •

Christ will be magnified in my body, whether by life or by death. For to me, to live is Christ, and to die is gain. But if I live on in the flesh, this will mean fruit from my labor; yet what I shall choose I cannot tell. For I am hard pressed between the two, having a desire to depart and be with Christ, which is far better. PHILIPPIANS 1:20–23 •

I through the law died to the law that I might live to God. I have been crucified with Christ; it is no longer I who live, but Christ lives in me; and the life which I now live in the flesh I live by faith in the Son of God, who loved me and gave Himself for me. GALATIANS 2:19–20 •

Evening Reading

God gave Solomon...largeness of heart like the sand on the seashore.
1 KINGS 4:29

Indeed a greater than Solomon is here. MATTHEW 12:42 • Prince of Peace. ISAIAH 9:6 •

Scarcely for a righteous man will one die; yet perhaps for a good man someone would even dare to die. But God demonstrates His own love toward us, in that while we were still sinners, Christ died for us. ROMANS 5:7–8 • Who, being in the form of God, did not consider it robbery to be equal with God, but made Himself of no reputation, taking the form of a bondservant, and coming in the likeness of men. And being found in appearance as a man, He humbled Himself and became obedient to the point of death, even the death of the cross. PHILIPPIANS 2:6–8 • The love of Christ...passes knowledge. EPHESIANS 3:19 •

Christ the power of God and the wisdom of God. 1 CORINTHIANS 1:24 • In whom are hidden all the treasures of wisdom and knowledge. COLOSSIANS 2:3 • The unsearchable riches of Christ. EPHESIANS 3:8 • Of Him you are in Christ Jesus, who became for us wisdom from God; and righteousness and sanctification and redemption. 1 CORINTHIANS 1:30 •

August 23

Morning Reading

I have loved you with an everlasting love; therefore with lovingkindness I have drawn you.
JEREMIAH 31:3

We are bound to give thanks to God always for you, brethren beloved by the Lord, because God from the beginning chose you for salvation through sanctification by the Spirit and belief in the truth, to which He called you by our gospel, for the obtaining of the glory of our Lord Jesus Christ. 2 THESSALONIANS 2:13–14 • [God] has saved us and called us with a holy calling, not according to our works, but according to His own purpose and grace which was given to us in Christ Jesus before time began. 2 TIMOTHY 1:9 • Your eyes saw my substance, being yet unformed. And in Your book they all were written, the days fashioned for me, when as yet there were none of them. PSALM 139:16 •

God so loved the world that He gave His only begotten Son, that whoever believes in Him should not perish but have everlasting life. JOHN 3:16 •

In this is love, not that we loved God, but that He loved us and sent His Son to be the propitiation for our sins. 1 JOHN 4:10 •

Evening Reading

I have made [you], *and I will bear* [you].
ISAIAH 46:4

Thus says the LORD, who created you, O Jacob, and He who formed you, O Israel: "Fear not, for I have redeemed you; I have called you by your name; you are Mine. When you pass through the waters, I will be with you; and through the rivers, they shall not overflow you." ISAIAH 43:1–2 • Even to your old age, I am He, and even to gray hairs I will carry you! ISAIAH 46:4 •

As an eagle stirs up its nest, hovers over its young, spreading out its wings, taking them up, carrying them on its wings, so the LORD alone led him. DEUTERONOMY 32:11–12 • He bore them and carried them all the days of old. ISAIAH 63:9 •

Jesus Christ is the same yesterday, today, and forever. HEBREWS 13:8 • For I am persuaded that neither...height nor depth, nor any other created thing, shall be able to separate us from the love of God which is in Christ Jesus our Lord. ROMANS 8:38–39 •

Can a woman forget her nursing child, and not have compassion on the son of her womb? Surely they may forget, yet I will not forget you. ISAIAH 49:15 •

August 24

Morning Reading

I know their sorrows.
EXODUS 3:7

A Man of sorrows and acquainted with grief. ISAIAH 53:3 • [Christ] sympathize[s] with our weaknesses. HEBREWS 4:15 •

He Himself took our infirmities and bore our sicknesses. MATTHEW 8:17 • Jesus therefore, being wearied from His journey, sat thus by the well. JOHN 4:6 •

When Jesus saw her weeping, and the Jews who came with her weeping, He groaned in the spirit and was troubled....Jesus wept. JOHN 11:33, 35 • For in that He Himself has suffered, being tempted, He is able to aid those who are tempted. HEBREWS 2:18 •

He looked down from the height of His sanctuary; from heaven the LORD viewed the earth, to hear the groaning of the prisoner, to release those appointed to death. PSALM 102:19–20 • He knows the way that I take; when He has tested me, I shall come forth as gold. JOB 23:10 • When my spirit was overwhelmed within me, then You knew my path. PSALM 142:3 •

He who touches you touches the apple of His eye. ZECHARIAH 2:8 • In all their affliction He was afflicted, and the Angel of His Presence saved them; in His love and in His pity He redeemed them; and He bore them and carried them all the days of old. ISAIAH 63:9 •

Evening Reading

I must work the works of Him who sent Me while it is day.
JOHN 9:4

The soul of a lazy man desires, and has nothing; but the soul of the diligent shall be made rich. PROVERBS 13:4 • He who waters will also be watered himself. PROVERBS 11:25 •

My food is to do the will of Him who sent Me, and to finish His work. Do you not say, "There are still four months and then comes the harvest"? Behold, I say to you, lift up your eyes and look at the fields, for they are already white for harvest! And he who reaps receives wages, and gathers fruit for eternal life, that both he who sows and he who reaps may rejoice together. JOHN 4:34–36 • The kingdom of heaven is like a landowner who went out early in the morning to hire laborers for his vineyard. Now when he had agreed with the laborers for a denarius a day, he sent them into his vineyard. MATTHEW 20:1–2 •

Preach the word! Be ready in season and out of season. 2 TIMOTHY 4:2 • Do business till I come. LUKE 19:13 •

I labored more abundantly than they all, yet not I, but the grace of God which was with me. 1 CORINTHIANS 15:10 •

August 25

Morning Reading

Look to the rock from which you were hewn,
and to the hole of the pit from which you were dug.
ISAIAH 51:1

Behold, I was brought forth in iniquity. PSALM 51:5 • No eye pitied you,...but you were thrown out into the open field, when you yourself were loathed on the day you were born. And when I passed by you and saw you struggling in your own blood, I said to you,..."Live!" EZEKIEL 16:5–6 •

He also brought me up out of a horrible pit, out of the miry clay, and set my feet upon a rock, and established my steps. He has put a new song in my mouth; praise to our God. PSALM 40:2–3 •

When we were still without strength, in due time Christ died for the ungodly. For scarcely for a righteous man will one die; yet perhaps for a good man someone would even dare to die. But God demonstrates His own love toward us, in that while we were still sinners, Christ died for us. ROMANS 5:6–8 • God, who is rich in mercy, because of His great love with which He loved us, even when we were dead in trespasses, made us alive together with Christ. EPHESIANS 2:4–5 •

Evening Reading

I will greatly rejoice in the LORD, my soul shall be joyful in my God.
ISAIAH 61:10

I will bless the LORD at all times; His praise shall continually be in my mouth. My soul shall make its boast in the LORD; the humble shall hear of it and be glad. Oh, magnify the LORD with me, and let us exalt His name together. PSALM 34:1–3 • The LORD will give grace and glory; no good thing will He withhold from those who walk uprightly. O LORD of hosts, blessed is the man who trusts in You! PSALM 84:11–12 • Bless the LORD, O my soul; and all that is within me, bless His holy name! PSALM 103:1 •

Is anyone cheerful? Let him sing psalms. JAMES 5:13 • Be filled with the Spirit, speaking to one another in psalms and hymns and spiritual songs, singing and making melody in your heart to the Lord, giving thanks always for all things. EPHESIANS 5:18–20 • Singing with grace in your hearts to the Lord. COLOSSIANS 3:16 •

At midnight Paul and Silas were praying and singing hymns to God, and the prisoners were listening to them. ACTS 16:25 • Rejoice in the Lord always. Again I will say, rejoice! PHILIPPIANS 4:4 •

 # August 26

Morning Reading

You shall also make a plate of pure gold and engrave on it,
like the engraving of a signet: HOLINESS TO THE LORD.
EXODUS 28:36

Pursue...holiness, without which no one will see the Lord. HEBREWS 12:14 • God is Spirit, and those who worship Him must worship in spirit and truth. JOHN 4:24 • We are all like an unclean thing, and all our righteousnesses are like filthy rags. ISAIAH 64:6 • By those who come near Me I must be regarded as holy; and before all the people I must be glorified. LEVITICUS 10:3 •

This is the law of the temple: the whole area surrounding the mountaintop is most holy. EZEKIEL 43:12 • Holiness adorns Your house, O LORD, forever. PSALM 93:5 •

For their sakes I sanctify Myself, that they also may be sanctified by the truth. JOHN 17:19 • Seeing then that we have a great High Priest who has passed through the heavens, Jesus the Son of God, let us...come boldly to the throne of grace, that we may obtain mercy and find grace to help in time of need. HEBREWS 4:14, 16 •

Evening Reading

My cup runs over.
PSALM 23:5

Oh, taste and see that the LORD is good; blessed is the man who trusts in Him! Oh, fear the LORD, you His saints! There is no want to those who fear Him. The young lions lack and suffer hunger; but those who seek the LORD shall not lack any good thing. PSALM 34:8–10 • His compassions fail not. They are new every morning; great is Your faithfulness. LAMENTATIONS 3:22–23 •

O LORD, You are the portion of my inheritance and my cup; You maintain my lot. The lines have fallen to me in pleasant places; yes, I have a good inheritance. PSALM 16:5–6 • Whether...the world or life or death, or things present or things to come; all are yours. 1 CORINTHIANS 3:22 • Blessed be the God and Father of our Lord Jesus Christ, who has blessed us with every spiritual blessing in the heavenly places in Christ. EPHESIANS 1:3 •

I have learned in whatever state I am, to be content. PHILIPPIANS 4:11 • Godliness with contentment is great gain. 1 TIMOTHY 6:6 • My God shall supply all your need according to His riches in glory by Christ Jesus. PHILIPPIANS 4:19 •

August 27

Morning Reading

Your word is a lamp to my feet and a light to my path.
PSALM 119:105

By the word of Your lips, I have kept away from the paths of the destroyer. Uphold my steps in Your paths, that my footsteps may not slip. PSALM 17:4–5 • When you roam, they will lead you; when you sleep, they will keep you; and when you awake, they will speak with you. For the commandment is a lamp, and the law a light. PROVERBS 6:22–23 • Your ears shall hear a word behind you, saying, "This is the way, walk in it," whenever you turn to the right hand or whenever you turn to the left. ISAIAH 30:21 •

I am the light of the world. He who follows Me shall not walk in darkness, but have the light of life. JOHN 8:12 • We have the prophetic word confirmed, which you do well to heed as a light that shines in a dark place. 2 PETER 1:19 • Now we see in a mirror, dimly, but then face to face. Now I know in part, but then I shall know just as I also am known. 1 CORINTHIANS 13:12 • They need no lamp nor light of the sun, for the Lord God gives them light. And they shall reign forever and ever. REVELATION 22:5 •

Evening Reading

What do you mean, sleeper? Arise.
JONAH 1:6

This is not your rest; because it is defiled, it shall destroy [you]. MICAH 2:10 • Set your mind on things above, not on things on the earth. COLOSSIANS 3:2 • If riches increase, do not set your heart on them. PSALM 62:10 • Set your heart and your soul to seek the LORD your God. Therefore arise. 1 CHRONICLES 22:19 •

Why do you sleep? Rise and pray, lest you enter into temptation. LUKE 22:46 • Take heed to yourselves, lest your hearts be weighed down with carousing, drunkenness, and cares of this life, and that Day come on you unexpectedly. LUKE 21:34 •

While the bridegroom was delayed, they all slumbered and slept. MATTHEW 25:5 • Yet a little while, and He who is coming will come and will not tarry. HEBREWS 10:37 • Now it is high time to awake out of sleep; for now our salvation is nearer than when we first believed. ROMANS 13:11 • Watch therefore, for you do not know when the master of the house is coming; in the evening, at midnight, at the crowing of the rooster, or in the morning; lest, coming suddenly, he find you sleeping. MARK 13:35–36 •

August 28

Morning Reading

The accuser of our brethren, who accused them before our God day and night, has been cast down.
REVELATION 12:10

They overcame him by the blood of the Lamb and by the word of their testimony. REVELATION 12:11 • Who shall bring a charge against God's elect? It is God who justifies. Who is he who condemns? It is Christ who died, and furthermore is also risen, who is even at the right hand of God, who also makes intercession for us. ROMANS 8:33–34 •

Having disarmed principalities and powers, He made a public spectacle of them, triumphing over them in it. COLOSSIANS 2:15 • That through death He might destroy him who had the power of death, that is, the devil, and release those who through fear of death were all their lifetime subject to bondage. HEBREWS 2:14–15 • In all these things we are more than conquerors through Him who loved us. ROMANS 8:37 • Put on the whole armor of God, that you may be able to stand against the wiles of the devil....And take the helmet of salvation, and the sword of the Spirit, which is the word of God. EPHESIANS 6:11, 17 • But thanks be to God, who gives us the victory through our Lord Jesus Christ. 1 CORINTHIANS 15:57 •

Evening Reading

The tree of life.
GENESIS 2:9

God has given us eternal life, and this life is in His Son. 1 JOHN 5:11 • He gave His only begotten Son, that whoever believes in Him should not perish but have everlasting life. JOHN 3:16 • As the Father raises the dead and gives life to them, even so the Son gives life to whom He will....As the Father has life in Himself, so He has granted the Son to have life in Himself. JOHN 5:21, 26 •

To him who overcomes I will give to eat from the tree of life, which is in the midst of the Paradise of God. REVELATION 2:7 • In the middle of its street, and on either side of the river, was the tree of life, which bore twelve fruits, each tree yielding its fruit every month. The leaves of the tree were for the healing of the nations. REVELATION 22:2 •

Happy is the man who finds wisdom....Length of days is in her right hand....She is a tree of life to those who take hold of her, and happy are all who retain her. PROVERBS 3:13, 16, 18 • Christ Jesus...became for us wisdom. 1 CORINTHIANS 1:30 •

August 29

Morning Reading

Whoever trusts in the LORD, happy is he.
PROVERBS 16:20

[Abraham] did not waver at the promise of God through unbelief, but was strengthened in faith, giving glory to God, and being fully convinced that what He had promised He was also able to perform. ROMANS 4:20–21 • The children of Israel were subdued at that time; and the children of Judah prevailed, because they relied on the LORD God of their fathers. 2 CHRONICLES 13:18 •

God is our refuge and strength, a very present help in trouble. Therefore we will not fear, even though the earth be removed, and though the mountains be carried into the midst of the sea. PSALM 46:1–2 • It is better to trust in the LORD than to put confidence in man. It is better to trust in the LORD than to put confidence in princes. PSALM 118:8–9 • The steps of a good man are ordered by the LORD, and He delights in his way. Though he fall, he shall not be utterly cast down; for the LORD upholds him with His hand. PSALM 37:23–24 •

Oh, taste and see that the LORD is good; blessed is the man who trusts in Him! Oh, fear the LORD, you His saints! There is no want to those who fear Him. PSALM 34:8–9 •

Evening Reading

I will both lie down in peace, and sleep;
for You alone, O LORD, make me dwell in safety.
PSALM 4:8

You shall not be afraid of the terror by night. PSALM 91:5 • He shall cover you with His feathers, and under His wings you shall take refuge. PSALM 91:4 • As a hen gathers her chicks under her wings. MATTHEW 23:37 • He will not allow your foot to be moved; He who keeps you will not slumber. Behold, He who keeps Israel shall neither slumber nor sleep. The LORD is your keeper; the LORD is your shade at your right hand. PSALM 121:3–5 •

I will abide in Your tabernacle forever; I will trust in the shelter of Your wings. PSALM 61:4 • The darkness shall not hide from You, but the night shines as the day; the darkness and the light are both alike to You. PSALM 139:12 •

He who did not spare His own Son, but delivered Him up for us all, how shall He not with Him also freely give us all things? ROMANS 8:32 • You are Christ's, and Christ is God's. 1 CORINTHIANS 3:23 • I will trust and not be afraid. ISAIAH 12:2 •

August 30

Morning Reading

The king held out to Esther the golden scepter that was in his hand. Then Esther went near and touched the top of the scepter.
ESTHER 5:2

It will be that when he cries to Me, I will hear, for I am gracious. EXODUS 22:27 •

We have known and believed the love that God has for us. God is love, and he who abides in love abides in God, and God in him. Love has been perfected among us in this: that we may have boldness in the day of judgment; because as He is, so are we in this world. There is no fear in love; but perfect love casts out fear, because fear involves torment. But he who fears has not been made perfect in love. We love Him because He first loved us. 1 JOHN 4:16–19 •

Let us draw near with a true heart in full assurance of faith, having our hearts sprinkled from an evil conscience and our bodies washed with pure water. HEBREWS 10:22 • For through Him we both have access by one Spirit to the Father. EPHESIANS 2:18 • We have boldness and access with confidence through faith in Him. EPHESIANS 3:12 • Let us therefore come boldly to the throne of grace, that we may obtain mercy and find grace to help in time of need. HEBREWS 4:16 •

Evening Reading

The children of Israel...said to one another, "What is it?" [Manna means "What is it?" in Hebrew.] *For they did not know what it was.*
EXODUS 16:15

Without controversy great is the mystery of godliness: God was manifested in the flesh. 1 TIMOTHY 3:16 • The bread of God is He who comes down from heaven and gives life to the world. JOHN 6:33 •

Your fathers ate the manna in the wilderness, and are dead....I am the living bread which came down from heaven. If anyone eats of this bread, he will live forever; and the bread that I shall give is My flesh, which I shall give for the life of the world....For My flesh is food indeed, and My blood is drink indeed. JOHN 6:49, 51, 55 •

The children of Israel...gathered, some more, some less....He who gathered little had no lack....They gathered it every morning, every man according to his need. EXODUS 16:17–18, 21 •

Do not worry, saying, "What shall we eat?" or "What shall we drink?"...Your heavenly Father knows that you need all these things. But seek first the kingdom of God and His righteousness, and all these things shall be added to you. MATTHEW 6:31–33 •

August 31

Morning Reading

*The free gift which came from many offenses
resulted in justification.*
ROMANS 5:16

Though your sins are like scarlet, they shall be as white as snow; though they are red like crimson, they shall be as wool. ISAIAH 1:18 • I, even I, am He who blots out your transgressions for My own sake; and I will not remember your sins. Put Me in remembrance; let us contend together; state your case, that you may be acquitted. ISAIAH 43:25–26 • I have blotted out, like a thick cloud, your transgressions, and like a cloud, your sins. Return to Me, for I have redeemed you. ISAIAH 44:22 •

God so loved the world that He gave His only begotten Son, that whoever believes in Him should not perish but have everlasting life. JOHN 3:16 • The free gift is not like the offense. For if by the one man's offense many died, much more the grace of God and the gift by the grace of the one Man, Jesus Christ, abounded to many. ROMANS 5:15 • And such were some of you. But you were washed, but you were sanctified, but you were justified in the name of the Lord Jesus and by the Spirit of our God. 1 CORINTHIANS 6:11 •

Evening Reading

Do business till I come.
LUKE 19:13

[The Son of Man] is like a man going to a far country, who left his house and gave authority to his servants, and to each his work, and commanded the doorkeeper to watch. MARK 13:34 • To one he gave five talents, to another two, and to another one, to each according to his own ability; and immediately he went on a journey. MATTHEW 25:15 •

I must work the works of Him who sent Me while it is day; the night is coming when no one can work. JOHN 9:4 • Did you not know that I must be about My Father's business? LUKE 2:49 • Leaving us an example, that you should follow His steps. 1 PETER 2:21 •

Preach the word! Be ready in season and out of season. Convince, rebuke, exhort, with all longsuffering and teaching. 2 TIMOTHY 4:2 • Each one's work will become clear; for the Day will declare it. 1 CORINTHIANS 3:13 • Therefore, my beloved brethren, be steadfast, immovable, always abounding in the work of the Lord, knowing that your labor is not in vain in the Lord. 1 CORINTHIANS 15:58 •

SEPTEMBER

September 1

Morning Reading

The fruit of the Spirit is...gentleness.
GALATIANS 5:22–23

The humble...shall increase their joy in the LORD, and the poor among men shall rejoice in the Holy One of Israel. ISAIAH 29:19 • Unless you are converted and become as little children, you will by no means enter the kingdom of heaven. Therefore whoever humbles himself as this little child is the greatest in the kingdom of heaven. MATTHEW 18:3–4 • The incorruptible beauty of a gentle and quiet spirit...is very precious in the sight of God. 1 PETER 3:4 • Love does not parade itself, is not puffed up. 1 CORINTHIANS 13:4 •

Pursue...gentleness. 1 TIMOTHY 6:11 • Take My yoke upon you and learn from Me, for I am gentle and lowly in heart. MATTHEW 11:29 • He was oppressed and He was afflicted, yet He opened not His mouth; He was led as a lamb to the slaughter, and as a sheep before its shearers is silent, so He opened not His mouth. ISAIAH 53:7 • Christ also suffered for us, leaving us an example, that you should follow His steps: "Who committed no sin, nor was deceit found in His mouth"; who, when He was reviled, did not revile in return,...but committed Himself to Him who judges righteously. 1 PETER 2:21–23 •

Evening Reading

If anyone desires to come after Me, let him deny himself,
and take up his cross daily, and follow Me.
LUKE 9:23

As ministers of God...[we receive both] honor and dishonor,...evil report and good report. 2 CORINTHIANS 6:4, 8 • All who desire to live godly in Christ Jesus will suffer persecution. 2 TIMOTHY 3:12 • Brethren, if I still preach circumcision, why do I still suffer persecution? Then the offense of the cross has ceased. GALATIANS 5:11 •

If I still pleased men, I would not be a bondservant of Christ. GALATIANS 1:10 •

If you are reproached for the name of Christ, blessed are you....But let none of you suffer as a murderer, a thief, an evildoer, or as a busybody in other people's matters. Yet if anyone suffers as a Christian, let him not be ashamed, but let him glorify God in this matter. 1 PETER 4:14–16 •

To you it has been granted on behalf of Christ, not only to believe in Him, but also to suffer for His sake. PHILIPPIANS 1:29 • If One died for all, then all died; and He died for all, that those who live should live no longer for themselves, but for Him who died for them and rose again. 2 CORINTHIANS 5:14–15 • If we endure, we shall also reign with Him. 2 TIMOTHY 2:12 •

September 2

Morning Reading

Wait on the LORD; be of good courage,
and He shall strengthen your heart.
PSALM 27:14

Have you not known? Have you not heard? The everlasting God, the LORD, the Creator of the ends of the earth, neither faints nor is weary....He gives power to the weak, and to those who have no might He increases strength. ISAIAH 40:28–29 • Fear not, for I am with you; be not dismayed, for I am your God. I will strengthen you, yes, I will help you, I will uphold you with My righteous right hand. ISAIAH 41:10 • You have been a strength to the poor, a strength to the needy in his distress, a refuge from the storm, a shade from the heat; for the blast of the terrible ones is as a storm against the wall. ISAIAH 25:4 •

The testing of your faith produces patience. But let patience have its perfect work, that you may be perfect and complete, lacking nothing. JAMES 1:3–4 • Therefore do not cast away your confidence, which has great reward. For you have need of endurance, so that after you have done the will of God, you may receive the promise. HEBREWS 10:35–36 •

Evening Reading

He makes me to lie down in green pastures.
PSALM 23:2

The wicked are like the troubled sea, when it cannot rest...."There is no peace," says my God, "for the wicked." ISAIAH 57:20–21 •

Come to Me, all you who labor and are heavy laden, and I will give you rest. MATTHEW 11:28 • Rest in the LORD. PSALM 37:7 • He who has entered His rest has himself also ceased from his works. HEBREWS 4:10 •

Do not be carried about with various and strange doctrines. For it is good that the heart be established by grace. HEBREWS 13:9 • That we should no longer be children, tossed to and fro and carried about with every wind of doctrine, by the trickery of men, in the cunning craftiness of deceitful plotting, but, speaking the truth in love, may grow up in all things into Him who is the head; [even] Christ. EPHESIANS 4:14–15 •

I sat down in his shade with great delight, and his fruit was sweet to my taste. He brought me to the banqueting house, and his banner over me was love. SONG OF SONGS 2:3–4 •

September 3

Morning Reading

Nor shall leaven be seen among you in all your quarters.
EXODUS 13:7

The fear of the LORD is to hate evil. PROVERBS 8:13 • Abhor what is evil. ROMANS 12:9 • Abstain from every form of evil. 1 THESSALONIANS 5:22 • Looking carefully lest anyone fall short of the grace of God; lest any root of bitterness springing up cause trouble, and by this many become defiled. HEBREWS 12:15 •

If I regard iniquity in my heart, the Lord will not hear. PSALM 66:18 •

Do you not know that a little leaven leavens the whole lump? Therefore purge out the old leaven, that you may be a new lump, since you truly are unleavened. For indeed Christ, our Passover, was sacrificed for us. Therefore let us keep the feast, not with old leaven, nor with the leaven of malice and wickedness, but with the unleavened bread of sincerity and truth. 1 CORINTHIANS 5:6–8 • Let a man examine himself, and so let him eat of the bread and drink of the cup. 1 CORINTHIANS 11:28 •

Let everyone who names the name of Christ depart from iniquity. 2 TIMOTHY 2:19 • Such a High Priest was fitting for us, who is holy, harmless, undefiled, separate from sinners. HEBREWS 7:26 • In Him there is no sin. 1 JOHN 3:5 •

Evening Reading

The serpent said to the woman, "You will not surely die....Your eyes will be opened, and you will be like God, knowing good and evil."
GENESIS 3:4–5

I fear, lest somehow, as the serpent deceived Eve by his craftiness, so your minds may be corrupted from the simplicity that is in Christ. 2 CORINTHIANS 11:3 •

My brethren, be strong in the Lord and in the power of His might. Put on the whole armor of God, that you may be able to stand against the wiles of the devil....Take up the whole armor of God, that you may be able to withstand in the evil day, and having done all, to stand. Stand therefore, having girded your waist with truth, having put on the breastplate of righteousness, and having shod your feet with the preparation of the gospel of peace; above all, taking the shield of faith with which you will be able to quench all the fiery darts of the wicked one. And take the helmet of salvation, and the sword of the Spirit, which is the word of God. EPHESIANS 6:10–11, 13–17 • Lest Satan should take advantage of us; for we are not ignorant of his devices. 2 CORINTHIANS 2:11 •

September 4

Morning Reading

Sit still, my daughter.
RUTH 3:18

Take heed, and be quiet; do not fear or be fainthearted. ISAIAH 7:4 • Be still, and know that I am God. PSALM 46:10 • Did I not say to you that if you would believe you would see the glory of God? JOHN 11:40 • The loftiness of man shall be bowed down, and the haughtiness of men shall be brought low; the LORD alone will be exalted in that day. ISAIAH 2:17 •

Mary...sat at Jesus' feet and heard His word....[Jesus said,] "Mary has chosen that good part, which will not be taken away from her." LUKE 10:39, 42 • In returning and rest you shall be saved; in quietness and confidence shall be your strength. ISAIAH 30:15 • Meditate within your heart on your bed, and be still. PSALM 4:4 •

Rest in the LORD, and wait patiently for Him; do not fret because of him who prospers in his way, because of the man who brings wicked schemes to pass. PSALM 37:7 •

He will not be afraid of evil tidings; his heart is steadfast, trusting in the LORD. His heart is established. PSALM 112:7–8 •

Whoever believes will not act hastily. ISAIAH 28:16 •

Evening Reading

What I am doing you do not understand now,
but you will know after this.
JOHN 13:7

You shall remember that the LORD your God led you all the way these forty years in the wilderness, to humble you and test you, to know what was in your heart, whether you would keep His commandments or not. DEUTERONOMY 8:2 •

"When I passed by you again and looked upon you, indeed your time was the time of love....Yes, I swore an oath to you and entered into a covenant with you, and you became Mine," says the Lord GOD. EZEKIEL 16:8 • Whom the LORD loves He chastens. HEBREWS 12:6 •

Beloved, do not think it strange concerning the fiery trial which is to try you, as though some strange thing happened to you; but rejoice to the extent that you partake of Christ's sufferings, that when His glory is revealed, you may also be glad with exceeding joy. 1 PETER 4:12–13 • Our light affliction, which is but for a moment, is working for us a far more exceeding and eternal weight of glory, while we do not look at the things which are seen, but at the things which are not seen. 2 CORINTHIANS 4:17–18 •

September 5

Morning Reading

As the body is one and has many members,...so also is Christ.
1 CORINTHIANS 12:12

He is the head of the body, the church. COLOSSIANS 1:18 • Head over all things to the church, which is His body, the fullness of Him who fills all in all. EPHESIANS 1:22–23 • We are members of His body, of His flesh and of His bones. EPHESIANS 5:30 •

A body You have prepared for Me. HEBREWS 10:5 • Your eyes saw my substance, being yet unformed. And in Your book they all were written, the days fashioned for me, when as yet there were none of them. PSALM 139:16 •

They were Yours, You gave them to Me. JOHN 17:6 • He chose us in Him before the foundation of the world. EPHESIANS 1:4 • Whom He foreknew, He also predestined to be conformed to the image of His Son. ROMANS 8:29 •

Grow up in all things into Him who is the head; Christ; from whom the whole body, joined and knit together by what every joint supplies,...causes growth of the body for the edifying of itself in love. EPHESIANS 4:15–16 •

Evening Reading

The fountain of living waters.
JEREMIAH 2:13

How precious is Your lovingkindness, O God! Therefore the children of men put their trust under the shadow of Your wings. They are abundantly satisfied with the fullness of Your house, and You give them drink from the river of Your pleasures. For with You is the fountain of life. PSALM 36:7–9 •

Thus says the Lord GOD: "Behold, My servants shall eat, but you shall be hungry; behold, My servants shall drink, but you shall be thirsty. ISAIAH 65:13 • Whoever drinks of the water that I shall give him will never thirst. But the water that I shall give him will become in him a fountain of water springing up into everlasting life. JOHN 4:14 • This He spoke concerning the Spirit, whom those believing in Him would receive. JOHN 7:39 •

Ho! Everyone who thirsts, come to the waters. ISAIAH 55:1 • The Spirit and the bride say, "Come!" And let him who hears say, "Come!" And let him who thirsts come. Whoever desires, let him take the water of life freely. REVELATION 22:17 •

September 6

Morning Reading

Let us lift our hearts and hands to God in heaven.
LAMENTATIONS 3:41

Who is like the LORD our God, who dwells on high, who humbles Himself to behold the things that are in the heavens and in the earth? PSALM 113:5–6 • To You, O LORD, I lift up my soul. PSALM 25:1 • I spread out my hands to You; my soul longs for You like a thirsty land....Do not hide Your face from me, lest I be like those who go down into the pit. Cause me to hear Your lovingkindness in the morning, for in You do I trust; cause me to know the way in which I should walk, for I lift up my soul to You. PSALM 143:6–8 •

Because Your lovingkindness is better than life, my lips shall praise You. Thus I will bless You while I live; I will lift up my hands in Your name. PSALM 63:3–4 • Rejoice the soul of Your servant, for to You, O Lord, I lift up my soul. For You, Lord, are good, and ready to forgive, and abundant in mercy to all those who call upon You. PSALM 86:4–5 •

Whatever you ask in My name, that I will do. JOHN 14:13 •

Evening Reading

Watchman, what of the night?
ISAIAH 21:11

It is high time to awake out of sleep; for now our salvation is nearer than when we first believed. The night is far spent, the day is at hand. Therefore let us cast off the works of darkness, and let us put on the armor of light. ROMANS 13:11–12 •

Learn this parable from the fig tree: when its branch has already become tender and puts forth leaves, you know that summer is near. So you also, when you see all these things, know that it is near; at the doors! MATTHEW 24:32–33 • Heaven and earth will pass away, but My words will by no means pass away. MATTHEW 24:35 •

I wait for the LORD, my soul waits, and in His word I do hope. My soul waits for the Lord more than those who watch for the morning; yes, more than those who watch for the morning. PSALM 130:5–6 •

He who testifies to these things says, "Surely I am coming quickly." Amen. Even so, come, Lord Jesus! REVELATION 22:20 •

Watch therefore, for you know neither the day nor the hour in which the Son of Man is coming. MATTHEW 25:13 •

September 7

Morning Reading

Rejoicing in hope.
ROMANS 12:12

The hope which is laid up for you in heaven. COLOSSIANS 1:5 • If in this life only we have hope in Christ, we are of all men the most pitiable. 1 CORINTHIANS 15:19 • We must through many tribulations enter the kingdom of God. ACTS 14:22 • Whoever does not bear his cross and come after Me cannot be My disciple. LUKE 14:27 • No one should be shaken by these afflictions; for you yourselves know that we are appointed to this. 1 THESSALONIANS 3:3 •

Rejoice in the Lord always. Again I will say, rejoice! PHILIPPIANS 4:4 • May the God of hope fill you with all joy and peace in believing, that you may abound in hope by the power of the Holy Spirit. ROMANS 15:13 • Blessed be the God and Father of our Lord Jesus Christ, who according to His abundant mercy has begotten us again to a living hope through the resurrection of Jesus Christ from the dead,...whom having not seen you love. Though now you do not see Him, yet believing, you rejoice with joy inexpressible and full of glory. 1 PETER 1:3, 8 • Through whom also we have access by faith into this grace in which we stand, and rejoice in hope of the glory of God. ROMANS 5:2 •

Evening Reading

I am poor and needy; yet the LORD thinks upon me.
PSALM 40:17

I know the thoughts that I think toward you, says the LORD, thoughts of peace and not of evil. JEREMIAH 29:11 • "My thoughts are not your thoughts, nor are your ways My ways," says the LORD. "For as the heavens are higher than the earth, so are My ways higher than your ways, and My thoughts than your thoughts." ISAIAH 55:8–9 •

How precious also are Your thoughts to me, O God! How great is the sum of them! If I should count them, they would be more in number than the sand; when I awake, I am still with You. PSALM 139:17–18 • O LORD, how great are Your works! Your thoughts are very deep. PSALM 92:5 • Many, O LORD my God, are Your wonderful works which You have done; and Your thoughts toward us. PSALM 40:5 •

Not many mighty, not many noble, are called. 1 CORINTHIANS 1:26 • Has God not chosen the poor of this world to be rich in faith and heirs of the kingdom? JAMES 2:5 • Having nothing, and yet possessing all things. 2 CORINTHIANS 6:10 • The unsearchable riches of Christ. EPHESIANS 3:8 •

September 8

Morning Reading

You have been weighed in the balances, and found wanting.
DANIEL 5:27

The LORD is the God of knowledge; and by Him actions are weighed. 1 SAMUEL 2:3 • What is highly esteemed among men is an abomination in the sight of God. LUKE 16:15 • The Lord does not see as man sees; for man looks at the outward appearance, but the LORD looks at the heart. 1 SAMUEL 16:7 • Do not be deceived, God is not mocked; for whatever a man sows, that he will also reap. For he who sows to his flesh will of the flesh reap corruption, but he who sows to the Spirit will of the Spirit reap everlasting life. GALATIANS 6:7–8 •

For what profit is it to a man if he gains the whole world, and loses his own soul? Or what will a man give in exchange for his soul? MATTHEW 16:26 • What things were gain to me, these I have counted loss for Christ. PHILIPPIANS 3:7 •

Behold, You desire truth in the inward parts. PSALM 51:6 • You have tested my heart; You have visited me in the night; You have tried me and have found nothing. PSALM 17:3 •

Evening Reading

Christ the firstfruits.
1 CORINTHIANS 15:23

Unless a grain of wheat falls into the ground and dies, it remains alone; but if it dies, it produces much grain. JOHN 12:24 • If the firstfruit is holy, the lump is also holy; and if the root is holy, so are the branches. ROMANS 11:16 • Now Christ is risen from the dead, and has become the firstfruits of those who have fallen asleep. 1 CORINTHIANS 15:20 • If we have been united together in the likeness of His death, certainly we also shall be in the likeness of His resurrection. ROMANS 6:5 • The Lord Jesus Christ...will transform our lowly body that it may be conformed to His glorious body, according to the working by which He is able even to subdue all things to Himself. PHILIPPIANS 3:20–21 •

The firstborn from the dead. COLOSSIANS 1:18 • If the Spirit of Him who raised Jesus from the dead dwells in you, He who raised Christ from the dead will also give life to your mortal bodies through His Spirit who dwells in you. ROMANS 8:11 •

I am the resurrection and the life. He who believes in Me, though he may die, he shall live. JOHN 11:25 •

September 9

Morning Reading

He has filled the hungry with good things,
and the rich He has sent away empty.
Luke 1:53

Because you say, "I am rich, have become wealthy, and have need of nothing"; and do not know that you are wretched, miserable, poor, blind, and naked; I counsel you to buy from Me gold refined in the fire, that you may be rich....As many as I love, I rebuke and chasten. Therefore be zealous and repent. Revelation 3:17–19 •

Blessed are those who hunger and thirst for righteousness, for they shall be filled. Matthew 5:6 • The poor and needy seek water, but there is none, their tongues fail for thirst. I, the Lord, will hear them; I, the God of Israel, will not forsake them. Isaiah 41:17 • I am the Lord your God.... Open your mouth wide, and I will fill it. Psalm 81:10 •

Why do you spend money for what is not bread, and your wages for what does not satisfy? Listen carefully to Me, and eat what is good, and let your soul delight itself in abundance. Isaiah 55:2 • I am the bread of life. He who comes to Me shall never hunger, and he who believes in Me shall never thirst. John 6:35 •

Evening Reading

My feet had almost stumbled; my steps had nearly slipped.
Psalm 73:2

If I say, "My foot slips," Your mercy, O Lord, will hold me up. Psalm 94:18 •

The Lord said, "Simon, Simon! Indeed, Satan has asked for you, that he may sift you as wheat. But I have prayed for you, that your faith should not fail." Luke 22:31–32 •

A righteous man may fall seven times and rise again. Proverbs 24:16 • Though he fall, he shall not be utterly cast down; for the Lord upholds him with His hand. Psalm 37:24 •

Do not rejoice over me, my enemy; when I fall, I will arise; when I sit in darkness, the Lord will be a light to me. Micah 7:8 • He shall deliver you in six troubles, yes, in seven no evil shall touch you. Job 5:19 •

If anyone sins, we have an Advocate with the Father, Jesus Christ the righteous. 1 John 2:1 • Therefore He is also able to save to the uttermost those who come to God through Him, since He always lives to make intercession for them. Hebrews 7:25 •

September 10

Morning Reading

I will give them one heart and one way, that they may fear
Me forever, for the good of them.
JEREMIAH 32:39

I will give you a new heart and put a new spirit within you. EZEKIEL 36:26 • Good and upright is the LORD; therefore He teaches sinners in the way. The humble He guides in justice, and the humble He teaches His way. All the paths of the LORD are mercy and truth, to such as keep His covenant and His testimonies. PSALM 25:8–10 •

That they all may be one, as You, Father, are in Me, and I in You; that they also may be one in Us, that the world may believe that You sent Me. JOHN 17:21 •

I...beseech you to walk worthy of the calling with which you were called, with all lowliness and gentleness,...endeavoring to keep the unity of the Spirit in the bond of peace. There is one body and one Spirit, just as you were called in one hope of your calling; one Lord, one faith, one baptism; one God and Father of all, who is above all, and through all, and in you all. EPHESIANS 4:1–6 •

Evening Reading

Those who wait on the LORD shall renew their strength.
ISAIAH 40:31

When I am weak, then I am strong. 2 CORINTHIANS 12:10 • My God shall be My strength. ISAIAH 49:5 • [The Lord Jesus] said to me, "My grace is sufficient for you, for My strength is made perfect in weakness." Therefore most gladly I will rather boast in my infirmities, that the power of Christ may rest upon me. 2 CORINTHIANS 12:9 • Let him take hold of My strength. ISAIAH 27:5 •

Cast your burden on the LORD, and He shall sustain you. PSALM 55:22 • The arms of his hands were made strong by the hands of the Mighty God of Jacob. GENESIS 49:24 •

I will not let You go unless You bless me! GENESIS 32:26 •

You come to me with a sword, with a spear, and with a javelin. But I come to you in the name of the LORD of hosts, the God of the armies of Israel, whom you have defied. 1 SAMUEL 17:45 • Plead my cause, O LORD, with those who strive with me; fight against those who fight against me. Take hold of shield and buckler, and stand up for my help. PSALM 35:1–2 •

September 11

Morning Reading

Do not be conformed to this world, but be transformed by the renewing of your mind.
ROMANS 12:2

You shall not follow a crowd to do evil. EXODUS 23:2 •

Do you not know that friendship with the world is enmity with God? Whoever therefore wants to be a friend of the world makes himself an enemy of God. JAMES 4:4 •

What fellowship has righteousness with lawlessness? And what communion has light with darkness? And what accord has Christ with Belial? Or what part has a believer with an unbeliever? And what agreement has the temple of God with idols? 2 CORINTHIANS 6:14–16 • Do not love the world or the things in the world. If anyone loves the world, the love of the Father is not in him....The world is passing away, and the lust of it; but he who does the will of God abides forever. 1 JOHN 2:15, 17 •

You once walked according to the course of this world, according to the prince of the power of the air, the spirit who now works in the sons of disobedience. EPHESIANS 2:2 • You have not so learned Christ, if indeed you have heard Him and have been taught by Him, as the truth is in Jesus. EPHESIANS 4:20–21 •

Evening Reading

Man goes out to his work and to his labor until the evening.
PSALM 104:23

In the sweat of your face you shall eat bread till you return to the ground. GENESIS 3:19 • We commanded you this: If anyone will not work, neither shall he eat. 2 THESSALONIANS 3:10 • Aspire to lead a quiet life, to mind your own business, and to work with your own hands. 1 THESSALONIANS 4:11 •

Whatever your hand finds to do, do it with your might; for there is no work or device or knowledge or wisdom in the grave where you are going. ECCLESIASTES 9:10 • The night is coming when no one can work. JOHN 9:4 •

Let us not grow weary while doing good, for in due season we shall reap if we do not lose heart. GALATIANS 6:9 • Always abounding in the work of the Lord, knowing that your labor is not in vain in the Lord. 1 CORINTHIANS 15:58 •

There remains therefore a rest for the people of God. HEBREWS 4:9 • To us who have borne the burden and the heat of the day. MATTHEW 20:12 • [God] said, "This is the rest with which you may cause the weary to rest," and, "This is the refreshing"; yet they would not hear. ISAIAH 28:12 •

September 12

Morning Reading

I have seen his ways, and will heal him.
ISAIAH 57:18

I am the LORD who heals you. EXODUS 15:26 • O LORD, You have searched me and known me. You know my sitting down and my rising up; You understand my thought afar off. You comprehend my path and my lying down, and are acquainted with all my ways. PSALM 139:1–3 • You have set our iniquities before You, our secret sins in the light of Your countenance. PSALM 90:8 • All things are naked and open to the eyes of Him to whom we must give account. HEBREWS 4:13 •

"Come now, and let us reason together," says the LORD, "though your sins are like scarlet, they shall be as white as snow; though they are red like crimson, they shall be as wool." ISAIAH 1:18 • He is gracious to him, and says, "Deliver him from going down to the Pit; I have found a ransom." JOB 33:24 • He was wounded for our transgressions, He was bruised for our iniquities; the chastisement for our peace was upon Him, and by His stripes we are healed. ISAIAH 53:5 • He has sent Me to heal the brokenhearted. ISAIAH 61:1 • Your faith has made you well. Go in peace, and be healed of your affliction. MARK 5:34 •

Evening Reading

The LORD is for me.
PSALM 118:7

May the LORD answer you in the day of trouble; may the name of the God of Jacob defend you; may He send you help from the sanctuary, and strengthen you out of Zion....We will rejoice in your salvation, and in the name of our God we will set up our banners! May the LORD fulfill all your petitions....Some trust in chariots, and some in horses; but we will remember the name of the LORD our God. They have bowed down and fallen; but we have risen and stand upright. PSALM 20:1–2, 5, 7–8 •

When the enemy comes in like a flood, the Spirit of the LORD will lift up a standard against him. ISAIAH 59:19 • No temptation has overtaken you except such as is common to man; but God is faithful, who will not allow you to be tempted beyond what you are able, but with the temptation will also make the way of escape, that you may be able to bear it. 1 CORINTHIANS 10:13 •

If God is for us, who can be against us? ROMANS 8:31 • The LORD is on my side; I will not fear. PSALM 118:6 •

Our God whom we serve is able to deliver us from the burning fiery furnace, and He will deliver us. DANIEL 3:17 •

September 13

Morning Reading

If anyone thirsts, let him come to Me and drink.
JOHN 7:37

My soul longs, yes, even faints for the courts of the LORD; my heart and my flesh cry out for the living God. PSALM 84:2 • O God, You are my God; early will I seek You; my soul thirsts for You; my flesh longs for You in a dry and thirsty land where there is no water. So I have looked for You in the sanctuary, to see Your power and Your glory. PSALM 63:1–2 •

Ho! Everyone who thirsts, come to the waters; and you who have no money, come, buy and eat. Yes, come, buy wine and milk without money and without price. ISAIAH 55:1 • The Spirit and the bride say, "Come!" And let him who hears say, "Come!" And let him who thirsts come. Whoever desires, let him take the water of life freely. REVELATION 22:17 • Whoever drinks of the water that I shall give him will never thirst. But the water that I shall give him will become in him a fountain of water springing up into everlasting life. JOHN 4:14 • My blood is drink indeed. JOHN 6:55 •

Eat, O friends! Drink, yes, drink deeply, O beloved ones! SONG OF SONGS 5:1 •

Evening Reading

You are the salt of the earth.
MATTHEW 5:13

Incorruptible. 1 PETER 3:4 • Having been born again, not of corruptible seed but incorruptible, through the word of God which lives and abides forever. 1 PETER 1:23 • He who believes in Me, though he may die, he shall live. JOHN 11:25 • Sons of God, being sons of the resurrection. LUKE 20:36 • The incorruptible God. ROMANS 1:23 •

If anyone does not have the Spirit of Christ, he is not His. And if Christ is in you, the body is dead because of sin, but the Spirit is life because of righteousness. But if the Spirit of Him who raised Jesus from the dead dwells in you, He who raised Christ from the dead will also give life to your mortal bodies through His Spirit who dwells in you. ROMANS 8:9–11 • The body is sown in corruption, it is raised in incorruption. 1 CORINTHIANS 15:42 •

Have salt in yourselves, and have peace with one another. MARK 9:50 • Let no corrupt word proceed out of your mouth, but what is good for necessary edification, that it may impart grace to the hearers. EPHESIANS 4:29 •

September 14

Morning Reading

I, even I, am He who comforts you.
ISAIAH 51:12

Blessed be the God and Father of our Lord Jesus Christ, the Father of mercies and God of all comfort, who comforts us in all our tribulation, that we may be able to comfort those who are in any trouble, with the comfort with which we ourselves are comforted by God. 2 CORINTHIANS 1:3–4 • As a father pities his children, so the LORD pities those who fear Him. For He knows our frame; He remembers that we are dust. PSALM 103:13–14 • As one whom his mother comforts, so I will comfort you. ISAIAH 66:13 • Casting all your care upon Him, for He cares for you. 1 PETER 5:7 •

You, O Lord, are a God full of compassion, and gracious, longsuffering and abundant in mercy and truth. PSALM 86:15 •

Another Helper, the Spirit of truth. JOHN 14:16–17 • The Spirit also helps in our weaknesses. ROMANS 8:26 •

God will wipe away every tear from their eyes; there shall be no more death, nor sorrow, nor crying. There shall be no more pain, for the former things have passed away. REVELATION 21:4 •

Evening Reading

You were called into the fellowship of His Son.
1 CORINTHIANS 1:9

He received from God the Father honor and glory when such a voice came to Him from the Excellent Glory: "This is My beloved Son, in whom I am well pleased." 2 PETER 1:17 • Behold what manner of love the Father has bestowed on us, that we should be called children of God! 1 JOHN 3:1 •

Be imitators of God as dear children. EPHESIANS 5:1 • If children, then heirs; heirs of God and joint heirs with Christ. ROMANS 8:17 •

The brightness of His glory and the express image of His person. HEBREWS 1:3 • Let your light so shine before men, that they may see your good works and glorify your Father in heaven. MATTHEW 5:16 •

Jesus, the author and finisher of our faith,...for the joy that was set before Him endured the cross, despising the shame. HEBREWS 12:2 • These things I speak in the world, that they may have My joy fulfilled in themselves. JOHN 17:13 • As the sufferings of Christ abound in us, so our consolation also abounds through Christ. 2 CORINTHIANS 1:5 •

September 15

Morning Reading

Sin shall not have dominion over you,
for you are not under law but under grace.
ROMANS 6:14

What then? Shall we sin because we are not under law but under grace? Certainly not! ROMANS 6:15 • My brethren, you also have become dead to the law through the body of Christ, that you may be married to another; to Him who was raised from the dead, that we should bear fruit to God. ROMANS 7:4 • Not being without law toward God, but under law toward Christ. 1 CORINTHIANS 9:21 • The sting of death is sin, and the strength of sin is the law. But thanks be to God, who gives us the victory through our Lord Jesus Christ. 1 CORINTHIANS 15:56–57 •

The law of the Spirit of life in Christ Jesus has made me free from the law of sin and death. ROMANS 8:2 • Whoever commits sin is a slave of sin. JOHN 8:34 • If the Son makes you free, you shall be free indeed. JOHN 8:36 •

Stand fast therefore in the liberty by which Christ has made us free, and do not be entangled again with a yoke of bondage. GALATIANS 5:1 •

Evening Reading

A double-minded man [is] *unstable in all his ways.*
JAMES 1:8

No one, having put his hand to the plow, and looking back, is fit for the kingdom of God. LUKE 9:62 •

He who comes to God must believe that He is, and that He is a rewarder of those who diligently seek Him. HEBREWS 11:6 • Let him ask in faith, with no doubting, for he who doubts is like a wave of the sea driven and tossed by the wind. For let not that man suppose that he will receive anything from the Lord. JAMES 1:6–7 • Whatever things you ask when you pray, believe that you receive them, and you will have them. MARK 11:24 •

No longer be children, tossed to and fro and carried about with every wind of doctrine, by the trickery of men, in the cunning craftiness of deceitful plotting, but, speaking the truth in love,...grow up in all things into Him who is the head; [even] Christ. EPHESIANS 4:14–15 •

Abide in Me. JOHN 15:4 • Be steadfast, immovable, always abounding in the work of the Lord, knowing that your labor is not in vain in the Lord. 1 CORINTHIANS 15:58 •

September 16

Morning Reading

The LORD weighs the hearts.
PROVERBS 21:2

The LORD knows the way of the righteous, but the way of the ungodly shall perish. PSALM 1:6 • The LORD will show who is His and who is holy. NUMBERS 16:5 • Your Father who sees in secret will Himself reward you openly. MATTHEW 6:4 •

Search me, O God, and know my heart; try me, and know my anxieties; and see if there is any wicked way in me, and lead me in the way everlasting. PSALM 139:23–24 • There is no fear in love; but perfect love casts out fear. 1 JOHN 4:18 •

Lord, all my desire is before You; and my sighing is not hidden from You. PSALM 38:9 • When my spirit was overwhelmed within me, then You knew my path. PSALM 142:3 • He who searches the hearts knows what the mind of the Spirit is, because He makes intercession for the saints according to the will of God. ROMANS 8:27 •

The solid foundation of God stands, having this seal: "The Lord knows those who are His," and, "Let everyone who names the name of Christ depart from iniquity." 2 TIMOTHY 2:19 •

Evening Reading

Weeping may endure for a night, but joy comes in the morning.
PSALM 30:5

No one should be shaken by these afflictions; for you yourselves know that we are appointed to this. For, in fact, we told you before when we were with you that we would suffer tribulation. 1 THESSALONIANS 3:3–4 • In Me you...have peace. In the world you will have tribulation; but be of good cheer, I have overcome the world. JOHN 16:33 •

I shall be satisfied when I awake in Your likeness. PSALM 17:15 • The night is far spent, the day is at hand. ROMANS 13:12 • He shall be like the light of the morning when the sun rises, a morning without clouds, like the tender grass springing out of the earth, by clear shining after rain. 2 SAMUEL 23:4 •

He will swallow up death forever, and the Lord GOD will wipe away tears from all faces. ISAIAH 25:8 • There shall be no more death, nor sorrow, nor crying. There shall be no more pain, for the former things have passed away. REVELATION 21:4 • We who are alive and remain shall be caught up together with them in the clouds to meet the Lord in the air. And thus we shall always be with the Lord. Therefore comfort one another with these words. 1 THESSALONIANS 4:17–18 •

September 17

Morning Reading

A bruised reed He will not break.
MATTHEW 12:20

The sacrifices of God are a broken spirit, a broken and a contrite heart; these, O God, You will not despise. PSALM 51:17 • He heals the brokenhearted and binds up their wounds. PSALM 147:3 • For thus says the High and Lofty One who inhabits eternity, whose name is Holy: "I dwell in the high and holy place, with him who has a contrite and humble spirit, to revive the spirit of the humble, and to revive the heart of the contrite ones. For I will not contend forever, nor will I always be angry; for the spirit would fail before Me, and the souls which I have made." ISAIAH 57:15–16 •

I will seek what was lost and bring back what was driven away, bind up the broken and strengthen what was sick. EZEKIEL 34:16 • Therefore strengthen the hands which hang down, and the feeble knees, and make straight paths for your feet, so that what is lame may not be dislocated, but rather be healed. HEBREWS 12:12–13 • Behold, your God...will come and save you. ISAIAH 35:4 •

Evening Reading

Oh, taste and see that the LORD is good;
blessed is the man who trusts in Him!
PSALM 34:8

When the master of the feast had tasted the water that was made wine, and did not know where it came from...he said,..."Every man at the beginning sets out the good wine, and when the guests have well drunk, then the inferior. You have kept the good wine until now!" JOHN 2:9–10 •

For the ear tests words as the palate tastes food. JOB 34:3 • I believed and therefore I spoke. 2 CORINTHIANS 4:13 • I know whom I have believed. 2 TIMOTHY 1:12 • I sat down in his shade with great delight, and his fruit was sweet to my taste. SONG OF SONGS 2:3 •

The goodness of God. ROMANS 2:4 • He who did not spare His own Son, but delivered Him up for us all, how shall He not with Him also freely give us all things? ROMANS 8:32 •

As newborn babes, desire the pure milk of the word, that you may grow thereby, if indeed you have tasted that the Lord is gracious. 1 PETER 2:2–3 •

Let all those rejoice who put their trust in You; let them ever shout for joy. PSALM 5:11 •

September 18

Morning Reading

Open my eyes, that I may see wondrous things from Your law.
PSALM 119:18

He opened their understanding, that they might comprehend the Scriptures. LUKE 24:45 • It has been given to you to know the mysteries of the kingdom of heaven, but to them it has not been given. MATTHEW 13:11 • I thank You, Father, Lord of heaven and earth, that You have hidden these things from the wise and prudent and have revealed them to babes. Even so, Father, for so it seemed good in Your sight. MATTHEW 11:25–26 • We have received, not the spirit of the world, but the Spirit who is from God, that we might know the things that have been freely given to us by God. 1 CORINTHIANS 2:12 • How precious also are Your thoughts to me, O God! How great is the sum of them! If I should count them, they would be more in number than the sand. PSALM 139:17–18 • Oh, the depth of the riches both of the wisdom and knowledge of God! How unsearchable are His judgments and His ways past finding out! For who has known the mind of the LORD? Or who has become His counselor?...For of Him and through Him and to Him are all things, to whom be glory forever. Amen. ROMANS 11:33–34, 36 •

Evening Reading

En Hakkore [Spring of the Caller].
JUDGES 15:19

If you knew the gift of God, and who it is who says to you, "Give Me a drink," you would have asked Him, and He would have given you living water. JOHN 4:10 • Jesus stood and cried out, saying, "If anyone thirsts, let him come to Me and drink."...This He spoke concerning the Spirit, whom those believing in Him would receive. JOHN 7:37, 39 •

"Try Me now in this," says the LORD of hosts, "if I will not open for you the windows of heaven and pour out for you such blessing that there will not be room enough to receive it." MALACHI 3:10 • If you then, being evil, know how to give good gifts to your children, how much more will your heavenly Father give the Holy Spirit to those who ask Him! LUKE 11:13 • Ask, and it will be given to you; seek, and you will find. LUKE 11:9 •

Because you are sons, God has sent forth the Spirit of His Son into your hearts, crying out, "Abba, Father!" GALATIANS 4:6 • You did not receive the spirit of bondage again to fear, but you received the Spirit of adoption by whom we cry out, "Abba, Father." ROMANS 8:15 •

September 19

Morning Reading

The God of all grace.
1 PETER 5:10

I will proclaim the name of the LORD before you. I will be gracious to whom I will be gracious. EXODUS 33:19 • He is gracious to him, and says, "Deliver him from going down to the Pit; I have found a ransom." JOB 33:24 • Being justified freely by His grace through the redemption that is in Christ Jesus, whom God set forth as a propitiation by His blood, through faith, to demonstrate His righteousness, because in His forbearance God had passed over the sins that were previously committed. ROMANS 3:24–25 • Grace and truth came through Jesus Christ. JOHN 1:17 •

By grace you have been saved through faith, and that not of yourselves; it is the gift of God. EPHESIANS 2:8 • Grace, mercy, and peace from God our Father and Jesus Christ our Lord. 1 TIMOTHY 1:2 • To each one of us grace was given according to the measure of Christ's gift. EPHESIANS 4:7 • As each one has received a gift, minister it to one another, as good stewards of the manifold grace of God. 1 PETER 4:10 • He gives more grace. Therefore He says: "God resists the proud, but gives grace to the humble." JAMES 4:6 •

Grow in the grace and knowledge of our Lord and Savior Jesus Christ. To Him be the glory both now and forever. Amen. 2 PETER 3:18 •

Evening Reading

I will lift up my eyes to the hills; from whence comes my help? My help comes from the LORD, who made heaven and earth.
PSALM 121:1–2

As the mountains surround Jerusalem, so the LORD surrounds His people from this time forth and forever. PSALM 125:2 •

Unto You I lift up my eyes, O You who dwell in the heavens. Behold, as the eyes of servants look to the hand of their masters, as the eyes of a maid to the hand of her mistress, so our eyes look to the LORD our God, until He has mercy on us. PSALM 123:1–2 • Because You have been my help, therefore in the shadow of Your wings I will rejoice. PSALM 63:7 •

O our God, will You not judge them? For we have no power against this great multitude that is coming against us; nor do we know what to do, but our eyes are upon You. 2 CHRONICLES 20:12 • My eyes are ever toward the LORD, for He shall pluck my feet out of the net. PSALM 25:15 • Our help is in the name of the LORD, who made heaven and earth. PSALM 124:8 •

September 20

Morning Reading

*Happy is the man who finds wisdom, and the man
who gains understanding.*
PROVERBS 3:13

Whoever finds [wisdom] finds life, and obtains favor from the Lord. PROVERBS 8:35 •

Thus says the Lord: "Let not the wise man glory in his wisdom, let not the mighty man glory in his might, nor let the rich man glory in his riches; but let him who glories glory in this, that he understands and knows Me, that I am the Lord." JEREMIAH 9:23–24 • The fear of the Lord is the beginning of wisdom. PROVERBS 9:10 •

What things were gain to me, these I have counted loss for Christ. Yet indeed I also count all things loss for the excellence of the knowledge of Christ Jesus my Lord, for whom I have suffered the loss of all things, and count them as rubbish, that I may gain Christ. PHILIPPIANS 3:7–8 • In whom are hidden all the treasures of wisdom and knowledge. COLOSSIANS 2:3 • Counsel is mine, and sound wisdom; I am understanding, I have strength. PROVERBS 8:14 •

Christ Jesus...became for us wisdom from God; and righteousness and sanctification and redemption. 1 CORINTHIANS 1:30 •

He who wins souls is wise. PROVERBS 11:30 •

Evening Reading

Poor, yet making many rich.
2 CORINTHIANS 6:10

You know the grace of our Lord Jesus Christ, that though He was rich, yet for your sakes He became poor, that you through His poverty might become rich. 2 CORINTHIANS 8:9 • Of His fullness we have all received, and grace for grace. JOHN 1:16 • My God shall supply all your need according to His riches in glory by Christ Jesus. PHILIPPIANS 4:19 • God is able to make all grace abound toward you, that you, always having all sufficiency in all things, may have an abundance for every good work. 2 CORINTHIANS 9:8 •

Has God not chosen the poor of this world to be rich in faith and heirs of the kingdom which He promised to those who love Him? JAMES 2:5 • Not many wise according to the flesh, not many mighty, not many noble, are called. But God has chosen the foolish things of the world to put to shame the wise, and God has chosen the weak things of the world to put to shame the things which are mighty. 1 CORINTHIANS 1:26–27 •

We have this treasure in earthen vessels, that the excellence of the power may be of God and not of us. 2 CORINTHIANS 4:7 •

September 21

Morning Reading

*We know that all things work together for good
to those who love God.*
ROMANS 8:28

Surely the wrath of man shall praise You; with the remainder of wrath You shall gird Yourself. PSALM 76:10 • You meant evil against me; but God meant it for good. GENESIS 50:20 •

All things are yours: whether...the world or life or death, or things present or things to come; all are yours. And you are Christ's, and Christ is God's. 1 CORINTHIANS 3:21–23 • All things are for your sakes, that grace, having spread through the many, may cause thanksgiving to abound to the glory of God. Therefore we do not lose heart. Even though our outward man is perishing, yet the inward man is being renewed day by day. For our light affliction, which is but for a moment, is working for us a far more exceeding and eternal weight of glory. 2 CORINTHIANS 4:15–17 •

My brethren, count it all joy when you fall into various trials, knowing that the testing of your faith produces patience. But let patience have its perfect work, that you may be perfect and complete, lacking nothing. JAMES 1:2–4 •

Evening Reading

The communion of the Holy Spirit be with you all.
2 CORINTHIANS 13:14

I will pray the Father, and He will give you another Helper, that He may abide with you forever; the Spirit of truth, whom the world cannot receive, because it neither sees Him nor knows Him; but you know Him, for He dwells with you and will be in you. JOHN 14:16–17 • He will not speak on His own authority, but whatever He hears He will speak; and He will tell you things to come. He will glorify Me, for He will take of what is Mine and declare it to you. JOHN 16:13–14 •

The love of God has been poured out in our hearts by the Holy Spirit who was given to us. ROMANS 5:5 •

He who is joined to the Lord is one spirit with Him....Do you not know that your body is the temple of the Holy Spirit who is in you, whom you have from God, and you are not your own? 1 CORINTHIANS 6:17, 19 •

Do not grieve the Holy Spirit of God, by whom you were sealed for the day of redemption. EPHESIANS 4:30 • The Spirit also helps in our weaknesses. For we do not know what we should pray for as we ought, but the Spirit Himself makes intercession for us with groanings which cannot be uttered. ROMANS 8:26 •

September 22

Morning Reading

May my meditation be sweet to Him; I will be glad in the LORD.
PSALM 104:34

Like an apple tree among the trees of the woods, so is my beloved among the sons. I sat down in his shade with great delight, and his fruit was sweet to my taste. SONG OF SONGS 2:3 • For who in the heavens can be compared to the LORD? Who among the sons of the mighty can be likened to the LORD? PSALM 89:6 •

My beloved is white and ruddy, chief among ten thousand. SONG OF SONGS 5:10 • One pearl of great price. MATTHEW 13:46 • The ruler over the kings of the earth. REVELATION 1:5 •

His head is like the finest gold; his locks are wavy, and black as a raven. SONG OF SONGS 5:11 • Head over all things. EPHESIANS 1:22 • The head of the body, the church. COLOSSIANS 1:18 •

His cheeks are like a bed of spices, banks of scented herbs. SONG OF SONGS 5:13 • He could not be hidden. MARK 7:24 •

His lips are lilies, dripping liquid myrrh. SONG OF SONGS 5:13 • No man ever spoke like this Man! JOHN 7:46 •

His countenance is like Lebanon, excellent as the cedars. SONG OF SONGS 5:15 • Make Your face shine upon Your servant. PSALM 31:16 • LORD, lift up the light of Your countenance upon us. PSALM 4:6 •

Evening Reading

My Father, if it is possible, let this cup pass from Me;
nevertheless, not as I will, but as You will.
MATTHEW 26:39

Now My soul is troubled, and what shall I say? "Father, save Me from this hour"? But for this purpose I came to this hour. JOHN 12:27 •

I have come down from heaven, not to do My own will, but the will of Him who sent Me. JOHN 6:38 • [Jesus]...became obedient to the point of death, even the death of the cross. PHILIPPIANS 2:8 • In the days of His flesh, when He had offered up prayers and supplications, with vehement cries and tears to Him who was able to save Him from death, and was heard because of His godly fear, though He was a Son, yet He learned obedience by the things which He suffered. HEBREWS 5:7–8 •

Do you think that I cannot now pray to My Father, and He will provide Me with more than twelve legions of angels? MATTHEW 26:53 • Thus it is written, and thus it was necessary for the Christ to suffer and to rise from the dead the third day, and that repentance and remission of sins should be preached in His name to all nations, beginning at Jerusalem. LUKE 24:46–47 •

September 23

Morning Reading

Our God did not forsake us.
Ezra 9:9

Beloved, do not think it strange concerning the fiery trial which is to try you, as though some strange thing happened to you. 1 Peter 4:12 • If you endure chastening, God deals with you as with sons; for what son is there whom a father does not chasten? But if you are without chastening, of which all have become partakers, then you are illegitimate and not sons. Hebrews 12:7–8 •

The Lord your God is testing you to know whether you love the Lord your God with all your heart and with all your soul. Deuteronomy 13:3 •

The Lord will not forsake His people, for His great name's sake, because it has pleased the Lord to make you His people. 1 Samuel 12:22 • Can a woman forget her nursing child, and not have compassion on the son of her womb? Surely they may forget, yet I will not forget you. Isaiah 49:15 • Happy is he who has the God of Jacob for his help, whose hope is in the Lord his God. Psalm 146:5 •

Shall God not avenge His own elect who cry out day and night to Him, though He bears long with them? I tell you that He will avenge them speedily. Luke 18:7–8 •

Evening Reading

He who overcomes shall inherit all things.
Revelation 21:7

If in this life only we have hope in Christ, we are of all men the most pitiable. 1 Corinthians 15:19 • Now they desire a better, that is, a heavenly country. Therefore God is not ashamed to be called their God, for He has prepared a city for them. Hebrews 11:16 • An inheritance incorruptible and undefiled and that does not fade away, reserved in heaven for you. 1 Peter 1:4 •

All things are yours:...the world or life or death, or things present or things to come; all are yours. 1 Corinthians 3:21–22 • Eye has not seen, nor ear heard, nor have entered into the heart of man the things which God has prepared for those who love Him. But God has revealed them to us through His Spirit. 1 Corinthians 2:9–10 •

Look to yourselves, that we do not lose those things we worked for, but that we may receive a full reward. 2 John 8 • Let us lay aside every weight, and the sin which so easily ensnares us, and let us run with endurance the race that is set before us. Hebrews 12:1 •

September 24

Morning Reading

It is good for me to draw near to God.
PSALM 73:28

LORD, I have loved the habitation of Your house, and the place where Your glory dwells. PSALM 26:8 • A day in Your courts is better than a thousand. I would rather be a doorkeeper in the house of my God than dwell in the tents of wickedness. PSALM 84:10 • Blessed is the man You choose, and cause to approach You, that he may dwell in Your courts. We shall be satisfied with the goodness of Your house, of Your holy temple. PSALM 65:4 •

The LORD is good to those who wait for Him, to the soul who seeks Him. LAMENTATIONS 3:25 • Therefore the LORD will wait, that He may be gracious to you; and therefore He will be exalted, that He may have mercy on you. For the LORD is a God of justice; blessed are all those who wait for Him. ISAIAH 30:18 •

Therefore, brethren, having boldness to enter the Holiest by the blood of Jesus, by a new and living way which He consecrated for us,... let us draw near with a true heart in full assurance of faith, having our hearts sprinkled from an evil conscience. HEBREWS 10:19–20, 22 •

Evening Reading

You know the grace of our Lord Jesus Christ.
2 CORINTHIANS 8:9

The Word became flesh and dwelt among us, and we beheld His glory, the glory as of the only begotten of the Father, full of grace and truth. JOHN 1:14 • You are fairer than the sons of men; grace is poured upon Your lips. PSALM 45:2 • All bore witness to Him, and marveled at the gracious words which proceeded out of His mouth. LUKE 4:22 •

You have tasted that the Lord is gracious. 1 PETER 2:3 • He who believes in the Son of God has the witness in himself. 1 JOHN 5:10 • We speak what We know and testify what We have seen. JOHN 3:11 •

Oh, taste and see that the LORD is good; blessed is the man who trusts in Him! PSALM 34:8 • I sat down in his shade with great delight, and his fruit was sweet to my taste. SONG OF SONGS 2:3 •

[The Lord Jesus] said to me, "My grace is sufficient for you, for My strength is made perfect in weakness." 2 CORINTHIANS 12:9 • To each one of us grace was given according to the measure of Christ's gift. EPHESIANS 4:7 • As each one has received a gift, minister it to one another, as good stewards of the manifold grace of God. 1 PETER 4:10 •

September 25

Morning Reading

*Let patience have its perfect work, that you may be perfect
and complete, lacking nothing.*
JAMES 1:4

Now for a little while, if need be, you have been grieved by various trials, that the genuineness of your faith, being much more precious than gold that perishes, though it is tested by fire, may be found to praise, honor, and glory at the revelation of Jesus Christ. 1 PETER 1:6–7 • We also glory in tribulations, knowing that tribulation produces perseverance; and perseverance, character; and character, hope. ROMANS 5:3–4 •

It is good that one should hope and wait quietly for the salvation of the LORD. LAMENTATIONS 3:26 • You have a better and an enduring possession for yourselves in heaven. Therefore do not cast away your confidence, which has great reward. For you have need of endurance, so that after you have done the will of God, you may receive the promise. HEBREWS 10:34–36 • May our Lord Jesus Christ Himself, and our God and Father, who has loved us and given us everlasting consolation and good hope by grace, comfort your hearts. 2 THESSALONIANS 2:16–17 •

Evening Reading

God will judge the secrets of men by Jesus Christ.
ROMANS 2:16

Judge nothing before the time, until the Lord comes, who will both bring to light the hidden things of darkness and reveal the counsels of the hearts. Then each one's praise will come from God. 1 CORINTHIANS 4:5 • The Father judges no one, but has committed all judgment to the Son,...because He is the Son of Man. JOHN 5:22, 27 • The Son of God...has eyes like a flame of fire. REVELATION 2:18 •

They say, "How does God know? And is there knowledge in the Most High?" PSALM 73:11 • These things you have done, and I kept silent; you thought that I was altogether like you; but I will rebuke you, and set them in order before your eyes. PSALM 50:21 • There is nothing covered that will not be revealed, nor hidden that will not be known. LUKE 12:2 •

Lord, all my desire is before You; and my sighing is not hidden from You. PSALM 38:9 • Examine me, O LORD, and prove me; try my mind and my heart. PSALM 26:2 •

September 26

Morning Reading

A God of truth and without injustice; righteous and upright is He.
DEUTERONOMY 32:4

Him who judges righteously. 1 PETER 2:23 • We must all appear before the judgment seat of Christ, that each one may receive the things done in the body, according to what he has done, whether good or bad. 2 CORINTHIANS 5:10 • Each of us shall give account of himself to God. ROMANS 14:12 • The soul who sins shall die. EZEKIEL 18:4 •

"Awake, O sword, against My Shepherd, against the Man who is My Companion," says the LORD of hosts. "Strike the Shepherd." ZECHARIAH 13:7 • The LORD has laid on Him the iniquity of us all. ISAIAH 53:6 • Mercy and truth have met together; righteousness and peace have kissed. PSALM 85:10 • Mercy triumphs over judgment. JAMES 2:13 • The wages of sin is death, but the gift of God is eternal life in Christ Jesus our Lord. ROMANS 6:23 •

A just God and a Savior; there is none besides Me. ISAIAH 45:21 • That He might be just and the justifier of the one who has faith in Jesus. ROMANS 3:26 • Justified freely by His grace through the redemption that is in Christ Jesus. ROMANS 3:24 •

Evening Reading

Death is swallowed up in victory.
1 CORINTHIANS 15:54

Thanks be to God, who gives us the victory through our Lord Jesus Christ. 1 CORINTHIANS 15:57 •

Inasmuch then as the children have partaken of flesh and blood, He Himself likewise shared in the same, that through death He might destroy him who had the power of death, that is, the devil, and release those who through fear of death were all their lifetime subject to bondage. HEBREWS 2:14-15 •

If we died with Christ, we believe that we shall also live with Him, knowing that Christ, having been raised from the dead, dies no more. Death no longer has dominion over Him. For the death that He died, He died to sin once for all; but the life that He lives, He lives to God. ROMANS 6:8-10 •

Likewise you also, reckon yourselves to be dead indeed to sin, but alive to God in Christ Jesus our Lord. ROMANS 6:11 •

In all these things we are more than conquerors through Him who loved us. ROMANS 8:37 •

September 27

Morning Reading

Therefore humble yourselves under the mighty hand of God, that He may exalt you in due time.
1 PETER 5:6

Everyone proud in heart is an abomination to the LORD; though they join forces, none will go unpunished. PROVERBS 16:5 •

O LORD, You are our Father; we are the clay, and You our potter; and all we are the work of Your hand. Do not be furious, O LORD, nor remember iniquity forever; indeed, please look; we all are Your people! ISAIAH 64:8–9 • You have chastised me, and I was chastised, like an untrained bull; restore me, and I will return, for You are the LORD my God. Surely, after my turning, I repented; and after I was instructed, I struck myself on the thigh; I was ashamed, yes, even humiliated, because I bore the reproach of my youth. JEREMIAH 31:18–19 • It is good for a man to bear the yoke in his youth. LAMENTATIONS 3:27 •

Affliction does not come from the dust, nor does trouble spring from the ground; yet man is born to trouble, as the sparks fly upward. JOB 5:6–7 •

Evening Reading

Has God indeed said...?
GENESIS 3:1

When the tempter came to Him, he said, "If You are the Son of God...." [Jesus] said, "It is written....It is written....It is written."...Then the devil left Him. MATTHEW 4:3–4, 7, 10–11 •

[The man of God] said, "I cannot return with you....For I have been told by the word of the LORD, 'You shall not eat bread nor drink water there, nor return by going the way you came.'" [The old prophet] said to him, "I too am a prophet as you are, and an angel spoke to me by the word of the LORD, saying, 'Bring him back with you to your house, that he may eat bread and drink water.'" (He was lying to him.) So he went back with him, and ate bread in his house, and drank water....The man of God...was disobedient to the word of the LORD. Therefore the LORD has delivered him to the lion, which has torn him and killed him, according to the word of the LORD. 1 KINGS 13:16–19, 26 • Even if we, or an angel from heaven, preach any other gospel to you than what we have preached to you, let him be accursed. GALATIANS 1:8 • Your word I have hidden in my heart, that I might not sin against You! PSALM 119:11 •

September 28

Morning Reading

They shall put My name on the children of Israel,
and I will bless them.
NUMBERS 6:27

We have become like those of old, over whom You never ruled, those who were never called by Your name. ISAIAH 63:19 • O LORD our God, masters besides You have had dominion over us; but by You only we make mention of Your name. ISAIAH 26:13 •

All peoples of the earth shall see that you are called by the name of the LORD, and they shall be afraid of you. DEUTERONOMY 28:10 • The LORD will not forsake His people, for His great name's sake, because it has pleased the LORD to make you His people. 1 SAMUEL 12:22 •

O Lord, hear! O Lord, forgive! O Lord, listen and act! Do not delay for Your own sake, my God, for Your city and Your people are called by Your name. DANIEL 9:19 • Help us, O God of our salvation, for the glory of Your name; and deliver us, and provide atonement for our sins, for Your name's sake! Why should the nations say, "Where is their God?" PSALM 79:9–10 •

The name of the LORD is a strong tower; the righteous run to it and are safe. PROVERBS 18:10 •

Evening Reading

The heavens declare the glory of God;
and the firmament shows His handiwork.
PSALM 19:1

Since the creation of the world His invisible attributes are clearly seen, being understood by the things that are made, even His eternal power and Godhead. ROMANS 1:20 • He did not leave Himself without witness. ACTS 14:17 • Day unto day utters speech, and night unto night reveals knowledge. There is no speech nor language where their voice is not heard. PSALM 19:2–3 •

When I consider Your heavens, the work of Your fingers, the moon and the stars, which You have ordained, what is man that You are mindful of him, and the son of man that You visit him? PSALM 8:3–4 •

There is one glory of the sun, another glory of the moon, and another glory of the stars; for one star differs from another star in glory. So also is the resurrection of the dead. 1 CORINTHIANS 15:41–42 • Those who are wise shall shine like the brightness of the firmament, and those who turn many to righteousness like the stars forever and ever. DANIEL 12:3 •

September 29

Morning Reading

By this we know love, because He laid down His life for us.
1 JOHN 3:16

The love of Christ which passes knowledge. EPHESIANS 3:19 • Greater love has no one than this, than to lay down one's life for his friends. JOHN 15:13 • You know the grace of our Lord Jesus Christ, that though He was rich, yet for your sakes He became poor, that you through His poverty might become rich. 2 CORINTHIANS 8:9 • Beloved, if God so loved us, we also ought to love one another. 1 JOHN 4:11 • Be kind to one another, tenderhearted, forgiving one another, just as God in Christ forgave you. EPHESIANS 4:32 • Bearing with one another, and forgiving one another, if anyone has a complaint against another; even as Christ forgave you, so you also must do. COLOSSIANS 3:13 • For even the Son of Man did not come to be served, but to serve, and to give His life a ransom for many. MARK 10:45 • Christ also suffered for us, leaving us an example, that you should follow His steps. 1 PETER 2:21 •

You also ought to wash one another's feet. For I have given you an example, that you should do as I have done to you. JOHN 13:14–15 • We also ought to lay down our lives for the brethren. 1 JOHN 3:16 •

Evening Reading

Whatever [the Father] *does, the Son also does in like manner.*
JOHN 5:19

The LORD gives wisdom; from His mouth come knowledge and understanding. PROVERBS 2:6 • I will give you a mouth and wisdom which all your adversaries will not be able to contradict or resist. LUKE 21:15 •

Wait on the LORD; be of good courage, and He shall strengthen your heart. PSALM 27:14 • My grace is sufficient for you, for My strength is made perfect in weakness. 2 CORINTHIANS 12:9 •

Those who are called, sanctified by God the Father. JUDE 1 • He who sanctifies and those who are being sanctified are all of one, for which reason He is not ashamed to call them brethren. HEBREWS 2:11 •

"Do I not fill heaven and earth?" says the LORD. JEREMIAH 23:24 • The fullness of Him who fills all in all. EPHESIANS 1:23 •

I, even I, am the LORD, and besides Me there is no savior. ISAIAH 43:11 • This is indeed the Christ, the Savior of the world. JOHN 4:42 •

Grace, mercy, and peace from God the Father and the Lord Jesus Christ our Savior. TITUS 1:4 •

September 30

Morning Reading

He knows the way that I take; when He has tested me,
I shall come forth as gold.
JOB 23:10

He knows our frame. PSALM 103:14 • He does not afflict willingly, nor grieve the children of men. LAMENTATIONS 3:33 •

The solid foundation of God stands, having this seal: "The Lord knows those who are His," and, "Let everyone who names the name of Christ depart from iniquity." But in a great house there are not only vessels of gold and silver, but also of wood and clay, some for honor and some for dishonor. Therefore if anyone cleanses himself from the latter, he will be a vessel for honor, sanctified and useful for the Master, prepared for every good work. 2 TIMOTHY 2:19–21 •

He will sit as a refiner and a purifier of silver; He will purify the sons of Levi, and purge them as gold and silver, that they may offer to the Lord an offering in righteousness. MALACHI 3:3 • I...will refine them as silver is refined....They will call on My name, and I will answer them. I will say, "This is My people"; and each one will say, "The Lord is my God." ZECHARIAH 13:9 •

Evening Reading

Show me Your ways, O LORD; teach me Your paths.
PSALM 25:4

Moses said to the LORD, "...I pray, if I have found grace in Your sight, show me now Your way, that I may know You and that I may find grace in Your sight...." And He said, "My Presence will go with you, and I will give you rest." EXODUS 33:12–14 • He made known His ways to Moses, his acts to the children of Israel. PSALM 103:7 •

The humble He guides in justice, and the humble He teaches His way....Who is the man that fears the LORD? Him shall He teach in the way He chooses. PSALM 25:9, 12 •

Trust in the LORD with all your heart, and lean not on your own understanding; in all your ways acknowledge Him, and He shall direct your paths. PROVERBS 3:5–6 •

You will show me the path of life; in Your presence is fullness of joy; at Your right hand are pleasures forevermore. PSALM 16:11 • I will instruct you and teach you in the way you should go; I will guide you with My eye. PSALM 32:8 • The path of the just is like the shining sun, that shines ever brighter unto the perfect day. PROVERBS 4:18 •

OCTOBER

October 1

Morning Reading

The fruit of the Spirit is...self-control.
GALATIANS 5:22–23

Everyone who competes for the prize is temperate in all things. Now they do it to obtain a perishable crown, but we for an imperishable crown. Therefore I run thus: not with uncertainty. Thus I fight: not as one who beats the air. But I discipline my body and bring it into subjection, lest, when I have preached to others, I myself should become disqualified. 1 CORINTHIANS 9:25–27 •

Do not be drunk with wine, in which is dissipation; but be filled with the Spirit. EPHESIANS 5:18 •

If anyone desires to come after Me, let him deny himself, and take up his cross, and follow Me. MATTHEW 16:24 •

Let us not sleep, as others do, but let us watch and be sober. For those who sleep, sleep at night, and those who get drunk are drunk at night. But let us who are of the day be sober, putting on the breastplate of faith and love, and as a helmet the hope of salvation. 1 THESSALONIANS 5:6–8 • Denying ungodliness and worldly lusts, we should live soberly, righteously, and godly in the present age, looking for the blessed hope and glorious appearing of our great God and Savior Jesus Christ. TITUS 2:12–13 •

Evening Reading

Grow up in all things into Him who is the head; [even] *Christ.*
EPHESIANS 4:15

First the blade, then the head, after that the full grain in the head. MARK 4:28 • Till we all come to the unity of the faith and of the knowledge of the Son of God, to a perfect man, to the measure of the stature of the fullness of Christ. EPHESIANS 4:13 •

They, measuring themselves by themselves, and comparing themselves among themselves, are not wise....But "he who glories, let him glory in the LORD." For not he who commends himself is approved, but whom the Lord commends. 2 CORINTHIANS 10:12, 17–18 •

The substance is of Christ. Let no one cheat you of your reward, taking delight in false humility and worship of angels, intruding into those things which he has not seen, vainly puffed up by his fleshly mind, and not holding fast to the Head, from whom all the body, nourished and knit together by joints and ligaments, grows with the increase that is from God. COLOSSIANS 2:17–19 •

Grow in the grace and knowledge of our Lord and Savior Jesus Christ. 2 PETER 3:18 •

October 2

Morning Reading

The goat shall bear on itself all their iniquities to an uninhabited land; and he shall release the goat in the wilderness.
LEVITICUS 16:22

As far as the east is from the west, so far has He removed our transgressions from us. PSALM 103:12 • "In those days and in that time," says the LORD, "the iniquity of Israel shall be sought, but there shall be none; and the sins of Judah, but they shall not be found; for I will pardon those whom I preserve." JEREMIAH 50:20 • You will cast all our sins into the depths of the sea. MICAH 7:19 • Who is a God like You, pardoning iniquity? MICAH 7:18 •

All we like sheep have gone astray; we have turned, every one, to his own way; and the LORD has laid on Him the iniquity of us all....He shall bear their iniquities. Therefore I will divide Him a portion with the great, and He shall divide the spoil with the strong, because He poured out His soul unto death, and He was numbered with the transgressors, and He bore the sin of many, and made intercession for the transgressors. ISAIAH 53:6, 11–12 • The Lamb of God who takes away the sin of the world! JOHN 1:29 •

Evening Reading

*Who makes you differ from another?
And what do you have that you did not receive?*
1 CORINTHIANS 4:7

By the grace of God I am what I am. 1 CORINTHIANS 15:10 • Of His own will He brought us forth by the word of truth. JAMES 1:18 • It is not of him who wills, nor of him who runs, but of God who shows mercy. ROMANS 9:16 • Where is boasting then? It is excluded. ROMANS 3:27 • Christ Jesus... became for us wisdom from God; and righteousness and sanctification and redemption; that, as it is written, "He who glories, let him glory in the LORD." 1 CORINTHIANS 1:30–31 •

You He made alive, who were dead in trespasses and sins, in which you once walked according to the course of this world, according to the prince of the power of the air, the spirit who now works in the sons of disobedience, among whom also we all once conducted ourselves in the lusts of our flesh, fulfilling the desires of the flesh and of the mind, and were by nature children of wrath, just as the others. EPHESIANS 2:1–3 • You were washed, but you were sanctified, but you were justified in the name of the Lord Jesus and by the Spirit of our God. 1 CORINTHIANS 6:11 •

October 3

Morning Reading

To Him who loved us and washed us from our
sins in His own blood.
REVELATION 1:5

Many waters cannot quench love, nor can the floods drown it. SONG OF SONGS 8:7 • Love is as strong as death. SONG OF SONGS 8:6 • Greater love has no one than this, than to lay down one's life for his friends. JOHN 15:13 •

Who Himself bore our sins in His own body on the tree, that we, having died to sins, might live for righteousness; by whose stripes you were healed. 1 PETER 2:24 • In Him we have redemption through His blood, the forgiveness of sins, according to the riches of His grace. EPHESIANS 1:7 •

You were washed,...you were sanctified,...you were justified in the name of the Lord Jesus and by the Spirit of our God. 1 CORINTHIANS 6:11 • You are a chosen generation, a royal priesthood, a holy nation, His own special people, that you may proclaim the praises of Him who called you out of darkness into His marvelous light. 1 PETER 2:9 • I beseech you therefore, brethren, by the mercies of God, that you present your bodies a living sacrifice, holy, acceptable to God, which is your reasonable service. ROMANS 12:1 •

Evening Reading

There are differences of ministries, but the same Lord.
1 CORINTHIANS 12:5

Azmaveth the son of Adiel was over the king's treasuries; and Jehonathan the son of Uzziah was over the storehouses....Ezri the son of Chelub was over those who did the work of the field for tilling the ground. And Shimei the Ramathite was over the vineyards....All these were the officials over King David's property. 1 CHRONICLES 27:25–27, 31 •

God has appointed these in the church: first apostles, second prophets, third teachers, after that miracles, then gifts of healings, helps, administrations, varieties of tongues. 1 CORINTHIANS 12:28 • One and the same Spirit works all these things, distributing to each one individually as He wills. 1 CORINTHIANS 12:11 •

As each one has received a gift, minister it to one another, as good stewards of the manifold grace of God. If anyone speaks, let him speak as the oracles of God. If anyone ministers, let him do it as with the ability which God supplies, that in all things God may be glorified through Jesus Christ, to whom belong the glory and the dominion forever and ever. 1 PETER 4:10–11 •

October 4

Morning Reading

Moses did not know that the skin of his face shone
while he talked with [God].
EXODUS 34:29

Not unto us, O LORD, not unto us, but to Your name give glory. PSALM 115:1 • Lord, when did we see You hungry and feed You, or thirsty and give You drink? MATTHEW 25:37 • In lowliness of mind let each esteem others better than himself. PHILIPPIANS 2:3 • Be clothed with humility. 1 PETER 5:5 •

[Jesus] was transfigured before them. His face shone like the sun, and His clothes became as white as the light. MATTHEW 17:2 • All who sat in the council, looking steadfastly at [Stephen], saw his face as the face of an angel. ACTS 6:15 • The glory which You gave Me I have given them. JOHN 17:22 • We all, with unveiled face, beholding as in a mirror the glory of the Lord, are being transformed into the same image from glory to glory, just as by the Spirit of the Lord. 2 CORINTHIANS 3:18 •

You are the light of the world. A city that is set on a hill cannot be hidden. Nor do they light a lamp and put it under a basket, but on a lampstand, and it gives light to all who are in the house. MATTHEW 5:14–15 •

Evening Reading

There are diversities of activities, but it is the same
God who works all in all.
1 CORINTHIANS 12:6

Some from Manasseh defected to David....And they helped David against the bands of raiders, for they were all mighty men of valor. 1 CHRONICLES 12:19, 21 • The manifestation of the Spirit is given to each one for the profit of all. 1 CORINTHIANS 12:7 •

The sons of Issachar...had understanding of the times, to know what Israel ought to do. 1 CHRONICLES 12:32 • To one is given the word of wisdom through the Spirit, to another the word of knowledge through the same Spirit. 1 CORINTHIANS 12:8 •

Of Zebulun there were fifty thousand who went out to battle, expert in war with all weapons of war, stouthearted men [not of double heart] who could keep ranks. 1 CHRONICLES 12:33 • A double-minded man [is] unstable in all his ways. JAMES 1:8 •

There should be no schism in the body, but...the members should have the same care for one another. And if one member suffers, all the members suffer with it; or if one member is honored, all the members rejoice with it. 1 CORINTHIANS 12:25–26 •

One Lord, one faith, one baptism. EPHESIANS 4:5 •

October 5

Morning Reading

Call upon Me in the day of trouble; I will deliver you,
and you shall glorify Me.
PSALM 50:15

Why are you cast down, O my soul? And why are you disquieted within me? Hope in God; for I shall yet praise Him, the help of my countenance and my God. PSALM 42:11 • Lord, You have heard the desire of the humble; You will prepare their heart; You will cause Your ear to hear. PSALM 10:17 • For You, Lord, are good, and ready to forgive, and abundant in mercy to all those who call upon You. PSALM 86:5 •

Jacob said to his household,..."Let us arise and go up to Bethel; and I will make an altar there to God, who answered me in the day of my distress and has been with me in the way which I have gone." GENESIS 35:2–3 • Bless the Lord, O my soul, and forget not all His benefits. PSALM 103:2 •

I love the Lord, because He has heard My voice and my supplications. Because He has inclined His ear to me, therefore I will call upon Him as long as I live. The pains of death surrounded me, and the pangs of Sheol laid hold of me; I found trouble and sorrow. Then I called upon the name of the Lord. PSALM 116:1–4 •

Evening Reading

Yet a little while, and He who is coming will
come and will not tarry.
HEBREWS 10:37

Write the vision and make it plain on tablets, that he may run who reads it. For the vision is yet for an appointed time; but at the end it will speak, and it will not lie. Though it tarries, wait for it; because it will surely come, it will not tarry. HABAKKUK 2:2–3 •

Beloved, do not forget this one thing, that with the Lord one day is as a thousand years, and a thousand years as one day. The Lord is not slack concerning His promise, as some count slackness, but is longsuffering toward us, not willing that any should perish but that all should come to repentance. 2 PETER 3:8–9 • You, O Lord, are a God full of compassion, and gracious, longsuffering and abundant in mercy and truth. PSALM 86:15 • Oh, that You would rend the heavens! That You would come down!...For since the beginning of the world men have not heard nor perceived by the ear, nor has the eye seen any God besides You, who acts for the one who waits for Him. ISAIAH 64:1, 4 •

October 6

Morning Reading

The Lord God Omnipotent reigns!
REVELATION 19:6

I know that You can do everything. JOB 42:2 • The things which are impossible with men are possible with God. LUKE 18:27 • He does according to His will in the army of heaven and among the inhabitants of the earth. No one can restrain His hand or say to Him, "What have You done?" DANIEL 4:35 • There is no one who can deliver out of My hand; I work, and who will reverse it? ISAIAH 43:13 • Abba, Father, all things are possible for You. MARK 14:36 •

Jesus said to [the blind men], "Do you believe that I am able to do this?" They said to Him, "Yes, Lord." Then He touched their eyes, saying, "According to your faith let it be to you." MATTHEW 9:28–29 • A leper came and worshiped Him, saying, "Lord, if You are willing, You can make me clean." Then Jesus put out His hand and touched him, saying, "I am willing; be cleansed." MATTHEW 8:2–3 • Mighty God. ISAIAH 9:6 • All authority has been given to Me in heaven and on earth. MATTHEW 28:18 •

Some trust in chariots, and some in horses; but we will remember the name of the LORD our God. PSALM 20:7 • Be strong and courageous; do not be afraid nor dismayed,...for there are more with us than with him. 2 CHRONICLES 32:7 •

Evening Reading

What is the word that the Lord spoke to you?
1 SAMUEL 3:17

He has shown you, O man, what is good; and what does the LORD require of you but to do justly, to love mercy, and to walk humbly with your God? MICAH 6:8 • And to keep the commandments of the LORD and His statutes which I command you today for your good? DEUTERONOMY 10:13 •

As many as are of the works of the law are under the curse; for it is written, "Cursed is everyone who does not continue in all things which are written in the book of the law, to do them." But that no one is justified by the law in the sight of God is evident, for "the just shall live by faith."...[The law] was added because of transgressions, till the Seed should come to whom the promise was made. GALATIANS 3:10–11, 19 •

God, who at various times and in various ways spoke in time past to the fathers by the prophets, has in these last days spoken to us by His Son. HEBREWS 1:1–2 •

Speak, LORD, for Your servant hears. 1 SAMUEL 3:9 •

October 7

Morning Reading

The humble He teaches His way.
PSALM 25:9

Blessed are the meek. MATTHEW 5:5 •

I returned and saw under the sun that; the race is not to the swift, nor the battle to the strong, nor bread to the wise, nor riches to men of understanding, nor favor to men of skill. ECCLESIASTES 9:11 • A man's heart plans his way, but the LORD directs his steps. PROVERBS 16:9 •

Unto You I lift up my eyes, O You who dwell in the heavens. Behold, as the eyes of servants look to the hand of their masters, as the eyes of a maid to the hand of her mistress, so our eyes look to the LORD our God. PSALM 123:1–2 • Cause me to know the way in which I should walk, for I lift up my soul to You. PSALM 143:8 •

O our God, will You not judge them? For we have no power against this great multitude that is coming against us; nor do we know what to do, but our eyes are upon You. 2 CHRONICLES 20:12 •

If any of you lacks wisdom, let him ask of God, who gives to all liberally and without reproach, and it will be given to him. JAMES 1:5 •

When He, the Spirit of truth, has come, He will guide you into all truth. JOHN 16:13 •

Evening Reading

Lord GOD,...with Your blessing let the house of Your
servant be blessed forever.
2 SAMUEL 7:29

You have blessed it, O LORD, and it shall be blessed forever. 1 CHRONICLES 17:27 • The blessing of the LORD makes one rich, and He adds no sorrow with it. PROVERBS 10:22 •

Remember the words of the Lord Jesus, that He said, "It is more blessed to give than to receive." ACTS 20:35 • When you give a feast, invite the poor, the maimed, the lame, the blind. And you will be blessed, because they cannot repay you; for you shall be repaid at the resurrection of the just. LUKE 14:13–14 • Come, you blessed of My Father, inherit the kingdom prepared for you from the foundation of the world: for I was hungry and you gave Me food; I was thirsty and you gave Me drink; I was a stranger and you took Me in; I was naked and you clothed Me; I was sick and you visited Me; I was in prison and you came to Me. MATTHEW 25:34–36 •

Blessed is he who considers the poor; the LORD will deliver him in time of trouble. PSALM 41:1 •

The LORD God is a sun and shield. PSALM 84:11 •

October 8

Morning Reading

I will not fear. What can man do to me?
HEBREWS 13:6

Who shall separate us from the love of Christ? Shall tribulation, or distress, or persecution, or famine, or nakedness, or peril, or sword?... In all these things we are more than conquerors through Him who loved us. ROMANS 8:35, 37 •

Do not be afraid of those who kill the body, and after that have no more that they can do. But I will show you whom you should fear: fear Him who, after He has killed, has power to cast into hell; yes, I say to you, fear Him! LUKE 12:4–5 •

Blessed are those who are persecuted for righteousness' sake, for theirs is the kingdom of heaven. Blessed are you when they revile and persecute you, and say all kinds of evil against you falsely for My sake. Rejoice and be exceedingly glad, for great is your reward in heaven. MATTHEW 5:10–12 • None of these things move me; nor do I count my life dear to myself, so that I may finish my race with joy. ACTS 20:24 • I will speak of Your testimonies also before kings, and will not be ashamed. PSALM 119:46 •

Evening Reading

He...set my feet upon a rock.
PSALM 40:2

That Rock was Christ. 1 CORINTHIANS 10:4 • Simon Peter...said, "You are the Christ, the Son of the living God."...[Jesus answered,] "On this rock I will build My church, and the gates of Hades shall not prevail against it." MATTHEW 16:16, 18 • Nor is there salvation in any other, for there is no other name under heaven given among men by which we must be saved. ACTS 4:12 •

Let us draw near...in full assurance of faith....Let us hold fast the confession of our hope without wavering. HEBREWS 10:22–23 • Let him ask in faith, with no doubting, for he who doubts is like a wave of the sea driven and tossed by the wind. JAMES 1:6 •

Who shall separate us from the love of Christ? Shall tribulation, or distress, or persecution, or famine, or nakedness, or peril, or sword?... In all these things we are more than conquerors through Him who loved us....[Neither] height nor depth, nor any other created thing, shall be able to separate us from the love of God which is in Christ Jesus our Lord. ROMANS 8:35, 37, 39 •

October 9

Morning Reading

You are God, ready to pardon, gracious and merciful.
NEHEMIAH 9:17

The Lord is not slack concerning His promise, as some count slackness, but is longsuffering toward us, not willing that any should perish but that all should come to repentance.....The longsuffering of our Lord is salvation. 2 PETER 3:9, 15 •

For this reason I obtained mercy, that in me first Jesus Christ might show all longsuffering, as a pattern to those who are going to believe on Him for everlasting life. 1 TIMOTHY 1:16 • Whatever things were written before were written for our learning, that we through the patience and comfort of the Scriptures might have hope. ROMANS 15:4 •

Do you despise the riches of His goodness, forbearance, and long-suffering, not knowing that the goodness of God leads you to repentance? ROMANS 2:4 • Rend your heart, and not your garments; return to the LORD your God, for He is gracious and merciful, slow to anger, and of great kindness; and He relents from doing harm. JOEL 2:13 •

Evening Reading

The words of the LORD are pure words.
PSALM 12:6

Your word is very pure; therefore Your servant loves it. PSALM 119:140 • The statutes of the LORD are right, rejoicing the heart; the commandment of the LORD is pure, enlightening the eyes. PSALM 19:8 • Every word of God is pure; He is a shield to those who put their trust in Him. Do not add to His words, lest He rebuke you, and you be found a liar. PROVERBS 30:5-6 •

Your word I have hidden in my heart, that I might not sin against You!...I will meditate on Your precepts, and contemplate Your ways. PSALM 119:11, 15 • Brethren, whatever things are true, whatever things are noble, whatever things are just, whatever things are pure, whatever things are lovely, whatever things are of good report, if there is any virtue and if there is anything praiseworthy; meditate on these things. PHILIPPIANS 4:8 • As newborn babes, desire the pure milk of the word, that you may grow thereby. 1 PETER 2:2 •

We are not, as so many, peddling the word of God; but as of sincerity, but as from God, we speak in the sight of God in Christ. 2 CORINTHIANS 2:17 • Not...handling the word of God deceitfully. 2 CORINTHIANS 4:2 •

October 10

Morning Reading

The whole family in heaven and earth.
EPHESIANS 3:15

One God and Father of all, who is above all, and through all, and in you all. EPHESIANS 4:6 • You are all sons of God through faith in Christ Jesus. GALATIANS 3:26 • That in the dispensation of the fullness of the times He might gather together in one all things in Christ, both which are in heaven and which are on earth; in Him. EPHESIANS 1:10 •

He is not ashamed to call them brethren. HEBREWS 2:11 • [Jesus] stretched out His hand toward His disciples and said, "Here are My mother and My brothers! For whoever does the will of My Father in heaven is My brother and sister and mother." MATTHEW 12:49–50 • Go to My brethren and say to them, "I am ascending to My Father and your Father, and to My God and your God." JOHN 20:17 •

I saw under the altar the souls of those who had been slain for the word of God and for the testimony which they held....Then a white robe was given to each of them; and it was said to them that they should rest a little while longer, until both the number of their fellow servants and their brethren, who would be killed as they were, was completed. REVELATION 6:9, 11 • That they should not be made perfect apart from us. HEBREWS 11:40 •

Evening Reading

In this manner, therefore, pray: Our Father in heaven,
hallowed be Your name.
MATTHEW 6:9

Jesus...lifted up His eyes to heaven, and said: "Father." JOHN 17:1 • My Father and your Father....My God and your God. JOHN 20:17 •

You are all sons of God through faith in Christ Jesus. GALATIANS 3:26 • You did not receive the spirit of bondage again to fear, but you received the Spirit of adoption by whom we cry out, "Abba, Father." The Spirit Himself bears witness with our spirit that we are children of God. ROMANS 8:15–16 •

Because you are sons, God has sent forth the Spirit of His Son into your hearts, crying out, "Abba, Father!" Therefore you are no longer a slave but a son. GALATIANS 4:6–7 •

Most assuredly, I say to you, whatever you ask the Father in My name He will give you. Until now you have asked nothing in My name. Ask, and you will receive, that your joy may be full. JOHN 16:23–24 •

I will receive you. I will be a Father to you, and you shall be My sons and daughters, says the LORD Almighty. 2 CORINTHIANS 6:17–18 •

October 11

Morning Reading

Be not far from Me, for trouble is near.
PSALM 22:11

How long, O LORD? Will You forget me forever? How long will You hide Your face from me? How long shall I take counsel in my soul, having sorrow in my heart daily? PSALM 13:1–2 • Do not hide Your face from me; do not turn Your servant away in anger; You have been my help; do not leave me nor forsake me, O God of my salvation. PSALM 27:9 •

He shall call upon Me, and I will answer him; I will be with him in trouble; I will deliver him and honor him. PSALM 91:15 • The LORD is near to all who call upon Him, to all who call upon Him in truth. He will fulfill the desire of those who fear Him; He also will hear their cry and save them. PSALM 145:18–19 •

I will not leave you orphans; I will come to you. JOHN 14:18 • Lo, I am with you always, even to the end of the age. MATTHEW 28:20 •

God is our refuge and strength, a very present help in trouble. PSALM 46:1 • Truly my soul silently waits for God; from Him comes my salvation....My soul, wait silently for God alone, for my expectation is from Him. PSALM 62:1, 5 •

Evening Reading

Hallowed be Your name.
MATTHEW 6:9

You shall worship no other god, for the LORD, whose name is Jealous, is a jealous God. EXODUS 34:14 •

Who is like You, O LORD, among the gods? Who is like You, glorious in holiness, fearful in praises, doing wonders? EXODUS 15:11 • Holy, holy, holy, Lord God Almighty. REVELATION 4:8 •

Worship the LORD in the beauty of holiness! 1 CHRONICLES 16:29 • I saw the Lord sitting on a throne, high and lifted up, and the train of His robe filled the temple. Above it stood seraphim; each one had six wings: with two he covered his face, with two he covered his feet, and with two he flew. And one cried to another and said: "Holy, holy, holy is the LORD of hosts; the whole earth is full of His glory!"...Woe is me, for I am undone! Because I am a man of unclean lips. ISAIAH 6:1–3, 5 • I have heard of You by the hearing of the ear, but now my eye sees You. Therefore I abhor myself, and repent in dust and ashes. JOB 42:5–6 •

The blood of Jesus Christ His Son cleanses us from all sin. 1 JOHN 1:7 • That we may be partakers of His holiness. HEBREWS 12:10 • Therefore, brethren, having boldness to enter the Holiest by the blood of Jesus,...let us draw near with a true heart. HEBREWS 10:19, 22 •

October 12

Morning Reading

God was in Christ reconciling the world to Himself,
not imputing their trespasses to them.
2 CORINTHIANS 5:19

It pleased the Father that in Him all the fullness should dwell, and by Him to reconcile all things to Himself,...having made peace through the blood of His cross. COLOSSIANS 1:19–20 • Mercy and truth have met together; righteousness and peace have kissed. PSALM 85:10 •

I know the thoughts that I think toward you, says the LORD, thoughts of peace and not of evil. JEREMIAH 29:11 • "Come now, and let us reason together," says the LORD, "though your sins are like scarlet, they shall be as white as snow; though they are red like crimson, they shall be as wool. ISAIAH 1:18 •

Who is a God like You, pardoning iniquity? MICAH 7:18 •

Now acquaint yourself with Him, and be at peace. JOB 22:21 • Work out your own salvation with fear and trembling; for it is God who works in you both to will and to do for His good pleasure. PHILIPPIANS 2:12–13 • LORD, You will establish peace for us, for You have also done all our works in us. ISAIAH 26:12 •

Evening Reading

Your kingdom come.
MATTHEW 6:10

In the days of these kings the God of heaven will set up a kingdom which shall never be destroyed; and the kingdom shall not be left to other people; it shall break in pieces and consume all these kingdoms, and it shall stand forever. DANIEL 2:44 • A stone...cut out without hands. DANIEL 2:34 • "Not by might nor by power, but by My Spirit," says the LORD of hosts. ZECHARIAH 4:6 • The kingdom of God does not come with observation; nor will they say, "See here!" or "See there!" For indeed, the kingdom of God is within you. LUKE 17:20–21 •

To you it has been given to know the mystery of the kingdom of God. MARK 4:11 • The kingdom of God is as if a man should scatter seed on the ground, and should sleep by night and rise by day, and the seed should sprout and grow, he himself does not know how....But when the grain ripens, immediately he puts in the sickle, because the harvest has come. MARK 4:26–27, 29 •

Be ready, for the Son of Man is coming at an hour you do not expect. MATTHEW 24:44 •

The Spirit and the bride say, "Come!" And let him who hears say, "Come!" REVELATION 22:17 •

October 13

Morning Reading

From the first day that you set your heart to understand, and to humble yourself before your God, your words were heard.
DANIEL 10:12

Thus says the High and Lofty One who inhabits eternity, whose name is Holy: "I dwell in the high and holy place, with him who has a contrite and humble spirit, to revive the spirit of the humble, and to revive the heart of the contrite ones." ISAIAH 57:15 • The sacrifices of God are a broken spirit, a broken and a contrite heart; these, O God, You will not despise. PSALM 51:17 • Though the LORD is on high, yet He regards the lowly; but the proud He knows from afar. PSALM 138:6 • Therefore humble yourselves under the mighty hand of God, that He may exalt you in due time. 1 PETER 5:6 • [The Scripture says,] "God resists the proud, but gives grace to the humble." Therefore submit to God. JAMES 4:6–7 •

You, Lord, are good, and ready to forgive, and abundant in mercy to all those who call upon You. Give ear, O LORD, to my prayer; and attend to the voice of my supplications. In the day of my trouble I will call upon You, for You will answer me. PSALM 86:5–7 •

Evening Reading

Your will be done on earth as it is in heaven.
MATTHEW 6:10

Understand what the will of the Lord is. EPHESIANS 5:17 •

It is not the will of your Father who is in heaven that one of these little ones should perish. MATTHEW 18:14 •

This is the will of God, [even] your sanctification. 1 THESSALONIANS 4:3 • That he no longer should live the rest of his time in the flesh for the lusts of men, but for the will of God. 1 PETER 4:2 • Of His own will He brought us forth by the word of truth....Therefore lay aside all filthiness. JAMES 1:18, 21 •

Be holy, for I am holy. 1 PETER 1:16 • [Jesus] said, "...Whoever does the will of God is My brother and My sister and mother." MARK 3:34–35 • Whoever hears these sayings of Mine, and does them, I will liken him to a wise man who built his house on the rock: and the rain descended, the floods came, and the winds blew and beat on that house; and it did not fall, for it was founded on the rock. MATTHEW 7:24–25 • The world is passing away, and the lust of it; but he who does the will of God abides forever. 1 JOHN 2:17 •

October 14

Morning Reading

Christ died and rose and lived again, that He might be Lord
of both the dead and the living.
ROMANS 14:9

Yet it pleased the LORD to bruise Him; He has put Him to grief. When You make His soul an offering for sin, He shall see His seed, He shall prolong His days, and the pleasure of the LORD shall prosper in His hand. He shall see the labor of His soul, and be satisfied. By His knowledge My righteous Servant shall justify many, for He shall bear their iniquities. ISAIAH 53:10–11 • Ought not the Christ to have suffered these things and to enter into His glory? LUKE 24:26 • We judge thus: that if One died for all, then all died; and He died for all, that those who live should live no longer for themselves, but for Him who died for them and rose again. 2 CORINTHIANS 5:14–15 •

Let all the house of Israel know assuredly that God has made this Jesus, whom you crucified, both Lord and Christ. ACTS 2:36 • He indeed was foreordained before the foundation of the world, but was manifest in these last times for you who through Him believe in God. 1 PETER 1:20–21 •

Evening Reading

Give us this day our daily bread.
MATTHEW 6:11

I have been young, and now am old; yet I have not seen the righteous forsaken, nor his descendants begging bread. PSALM 37:25 • Bread will be given him, his water will be sure. ISAIAH 33:16 • The ravens brought [Elijah] bread and meat in the morning, and bread and meat in the evening; and he drank from the brook. 1 KINGS 17:6 •

My God shall supply all your need according to His riches in glory by Christ Jesus. PHILIPPIANS 4:19 • Be content with such things as you have. For He Himself has said, "I will never leave you nor forsake you." HEBREWS 13:5 •

He humbled you, allowed you to hunger, and fed you with manna,... that He might make you know that man shall not live by bread alone; but man lives by every word that proceeds from the mouth of the LORD. DEUTERONOMY 8:3 • Jesus said to them, "Most assuredly, I say to you, Moses did not give you the bread from heaven, but My Father gives you the true bread from heaven. For the bread of God is He who comes down from heaven and gives life to the world." Then they said to Him, "Lord, give us this bread always." JOHN 6:32–34 •

October 15

Morning Reading

God is my defense.
PSALM 59:9

The LORD is my rock and my fortress and my deliverer; the God of my strength, in whom I will trust; my shield and the horn of my salvation, my stronghold and my refuge; my Savior. 2 SAMUEL 22:2–3 • The LORD is my strength and my shield; my heart trusted in Him, and I am helped; therefore my heart greatly rejoices, and with my song I will praise Him. PSALM 28:7 •

When the enemy comes in like a flood, the Spirit of the LORD will lift up a standard against him. ISAIAH 59:19 • We may boldly say: "The LORD is my helper; I will not fear. What can man do to me?" HEBREWS 13:6 •

The LORD is my light and my salvation; whom shall I fear? The LORD is the strength of my life; of whom shall I be afraid? PSALM 27:1 •

As the mountains surround Jerusalem, so the LORD surrounds His people from this time forth and forever. PSALM 125:2 • Because You have been my help, therefore in the shadow of Your wings I will rejoice. PSALM 63:7 •

For Your name's sake, lead me and guide me. PSALM 31:3 •

Evening Reading

Forgive us our debts, as we forgive our debtors.
MATTHEW 6:12

Then Peter came to Him and said, "Lord, how often shall my brother sin against me, and I forgive him? Up to seven times?" Jesus said to him, "I do not say to you, up to seven times, but up to seventy times seven." MATTHEW 18:21–22 • Then his master, after he had called him, said to him, "You wicked servant! I forgave you all that debt because you begged me. Should you not also have had compassion on your fellow servant, just as I had pity on you?" And his master was angry, and delivered him to the torturers until he should pay all that was due to him. So My heavenly Father also will do to you if each of you, from his heart, does not forgive his brother his trespasses. MATTHEW 18:32–35 • Be kind to one another, tenderhearted, forgiving one another, just as God in Christ forgave you. EPHESIANS 4:32 • You...He has made alive,...having forgiven you all trespasses, having wiped out the handwriting of requirements that was against us, which was contrary to us. And He has taken it out of the way, having nailed it to the cross. COLOSSIANS 2:13–14 • Even as Christ forgave you, so you also must do. COLOSSIANS 3:13 •

October 16

Morning Reading

Not lagging in diligence, fervent in spirit, serving the Lord.
ROMANS 12:11

Whatever your hand finds to do, do it with your might; for there is no work or device or knowledge or wisdom in the grave where you are going. ECCLESIASTES 9:10 • Whatever you do, do it heartily, as to the Lord and not to men, knowing that from the Lord you will receive the reward of the inheritance; for you serve the Lord Christ. COLOSSIANS 3:23–24 • Whatever good anyone does, he will receive the same from the Lord. EPHESIANS 6:8 •

I must work the works of Him who sent Me while it is day; the night is coming when no one can work. JOHN 9:4 • Did you not know that I must be about My Father's business? LUKE 2:49 • Zeal for Your house has eaten Me up. JOHN 2:17 •

Brethren, be even more diligent to make your call and election sure, for if you do these things you will never stumble. 2 PETER 1:10 • We desire that each one of you show the same diligence to the full assurance of hope until the end, that you do not become sluggish, but imitate those who through faith and patience inherit the promises. HEBREWS 6:11–12 • Run in such a way that you may obtain [the prize]. 1 CORINTHIANS 9:24 •

Evening Reading

Do not lead us into temptation, but deliver us from the evil one.
MATTHEW 6:13

He who trusts in his own heart is a fool, but whoever walks wisely will be delivered. PROVERBS 28:26 •

Let no one say when he is tempted, "I am tempted by God"; for God cannot be tempted by evil, nor does He Himself tempt anyone. But each one is tempted when he is drawn away by his own desires and enticed. JAMES 1:13–14 • Therefore "Come out from among them and be separate, says the Lord. Do not touch what is unclean, and I will receive you." 2 CORINTHIANS 6:17 •

Lot lifted his eyes and saw all the plain of Jordan, that it was well watered everywhere...like the garden of the LORD....Then Lot chose for himself all the plain of Jordan....But the men of Sodom were exceedingly wicked and sinful against the LORD. GENESIS 13:10–11, 13 •

[The Lord] delivered righteous Lot, who was oppressed by the filthy conduct of the wicked....The Lord knows how to deliver the godly out of temptations. 2 PETER 2:7, 9 • Indeed, he will be made to stand, for God is able to make him stand. ROMANS 14:4 •

 *October 17*

Morning Reading

In Your name they rejoice all day long,
and in Your righteousness they are exalted.
PSALM 89:16

In the LORD I have righteousness and strength. To Him men shall come, and all shall be ashamed who are incensed against Him. In the LORD all the descendants of Israel shall be justified, and shall glory. ISAIAH 45:24–25 • Be glad in the LORD and rejoice, you righteous; and shout for joy, all you upright in heart! PSALM 32:11 •

The righteousness of God apart from the law is revealed, being witnessed by the Law and the Prophets, even the righteousness of God, through faith in Jesus Christ, to all and on all who believe,...to demonstrate at the present time His righteousness, that He might be just and the justifier of the one who has faith in Jesus. ROMANS 3:21–22, 26 •

Rejoice in the Lord always. Again I will say, rejoice! PHILIPPIANS 4:4 • Whom having not seen you love. Though now you do not see Him, yet believing, you rejoice with joy inexpressible and full of glory. 1 PETER 1:8 •

Evening Reading

For Yours is the kingdom and the power and the glory forever.
MATTHEW 6:13

The LORD reigns, He is clothed with majesty;...Your throne is established from of old; You are from everlasting. PSALM 93:1–2 •

The LORD is...great in power. NAHUM 1:3 • If God is for us, who can be against us? ROMANS 8:31 • Our God whom we serve is able to deliver us. DANIEL 3:17 • My Father, who has given them to Me, is greater than all; and no one is able to snatch them out of My Father's hand. JOHN 10:29 • He who is in you is greater than he who is in the world. 1 JOHN 4:4 •

Not unto us, O LORD, not unto us, but to Your name give glory. PSALM 115:1 • Yours, O LORD, is the greatness, the power and the glory, the victory and the majesty; for all that is in heaven and in earth is Yours; Yours is the kingdom, O LORD, and You are exalted as head over all....Now therefore, our God, we thank You and praise Your glorious name. But who am I, and who are my people, that we should be able to offer so willingly as this? For all things come from You, and of Your own we have given You. 1 CHRONICLES 29:11, 13–14 •

October 18

Morning Reading

One of the soldiers pierced His side with a spear,
and immediately blood and water came out.
JOHN 19:34

This is the blood of the covenant which the LORD has made with you. EXODUS 24:8 • The life of the flesh is in the blood, and I have given it to you upon the altar to make atonement for your souls. LEVITICUS 17:11 • It is not possible that the blood of bulls and goats could take away sins. HEBREWS 10:4 •

[Jesus] said to them, "This is My blood of the new covenant, which is shed for many." MARK 14:24 • With His own blood He entered the Most Holy Place once for all, having obtained eternal redemption [for us]. HEBREWS 9:12 • Having made peace through the blood of His cross. COLOSSIANS 1:20 •

Knowing that you were not redeemed with corruptible things, like silver or gold,...but with the precious blood of Christ, as of a lamb without blemish and without spot,...manifest in these last times for you. 1 PETER 1:18–20 •

Then I will sprinkle clean water on you, and you shall be clean; I will cleanse you from all...your idols. EZEKIEL 36:25 • Let us draw near with a true heart in full assurance of faith, having our hearts sprinkled from an evil conscience. HEBREWS 10:22 •

Evening Reading

Amen.
MATTHEW 6:13

Amen! May the LORD God...say so too. 1 KINGS 1:36 • [The Sovereign Lord says,] "He who blesses himself in the earth shall bless himself in the God of truth; and he who swears in the earth shall swear by the God of truth; because the former troubles are forgotten, and because they are hidden from My eyes." ISAIAH 65:16 •

When God made a promise to Abraham, because He could swear by no one greater, He swore by Himself....For men indeed swear by the greater, and an oath for confirmation is for them an end of all dispute. Thus God, determining to show more abundantly to the heirs of promise the immutability of His counsel, confirmed it by an oath, that by two immutable things, in which it is impossible for God to lie, we might have strong consolation, who have fled for refuge to lay hold of the hope set before us. HEBREWS 6:13, 16–18 •

These things says the Amen, the Faithful and True Witness. REVELATION 3:14 • For all the promises of God in Him are Yes, and in Him Amen, to the glory of God through us. 2 CORINTHIANS 1:20 •

Blessed be the LORD God, the God of Israel, who only does wondrous things! And blessed be His glorious name forever!...Amen and Amen. PSALM 72:18–19 •

October 19

Morning Reading

The LORD will be your confidence, and will keep
your foot from being caught.
PROVERBS 3:26

Surely the wrath of man shall praise You; with the remainder of wrath You shall gird Yourself. PSALM 76:10 • The king's heart is in the hand of the LORD, like the rivers of water; He turns it wherever He wishes. PROVERBS 21:1 • When a man's ways please the LORD, He makes even his enemies to be at peace with him. PROVERBS 16:7 •

I wait for the LORD, my soul waits, and in His word I do hope. My soul waits for the Lord more than those who watch for the morning; yes, more than those who watch for the morning. PSALM 130:5–6 • I sought the LORD, and He heard me, and delivered me from all my fears. PSALM 34:4 •

The eternal God is your refuge, and underneath are the everlasting arms; He will thrust out the enemy from before you, and will say, "Destroy!" DEUTERONOMY 33:27 • Blessed is the man who trusts in the LORD, and whose hope is the LORD. JEREMIAH 17:7 •

What then shall we say to these things? If God is for us, who can be against us? ROMANS 8:31 •

Evening Reading

Consolation in Christ,...comfort of love,...fellowship of the Spirit.
PHILIPPIANS 2:1

Man who is born of woman is of few days and full of trouble. He comes forth like a flower and fades away; he flees like a shadow and does not continue. JOB 14:1–2 • My flesh and my heart fail; but God is the strength of my heart and my portion forever. PSALM 73:26 •

The Father...will give you another Helper, that He may abide with you forever....The Holy Spirit, whom the Father will send in My name. JOHN 14:16, 26 • Blessed be the God and Father of our Lord Jesus Christ, the Father of mercies and God of all comfort, who comforts us in all our tribulation, that we may be able to comfort those who are in any trouble, with the comfort with which we ourselves are comforted by God. 2 CORINTHIANS 1:3–4 •

If we believe that Jesus died and rose again, even so God will bring with Him those who sleep in Jesus....And thus we shall always be with the Lord. Therefore comfort one another with these words. 1 THESSALONIANS 4:14, 17–18 •

October 20

Morning Reading

I delight in the law of God according to the inward man.
ROMANS 7:22

Oh, how I love Your law! It is my meditation all the day. PSALM 119:97 • Your words were found, and I ate them, and Your word was to me the joy and rejoicing of my heart. JEREMIAH 15:16 • I sat down in his shade with great delight, and his fruit was sweet to my taste. SONG OF SONGS 2:3 • I have treasured the words of His mouth more than my necessary food. JOB 23:12 •

I delight to do Your will, O my God, and Your law is within my heart. PSALM 40:8 • My food is to do the will of Him who sent Me, and to finish His work. JOHN 4:34 •

The statutes of the LORD are right, rejoicing the heart; the commandment of the LORD is pure, enlightening the eyes....More to be desired are they than gold, yea, than much fine gold; sweeter also than honey and the honeycomb. PSALM 19:8, 10 • Be doers of the word, and not hearers only, deceiving yourselves. For if anyone is a hearer of the word and not a doer, he is like a man observing his natural face in a mirror; for he observes himself, goes away, and immediately forgets what kind of man he was. JAMES 1:22–24 •

Evening Reading

May the LORD your God accept you.
2 SAMUEL 24:23

With what shall I come before the LORD, and bow myself before the High God? Shall I come before Him with burnt offerings, with calves a year old? Will the LORD be pleased with thousands of rams, ten thousand rivers of oil? Shall I give my firstborn for my transgression, the fruit of my body for the sin of my soul? He has shown you, O man, what is good; and what does the LORD require of you but to do justly, to love mercy, and to walk humbly with your God? MICAH 6:6–8 •

We are all like an unclean thing, and all our righteousnesses are like filthy rags. ISAIAH 64:6 • There is none righteous, no, not one;...for all have sinned and fall short of the glory of God, being justified freely by His grace through the redemption that is in Christ Jesus, whom God set forth as a propitiation by His blood, through faith, to demonstrate His righteousness, because in His forbearance God had passed over the sins that were previously committed, to demonstrate at the present time His righteousness, that He might be just and the justifier of the one who has faith in Jesus. ROMANS 3:10, 23–26 •

He has made us accepted in the Beloved. EPHESIANS 1:6 • You are complete in Him. COLOSSIANS 2:10 •

October 21

Morning Reading

Of His fullness we have all received, and grace for grace.
JOHN 1:16

This is My beloved Son, in whom I am well pleased. MATTHEW 17:5 • Behold what manner of love the Father has bestowed on us, that we should be called children of God! 1 JOHN 3:1 •

His Son, whom He has appointed heir of all things. HEBREWS 1:2 • If children, then heirs; heirs of God and joint heirs with Christ, if indeed we suffer with Him, that we may also be glorified together. ROMANS 8:17 •

I and My Father are one....The Father is in Me, and I in Him. JOHN 10:30, 38 • My Father and your Father,...My God and your God. JOHN 20:17 • I in them, and You in Me; that they may be made perfect in one. JOHN 17:23 •

The church, which is His body, the fullness of Him who fills all in all. EPHESIANS 1:22–23 •

Having these promises, beloved, let us cleanse ourselves from all filthiness of the flesh and spirit, perfecting holiness in the fear of God. 2 CORINTHIANS 7:1 •

Evening Reading

A servant is not greater than his master; nor is he who is sent greater than he who sent him. If you know these things, blessed are you if you do them.
JOHN 13:16–17

There was also a dispute among [Jesus' disciples], as to which of them should be considered the greatest. And He said to them, "The kings of the Gentiles exercise lordship over them, and those who exercise authority over them are called 'benefactors.' But not so among you; on the contrary, he who is greatest among you, let him be as the younger, and he who governs as he who serves. For who is greater, he who sits at the table, or he who serves? Is it not he who sits at the table? Yet I am among you as the One who serves." LUKE 22:24–27 • Just as the Son of Man did not come to be served, but to serve, and to give His life a ransom for many. MATTHEW 20:28 •

Jesus, knowing that the Father had given all things into His hands, and that He had come from God and was going to God, rose from supper and laid aside His garments, took a towel and girded Himself. After that, He poured water into a basin and began to wash the disciples' feet, and to wipe them with the towel with which He was girded. JOHN 13:3–5 •

October 22

Morning Reading

God, my heart is steadfast.
PSALM 108:1

The LORD is my light and my salvation; whom shall I fear? The LORD is the strength of my life; of whom shall I be afraid? PSALM 27:1 •

You will keep him in perfect peace, whose mind is stayed on You, because he trusts in You. ISAIAH 26:3 • He will not be afraid of evil tidings; his heart is steadfast, trusting in the LORD. His heart is established; he will not be afraid, until he sees his desire upon his enemies. PSALM 112:7–8 •

Whenever I am afraid, I will trust in You. PSALM 56:3 • In the time of trouble He shall hide me in His pavilion; in the secret place of His tabernacle He shall hide me; He shall set me high upon a rock. And now my head shall be lifted up above my enemies all around me; therefore I will offer sacrifices of joy in His tabernacle; I will sing, yes, I will sing praises to the LORD. PSALM 27:5–6 •

May the God of all grace, who called us to His eternal glory by Christ Jesus, after you have suffered a while, perfect, establish, strengthen, and settle you. To Him be the glory and the dominion forever and ever. 1 PETER 5:10–11 •

Evening Reading

The LORD has established His throne in heaven,
and His kingdom rules over all.
PSALM 103:19

The lot is cast into the lap, but its every decision is from the LORD. PROVERBS 16:33 • If there is calamity in a city, will not the LORD have done it? AMOS 3:6 •

I am the LORD, and there is no other; there is no God besides Me. I will gird you, though you have not known Me, that they may know from the rising of the sun to its setting that there is none besides Me. I am the LORD, and there is no other; I form the light and create darkness, I make peace and create calamity; I, the LORD, do all these things. ISAIAH 45:5–7 •

He does according to His will in the army of heaven and among the inhabitants of the earth. No one can restrain His hand or say to Him, "What have You done?" DANIEL 4:35 • If God is for us, who can be against us? ROMANS 8:31 •

He must reign till He has put all enemies under His feet. 1 CORINTHIANS 15:25 • Do not fear, little flock, for it is your Father's good pleasure to give you the kingdom. LUKE 12:32 •

Daily Light on the Daily Path

October 23

Morning Reading

One's life does not consist in the abundance
of the things he possesses.
LUKE 12:15

A little that a righteous man has is better than the riches of many wicked. PSALM 37:16 • Better is a little with the fear of the LORD, than great treasure with trouble. PROVERBS 15:16 • Godliness with contentment is great gain....Having food and clothing, with these we shall be content. 1 TIMOTHY 6:6, 8 •

Give me neither poverty nor riches; feed me with the food allotted to me; lest I be full and deny You, and say, "Who is the LORD?" Or lest I be poor and steal, and profane the name of my God. PROVERBS 30:8–9 • Give us this day our daily bread. MATTHEW 6:11 •

Do not worry about your life, what you will eat or what you will drink; nor about your body, what you will put on. Is not life more than food and the body more than clothing? MATTHEW 6:25 • [Jesus] said to [His disciples], "When I sent you without money bag, knapsack, and sandals, did you lack anything?" So they said, "Nothing." LUKE 22:35 • Let your conduct be without covetousness; be content with such things as you have. For He Himself has said, "I will never leave you nor forsake you." HEBREWS 13:5 •

Evening Reading

It is the Spirit who gives life.
JOHN 6:63

It is written, "The first man Adam became a living being." The last Adam became a life-giving spirit. 1 CORINTHIANS 15:45 • That which is born of the flesh is flesh, and that which is born of the Spirit is spirit. JOHN 3:6 • Not by works of righteousness which we have done, but according to His mercy He saved us, through the washing of regeneration and renewing of the Holy Spirit. TITUS 3:5 •

If anyone does not have the Spirit of Christ, he is not His. And if Christ is in you, the body is dead because of sin, but the Spirit is life because of righteousness. But if the Spirit of Him who raised Jesus from the dead dwells in you, He who raised Christ from the dead will also give life to your mortal bodies through His Spirit who dwells in you. ROMANS 8:9–11 •

It is no longer I who live, but Christ lives in me; and the life which I now live in the flesh I live by faith in the Son of God. GALATIANS 2:20 • Reckon yourselves to be dead indeed to sin, but alive to God in Christ Jesus our Lord. ROMANS 6:11 •

October 24

Morning Reading

I have been cast out of Your sight;
yet I will look again toward Your holy temple.
JONAH 2:4

Zion said, "The LORD has forsaken me, and my Lord has forgotten me." [The Lord says,] "Can a woman forget her nursing child, and not have compassion on the son of her womb? Surely they may forget, yet I will not forget you." ISAIAH 49:14–15 •

I have forgotten prosperity. And I said, "My strength and my hope have perished from the LORD." LAMENTATIONS 3:17–18 • Awake! Why do You sleep, O Lord? Arise! Do not cast us off forever. PSALM 44:23 • Why do you say, O Jacob, and speak, O Israel: "My way is hidden from the LORD, and my just claim is passed over by my God"? ISAIAH 40:27 • "With a little wrath I hid My face from you for a moment; but with everlasting kindness I will have mercy on you," says the LORD, your Redeemer. ISAIAH 54:8 •

Why are you cast down, O my soul? And why are you disquieted within me? Hope in God; for I shall yet praise Him, the help of my countenance and my God. PSALM 43:5 • We are hard pressed on every side, yet not crushed; we are perplexed, but not in despair; persecuted, but not forsaken; struck down, but not destroyed. 2 CORINTHIANS 4:8–9 •

Evening Reading

The poor and needy seek water, but there is none, their tongues fail for
thirst. I, the LORD, will hear them.
ISAIAH 41:17

There are many who say, "Who will show us any good?" PSALM 4:6 • What has man for all his labor, and for the striving of his heart with which he has toiled under the sun? For all his days are sorrowful, and his work burdensome; even in the night his heart takes no rest. ECCLESIASTES 2:22–23 • All is vanity and grasping for the wind. ECCLESIASTES 2:17 • They have forsaken Me, the fountain of living waters, and hewn themselves cisterns; broken cisterns that can hold no water. JEREMIAH 2:13 •

The one who comes to Me I will by no means cast out. JOHN 6:37 • I will pour water on him who is thirsty. ISAIAH 44:3 • Blessed are those who hunger and thirst for righteousness, for they shall be filled. MATTHEW 5:6 •

O God, You are my God; early will I seek You; my soul thirsts for You; my flesh longs for You in a dry and thirsty land where there is no water. PSALM 63:1 •

October 25

Morning Reading

Lo, I am with you always, even to the end of the age.
MATTHEW 28:20

If two of you agree on earth concerning anything that they ask, it will be done for them by My Father in heaven. For where two or three are gathered together in My name, I am there in the midst of them. MATTHEW 18:19–20 • He who has My commandments and keeps them, it is he who loves Me. And he who loves Me will be loved by My Father, and I will love him and manifest Myself to him. JOHN 14:21 •

Judas (not Iscariot) said to Him, "Lord, how is it that You will manifest Yourself to us, and not to the world?" Jesus answered,..."If anyone loves Me, he will keep My word; and My Father will love him, and We will come to him and make Our home with him." JOHN 14:22–23 •

To Him who is able to keep you from stumbling, and to present you faultless before the presence of His glory with exceeding joy, to God our Savior, who alone is wise, be glory and majesty, dominion and power, both now and forever. Amen. JUDE 24–25 •

Evening Reading

The end of all things is at hand.
1 PETER 4:7

I saw a great white throne and Him who sat on it, from whose face the earth and the heaven fled away. REVELATION 20:11 • The heavens and the earth which are now preserved,...are reserved for fire until the day of judgment. 2 PETER 3:7 •

God is our refuge and strength, a very present help in trouble. Therefore we will not fear, even though the earth be removed, and though the mountains be carried into the midst of the sea; though its waters roar and be troubled, though the mountains shake with its swelling. PSALM 46:1–3 • You will hear of wars and rumors of wars. See that you are not troubled. MATTHEW 24:6 •

We have a building from God, a house not made with hands, eternal in the heavens. 2 CORINTHIANS 5:1 • We...look for new heavens and a new earth in which righteousness dwells. Therefore, beloved, looking forward to these things, be diligent to be found by Him in peace, without spot and blameless. 2 PETER 3:13–14 •

October 26

Morning Reading

The LORD reigns.
PSALM 99:1

"Do you not fear Me?" says the LORD. "Will you not tremble at My presence, who have placed the sand as the bound of the sea, by a perpetual decree, that it cannot pass beyond it? And though its waves toss to and fro, yet they cannot prevail; though they roar, yet they cannot pass over it." JEREMIAH 5:22 • Exaltation comes neither from the east nor from the west nor from the south. But God is the Judge: He puts down one, and exalts another. PSALM 75:6–7 •

He changes the times and the seasons; He removes kings and raises up kings; He gives wisdom to the wise and knowledge to those who have understanding. DANIEL 2:21 • You will hear of wars and rumors of wars. See that you are not troubled. MATTHEW 24:6 •

If God is for us, who can be against us? ROMANS 8:31 • Are not two sparrows sold for a copper coin? And not one of them falls to the ground apart from your Father's will. But the very hairs of your head are all numbered. Do not fear therefore; you are of more value than many sparrows. MATTHEW 10:29–31 •

Evening Reading

Take heed to your spirit.
MALACHI 2:15

John...said, "Master, we saw someone casting out demons in Your name, and we forbade him because he does not follow with us." But Jesus said to him, "Do not forbid him, for he who is not against us is on our side." LUKE 9:49–50 • James and John...said, "Lord, do You want us to command fire to come down from heaven and consume [the Samaritan village], just as Elijah did?" But He turned and rebuked them, and said, "You do not know what manner of spirit you are of." LUKE 9:54–55 •

A young man...told Moses,..."Eldad and Medad are prophesying in the camp." So Joshua the son of Nun...said, "Moses my lord, forbid them!" Then Moses said to him, "Are you zealous for my sake? Oh, that all the Lord's people were prophets and that the LORD would put His Spirit upon them!" NUMBERS 11:27–29 •

The fruit of the Spirit is love, joy, peace, longsuffering, kindness, goodness, faithfulness, gentleness, self-control....Those who are Christ's have crucified the flesh with its passions and desires. If we live in the Spirit, let us also walk in the Spirit. Let us not become conceited, provoking one another, envying one another. GALATIANS 5:22–26 •

October 27

Morning Reading

He Himself took our infirmities and bore our sicknesses.
MATTHEW 8:17

Then the priest shall command to take for him who is to be cleansed two living and clean birds, cedar wood, scarlet, and hyssop. And the priest shall command that one of the birds be killed in an earthen vessel over running water. As for the living bird, he shall take it, the cedar wood and the scarlet and the hyssop, and dip them and the living bird in the blood of the bird that was killed over the running water. And he shall sprinkle it seven times on him who is to be cleansed from the leprosy, and shall pronounce him clean, and shall let the living bird loose in the open field. LEVITICUS 14:4–7 •

Behold, a man who was full of leprosy saw Jesus; and he fell on his face and implored Him, saying, "Lord, if You are willing, You can make me clean." LUKE 5:12 • Then Jesus, moved with compassion, stretched out His hand and touched him, and said to him, "I am willing; be cleansed." As soon as He had spoken, immediately the leprosy left him, and he was cleansed. MARK 1:41–42 •

Evening Reading

He whom you bless is blessed.
NUMBERS 22:6

Blessed are the poor in spirit, for theirs is the kingdom of heaven. Blessed are those who mourn, for they shall be comforted. Blessed are the meek, for they shall inherit the earth. Blessed are those who hunger and thirst for righteousness, for they shall be filled. Blessed are the merciful, for they shall obtain mercy. Blessed are the pure in heart, for they shall see God. Blessed are the peacemakers, for they shall be called sons of God. Blessed are those who are persecuted for righteous-ness' sake, for theirs is the kingdom of heaven. Blessed are you when they revile and persecute you, and say all kinds of evil against you falsely for My sake. Rejoice and be exceedingly glad, for great is your reward in heaven, for so they persecuted the prophets who were before you. MATTHEW 5:3–12 • Blessed are those who hear the word of God and keep it! LUKE 11:28 •

Blessed are those who do His commandments, that they may have the right to the tree of life, and may enter through the gates into the city. REVELATION 22:14 •

October 28

Morning Reading

He saw that there was no man, and wondered that there was no inter-cessor; therefore His own arm brought salvation for Him.
ISAIAH 59:16

Sacrifice and offering You did not desire; my ears You have opened. Burnt offering and sin offering You did not require. Then I said, "Behold, I come; in the scroll of the book it is written of me. I delight to do Your will, O my God, and Your law is within my heart." PSALM 40:6–8 • I lay down My life that I may take it again. No one takes it from Me, but I lay it down of Myself. I have power to lay it down, and I have power to take it again. JOHN 10:17–18 •

There is no other God besides Me, a just God and a Savior; there is none besides Me. Look to Me, and be saved, all you ends of the earth! For I am God, and there is no other. ISAIAH 45:21–22 • There is no other name under heaven given among men by which we must be saved. ACTS 4:12 •

You know the grace of our Lord Jesus Christ, that though He was rich, yet for your sakes He became poor, that you through His poverty might become rich. 2 CORINTHIANS 8:9 •

Evening Reading

The enemy.
LUKE 10:19

Be sober, be vigilant; because your adversary the devil walks about like a roaring lion, seeking whom he may devour. 1 PETER 5:8 • Resist the devil and he will flee from you. JAMES 4:7 •

Put on the whole armor of God, that you may be able to stand against the wiles of the devil. For we do not wrestle against flesh and blood, but against principalities, against powers, against the rulers of the darkness of this age, against spiritual hosts of wickedness in the heavenly places. Therefore take up the whole armor of God, that you may be able to withstand in the evil day, and having done all, to stand. Stand therefore, having girded your waist with truth, having put on the breastplate of righteousness, and having shod your feet with the preparation of the gospel of peace; above all, taking the shield of faith with which you will be able to quench all the fiery darts of the wicked one. EPHESIANS 6:11–16 •

Do not rejoice over me, my enemy; when I fall, I will arise; when I sit in darkness, the LORD will be a light to me. MICAH 7:8 •

October 29

Morning Reading

He is altogether lovely.
SONG OF SONGS 5:16

May my meditation be sweet to Him. PSALM 104:34 • My beloved is... chief among ten thousand. SONG OF SONGS 5:10 • [Jesus is] a chief cornerstone, elect, precious, and he who believes on Him will by no means be put to shame. 1 PETER 2:6 • You are fairer than the sons of men; grace is poured upon Your lips. PSALM 45:2 • God also has highly exalted [Jesus] and given Him the name which is above every name. PHILIPPIANS 2:9 • It pleased the Father that in Him all the fullness should dwell. COLOSSIANS 1:19 •

Whom having not seen you love. Though now you do not see Him, yet believing, you rejoice with joy inexpressible and full of glory. 1 PETER 1:8 •

I also count all things loss for the excellence of the knowledge of Christ Jesus my Lord, for whom I have suffered the loss of all things, and count them as rubbish, that I may gain Christ and be found in Him, not having my own righteousness, which is from the law, but that which is through faith in Christ, the righteousness which is from God by faith. PHILIPPIANS 3:8–9 •

Evening Reading

David strengthened himself in the LORD his God.
1 SAMUEL 30:6

Lord, to whom shall we go? You have the words of eternal life. JOHN 6:68 • I know whom I have believed and am persuaded that He is able to keep what I have committed to Him until that Day. 2 TIMOTHY 1:12 •

In my distress I called upon the LORD, and cried out to my God; He heard my voice from His temple, and my cry came before Him, even to His ears. PSALM 18:6 • They confronted me in the day of my calamity, but the LORD was my support. He also brought me out into a broad place; He delivered me because He delighted in me. PSALM 18:18–19 •

I will bless the LORD at all times; His praise shall continually be in my mouth. My soul shall make its boast in the LORD; the humble shall hear of it and be glad. Oh, magnify the LORD with me, and let us exalt His name together. I sought the LORD, and He heard me, and delivered me from all my fears....Oh, taste and see that the LORD is good; blessed is the man who trusts in Him! PSALM 34:1–4, 8 •

Morning Reading

It is good that one should hope and wait quietly
for the salvation of the LORD.
LAMENTATIONS 3:26

Has God forgotten to be gracious? Has He in anger shut up His tender mercies? PSALM 77:9 • I said in my haste, "I am cut off from before Your eyes"; nevertheless You heard the voice of my supplications when I cried out to You. PSALM 31:22 •

Shall God not avenge His own elect who cry out day and night to Him, though He bears long with them? I tell you that He will avenge them speedily. LUKE 18:7–8 • Wait for the LORD, and He will save you. PROVERBS 20:22 • Rest in the LORD, and wait patiently for Him; do not fret because of him who prospers in his way, because of the man who brings wicked schemes to pass. PSALM 37:7 •

You will not need to fight in this battle. Position yourselves, stand still and see the salvation of the LORD. 2 CHRONICLES 20:17 •

Let us not grow weary while doing good, for in due season we shall reap if we do not lose heart. GALATIANS 6:9 • See how the farmer waits for the precious fruit of the earth, waiting patiently for it until it receives the early and latter rain. JAMES 5:7 •

Evening Reading

Catch us the foxes, the little foxes that spoil the vines,
for our vines have tender grapes.
SONG OF SONGS 2:15

Who can understand his errors? Cleanse me from secret faults. PSALM 19:12 • Looking carefully lest anyone fall short of the grace of God; lest any root of bitterness springing up cause trouble, and by this many become defiled. HEBREWS 12:15 • You ran well. Who hindered you from obeying the truth? GALATIANS 5:7 •

He who has begun a good work in you will complete it until the day of Jesus Christ. PHILIPPIANS 1:6 • Let your conduct be worthy of the gospel of Christ. PHILIPPIANS 1:27 • The tongue is a little member and boasts great things. See how great a forest a little fire kindles! And the tongue is a fire, a world of iniquity. The tongue is so set among our members that it defiles the whole body, and sets on fire the course of nature; and it is set on fire by hell....No man can tame the tongue. It is an unruly evil, full of deadly poison. JAMES 3:5–6, 8 • Let your speech always be with grace, seasoned with salt. COLOSSIANS 4:6 •

October 31

Morning Reading

"Not by might nor by power, but by My Spirit,"
says the LORD of hosts.
ZECHARIAH 4:6

Who has directed the Spirit of the LORD, or as His counselor has taught Him? ISAIAH 40:13 •

God has chosen the foolish things of the world to put to shame the wise, and God has chosen the weak things of the world to put to shame the things which are mighty; and the base things of the world and the things which are despised God has chosen, and the things which are not, to bring to nothing the things that are, that no flesh should glory in His presence. 1 CORINTHIANS 1:27–29 •

The wind blows where it wishes, and you hear the sound of it, but cannot tell where it comes from and where it goes. So is everyone who is born of the Spirit. JOHN 3:8 • Born, not of blood, nor of the will of the flesh, nor of the will of man, but of God. JOHN 1:13 •

My Spirit remains among you; do not fear! HAGGAI 2:5 • The battle is not yours, but God's. 2 CHRONICLES 20:15 •

The LORD does not save with sword and spear; for the battle is the Lord's, and He will give you into our hands. 1 SAMUEL 17:47 •

Evening Reading

Do as You have said.
2 SAMUEL 7:25

Establish Your word to Your servant, who is devoted to fearing You. PSALM 119:38 • So shall I have an answer for him who reproaches me, for I trust in Your word. PSALM 119:42 • Remember the word to Your servant, upon which You have caused me to hope. PSALM 119:49 • Your statutes have been my songs in the house of my pilgrimage. PSALM 119:54 • The law of Your mouth is better to me than thousands of coins of gold and silver. PSALM 119:72 • Forever, O LORD, Your word is settled in heaven. Your faithfulness endures to all generations. PSALM 119:89–90 •

God, determining to show more abundantly to the heirs of promise the immutability of His counsel, confirmed it by an oath, that by two immutable things, in which it is impossible for God to lie, we might have strong consolation, who have fled for refuge to lay hold of the hope set before us. This hope we have as an anchor of the soul, both sure and steadfast, and which enters the Presence behind the veil, where the forerunner has entered for us, even Jesus. HEBREWS 6:17–20 •

Exceedingly great and precious promises. 2 PETER 1:4 •

NOVEMBER

November 1

Morning Reading

Blessed is the man who listens to me, watching daily at my gates, waiting at the posts of my doors.
PROVERBS 8:34

Behold, as the eyes of servants look to the hand of their masters, as the eyes of a maid to the hand of her mistress, so our eyes look to the LORD our God, until He has mercy on us. PSALM 123:2 •

This shall be a continual burnt offering throughout your generations at the door of the tabernacle of meeting before the LORD, where I will meet you to speak with you. EXODUS 29:42 • In every place where I record My name I will come to you, and I will bless you. EXODUS 20:24 •

For where two or three are gathered together in My name, I am there in the midst of them. MATTHEW 18:20 •

The hour is coming, and now is, when the true worshipers will worship the Father in spirit and truth; for the Father is seeking such to worship Him. God is Spirit, and those who worship Him must worship in spirit and truth. JOHN 4:23–24 •

Praying always with all prayer and supplication in the Spirit. EPHESIANS 6:18 • Pray without ceasing. 1 THESSALONIANS 5:17 •

Evening Reading

His name will be called...Counselor.
ISAIAH 9:6

The Spirit of the LORD shall rest upon Him, the Spirit of wisdom and understanding, the Spirit of counsel and might, the Spirit of knowledge and of the fear of the LORD. His delight is in the fear of the LORD. ISAIAH 11:2–3 •

Does not wisdom cry out, and understanding lift up her voice?...[Wisdom says,] "To you, O men, I call, and my voice is to the sons of men. O you simple ones, understand prudence, and you fools, be of an understanding heart. Listen, for I will speak of excellent things, and from the opening of my lips will come right things....Counsel is mine, and sound wisdom; I am understanding, I have strength." PROVERBS 8:1, 4–6, 14 •

The LORD of hosts...is wonderful in counsel and excellent in guidance. ISAIAH 28:29 • If any of you lacks wisdom, let him ask of God, who gives to all liberally and without reproach, and it will be given to him. JAMES 1:5 • Trust in the LORD with all your heart, and lean not on your own understanding; in all your ways acknowledge Him, and He shall direct your paths. PROVERBS 3:5–6 •

November 2

Morning Reading

Always pursue what is good.
1 THESSALONIANS 5:15

For to this you were called, because Christ also suffered for us, leaving us an example, that you should follow His steps: "Who committed no sin, nor was deceit found in His mouth"; who, when He was reviled, did not revile in return...but committed Himself to Him who judges righteously. 1 PETER 2:21–23 • Consider Him who endured such hostility from sinners against Himself, lest you become weary and discouraged in your souls. HEBREWS 12:3 •

Let us lay aside every weight, and the sin which so easily ensnares us, and let us run with endurance the race that is set before us, looking unto Jesus, the author and finisher of our faith, who for the joy that was set before Him endured the cross, despising the shame, and has sat down at the right hand of the throne of God. HEBREWS 12:1–2 •

Finally, brethren, whatever things are true, whatever things are noble, whatever things are just, whatever things are pure, whatever things are lovely, whatever things are of good report, if there is any virtue and if there is anything praiseworthy; meditate on these things. PHILIPPIANS 4:8 •

Evening Reading

Mighty God.
ISAIAH 9:6

You are fairer than the sons of men; grace is poured upon Your lips; therefore God has blessed You forever. Gird Your sword upon Your thigh, O Mighty One, with Your glory and Your majesty. And in Your majesty ride prosperously....Your throne, O God, is forever and ever; a scepter of righteousness is the scepter of Your kingdom. PSALM 45:2–4, 6 • You spoke in a vision to Your holy one, and said: "I have given help to one who is mighty." PSALM 89:19 • "The Man who is My Companion," says the LORD of hosts. ZECHARIAH 13:7 •

Behold, God is my salvation, I will trust and not be afraid; "For YAH, the LORD, is my strength and song; He also has become my salvation." ISAIAH 12:2 • Thanks be to God who always leads us in triumph in Christ. 2 CORINTHIANS 2:14 •

Now to Him who is able to keep you from stumbling, and to present you faultless before the presence of His glory with exceeding joy, to God our Savior, who alone is wise, be glory and majesty, dominion and power, both now and forever. JUDE 24–25 •

November 3

Morning Reading

The ways of the LORD are right; the righteous walk in them,
but transgressors stumble in them.
HOSEA 14:9

To you who believe, He is precious; but to those who are disobedient,...[He is] "a stone of stumbling and a rock of offense." 1 PETER 2:7–8 • The way of the LORD is strength for the upright, but destruction will come to the workers of iniquity. PROVERBS 10:29 •

He who has ears to hear, let him hear! MATTHEW 11:15 • Whoever is wise will observe these things, and they will understand the loving-kindness of the LORD. PSALM 107:43 • The lamp of the body is the eye. If therefore your eye is good, your whole body will be full of light. MATTHEW 6:22 • If anyone wants to do His will, he shall know concerning the doctrine, whether it is from God. JOHN 7:17 • Whoever has, to him more will be given, and he will have abundance. MATTHEW 13:12 •

He who is of God hears God's words; therefore you do not hear, because you are not of God. JOHN 8:47 • You are not willing to come to Me that you may have life. JOHN 5:40 • My sheep hear My voice, and I know them, and they follow Me. JOHN 10:27 •

Evening Reading

Everlasting Father.
ISAIAH 9:6

Hear, O Israel: The LORD our God, the LORD is one! DEUTERONOMY 6:4 •
I and My Father are one....The Father is in Me, and I in Him. JOHN 10:30, 38 • If you had known Me, you would have known My Father also. JOHN 8:19 • Philip said to Him, "Lord, show us the Father, and it is sufficient for us." Jesus said to him, "Have I been with you so long, and yet you have not known Me, Philip? He who has seen Me has seen the Father." JOHN 14:8–9 • Here am I and the children whom God has given Me. HEBREWS 2:13 • He shall see the labor of His soul, and be satisfied. ISAIAH 53:11 • "I am the Alpha and the Omega, the Beginning and the End," says the Lord, "who is and who was and who is to come, the Almighty." REVELATION 1:8 • Before Abraham was, I AM. JOHN 8:58 • God said to Moses, "I AM WHO I AM." And He said, "Thus you shall say to the children of Israel, 'I AM has sent me to you.'" EXODUS 3:14 •

To the Son He says: "Your throne, O God, is forever and ever." HEBREWS 1:8 • He is before all things, and in Him all things consist. COLOSSIANS 1:17 • In Him dwells all the fullness of the Godhead bodily. COLOSSIANS 2:9 •

November 4

Morning Reading

*Now for a little while, if need be, you have been
grieved by various trials.*
1 PETER 1:6

Beloved, do not think it strange concerning the fiery trial which is
to try you, as though some strange thing happened to you; but rejoice
to the extent that you partake of Christ's sufferings, that when His glory
is revealed, you may also be glad with exceeding joy. 1 PETER 4:12–13 • The
exhortation which speaks to you as to sons: "My son, do not despise the
chastening of the LORD, nor be discouraged when you are rebuked by
Him."...Now no chastening seems to be joyful for the present, but painful; nevertheless, afterward it yields the peaceable fruit of righteousness
to those who have been trained by it. HEBREWS 12:5, 11 •

We do not have a High Priest who cannot sympathize with our
weaknesses, but was in all points tempted as we are, yet without sin.
HEBREWS 4:15 • For in that He Himself has suffered, being tempted, He
is able to aid those who are tempted. HEBREWS 2:18 • God is faithful, who
will not allow you to be tempted beyond what you are able. 1 CORINTHIANS
10:13 •

Evening Reading

Prince of Peace.
ISAIAH 9:6

He will judge Your people with righteousness, and Your poor with
justice. The mountains will bring peace to the people, and the little
hills, by righteousness....He shall come down like rain upon the grass
before mowing, like showers that water the earth. In His days the righteous shall flourish, and abundance of peace, until the moon is no
more. PSALM 72:2–3, 6–7 • Glory to God,...and on earth peace, goodwill
toward men! LUKE 2:14 •

Through the tender mercy of our God, with which the Dayspring
from on high has visited us; to give light to those who sit in darkness
and the shadow of death, to guide our feet into the way of peace. LUKE
1:78–79 • Peace through Jesus Christ; He is Lord of all. ACTS 10:36 •

These things I have spoken to you, that in Me you may have peace.
In the world you will have tribulation; but be of good cheer, I have
overcome the world. JOHN 16:33 • Peace I leave with you, My peace I give
to you; not as the world gives do I give to you. JOHN 14:27 • The peace of
God, which surpasses all understanding, will guard your hearts and
minds through Christ Jesus. PHILIPPIANS 4:7 •

November 5

Morning Reading

*Also take for yourself quality spices....And you
shall make from these a holy anointing oil.*
EXODUS 30:23, 25

It shall not be poured on man's flesh; nor shall you make any other like it, according to its composition. It is holy, and it shall be holy to you. EXODUS 30:32 • One Spirit. EPHESIANS 4:4 • There are diversities of gifts, but the same Spirit. 1 CORINTHIANS 12:4 •

God, Your God, has anointed You with the oil of gladness more than Your companions. PSALM 45:7 • God anointed Jesus of Nazareth with the Holy Spirit and with power. ACTS 10:38 • God does not give the Spirit by measure [to Him]. JOHN 3:34 •

Of His fullness we have all received. JOHN 1:16 • As the same anointing teaches you concerning all things, and is true, and is not a lie, and just as it has taught you, you will abide in Him. 1 JOHN 2:27 • He who establishes us with you in Christ and has anointed us is God, who also has sealed us and given us the Spirit in our hearts. 2 CORINTHIANS 1:21–22 •

The fruit of the Spirit is love, joy, peace, longsuffering, kindness, goodness, faithfulness, gentleness, self-control. Against such there is no law. GALATIANS 5:22–23 •

Evening Reading

The form of this world is passing away.
1 CORINTHIANS 7:31

All the days of Methuselah were nine hundred and sixty-nine years; and he died. GENESIS 5:27 •

Let the lowly brother glory in his exaltation, but the rich in his humiliation, because as a flower of the field he will pass away. For no sooner has the sun risen with a burning heat than it withers the grass; its flower falls, and its beautiful appearance perishes. So the rich man also will fade away in his pursuits. JAMES 1:9–11 • For what is your life? It is even a vapor that appears for a little time and then vanishes away. JAMES 4:14 • The world is passing away, and the lust of it; but he who does the will of God abides forever. 1 JOHN 2:17 •

LORD, make me to know my end, and what is the measure of my days, that I may know how frail I am. PSALM 39:4 • When they say, "Peace and safety!" then sudden destruction comes upon them, as labor pains upon a pregnant woman. And they shall not escape. But you, brethren, are not in darkness, so that this Day should overtake you as a thief. 1 THESSALONIANS 5:3–4 •

November 6

Morning Reading

When Christ who is our life appears, then you also
will appear with Him in glory.
COLOSSIANS 3:4

I am the resurrection and the life. He who believes in Me, though he may die, he shall live. JOHN 11:25 • God has given us eternal life, and this life is in His Son. He who has the Son has life; he who does not have the Son of God does not have life. 1 JOHN 5:11–12 •

The Lord Himself will descend from heaven with a shout, with the voice of an archangel, and with the trumpet of God. And the dead in Christ will rise first. Then we who are alive and remain shall be caught up together with them in the clouds to meet the Lord in the air. And thus we shall always be with the Lord. Therefore comfort one another with these words. 1 THESSALONIANS 4:16–18 • When He is revealed, we shall be like Him, for we shall see Him as He is. 1 JOHN 3:2 • [The body] is sown in dishonor, it is raised in glory. It is sown in weakness, it is raised in power. 1 CORINTHIANS 15:43 •

If I go and prepare a place for you, I will come again and receive you to Myself; that where I am, there you may be also. JOHN 14:3 •

Evening Reading

Lead me in Your truth and teach me.
PSALM 25:5

When...the Spirit of truth, has come, He will guide you into all truth. JOHN 16:13 • You have an anointing from the Holy One, and you know all things. 1 JOHN 2:20 •

To the law and to the testimony! If they do not speak according to this word, it is because there is no light in them. ISAIAH 8:20 • All Scripture is given by inspiration of God, and is profitable for doctrine, for reproof, for correction, for instruction in righteousness, that the man of God may be complete, thoroughly equipped for every good work. 2 TIMOTHY 3:16–17 • The Holy Scriptures...are able to make you wise for salvation through faith which is in Christ Jesus. 2 TIMOTHY 3:15 •

I will instruct you and teach you in the way you should go; I will guide you with My eye. PSALM 32:8 • The lamp of the body is the eye. If therefore your eye is good, your whole body will be full of light. MATTHEW 6:22 • If anyone wants to do His will, he shall know concerning the doctrine, whether it is from God. JOHN 7:17 • Whoever walks the road, although a fool, shall not go astray. ISAIAH 35:8 •

November 7

Morning Reading

*Oh, that men would give thanks to the LORD for His goodness,
and for His wonderful works to the children of men!*
PSALM 107:8

Oh, taste and see that the LORD is good; blessed is the man who trusts in Him! PSALM 34:8 • Oh, how great is Your goodness, which You have laid up for those who fear You. PSALM 31:19 •

This people I have formed for Myself; they shall declare My praise. ISAIAH 43:21 • [God] predestined us to adoption as sons by Jesus Christ to Himself, according to the good pleasure of His will, to the praise of the glory of His grace, by which He has made us accepted in the Beloved,... that we who first trusted in Christ should be to the praise of His glory. EPHESIANS 1:5–6, 12 •

How great is its goodness and how great its beauty! ZECHARIAH 9:17 • The LORD is good to all, and His tender mercies are over all His works. All Your works shall praise You, O LORD, and Your saints shall bless You. They shall speak of the glory of Your kingdom, and talk of Your power, to make known to the sons of men His mighty acts, and the glorious majesty of His kingdom. PSALM 145:9–12 •

Evening Reading

Indeed we count them blessed who endure.
JAMES 5:11

We also glory in tribulations, knowing that tribulation produces perseverance; and perseverance, character; and character, hope. Now hope does not disappoint, because the love of God has been poured out in our hearts by the Holy Spirit who was given to us. ROMANS 5:3–5 • No chastening seems to be joyful for the present, but painful; nevertheless, afterward it yields the peaceable fruit of righteousness to those who have been trained by it. HEBREWS 12:11 • My brethren, count it all joy when you fall into various trials, knowing that the testing of your faith produces patience. But let patience have its perfect work, that you may be perfect and complete, lacking nothing....Blessed is the man who endures temptation; for when he has been approved, he will receive the crown of life which the Lord has promised to those who love Him. JAMES 1:2–4, 12 • Therefore most gladly I will rather boast in my infirmities, that the power of Christ may rest upon me....For when I am weak, then I am strong. 2 CORINTHIANS 12:9–10 •

November 8

Morning Reading

*Let us who are of the day be sober, putting on the breastplate of faith
and love, and as a helmet the hope of salvation.*
1 THESSALONIANS 5:8

Gird up the loins of your mind, be sober, and rest your hope fully
upon the grace that is to be brought to you at the revelation of Jesus
Christ. 1 PETER 1:13 • Stand therefore, having girded your waist with
truth, having put on the breastplate of righteousness,...[and] above all,
taking the shield of faith with which you will be able to quench all the
fiery darts of the wicked one. And take the helmet of salvation, and the
sword of the Spirit, which is the word of God. EPHESIANS 6:14, 16–17 •

He will swallow up death forever, and the Lord GOD will wipe away
tears from all faces; the rebuke of His people He will take away from
all the earth; for the LORD has spoken. And it will be said in that day:
"Behold, this is our God; we have waited for Him, and He will save us.
This is the LORD;...we will be glad and rejoice in His salvation." ISAIAH
25:8–9 •

Faith is the substance of things hoped for, the evidence of things
not seen. HEBREWS 11:1 •

Evening Reading

*The children of Israel encamped before them like two little flocks of
goats, while the Syrians filled the countryside.*
1 KINGS 20:27

Thus says the LORD: "Because the Syrians have said, 'The LORD
is God of the hills, but He is not God of the valleys,' therefore I will
deliver all this great multitude into your hand, and you shall know
that I am the LORD." And they encamped opposite each other for seven
days. So it was that on the seventh day the battle was joined; and the
children of Israel killed one hundred thousand foot soldiers of the
Syrians in one day. 1 KINGS 20:28–29 • You are of God, little children, and
have overcome them, because He who is in you is greater than he who
is in the world. 1 JOHN 4:4 •

Fear not, for I am with you; be not dismayed, for I am your God.
I will strengthen you, yes, I will help you, I will uphold you with My
righteous right hand. ISAIAH 41:10 •

"They will fight against you, but they shall not prevail against you.
For I am with you," says the LORD, "to deliver you." JEREMIAH 1:19 •

November 9

Morning Reading

I have given help to one who is mighty; I have exalted one chosen from the people.
PSALM 89:19

I, even I, am the LORD, and besides Me there is no savior. ISAIAH 43:11 • There is one God and one Mediator between God and men, the Man Christ Jesus. 1 TIMOTHY 2:5 • There is no other name under heaven given among men by which we must be saved. ACTS 4:12 •

Mighty God. ISAIAH 9:6 • [Christ] made Himself of no reputation, taking the form of a bondservant, and coming in the likeness of men. And being found in appearance as a man, He humbled Himself and became obedient to the point of death, even the death of the cross. Therefore God also has highly exalted Him and given Him the name which is above every name. PHILIPPIANS 2:7–9 • We see Jesus, who was made a little lower than the angels, for the suffering of death crowned with glory and honor, that He, by the grace of God, might taste death for everyone. HEBREWS 2:9 • Inasmuch then as the children have partaken of flesh and blood, He Himself likewise shared in the same. HEBREWS 2:14 •

Evening Reading

Gather My saints together to Me, those who have made a covenant with Me by sacrifice.
PSALM 50:5

Christ was offered once to bear the sins of many. To those who eagerly wait for Him He will appear a second time, apart from sin, for salvation. HEBREWS 9:28 • He is the Mediator of the new covenant, by means of death,...that those who are called may receive the promise of the eternal inheritance. HEBREWS 9:15 •

Father, I desire that they also whom You gave Me may be with Me where I am. JOHN 17:24 • Then He will send His angels, and gather together His elect from the four winds, from the farthest part of earth to the farthest part of heaven. MARK 13:27 • If any of you are driven out to the farthest parts under heaven, from there the LORD your God will gather you, and from there He will bring you. DEUTERONOMY 30:4 •

The dead in Christ will rise first. Then we who are alive and remain shall be caught up together with them in the clouds to meet the Lord in the air. And thus we shall always be with the Lord. 1 THESSALONIANS 4:16–17 •

November 10

Morning Reading

*Fruitful in every good work and increasing in
the knowledge of God.*
Colossians 1:10

I beseech you therefore, brethren, by the mercies of God, that you present your bodies a living sacrifice, holy, acceptable to God, which is your reasonable service. And do not be conformed to this world, but be transformed by the renewing of your mind, that you may prove what is that good and acceptable and perfect will of God. Romans 12:1–2 • As you presented your members as slaves of uncleanness, and of lawlessness leading to more lawlessness, so now present your members as slaves of righteousness for holiness. Romans 6:19 • In Christ Jesus neither circumcision nor uncircumcision avails anything, but a new creation. And as many as walk according to this rule, peace and mercy be upon them. Galatians 6:15–16 •

By this My Father is glorified, that you bear much fruit; so you will be My disciples....I chose you and appointed you that you should go and bear fruit, and that your fruit should remain, that whatever you ask the Father in My name He may give you. John 15:8, 16 •

Evening Reading

I sought him, but I did not find him.
Song of Songs 3:1

Return to the Lord your God, for you have stumbled because of your iniquity; take words with you, and return to the Lord. Say to Him, "Take away all iniquity; receive us graciously." Hosea 14:1–2 •

Let no one say when he is tempted, "I am tempted by God."...But each one is tempted when he is drawn away by his own desires and enticed. James 1:13–14 • Do not be deceived, my beloved brethren. Every good gift and every perfect gift is from above, and comes down from the Father of lights, with whom there is no variation or shadow of turning. James 1:16–17 •

Wait on the Lord; be of good courage, and He shall strengthen your heart; wait, I say, on the Lord! Psalm 27:14 • It is good that one should hope and wait quietly for the salvation of the Lord. Lamentations 3:26 • Shall God not avenge His own elect who cry out day and night to Him, though He bears long with them? Luke 18:7 •

Truly my soul silently waits for God; from Him comes my salvation....My soul, wait silently for God alone, for my expectation is from Him. Psalm 62:1, 5 •

November 11

Morning Reading

He led them on safely.
PSALM 78:53

I traverse the way of righteousness, in the midst of the paths of justice. PROVERBS 8:20 •

Behold, I send an Angel before you to keep you in the way and to bring you into the place which I have prepared. EXODUS 23:20 • In all their affliction He was afflicted, and the Angel of His Presence saved them; in His love and in His pity He redeemed them; and He bore them and carried them all the days of old. ISAIAH 63:9 •

They did not gain possession of the land by their own sword, nor did their own arm save them; but it was Your right hand, Your arm, and the light of Your countenance, because You favored them. PSALM 44:3 • So You lead Your people, to make Yourself a glorious name. ISAIAH 63:14 •

Lead me, O LORD, in Your righteousness because of my enemies; make Your way straight before my face. PSALM 5:8 • Oh, send out Your light and Your truth! Let them lead me; let them bring me to Your holy hill and to Your tabernacle. Then I will go to the altar of God, to God my exceeding joy; and on the harp I will praise You, O God, my God. PSALM 43:3–4 •

Evening Reading

You were washed,...you were sanctified,...you were justified.
1 CORINTHIANS 6:11

The blood of Jesus Christ His Son cleanses us from all sin. 1 JOHN 1:7 • The chastisement for our peace was upon Him, and by His stripes we are healed. ISAIAH 53:5 •

Christ also loved the church and gave Himself for her, that He might sanctify and cleanse her with the washing of water by the word, that He might present her to Himself a glorious church, not having spot or wrinkle or any such thing, but that she should be holy and without blemish. EPHESIANS 5:25–27 • To her it was granted to be arrayed in fine linen, clean and bright, for the fine linen is the righteous acts of the saints. REVELATION 19:8 • Let us draw near with a true heart in full assurance of faith, having our hearts sprinkled from an evil conscience and our bodies washed with pure water. HEBREWS 10:22 •

Who shall bring a charge against God's elect? It is God who justifies. ROMANS 8:33 • Blessed is he whose transgression is forgiven, whose sin is covered. Blessed is the man to whom the LORD does not impute iniquity, and in whose spirit there is no deceit. PSALM 32:1–2 •

November 12

Morning Reading

Godly sorrow produces repentance leading to
salvation, not to be regretted.
2 CORINTHIANS 7:10

Peter remembered the word of Jesus who had said to him, "Before the rooster crows, you will deny Me three times." So he went out and wept bitterly. MATTHEW 26:75 • If we confess our sins, He is faithful and just to forgive us our sins and to cleanse us from all unrighteousness. 1 JOHN 1:9 • The blood of Jesus Christ His Son cleanses us from all sin. 1 JOHN 1:7 •

My iniquities have overtaken me, so that I am not able to look up; they are more than the hairs of my head; therefore my heart fails me. Be pleased, O LORD, to deliver me; O LORD, make haste to help me! PSALM 40:12–13 •

By the help of your God, return; observe mercy and justice, and wait on your God continually. HOSEA 12:6 •

The sacrifices of God are a broken spirit, a broken and a contrite heart; these, O God, You will not despise. PSALM 51:17 • He heals the brokenhearted and binds up their wounds. PSALM 147:3 • He has shown you, O man, what is good; and what does the LORD require of you but to do justly, to love mercy, and to walk humbly with your God? MICAH 6:8 •

Evening Reading

Say to her, "Is it well with you?"…And she answered, "It is well."
2 KINGS 4:26

We have the same spirit of faith. 2 CORINTHIANS 4:13 •

As chastened, and yet not killed; as sorrowful, yet always rejoicing; as poor, yet making many rich; as having nothing, and yet possessing all things. 2 CORINTHIANS 6:9–10 •

We are hard pressed on every side, yet not crushed; we are perplexed, but not in despair; persecuted, but not forsaken; struck down, but not destroyed; always carrying about in the body the dying of the Lord Jesus, that the life of Jesus also may be manifested in our body.… Therefore we do not lose heart. Even though our outward man is perishing, yet the inward man is being renewed day by day. For our light affliction, which is but for a moment, is working for us a far more exceeding and eternal weight of glory, while we do not look at the things which are seen, but at the things which are not seen. 2 CORINTHIANS 4:8–10, 16–18 •

Beloved, I pray that you may prosper in all things and be in health, just as your soul prospers. 3 JOHN 2 •

November 13

Morning Reading

Christ also loved the church and gave Himself for her,
that He might sanctify and cleanse her with the
washing of water by the word.
EPHESIANS 5:25–26

Walk in love, as Christ also has loved us and given Himself for us, an offering and a sacrifice to God for a sweet-smelling aroma. EPHESIANS 5:2 •

Having been born again, not of corruptible seed but incorruptible, through the word of God which lives and abides forever. 1 PETER 1:23 • Sanctify them by Your truth. Your word is truth. JOHN 17:17 • Unless one is born of water and the Spirit, he cannot enter the kingdom of God. JOHN 3:5 • Not by works of righteousness which we have done, but according to His mercy He saved us, through the washing of regeneration and renewing of the Holy Spirit. TITUS 3:5 • Your word has given me life. PSALM 119:50 •

The law of the LORD is perfect, converting the soul; the testimony of the LORD is sure, making wise the simple; the statutes of the LORD are right, rejoicing the heart; the commandment of the LORD is pure, enlightening the eyes. PSALM 19:7–8 •

Evening Reading

Through Him we both have access by one Spirit to the Father.
EPHESIANS 2:18

I in them, and You in Me; that they may be made perfect in one. JOHN 17:23 •

Whatever you ask in My name, that I will do, that the Father may be glorified in the Son. If you ask anything in My name, I will do it.... And I will pray the Father, and He will give you another Helper, that He may abide with you forever; the Spirit of truth, whom the world cannot receive, because it neither sees Him nor knows Him; but you know Him, for He dwells with you and will be in you. JOHN 14:13–14, 16–17 • There is one body and one Spirit, just as you were called in one hope of your calling; one Lord, one faith, one baptism; one God and Father of all, who is above all, and through all, and in you all. EPHESIANS 4:4–6 • When you pray, say: Our Father in heaven. LUKE 11:2 •

Therefore, brethren, having boldness to enter the Holiest by the blood of Jesus, by a new and living way,...let us draw near. HEBREWS 10:19–20, 22 •

November 14

Morning Reading

You are my help and my deliverer; do not delay, O my God.
PSALM 40:17

The steps of a good man are ordered by the LORD, and He delights in his way. Though he fall, he shall not be utterly cast down; for the LORD upholds him with His hand. PSALM 37:23–24 • In the fear of the LORD there is strong confidence, and His children will have a place of refuge. PROVERBS 14:26 •

Who are you that you should be afraid of a man who will die, and of the son of a man who will be made like grass? And you forget the LORD your Maker. ISAIAH 51:12–13 •

I am with you to deliver you. JEREMIAH 1:8 • Be strong and of good courage, do not fear nor be afraid of them; for the LORD your God, He is the One who goes with you. He will not leave you nor forsake you. DEUTERONOMY 31:6 •

I will sing of Your power; yes, I will sing aloud of Your mercy in the morning; for You have been my defense and refuge in the day of my trouble. PSALM 59:16 • You are my hiding place; You shall preserve me from trouble; You shall surround me with songs of deliverance. PSALM 32:7 •

Evening Reading

How will you do in the floodplain of the Jordan?
JEREMIAH 12:5

For the Jordan overflows all its banks during the whole time of harvest. JOSHUA 3:15 •

The priests who bore the ark of the covenant of the LORD stood firm on dry ground in the midst of the Jordan; and all Israel crossed over on dry ground, until all the people had crossed completely over the Jordan. JOSHUA 3:17 •

We see Jesus, who was made a little lower than the angels, for the suffering of death crowned with glory and honor, that He, by the grace of God, might taste death for everyone. HEBREWS 2:9 •

Though I walk through the valley of the shadow of death, I will fear no evil; for You are with me; Your rod and Your staff, they comfort me. PSALM 23:4 • When you pass through the waters, I will be with you. ISAIAH 43:2 •

Do not be afraid; I am the First and the Last. I am He who lives, and was dead, and behold, I am alive forevermore. Amen. And I have the keys of Hades and of Death. REVELATION 1:17–18 •

November 15

Morning Reading

God is faithful, by whom you were called into the fellowship
of His Son, Jesus Christ our Lord.
1 CORINTHIANS 1:9

Let us hold fast the confession of our hope without wavering, for He who promised is faithful. HEBREWS 10:23 • God has said: "I will dwell in them and walk among them. I will be their God, and they shall be My people." 2 CORINTHIANS 6:16 • Truly our fellowship is with the Father and with His Son Jesus Christ. 1 JOHN 1:3 • Rejoice to the extent that you partake of Christ's sufferings, that when His glory is revealed, you may also be glad with exceeding joy. 1 PETER 4:13 •

That you, being rooted and grounded in love, may be able to comprehend with all the saints what is the width and length and depth and height; to know the love of Christ which passes knowledge; that you may be filled with all the fullness of God. EPHESIANS 3:17–19 •

Whoever confesses that Jesus is the Son of God, God abides in him, and he in God. 1 JOHN 4:15 • Now he who keeps His commandments abides in Him, and He in him. 1 JOHN 3:24 •

Evening Reading

We are His workmanship.
EPHESIANS 2:10

The king commanded them to quarry large stones, costly stones, and hewn stones, to lay the foundation of the temple. 1 KINGS 5:17 • The temple, when it was being built, was built with stone finished at the quarry, so that no hammer or chisel or any iron tool was heard in the temple while it was being built. 1 KINGS 6:7 •

You also, as living stones, are being built up a spiritual house. 1 PETER 2:5 • Having been built on the foundation of the apostles and prophets, Jesus Christ Himself being the chief cornerstone, in whom the whole building, being joined together, grows into a holy temple in the Lord, in whom you also are being built together for a dwelling place of God in the Spirit. EPHESIANS 2:20–22 • Who once were not a people but are now the people of God. 1 PETER 2:10 •

You are God's building. 1 CORINTHIANS 3:9 • Therefore, if anyone is in Christ, he is a new creation; old things have passed away; behold, all things have become new. 2 CORINTHIANS 5:17 • Now He who has prepared us for this very thing is God, who also has given us the Spirit as a guarantee. 2 CORINTHIANS 5:5 •

November 16

Morning Reading

Sanctify them by Your truth. Your word is truth.
JOHN 17:17

You are already clean because of the word which I have spoken to you. JOHN 15:3 • Let the word of Christ dwell in you richly in all wisdom. COLOSSIANS 3:16 •

How can a young man cleanse his way? By taking heed according to Your word. With my whole heart I have sought You; oh, let me not wander from Your commandments! PSALM 119:9–10 •

When wisdom enters your heart, and knowledge is pleasant to your soul, discretion will preserve you; understanding will keep you. PROVERBS 2:10–11 •

My foot has held fast to His steps; I have kept His way and not turned aside. I have not departed from the commandment of His lips; I have treasured the words of His mouth more than my necessary food. JOB 23:11–12 • I have more understanding than all my teachers, for Your testimonies are my meditation. PSALM 119:99 • If you abide in My word, you are My disciples indeed. And you shall know the truth, and the truth shall make you free. JOHN 8:31–32 •

Evening Reading

Fellow citizens with the saints.
EPHESIANS 2:19

You have come to Mount Zion and to the city of the living God, the heavenly Jerusalem, to an innumerable company of angels, to the general assembly and church of the firstborn who are registered in heaven, to God the Judge of all, to the spirits of just men made perfect. HEBREWS 12:22–23 •

These all died in faith, not having received the promises, but having seen them afar off were assured of them, embraced them and confessed that they were strangers and pilgrims on the earth. HEBREWS 11:13 • Our citizenship is in heaven, from which we also eagerly wait for the Savior, the Lord Jesus Christ, who will transform our lowly body that it may be conformed to His glorious body, according to the working by which He is able even to subdue all things to Himself. PHILIPPIANS 3:20–21 • [The Father] has delivered us from the power of darkness and conveyed us into the kingdom of the Son of His love. COLOSSIANS 1:13 •

As sojourners and pilgrims, abstain from fleshly lusts which war against the soul. 1 PETER 2:11 •

November 17

Morning Reading

Your thoughts are very deep.
PSALM 92:5

We...do not cease to pray for you, and to ask that you may be filled with the knowledge of His will in all wisdom and spiritual understanding. COLOSSIANS 1:9 • That Christ may dwell in your hearts through faith; that you, being rooted and grounded in love, may be able to comprehend with all the saints what is the width and length and depth and height; to know the love of Christ which passes knowledge; that you may be filled with all the fullness of God. EPHESIANS 3:17–19 •

Oh, the depth of the riches both of the wisdom and knowledge of God! How unsearchable are His judgments and His ways past finding out! ROMANS 11:33 • "For My thoughts are not your thoughts, nor are your ways My ways," says the LORD. "For as the heavens are higher than the earth, so are My ways higher than your ways, and My thoughts than your thoughts." ISAIAH 55:8–9 • Many, O LORD my God, are Your wonderful works which You have done; and Your thoughts toward us cannot be recounted to You in order; if I would declare and speak of them, they are more than can be numbered. PSALM 40:5 •

Evening Reading

Whatever a man sows, that he will also reap.
GALATIANS 6:7

Those who plow iniquity and sow trouble reap the same. JOB 4:8 • They sow the wind, and reap the whirlwind. HOSEA 8:7 • He who sows to his flesh will of the flesh reap corruption. GALATIANS 6:8 •

He who sows righteousness will have a sure reward. PROVERBS 11:18 • He who sows to the Spirit will of the Spirit reap everlasting life. And let us not grow weary while doing good, for in due season we shall reap if we do not lose heart. Therefore, as we have opportunity, let us do good to all, especially to those who are of the household of faith. GALATIANS 6:8–10 •

There is one who scatters, yet increases more; and there is one who withholds more than is right, but it leads to poverty. The generous soul will be made rich, and he who waters will also be watered himself. PROVERBS 11:24–25 • He who sows sparingly will also reap sparingly, and he who sows bountifully will also reap bountifully. 2 CORINTHIANS 9:6 •

November 18

Morning Reading

He removes it by His rough wind in the day of the east wind.
ISAIAH 27:8

Let us fall into the hand of the LORD, for His mercies are great. 2 SAMUEL 24:14 • I will correct you in justice, and will not let you go altogether unpunished. JEREMIAH 30:11 • He will not always strive with us, nor will He keep His anger forever. He has not dealt with us according to our sins, nor punished us according to our iniquities....For He knows our frame; He remembers that we are dust. PSALM 103:9–10, 14 • I will spare them as a man spares his own son who serves him. MALACHI 3:17 •

God is faithful, who will not allow you to be tempted beyond what you are able, but with the temptation will also make the way of escape, that you may be able to bear it. 1 CORINTHIANS 10:13 • Satan has asked for you, that he may sift you as wheat. But I have prayed for you, that your faith should not fail. LUKE 22:31–32 •

You have been a strength to the poor, a strength to the needy in his distress, a refuge from the storm, a shade from the heat; for the blast of the terrible ones is as a storm against the wall. ISAIAH 25:4 •

Evening Reading

I did not believe the words until I came and saw with my own eyes;
and indeed the half was not told me.
1 KINGS 10:7

The queen of the South will rise up in the judgment with this generation and condemn it, for she came from the ends of the earth to hear the wisdom of Solomon; and indeed a greater than Solomon is here. MATTHEW 12:42 • We beheld His glory, the glory as of the only begotten of the Father, full of grace and truth. JOHN 1:14 •

My speech and my preaching were...in demonstration of the Spirit and of power, that your faith should not be in the wisdom of men but in the power of God. 1 CORINTHIANS 2:4–5 • As it is written: "Eye has not seen, nor ear heard, nor have entered into the heart of man the things which God has prepared for those who love Him." But God has revealed them to us through His Spirit. For the Spirit searches all things, yes, the deep things of God. 1 CORINTHIANS 2:9–10 •

Your eyes will see the King in His beauty. ISAIAH 33:17 • We shall see Him as He is. 1 JOHN 3:2 • In my flesh I shall see God. JOB 19:26 • I shall be satisfied when I awake in Your likeness. PSALM 17:15 •

November 19

Morning Reading

By their fruits you will know them.
MATTHEW 7:20

Little children, let no one deceive you. He who practices righteousness is righteous, just as He is righteous. 1 JOHN 3:7 • Does a spring send forth fresh water and bitter from the same opening? Can a fig tree, my brethren, bear olives, or a grapevine bear figs? Thus no spring yields both salt water and fresh. Who is wise and understanding among you? Let him show by good conduct that his works are done in the meekness of wisdom. JAMES 3:11–13 • Having your conduct honorable among the Gentiles, that when they speak against you as evildoers, they may, by your good works which they observe, glorify God in the day of visitation. 1 PETER 2:12 •

Either make the tree good and its fruit good, or else make the tree bad and its fruit bad; for a tree is known by its fruit....A good man out of the good treasure of his heart brings forth good things, and an evil man out of the evil treasure brings forth evil things. MATTHEW 12:33, 35 •

What more could have been done to My vineyard that I have not done in it? ISAIAH 5:4 •

Evening Reading

I will make the place of My feet glorious.
ISAIAH 60:13

Thus says the LORD: "Heaven is My throne, and earth is My footstool." ISAIAH 66:1 •

Will God indeed dwell with men on the earth? Behold, heaven and the heaven of heavens cannot contain You. How much less this temple which I have built! 2 CHRONICLES 6:18 •

Thus says the LORD of hosts: "Once more (it is a little while) I will shake heaven and earth, the sea and dry land; and I will shake all nations, and they shall come to the Desire of All Nations, and I will fill this temple with glory," says the LORD of hosts...."The glory of this latter temple shall be greater than the former," says the LORD of hosts. "And in this place I will give peace," says the LORD of hosts. HAGGAI 2:6–7, 9 •

I saw a new heaven and a new earth, for the first heaven and the first earth had passed away. Also there was no more sea....And I heard a loud voice from heaven saying, "Behold, the tabernacle of God is with men, and He will dwell with them, and they shall be His people. God Himself will be with them and be their God." REVELATION 21:1, 3 •

November 20

Morning Reading

When I sit in darkness, the LORD will be a light to me.
MICAH 7:8

When you pass through the waters, I will be with you; and through the rivers, they shall not overflow you. When you walk through the fire, you shall not be burned, nor shall the flame scorch you. For I am the LORD your God, the Holy One of Israel, your Savior. ISAIAH 43:2–3 • I will bring the blind by a way they did not know; I will lead them in paths they have not known. I will make darkness light before them, and crooked places straight. These things I will do for them, and not forsake them. ISAIAH 42:16 •

Yea, though I walk through the valley of the shadow of death, I will fear no evil; for You are with me; Your rod and Your staff, they comfort me. PSALM 23:4 • Whenever I am afraid, I will trust in You. In God (I will praise His word), in God I have put my trust; I will not fear. What can flesh do to me? PSALM 56:3–4 • The LORD is my light and my salvation; whom shall I fear? The LORD is the strength of my life; of whom shall I be afraid? PSALM 27:1 •

Evening Reading

There is one God and one Mediator between God and men,
the Man Christ Jesus.
1 TIMOTHY 2:5

Hear, O Israel: The LORD our God, the LORD is one! DEUTERONOMY 6:4 • Now a mediator does not mediate for one only, but God is one. GALATIANS 3:20 •

We have sinned with our fathers, we have committed iniquity, we have done wickedly. Our fathers in Egypt did not understand Your wonders; they did not remember the multitude of Your mercies.... Therefore He said that He would destroy them, had not Moses His chosen one stood before Him in the breach, to turn away His wrath, lest He destroy them. PSALM 106:6–7, 23 •

Therefore, holy brethren, partakers of the heavenly calling, consider the Apostle and High Priest of our confession, Christ Jesus, who was faithful to Him who appointed Him, as Moses also was faithful in all His house. HEBREWS 3:1–2 •

He is also Mediator of a better covenant, which was established on better promises....[As God said,] "I will be merciful to their unrighteousness, and their sins and their lawless deeds I will remember no more." HEBREWS 8:6, 12 •

Daily Light on the Daily Path

November 21

Morning Reading

The one who comes to Me I will by no means cast out.
JOHN 6:37

It will be that when he cries to Me, I will hear, for I am gracious. EXODUS 22:27 • I will not cast them away, nor shall I abhor them, to utterly destroy them and break My covenant with them; for I am the LORD their God. LEVITICUS 26:44 • I will remember My covenant with you in the days of your youth, and I will establish an everlasting covenant with you. EZEKIEL 16:60 •

"Come now, and let us reason together," says the LORD, "though your sins are like scarlet, they shall be as white as snow; though they are red like crimson, they shall be as wool." ISAIAH 1:18 • Let the wicked forsake his way, and the unrighteous man his thoughts; let him return to the LORD, and He will have mercy on him; and to our God, for He will abundantly pardon. ISAIAH 55:7 • Then [the thief on the cross] said to Jesus, "Lord, remember me when You come into Your kingdom." And Jesus said to him, "Assuredly, I say to you, today you will be with Me in Paradise." LUKE 23:42–43 •

A bruised reed He will not break, and smoking flax He will not quench. ISAIAH 42:3 •

Evening Reading

The Son of His love.
COLOSSIANS 1:13

A voice came from heaven, saying, "This is My beloved Son, in whom I am well pleased." MATTHEW 3:17 • Behold! My Servant whom I uphold, My Elect One in whom My soul delights! ISAIAH 42:1 • The only begotten Son, who is in the bosom of the Father. JOHN 1:18 •

In this the love of God was manifested toward us, that God has sent His only begotten Son into the world, that we might live through Him. In this is love, not that we loved God, but that He loved us and sent His Son to be the propitiation for our sins....And we have known and believed the love that God has for us. God is love, and he who abides in love abides in God, and God in him. 1 JOHN 4:9–10, 16 •

The glory which You gave Me I have given them, that they may be one just as We are one: I in them, and You in Me; that they may be made perfect in one, and that the world may know that You have sent Me, and have loved them as You have loved Me. JOHN 17:22–24 • Behold what manner of love the Father has bestowed on us, that we should be called children of God! 1 JOHN 3:1 •

November 22

Morning Reading

Praying in the Holy Spirit.
JUDE 20

God is Spirit, and those who worship Him must worship in spirit and truth. JOHN 4:24 • We both have access by one Spirit to the Father. EPHESIANS 2:18 •

O My Father, if it is possible, let this cup pass from Me; nevertheless, not as I will, but as You will. MATTHEW 26:39 •

The Spirit also helps in our weaknesses. For we do not know what we should pray for as we ought, but the Spirit Himself makes intercession for us with groanings which cannot be uttered. Now He who searches the hearts knows what the mind of the Spirit is, because He makes intercession for the saints according to the will of God. ROMANS 8:26–27 • This is the confidence that we have in Him, that if we ask anything according to His will, He hears us. 1 JOHN 5:14 • When He, the Spirit of truth, has come, He will guide you into all truth. JOHN 16:13 •

Praying always with all prayer and supplication in the Spirit, being watchful to this end with all perseverance and supplication. EPHESIANS 6:18 •

Evening Reading

There is hope for a tree, if it is cut down, that it will sprout again, and that its tender shoots will not cease.
JOB 14:7

A bruised reed He will not break. ISAIAH 42:3 • He restores my soul. PSALM 23:3 •

Godly sorrow produces repentance leading to salvation, not to be regretted; but the sorrow of the world produces death. 2 CORINTHIANS 7:10 • No chastening seems to be joyful for the present, but painful; nevertheless, afterward it yields the peaceable fruit of righteousness to those who have been trained by it. HEBREWS 12:11 •

Before I was afflicted I went astray, but now I keep Your word. PSALM 119:67 • After all that has come upon us for our evil deeds and for our great guilt, since You our God have punished us less than our iniquities deserve, and have given us such deliverance as this. EZRA 9:13 •

Do not rejoice over me, my enemy; when I fall, I will arise; when I sit in darkness, the LORD will be a light to me....He will bring me forth to the light; I will see His righteousness. MICAH 7:8–9 •

November 23

Morning Reading

*Whoever listens to me will dwell safely, and will be
secure, without fear of evil.*
PROVERBS 1:33

LORD, You have been our dwelling place in all generations. PSALM 90:1 • He who dwells in the secret place of the Most High shall abide under the shadow of the Almighty....His truth shall be your shield and buckler. PSALM 91:1, 4

Your life is hidden with Christ in God. COLOSSIANS 3:3 • He who touches you touches the apple of His eye. ZECHARIAH 2:8 • Do not be afraid. Stand still, and see the salvation of the LORD....The LORD will fight for you, and you shall hold your peace. EXODUS 14:13–14 • God is our refuge and strength, a very present help in trouble. Therefore we will not fear. PSALM 46:1–2

Jesus spoke to [His disciples], saying, "Be of good cheer! It is I; do not be afraid." MATTHEW 14:27 • Why are you troubled? And why do doubts arise in your hearts? Behold My hands and My feet, that it is I Myself. Handle Me and see, for a spirit does not have flesh and bones as you see I have. LUKE 24:38–39 • I know whom I have believed and am persuaded that He is able to keep what I have committed to Him until that Day. 2 TIMOTHY 1:12 •

Evening Reading

My kingdom is not of this world.
JOHN 18:36

This Man, after He had offered one sacrifice for sins forever, sat down at the right hand of God, from that time waiting till His enemies are made His footstool. HEBREWS 10:12-13 • Hereafter you will see the Son of Man sitting at the right hand of the Power, and coming on the clouds of heaven. MATTHEW 26:64 •

He must reign till He has put all enemies under His feet. 1 CORINTHIANS 15:25 •

Thanks be to God, who gives us the victory through our Lord Jesus Christ. 1 CORINTHIANS 15:57 • He raised Him from the dead and seated Him at His right hand in the heavenly places, far above all principality and power and might and dominion, and every name that is named, not only in this age but also in that which is to come. And He put all things under His feet, and gave Him to be head over all things to the church, which is His body, the fullness of Him who fills all in all. EPHESIANS 1:20–23 • He will manifest in His own time, He who is the blessed and only Potentate, the King of kings and Lord of lords. 1 TIMOTHY 6:15 •

November 24

Morning Reading

My mother and My brothers are these who
hear the word of God and do it.
Luke 8:21

Both He who sanctifies and those who are being sanctified are all of one, for which reason He is not ashamed to call them brethren, saying: "I will declare Your name to My brethren; in the midst of the assembly I will sing praise to You." Hebrews 2:11–12 • In Christ Jesus neither circumcision nor uncircumcision avails anything, but faith working through love. Galatians 5:6 • You are My friends if you do whatever I command you. John 15:14 • Blessed are those who hear the word of God and keep it! Luke 11:28 •

Not everyone who says to Me, "Lord, Lord," shall enter the kingdom of heaven, but he who does the will of My Father in heaven. Matthew 7:21 • My food is to do the will of Him who sent Me, and to finish His work. John 4:34 •

If we say that we have fellowship with Him, and walk in darkness, we lie and do not practice the truth. 1 John 1:6 • Whoever keeps His word, truly the love of God is perfected in him. By this we know that we are in Him. 1 John 2:5 •

Evening Reading

What are you doing here, Elijah?
1 Kings 19:9

He knows the way that I take. Job 23:10 • O Lord, You have searched me and known me. You know my sitting down and my rising up; You understand my thought afar off. You comprehend my path and my lying down, and are acquainted with all my ways. Psalm 139:1–3 • Where can I go from Your Spirit? Or where can I flee from Your presence?... If I take the wings of the morning, and dwell in the uttermost parts of the sea, even there Your hand shall lead me, and Your right hand shall hold me. Psalm 139:7, 9–10 •

Elijah was a man with a nature like ours. James 5:17 • The fear of man brings a snare, but whoever trusts in the Lord shall be safe. Proverbs 29:25 • Though he fall, he shall not be utterly cast down; for the Lord upholds him with His hand. Psalm 37:24 • A righteous man may fall seven times and rise again. Proverbs 24:16 •

Let us not grow weary while doing good, for in due season we shall reap if we do not lose heart. Galatians 6:9 • The spirit indeed is willing, but the flesh is weak. Matthew 26:41 • As a father pities his children, so the Lord pities those who fear Him. Psalm 103:13 •

November 25

Morning Reading

Having been set free from sin,
you became slaves of righteousness.
ROMANS 6:18

You cannot serve God and mammon. MATTHEW 6:24 • When you were slaves of sin, you were free in regard to righteousness. What fruit did you have then in the things of which you are now ashamed? For the end of those things is death. But now having been set free from sin, and having become slaves of God, you have your fruit to holiness, and the end, everlasting life. ROMANS 6:20–22 •

Christ is the end of the law for righteousness to everyone who believes. ROMANS 10:4 •

If anyone serves Me, let him follow Me; and where I am, there My servant will be also. If anyone serves Me, him My Father will honor. JOHN 12:26 • Take My yoke upon you and learn from Me, for I am gentle and lowly in heart, and you will find rest for your souls. For My yoke is easy and My burden is light. MATTHEW 11:29–30 •

O LORD our God, masters besides You have had dominion over us; but by You only we make mention of Your name. ISAIAH 26:13 • I will run the course of Your commandments, for You shall enlarge my heart. PSALM 119:32 •

Evening Reading

Whoever calls on the name of the LORD shall be saved.
ACTS 2:21

[Manasseh] did evil in the sight of the LORD, according to the abominations of the nations....He raised up altars for Baal,...and he built altars for all the host of heaven in the two courts of the house of the LORD. Also he made his son pass through the fire, practiced soothsaying, used witchcraft, and consulted spiritists and mediums. He did much evil in the sight of the LORD, to provoke Him to anger. 2 KINGS 21:2–3, 5–6 • Now when [Manasseh] was in affliction, he implored the LORD his God, and humbled himself greatly before the God of his fathers, and prayed to Him; and He received his entreaty, heard his supplication. 2 CHRONICLES 33:12–13 •

"Come now, and let us reason together," says the LORD, "though your sins are like scarlet, they shall be as white as snow; though they are red like crimson, they shall be as wool." ISAIAH 1:18 • The Lord is...longsuffering toward us, not willing that any should perish but that all should come to repentance. 2 PETER 3:9 •

November 26

Morning Reading

The LORD delights in you.
ISAIAH 62:4

Thus says the LORD, who created you,..."Fear not, for I have redeemed you; I have called you by your name; You are Mine." ISAIAH 43:1 • Can a woman forget her nursing child, and not have compassion on the son of her womb? Surely they may forget, yet I will not forget you. See, I have inscribed you on the palms of My hands; your walls are continually before Me. ISAIAH 49:15–16 •

The steps of a good man are ordered by the LORD, and He delights in his way. PSALM 37:23 • My delight was with the sons of men. PROVERBS 8:31 • The LORD takes pleasure in those who fear Him, in those who hope in His mercy. PSALM 147:11 • "They shall be Mine," says the LORD of hosts, "on the day that I make them My jewels. And I will spare them as a man spares his own son who serves him." MALACHI 3:17 •

You, who once were alienated and enemies in your mind by wicked works, yet now He has reconciled in the body of His flesh through death, to present you holy, and blameless, and above reproach in His sight. COLOSSIANS 1:21–22 •

Evening Reading

The sorrow of the world produces death.
2 CORINTHIANS 7:10

When Ahithophel saw that his advice was not followed, he saddled a donkey, and arose and went home to his house, to his city. Then he put his household in order, and hanged himself, and died. 2 SAMUEL 17:23 • Who can bear a broken spirit? PROVERBS 18:14 •

Is there no balm in Gilead, is there no physician there? Why then is there no recovery for the health of the daughter of my people? JEREMIAH 8:22 • The LORD has anointed Me to preach good tidings to the poor; He has sent Me to heal the brokenhearted,...to comfort all who mourn, to console those who mourn in Zion, to give them beauty for ashes, the oil of joy for mourning, the garment of praise for the spirit of heaviness. ISAIAH 61:1–3 • Come to Me, all you who labor and are heavy laden, and I will give you rest. Take My yoke upon you and learn from Me, for I am gentle and lowly in heart, and you will find rest for your souls. For My yoke is easy and My burden is light. MATTHEW 11:28–30 •

Philip...preached Jesus to him. ACTS 8:35 • He heals the brokenhearted and binds up their wounds. PSALM 147:3 •

November 27

Morning Reading

The glory which You gave Me I have given them.
JOHN 17:22

I saw the Lord sitting on a throne, high and lifted up, and the train of His robe filled the temple. Above it stood seraphim....And one cried to another and said: "Holy, holy, holy is the LORD of hosts; the whole earth is full of His glory!" ISAIAH 6:1–3 • These things Isaiah said when he saw His glory and spoke of Him. JOHN 12:41 • On the likeness of the throne was a likeness...of a man high above it....Like the appearance of a rainbow in a cloud on a rainy day, so was the appearance of the brightness all around it. This was the appearance of the likeness of the glory of the LORD. EZEKIEL 1:26, 28 •

[Moses] said, "Please, show me Your glory."...But [God] said, "You cannot see My face; for no man shall see Me, and live." EXODUS 33:18, 20 • No one has seen God at any time. The only begotten Son, who is in the bosom of the Father, He has declared Him. JOHN 1:18 • God who commanded light to shine out of darkness,...has shone in our hearts to give the light of the knowledge of the glory of God in the face of Jesus Christ. 2 CORINTHIANS 4:6 •

Evening Reading

My son, if sinners entice you, do not consent.
PROVERBS 1:10

[Eve] took of its fruit and ate. She also gave to her husband with her, and he ate. GENESIS 3:6 • Did not Achan the son of Zerah commit a trespass in the accursed thing, and wrath fell on all the congregation of Israel? And that man did not perish alone in his iniquity. JOSHUA 22:20 •

You shall not follow a crowd to do evil. EXODUS 23:2 •

Wide is the gate and broad is the way that leads to destruction, and there are many who go in by it. MATTHEW 7:13 •

None of us lives to himself. ROMANS 14:7 • You, brethren, have been called to liberty; only do not use liberty as an opportunity for the flesh, but through love serve one another. GALATIANS 5:13 • Beware lest somehow this liberty of yours become a stumbling block to those who are weak. 1 CORINTHIANS 8:9 • When you thus sin against the brethren, and wound their weak conscience, you sin against Christ. 1 CORINTHIANS 8:12 •

All we like sheep have gone astray; we have turned, every one, to his own way; and the LORD has laid on Him the iniquity of us all. ISAIAH 53:6 •

November 28

Morning Reading

As the body without the spirit is dead,
so faith without works is dead also.
JAMES 2:26

Not everyone who says to Me, "Lord, Lord," shall enter the kingdom of heaven, but he who does the will of My Father in heaven. MATTHEW 7:21 • Pursue...holiness, without which no one will see the Lord. HEBREWS 12:14 • Add to your faith virtue, to virtue knowledge, to knowledge self-control, to self-control perseverance, to perseverance godliness, to godliness brotherly kindness, and to brotherly kindness love. For if these things are yours and abound, you will be neither barren nor unfruitful in the knowledge of our Lord Jesus Christ. For he who lacks these things is shortsighted, even to blindness, and has forgotten that he was cleansed from his old sins. Therefore, brethren, be even more diligent to make your call and election sure, for if you do these things you will never stumble. 2 PETER 1:5–10 •

By grace you have been saved through faith, and that not of yourselves; it is the gift of God, not of works, lest anyone should boast. EPHESIANS 2:8–9 •

Evening Reading

As the children have partaken of flesh and blood, He Himself likewise
shared in the same, that...He might...release those who through fear of
death were all their lifetime subject to bondage.
HEBREWS 2:14–15

O Death, where is your sting? O Hades, where is your victory?... Thanks be to God, who gives us the victory through our Lord Jesus Christ. 1 CORINTHIANS 15:55, 57 • Therefore we do not lose heart. Even though our outward man is perishing, yet the inward man is being renewed day by day. 2 CORINTHIANS 4:16 •

We know that if our earthly house, this tent, is destroyed, we have a building from God, a house not made with hands, eternal in the heavens....So we are always confident, knowing that while we are at home in the body we are absent from the Lord....We are...well pleased rather to be absent from the body and to be present with the Lord. 2 CORINTHIANS 5:1, 6–8 •

Let not your heart be troubled; you believe in God, believe also in Me. In My Father's house are many mansions; if it were not so, I would have told you. I go to prepare a place for you. And if I go and prepare a place for you, I will come again and receive you to Myself; that where I am, there you may be also. JOHN 14:1–3 •

November 29

Morning Reading

We shall be satisfied with the goodness of Your house.
PSALM 65:4

One thing I have desired of the LORD, that will I seek: that I may dwell in the house of the LORD all the days of my life, to behold the beauty of the LORD, and to inquire in His temple. PSALM 27:4 •

Blessed are those who hunger and thirst for righteousness, for they shall be filled. MATTHEW 5:6 • He has filled the hungry with good things, and the rich He has sent away empty. LUKE 1:53 •

He satisfies the longing soul, and fills the hungry soul with goodness. PSALM 107:9 • I am the bread of life. He who comes to Me shall never hunger, and he who believes in Me shall never thirst. JOHN 6:35 •

How precious is Your lovingkindness, O God! Therefore the children of men put their trust under the shadow of Your wings. They are abundantly satisfied with the fullness of Your house, and You give them drink from the river of Your pleasures. For with You is the fountain of life; in Your light we see light. PSALM 36:7–9 •

Evening Reading

Do you now believe?
JOHN 16:31

What does it profit, my brethren, if someone says he has faith but does not have works? Can faith save him?...Thus also faith by itself, if it does not have works, is dead. JAMES 2:14, 17 •

By faith Abraham, when he was tested, offered up Isaac, and he who had received the promises offered up his only begotten son, of whom it was said, "In Isaac your seed shall be called," concluding that God was able to raise him up, even from the dead. HEBREWS 11:17–19 • Was not Abraham our father justified by works when he offered Isaac his son on the altar?...You see then that a man is justified by works, and not by faith only. JAMES 2:21, 24 •

He who looks into the perfect law of liberty and continues in it, and is not a forgetful hearer but a doer of the work, this one will be blessed in what he does. JAMES 1:25 •

By their fruits you will know them. Not everyone who says to Me, "Lord, Lord," shall enter the kingdom of heaven, but he who does the will of My Father in heaven. MATTHEW 7:20–21 • If you know these things, blessed are you if you do them. JOHN 13:17 •

November 30

Morning Reading

Now may the Lord of peace Himself give you peace always in every way. The Lord be with you all.
2 THESSALONIANS 3:16

Peace from Him who is and who was and who is to come. REVELATION 1:4 • The peace of God, which surpasses all understanding, will guard your hearts and minds through Christ Jesus. PHILIPPIANS 4:7 •

Jesus Himself stood in the midst of [His disciples], and said to them, "Peace to you." LUKE 24:36 • Peace I leave with you, My peace I give to you; not as the world gives do I give to you. Let not your heart be troubled, neither let it be afraid. JOHN 14:27 •

The Helper,...[even] the Spirit of truth. JOHN 15:26 • The fruit of the Spirit is love, joy, peace. GALATIANS 5:22 • The Spirit Himself bears witness with our spirit that we are children of God. ROMANS 8:16 •

And [God] said, "My Presence will go with you, and I will give you rest." Then [Moses] said to Him, "If Your Presence does not go with us, do not bring us up from here. For how then will it be known that Your people and I have found grace in Your sight, except You go with us?" EXODUS 33:14–16 •

Evening Reading

We...glory in tribulations.
ROMANS 5:3

If in this life only we have hope in Christ, we are of all men the most pitiable. 1 CORINTHIANS 15:19 •

Beloved, do not think it strange concerning the fiery trial which is to try you, as though some strange thing happened to you; but rejoice to the extent that you partake of Christ's sufferings, that when His glory is revealed, you may also be glad with exceeding joy. 1 PETER 4:12–13 • Sorrowful, yet always rejoicing. 2 CORINTHIANS 6:10 •

Rejoice in the Lord always. Again I will say, rejoice! PHILIPPIANS 4:4 • They departed from the presence of the council, rejoicing that they were counted worthy to suffer shame for His name. ACTS 5:41 •

May the God of hope fill you with all joy and peace in believing. ROMANS 15:13 •

Though the fig tree may not blossom, nor fruit be on the vines; though the labor of the olive may fail, and the fields yield no food; though the flock may be cut off from the fold, and there be no herd in the stalls; yet I will rejoice in the LORD, I will joy in the God of my salvation. HABAKKUK 3:17–18 •

DECEMBER

December 1

Morning Reading

A man will be as a hiding place from the wind,
and a cover from the tempest.
ISAIAH 32:2

Inasmuch then as the children have partaken of flesh and blood, He Himself likewise shared in the same. HEBREWS 2:14 • "The Man who is My Companion," says the LORD of hosts. ZECHARIAH 13:7 • I and My Father are one. JOHN 10:30 •

He who dwells in the secret place of the Most High shall abide under the shadow of the Almighty. PSALM 91:1 • There will be a tabernacle for shade in the daytime from the heat, for a place of refuge, and for a shelter from storm and rain. ISAIAH 4:6 • The LORD is your shade at your right hand. The sun shall not strike you by day, nor the moon by night. PSALM 121:5–6 • When my heart is overwhelmed; lead me to the rock that is higher than I. PSALM 61:2 • You are my hiding place; You shall preserve me from trouble. PSALM 32:7 • You have been a strength to the poor, a strength to the needy in his distress, a refuge from the storm, a shade from the heat; for the blast of the terrible ones is as a storm against the wall. ISAIAH 25:4 •

Evening Reading

Behold, I create new heavens and a new earth.
ISAIAH 65:17

"The new heavens and the new earth which I will make shall remain before Me," says the LORD, "so shall your descendants and your name remain." ISAIAH 66:22 •

We, according to His promise, look for new heavens and a new earth in which righteousness dwells. 2 PETER 3:13 •

I saw a new heaven and a new earth, for the first heaven and the first earth had passed away. Also there was no more sea. Then I, John, saw the holy city, New Jerusalem, coming down out of heaven from God, prepared as a bride adorned for her husband. And I heard a loud voice from heaven saying, "Behold, the tabernacle of God is with men, and He will dwell with them, and they shall be His people. God Himself will be with them and be their God. And God will wipe away every tear from their eyes; there shall be no more death, nor sorrow, nor crying. There shall be no more pain, for the former things have passed away." Then He who sat on the throne said, "Behold, I make all things new." REVELATION 21:1–5 •

December 2

Morning Reading

You have an anointing from the Holy One,
and you know all things.
1 JOHN 2:20

God anointed Jesus of Nazareth with the Holy Spirit and with power. ACTS 10:38 • It pleased the Father that in Him all the fullness should dwell. COLOSSIANS 1:19 • Of His fullness we have all received, and grace for grace. JOHN 1:16 •

You anoint my head with oil. PSALM 23:5 • The anointing which you have received from Him abides in you, and you do not need that anyone teach you; but as the same anointing teaches you concerning all things, and is true, and is not a lie, and just as it has taught you, you will abide in Him. 1 JOHN 2:27 •

The Helper, the Holy Spirit, whom the Father will send in My name, He will teach you all things, and bring to your remembrance all things that I said to you. JOHN 14:26 •

The Spirit also helps in our weaknesses. For we do not know what we should pray for as we ought, but the Spirit Himself makes intercession for us with groanings which cannot be uttered. ROMANS 8:26 •

Evening Reading

Having our hearts sprinkled from an evil conscience.
HEBREWS 10:22

If the blood of bulls and goats and the ashes of a heifer, sprinkling the unclean, sanctifies for the purifying of the flesh, how much more shall the blood of Christ, who through the eternal Spirit offered Himself without spot to God, cleanse your conscience from dead works to serve the living God? HEBREWS 9:13–14 • The blood of sprinkling that speaks better things than that of Abel. HEBREWS 12:24 •

We have redemption through His blood, the forgiveness of sins, according to the riches of His grace. EPHESIANS 1:7 •

When Moses had spoken every precept to all the people according to the law, he took the blood of calves and goats, with water, scarlet wool, and hyssop, and sprinkled both the book itself and all the people....Then likewise he sprinkled with blood both the tabernacle and all the vessels of the ministry. And according to the law almost all things are purified with blood, and without shedding of blood there is no remission. HEBREWS 9:19, 21–22 •

December 3

Morning Reading

I would seek God, and to God I would commit my cause.
Job 5:8

Is anything too hard for the LORD? Genesis 18:14 • Commit your way to the LORD, trust also in Him, and He shall bring it to pass. Psalm 37:5 • Be anxious for nothing, but in everything by prayer and supplication, with thanksgiving, let your requests be made known to God. Philippians 4:6 • Casting all your care upon Him, for He cares for you. 1 Peter 5:7 •

Hezekiah received the letter from the hand of the messengers, and read it; and Hezekiah went up to the house of the LORD, and spread it before the LORD. Then Hezekiah prayed to the LORD. Isaiah 37:14–15 •

It shall come to pass that before they call, I will answer; and while they are still speaking, I will hear. Isaiah 65:24 • The effective, fervent prayer of a righteous man avails much. James 5:16 •

I love the LORD, because He has heard My voice and my supplications. Because He has inclined His ear to me, therefore I will call upon Him as long as I live. Psalm 116:1–2 •

Evening Reading

Our bodies washed with pure water.
Hebrews 10:22

You shall also make a laver of bronze....You shall put it between the tabernacle of meeting and the altar. And you shall put water in it, for Aaron and his sons shall wash their hands and their feet in water from it. When they go into the tabernacle of meeting,...they shall wash with water, lest they die. So they shall wash their hands and their feet, lest they die. Exodus 30:18–21 • Your body is the temple of the Holy Spirit who is in you. 1 Corinthians 6:19 • If anyone defiles the temple of God, God will destroy him. For the temple of God is holy, which temple you are. 1 Corinthians 3:17 •

In my flesh I shall see God, whom I shall see for myself, and my eyes shall behold, and not another. Job 19:26–27 • There shall by no means enter it anything that defiles. Revelation 21:27 • You are of purer eyes than to behold evil, and cannot look on wickedness. Habakkuk 1:13 • I beseech you therefore, brethren, by the mercies of God, that you present your bodies a living sacrifice, holy, acceptable to God, which is your reasonable service. Romans 12:1 •

December 4

Morning Reading

Where can wisdom be found?
JOB 28:12

If any of you lacks wisdom, let him ask of God, who gives to all liberally and without reproach, and it will be given to him. But let him ask in faith, with no doubting, for he who doubts is like a wave of the sea driven and tossed by the wind. JAMES 1:5–6 • Trust in the LORD with all your heart, and lean not on your own understanding; in all your ways acknowledge Him, and He shall direct your paths. PROVERBS 3:5–6 • God...alone is wise. 1 TIMOTHY 1:17 • Do not be wise in your own eyes. PROVERBS 3:7 •

Then said I: "Ah, Lord GOD! Behold, I cannot speak, for I am a youth." But the LORD said to me: "Do not say, 'I am a youth,' for you shall go to all to whom I send you, and whatever I command you, you shall speak. Do not be afraid of their faces, for I am with you to deliver you," says the LORD. JEREMIAH 1:6–8 •

Whatever you ask the Father in My name He will give you. Until now you have asked nothing in My name. Ask, and you will receive, that your joy may be full. JOHN 16:23–24 • Whatever things you ask in prayer, believing, you will receive. MATTHEW 21:22 •

Evening Reading

I would not live forever.
JOB 7:16

I said, "Oh, that I had wings like a dove! I would fly away and be at rest....I would hasten my escape from the windy storm and tempest." PSALM 55:6, 8 •

In this we groan, earnestly desiring to be clothed with our habitation which is from heaven....For we who are in this tent groan, being burdened, not because we want to be unclothed, but further clothed, that mortality may be swallowed up by life. 2 CORINTHIANS 5:2, 4 • Having a desire to depart and be with Christ, which is far better. PHILIPPIANS 1:23 •

Let us run with endurance the race that is set before us, looking unto Jesus, the author and finisher of our faith, who for the joy that was set before Him endured the cross, despising the shame, and has sat down at the right hand of the throne of God. For consider Him who endured such hostility from sinners against Himself, lest you become weary and discouraged in your souls. HEBREWS 12:1–3 •

Let not your heart be troubled, neither let it be afraid. JOHN 14:27 •

December 5

Morning Reading

It is good for me that I have been afflicted,
that I may learn Your statutes.
PSALM 119:71

Though He was a Son, yet He learned obedience by the things which He suffered. HEBREWS 5:8 • We suffer with Him, that we may also be glorified together. For I consider that the sufferings of this present time are not worthy to be compared with the glory which shall be revealed in us. ROMANS 8:17–18 •

He knows the way that I take; when He has tested me, I shall come forth as gold. My foot has held fast to His steps; I have kept His way and not turned aside. JOB 23:10–11 •

You shall remember that the LORD your God led you all the way these forty years in the wilderness, to humble you and test you, to know what was in your heart, whether you would keep His commandments or not....You should know in your heart that as a man chastens his son, so the LORD your God chastens you. Therefore you shall keep the commandments of the LORD your God, to walk in His ways and to fear Him. DEUTERONOMY 8:2, 5–6 •

Evening Reading

By strength no man shall prevail.
1 SAMUEL 2:9

Then David said to the Philistine, "You come to me with a sword, with a spear, and with a javelin. But I come to you in the name of the LORD of hosts, the God of the armies of Israel, whom you have defied."... Then David put his hand in his bag and took out a stone; and he slung it and struck the Philistine in his forehead, so that the stone sank into his forehead, and he fell on his face to the earth. So David prevailed over the Philistine with a sling and a stone. 1 SAMUEL 17:45, 49–50 •

No king is saved by the multitude of an army; a mighty man is not delivered by great strength....Behold, the eye of the LORD is on those who fear Him, on those who hope in His mercy. PSALM 33:16, 18 • Both riches and honor come from You, and You reign over all. In Your hand is power and might; in Your hand it is to make great and to give strength to all. 1 CHRONICLES 29:12 •

I...boast in my infirmities, that the power of Christ may rest upon me. Therefore I take pleasure in infirmities, in reproaches, in needs, in persecutions, in distresses, for Christ's sake. For when I am weak, then I am strong. 2 CORINTHIANS 12:9–10 •

December 6

Morning Reading

It is God who works in you.
PHILIPPIANS 2:13

Not that we are sufficient of ourselves to think of anything as being from ourselves, but our sufficiency is from God. 2 CORINTHIANS 3:5 • A man can receive nothing unless it has been given to him from heaven. JOHN 3:27 • No one can come to Me unless the Father who sent Me draws him; and I will raise him up at the last day. JOHN 6:44 • I will give them one heart and one way, that they may fear Me forever. JEREMIAH 32:39 •

Do not be deceived, my beloved brethren. Every good gift and every perfect gift is from above, and comes down from the Father of lights, with whom there is no variation or shadow of turning. Of His own will He brought us forth by the word of truth, that we might be a kind of firstfruits of His creatures. JAMES 1:16–18 •

For we are His workmanship, created in Christ Jesus for good works, which God prepared beforehand that we should walk in them. EPHESIANS 2:10 •

LORD, You will establish peace for us, for You have also done all our works in us. ISAIAH 26:12 •

Evening Reading

The spirit indeed is willing, but the flesh is weak.
MATTHEW 26:41

In the way of Your judgments, O LORD, we have waited for You; the desire of our soul is for Your name and for the remembrance of You. With my soul I have desired You in the night, yes, by my spirit within me I will seek You early. ISAIAH 26:8–9 •

I know that in me (that is, in my flesh) nothing good dwells; for to will is present with me, but how to perform what is good I do not find....For I delight in the law of God according to the inward man. But I see another law in my members, warring against the law of my mind, and bringing me into captivity to the law of sin which is in my members. ROMANS 7:18, 22–23 • The flesh lusts against the Spirit, and the Spirit against the flesh; and these are contrary to one another, so that you do not do the things that you wish. GALATIANS 5:17 •

I can do all things through Christ who strengthens me. PHILIPPIANS 4:13 • Our sufficiency is from God. 2 CORINTHIANS 3:5 • My grace is sufficient for you. 2 CORINTHIANS 12:9 •

December 7

Morning Reading

He made Him who knew no sin to be sin for us,
that we might become the righteousness of God in Him.
2 CORINTHIANS 5:21

The LORD has laid on Him the iniquity of us all. ISAIAH 53:6 • Who Himself bore our sins in His own body on the tree, that we, having died to sins, might live for righteousness; by whose stripes you were healed. 1 PETER 2:24 • As by one man's disobedience many were made sinners, so also by one Man's obedience many will be made righteous. ROMANS 5:19 •

But when the kindness and the love of God our Savior toward man appeared, not by works of righteousness which we have done, but according to His mercy He saved us, through the washing of regeneration and renewing of the Holy Spirit, whom He poured out on us abundantly through Jesus Christ our Savior, that having been justified by His grace we should become heirs according to the hope of eternal life. TITUS 3:4–7 • There is therefore now no condemnation to those who are in Christ Jesus, who do not walk according to the flesh, but according to the Spirit. ROMANS 8:1 •

THE LORD OUR RIGHTEOUSNESS. JEREMIAH 23:6 •

Evening Reading

I will be like the dew to Israel.
HOSEA 14:5

The meekness and gentleness of Christ. 2 CORINTHIANS 10:1 •

A bruised reed He will not break, and smoking flax He will not quench. ISAIAH 42:3 •

[Jesus read from the book of Isaiah,] "The Spirit of the LORD is upon Me, because He has anointed Me to preach the gospel to the poor; He has sent Me to heal the brokenhearted, to proclaim liberty to the captives and recovery of sight to the blind, to set at liberty those who are oppressed; to proclaim the acceptable year of the LORD."... And He began to say to them, "Today this Scripture is fulfilled in your hearing." So all bore witness to Him, and marveled at the gracious words which proceeded out of His mouth. LUKE 4:18–19, 21–22 •

And the Lord turned and looked at Peter. And Peter remembered the word of the Lord, how He had said to him, "Before the rooster crows, you will deny Me three times." So Peter went out and wept bitterly. LUKE 22:61–62 •

He will feed His flock like a shepherd; He will gather the lambs with His arm, and carry them in His bosom, and gently lead those who are with young. ISAIAH 40:11 •

December 8

Morning Reading

Through love serve one another.
GALATIANS 5:13

Brethren, if a man is overtaken in any trespass, you who are spiritual restore such a one in a spirit of gentleness, considering yourself lest you also be tempted. Bear one another's burdens, and so fulfill the law of Christ. GALATIANS 6:1–2 •

Brethren, if anyone among you wanders from the truth, and someone turns him back, let him know that he who turns a sinner from the error of his way will save a soul from death and cover a multitude of sins. JAMES 5:19–20 • Since you have purified your souls in obeying the truth through the Spirit in sincere love of the brethren, love one another fervently with a pure heart. 1 PETER 1:22 • Owe no one anything except to love one another, for he who loves another has fulfilled the law. ROMANS 13:8 • Be kindly affectionate to one another with brotherly love, in honor giving preference to one another. ROMANS 12:10 • Yes, all of you be submissive to one another, and be clothed with humility, for "God resists the proud, but gives grace to the humble." 1 PETER 5:5 •

We then who are strong ought to bear with the scruples of the weak, and not to please ourselves. ROMANS 15:1 •

Evening Reading

The dust will return to the earth as it was.
ECCLESIASTES 12:7

The body is sown in corruption....It is sown in dishonor....It is sown in weakness, it is raised in power. It is sown a natural body. 1 CORINTHIANS 15:42–44 • The first man was of the earth, made of dust. 1 CORINTHIANS 15:47 •

Dust you are, and to dust you shall return. GENESIS 3:19 • One dies in his full strength, being wholly at ease and secure....Another man dies in the bitterness of his soul, never having eaten with pleasure. They lie down alike in the dust, and worms cover them. JOB 21:23, 25–26 •

My flesh also will rest in hope. PSALM 16:9 • After my skin is destroyed, this I know, that in my flesh I shall see God. JOB 19:26 • The Lord Jesus Christ...will transform our lowly body that it may be conformed to His glorious body, according to the working by which He is able even to subdue all things to Himself. PHILIPPIANS 3:20–21 •

LORD, make me to know my end, and what is the measure of my days, that I may know how frail I am. PSALM 39:4 • So teach us to number our days, that we may gain a heart of wisdom. PSALM 90:12 •

December 9

Morning Reading

*To do righteousness and justice is more acceptable
to the LORD than sacrifice.*
PROVERBS 21:3

He has shown you, O man, what is good; and what does the LORD require of you but to do justly, to love mercy, and to walk humbly with your God? MICAH 6:8 • Has the LORD as great delight in burnt offerings and sacrifices, as in obeying the voice of the LORD? Behold, to obey is better than sacrifice, and to heed than the fat of rams. 1 SAMUEL 15:22 • To love Him with all the heart, with all the understanding, with all the soul, and with all the strength, and to love one's neighbor as oneself, is more than all the whole burnt offerings and sacrifices. MARK 12:33 •

So you, by the help of your God, return; observe mercy and justice, and wait on your God continually. HOSEA 12:6 • Mary...sat at Jesus' feet and heard His word. LUKE 10:39 • One thing is needed, and Mary has chosen that good part, which will not be taken away from her. LUKE 10:42 •

It is God who works in you both to will and to do for His good pleasure. PHILIPPIANS 2:13 •

Evening Reading

The spirit will return to God who gave it.
ECCLESIASTES 12:7

The LORD God formed man of the dust of the ground, and breathed into his nostrils the breath of life; and man became a living being. GENESIS 2:7 • There is a spirit in man, and the breath of the Almighty gives him understanding. JOB 32:8 • The first man Adam became a living being. 1 CORINTHIANS 15:45 • The spirit of the sons of men, which goes upward. ECCLESIASTES 3:21 •

While we are at home in the body we are absent from the Lord....We are confident, yes, well pleased rather to be absent from the body and to be present with the Lord. 2 CORINTHIANS 5:6, 8 • To...be with Christ, which is far better. PHILIPPIANS 1:23 • I do not want you to be ignorant, brethren, concerning those who have fallen asleep, lest you sorrow as others who have no hope. For if we believe that Jesus died and rose again, even so God will bring with Him those who sleep in Jesus. 1 THESSALONIANS 4:13–14 •

I go to prepare a place for you. And if I go and prepare a place for you, I will come again and receive you to Myself; that where I am, there you may be also. JOHN 14:2–3 •

December 10

Morning Reading

No one is able to snatch them out of My Father's hand.
JOHN 10:29

I know whom I have believed and am persuaded that He is able to keep what I have committed to Him until that Day. 2 TIMOTHY 1:12 • The Lord will deliver me from every evil work and preserve me for His heavenly kingdom. 2 TIMOTHY 4:18 • We are more than conquerors through Him who loved us. For I am persuaded that neither death nor life, nor angels nor principalities nor powers, nor things present nor things to come, nor height nor depth, nor any other created thing, shall be able to separate us from the love of God which is in Christ Jesus our Lord. ROMANS 8:37–39 • Your life is hidden with Christ in God. COLOSSIANS 3:3 •

Has God not chosen the poor of this world to be rich in faith and heirs of the kingdom which He promised to those who love Him? JAMES 2:5 •

May our Lord Jesus Christ Himself, and our God and Father, who has loved us and given us everlasting consolation and good hope by grace, comfort your hearts and establish you in every good word and work. 2 THESSALONIANS 2:16–17 •

Evening Reading

The perfect law of liberty.
JAMES 1:25

You shall know the truth, and the truth shall make you free....Most assuredly, I say to you, whoever commits sin is a slave of sin....Therefore if the Son makes you free, you shall be free indeed. JOHN 8:32, 34, 36 •

Stand fast therefore in the liberty by which Christ has made us free, and do not be entangled again with a yoke of bondage....For you, brethren, have been called to liberty; only do not use liberty as an opportunity for the flesh, but through love serve one another. For all the law is fulfilled in one word, even in this: "You shall love your neighbor as yourself." GALATIANS 5:1, 13–14 • Having been set free from sin, you became slaves of righteousness. ROMANS 6:18 • For the woman who has a husband is bound by the law to her husband as long as he lives. But if the husband dies, she is released from the law of her husband. ROMANS 7:2 •

The law of the Spirit of life in Christ Jesus has made me free from the law of sin and death. ROMANS 8:2 • I will walk at liberty, for I seek Your precepts. PSALM 119:45 •

December 11

Morning Reading

Do not let your good be spoken of as evil.
ROMANS 14:16

Abstain from every form of evil. 1 THESSALONIANS 5:22 • Providing honorable things, not only in the sight of the Lord, but also in the sight of men. 2 CORINTHIANS 8:21 • For this is the will of God, that by doing good you may put to silence the ignorance of foolish men. 1 PETER 2:15 •

Let none of you suffer as a murderer, a thief, an evildoer, or as a busybody in other people's matters. Yet if anyone suffers as a Christian, let him not be ashamed, but let him glorify God in this matter. 1 PETER 4:15–16 •

You, brethren, have been called to liberty; only do not use liberty as an opportunity for the flesh, but through love serve one another. GALATIANS 5:13 • Beware lest somehow this liberty of yours become a stumbling block to those who are weak. 1 CORINTHIANS 8:9 • Whoever causes one of these little ones who believe in Me to sin, it would be better for him if a millstone were hung around his neck, and he were drowned in the depth of the sea. MATTHEW 18:6 • Inasmuch as you did it to one of the least of these My brethren, you did it to Me. MATTHEW 25:40 •

Evening Reading

Awake, you who sleep, arise from the dead,
and Christ will give you light.
EPHESIANS 5:14

It is high time to awake out of sleep; for now our salvation is nearer than when we first believed. ROMANS 13:11 • Therefore let us not sleep, as others do, but let us watch and be sober. For those who sleep, sleep at night, and those who get drunk are drunk at night. But let us who are of the day be sober, putting on the breastplate of faith and love, and as a helmet the hope of salvation. 1 THESSALONIANS 5:6–8 •

Arise, shine; for your light has come! And the glory of the LORD is risen upon you. For behold, the darkness shall cover the earth, and deep darkness the people; but the LORD will arise over you, and His glory will be seen upon you. ISAIAH 60:1–2 •

Therefore gird up the loins of your mind, be sober, and rest your hope fully upon the grace that is to be brought to you at the revelation of Jesus Christ. 1 PETER 1:13 • Let your waist be girded and your lamps burning; and you yourselves be like men who wait for their master. LUKE 12:35–36 •

December 12

Morning Reading

The LORD, is in your midst.
ZEPHANIAH 3:15

Fear not, for I am with you; be not dismayed, for I am your God. I will strengthen you, yes, I will help you, I will uphold you with My righteous right hand. ISAIAH 41:10 • Strengthen the weak hands, and make firm the feeble knees. Say to those who are fearful-hearted, "Be strong, do not fear! Behold, your God will come with vengeance, with the recompense of God; He will come and save you." ISAIAH 35:3–4 • The LORD your God in your midst, the Mighty One, will save; He will rejoice over you with gladness, He will quiet you with His love, He will rejoice over you with singing. ZEPHANIAH 3:17 • Wait on the LORD; be of good courage, and He shall strengthen your heart; wait, I say, on the LORD! PSALM 27:14 •

I heard a loud voice from heaven saying, "Behold, the tabernacle of God is with men, and He will dwell with them, and they shall be His people. God Himself will be with them and be their God. And God will wipe away every tear from their eyes; there shall be no more death, nor sorrow, nor crying. There shall be no more pain, for the former things have passed away." REVELATION 21:3–4 •

Evening Reading

The LORD said to Moses, "Why do you cry to Me?
Tell the children of Israel to go forward."
EXODUS 14:15

Be of good courage, and let us be strong for our people and for the cities of our God. And may the LORD do what is good in His sight. 1 CHRONICLES 19:13 • We made our prayer to our God, and because of them we set a watch against them day and night. NEHEMIAH 4:9 •

Not everyone who says to Me, "Lord, Lord," shall enter the kingdom of heaven, but he who does the will of My Father in heaven. MATTHEW 7:21 • If anyone wants to do His will, he shall know concerning the doctrine, whether it is from God. JOHN 7:17 • Let us know, let us pursue the knowledge of the LORD. HOSEA 6:3 •

Watch and pray, lest you enter into temptation. MATTHEW 26:41 • Watch, stand fast in the faith, be brave, be strong. 1 CORINTHIANS 16:13 • Not lagging in diligence, fervent in spirit, serving the Lord. ROMANS 12:11 •

Strengthen the weak hands, and make firm the feeble knees. Say to those who are fearful-hearted, "Be strong, do not fear!" ISAIAH 35:3–4 •

December 13

Morning Reading

Be strong in the grace that is in Christ Jesus.
2 TIMOTHY 2:1

Strengthened with all might, according to His glorious power. COLOSSIANS 1:11 • As you have therefore received Christ Jesus the Lord, so walk in Him, rooted and built up in Him and established in the faith, as you have been taught, abounding in it with thanksgiving. COLOSSIANS 2:6–7 • That they may be called trees of righteousness, the planting of the LORD, that He may be glorified. ISAIAH 61:3 • Built on the foundation of the apostles and prophets, Jesus Christ Himself being the chief cornerstone, in whom the whole building, being joined together, grows into a holy temple in the Lord, in whom you also are being built together for a dwelling place of God in the Spirit. EPHESIANS 2:20–22 •

I commend you to God and to the word of His grace, which is able to build you up and give you an inheritance among all those who are sanctified. ACTS 20:32 • Being filled with the fruits of righteousness which are by Jesus Christ, to the glory and praise of God. PHILIPPIANS 1:11 •

Fight the good fight of faith. 1 TIMOTHY 6:12 • Not in any way terrified by your adversaries. PHILIPPIANS 1:28 •

Evening Reading

You render to each one according to his work.
PSALM 62:12

For no other foundation can anyone lay than that which is laid, which is Jesus Christ....If anyone's work which he has built on it endures, he will receive a reward. If anyone's work is burned, he will suffer loss; but he himself will be saved, yet so as through fire. 1 CORINTHIANS 3:11, 14–15 • We must all appear before the judgment seat of Christ, that each one may receive the things done in the body, according to what he has done, whether good or bad. 2 CORINTHIANS 5:10 •

When you do a charitable deed, do not let your left hand know what your right hand is doing, that your charitable deed may be in secret; and your Father who sees in secret will Himself reward you openly. MATTHEW 6:3–4 • After a long time the lord of those servants came and settled accounts with them. MATTHEW 25:19 •

Not that we are sufficient of ourselves to think of anything as being from ourselves, but our sufficiency is from God. 2 CORINTHIANS 3:5 • LORD, You will establish peace for us, for You have also done all our works in us. ISAIAH 26:12 •

December 14

Morning Reading

Make His praise glorious.
PSALM 66:2

This people I have formed for Myself; they shall declare My praise. ISAIAH 43:21 • I will cleanse them from all their iniquity by which they have sinned against Me, and I will pardon all their iniquities by which they have sinned and by which they have transgressed against Me. Then it shall be to Me a name of joy, a praise, and an honor before all nations of the earth. JEREMIAH 33:8–9 • Therefore by Him let us continually offer the sacrifice of praise to God, that is, the fruit of our lips, giving thanks to His name. HEBREWS 13:15 •

I will praise You, O Lord my God, with all my heart, and I will glorify Your name forevermore. For great is Your mercy toward me, and You have delivered my soul from the depths of Sheol. PSALM 86:12–13 • Who is like You, O LORD,...glorious in holiness, fearful in praises, doing wonders? EXODUS 15:11 • I will praise the name of God with a song, and will magnify Him with thanksgiving. PSALM 69:30 • They sing the song of Moses, the servant of God, and the song of the Lamb, saying: "Great and marvelous are Your works, Lord God Almighty!" REVELATION 15:3 •

Evening Reading

We...were by nature children of wrath, just as the others.
EPHESIANS 2:3

We ourselves were also once foolish, disobedient, deceived, serving various lusts and pleasures, living in malice and envy, hateful and hating one another. TITUS 3:3 • Do not marvel that I said to you, "You must be born again." JOHN 3:7 •

Job answered the LORD and said: "Behold, I am vile; what shall I answer You? I lay my hand over my mouth." JOB 40:3–4 • The LORD said to Satan, "Have you considered My servant Job, that there is none like him on the earth, a blameless and upright man, one who fears God and shuns evil?" JOB 1:8 •

Behold, I [David] was brought forth in iniquity, and in sin my mother conceived me. PSALM 51:5 • David...to whom also [God] gave testimony and said, "I have found David the son of Jesse, a man after My own heart, who will do all My will." ACTS 13:22 •

I [Paul] was formerly a blasphemer, a persecutor, and an insolent man; but I obtained mercy. 1 TIMOTHY 1:13 •

That which is born of the flesh is flesh, and that which is born of the Spirit is spirit. JOHN 3:6 •

Morning Reading

Bear one another's burdens, and so fulfill the law of Christ.
GALATIANS 6:2

Let each of you look out not only for his own interests, but also for the interests of others. Let this mind be in you which was also in Christ Jesus,...[who took] the form of a bondservant. PHILIPPIANS 2:4–5, 7 • Even the Son of Man did not come to be served, but to serve, and to give His life a ransom for many. MARK 10:45 • He died for all, that those who live should live no longer for themselves, but for Him who died for them and rose again. 2 CORINTHIANS 5:15 •

When Jesus saw her weeping, and the Jews who came with her weeping, He groaned in the spirit and was troubled. JOHN 11:33 • Jesus wept. JOHN 11:35 • Rejoice with those who rejoice, and weep with those who weep. ROMANS 12:15 •

All of you be of one mind, having compassion for one another; love as brothers, be tenderhearted, be courteous; not returning evil for evil or reviling for reviling, but on the contrary blessing, knowing that you were called to this, that you may inherit a blessing. 1 PETER 3:8–9 •

Evening Reading

Son, go, work today in my vineyard.
MATTHEW 21:28

You are no longer a slave but a son, and if a son, then an heir of God through Christ. GALATIANS 4:7 •

Reckon yourselves to be dead indeed to sin, but alive to God in Christ Jesus our Lord. Therefore do not let sin reign in your mortal body, that you should obey it in its lusts. And do not present your members as instruments of unrighteousness to sin, but present yourselves to God as being alive from the dead, and your members as instruments of righteousness to God. ROMANS 6:11–13 • [Be] obedient children, not conforming yourselves to the former lusts, as in your ignorance; but as He who called you is holy, you also be holy in all your conduct, because it is written, "Be holy, for I am holy." 1 PETER 1:14–16 • Sanctified and useful for the Master, prepared for every good work. 2 TIMOTHY 2:21 •

Therefore, my beloved brethren, be steadfast, immovable, always abounding in the work of the Lord, knowing that your labor is not in vain in the Lord. 1 CORINTHIANS 15:58 •

December 16

Morning Reading

Having loved His own who were in the world,
He loved them to the end.
JOHN 13:1

I pray for them. I do not pray for the world but for those whom You have given Me, for they are Yours. And all Mine are Yours, and Yours are Mine, and I am glorified in them....I do not pray that You should take them out of the world, but that You should keep them from the evil one. They are not of the world, just as I am not of the world. JOHN 17:9–10, 15–16 •

As the Father loved Me, I also have loved you; abide in My love. JOHN 15:9 • Greater love has no one than this, than to lay down one's life for his friends. You are My friends if you do whatever I command you. JOHN 15:13–14 • A new commandment I give to you, that you love one another; as I have loved you, that you also love one another. JOHN 13:34 •

He who has begun a good work in you will complete it until the day of Jesus Christ. PHILIPPIANS 1:6 • Christ also loved the church and gave Himself for her, that He might sanctify and cleanse her with the washing of water by the word. EPHESIANS 5:25–26 •

Evening Reading

The deep things of God.
1 CORINTHIANS 2:10

No longer do I call you servants, for a servant does not know what his master is doing; but I have called you friends, for all things that I heard from My Father I have made known to you. JOHN 15:15 • It has been given to you to know the mysteries of the kingdom of heaven. MATTHEW 13:11 •

We have received, not the spirit of the world, but the Spirit who is from God, that we might know the things that have been freely given to us by God. 1 CORINTHIANS 2:12 •

For this reason I bow my knees to the Father of our Lord Jesus Christ, from whom the whole family in heaven and earth is named, that He would grant you, according to the riches of His glory, to be strengthened with might through His Spirit in the inner man, that Christ may dwell in your hearts through faith; that you, being rooted and grounded in love, may be able to comprehend with all the saints what is the width and length and depth and height; to know the love of Christ which passes knowledge; that you may be filled with all the fullness of God. EPHESIANS 3:14–19 •

December 17

Morning Reading

Revive us, and we will call upon Your name.
PSALM 80:18

It is the Spirit who gives life. JOHN 6:63 • The Spirit also helps in our weaknesses. For we do not know what we should pray for as we ought, but the Spirit Himself makes intercession for us with groanings which cannot be uttered. Now He who searches the hearts knows what the mind of the Spirit is, because He makes intercession for the saints according to the will of God. ROMANS 8:26–27 • Praying always with all prayer and supplication in the Spirit, being watchful to this end with all perseverance. EPHESIANS 6:18 •

I will never forget Your precepts, for by them You have given me life. PSALM 119:93 • The words that I speak to you are spirit, and they are life. JOHN 6:63 • The letter kills, but the Spirit gives life. 2 CORINTHIANS 3:6 • If you abide in Me, and My words abide in you, you will ask what you desire, and it shall be done for you. JOHN 15:7 • This is the confidence that we have in Him, that if we ask anything according to His will, He hears us. 1 JOHN 5:14 •

No one can say that Jesus is Lord except by the Holy Spirit. 1 CORINTHIANS 12:3 •

Evening Reading

Have no fellowship with the unfruitful works of darkness,
but rather expose them.
EPHESIANS 5:11

Do not be deceived: "Evil company corrupts good habits." 1 CORINTHIANS 15:33 •

Do you not know that a little leaven leavens the whole lump? Therefore purge out the old leaven....I wrote to you in my epistle not to keep company with sexually immoral people. Yet I certainly did not mean with the sexually immoral people of this world, or with the covetous, or extortioners, or idolaters, since then you would need to go out of the world. But now I have written to you not to keep company with anyone named a brother, who is sexually immoral, or covetous, or an idolater, or a reviler, or a drunkard, or an extortioner; not even to eat with such a person. 1 CORINTHIANS 5:6–7, 9–11 • That you may become blameless and harmless, children of God without fault in the midst of a crooked and perverse generation, among whom you shine as lights in the world. PHILIPPIANS 2:15 •

In a great house there are not only vessels of gold and silver, but also of wood and clay, some for honor and some for dishonor. 2 TIMOTHY 2:20 •

December 18

Morning Reading

*Let us therefore come boldly to the throne of grace, that we may obtain
mercy and find grace to help in time of need.*
HEBREWS 4:16

Be anxious for nothing, but in everything by prayer and supplication, with thanksgiving, let your requests be made known to God; and the peace of God, which surpasses all understanding, will guard your hearts and minds through Christ Jesus. PHILIPPIANS 4:6–7 • You did not receive the spirit of bondage again to fear, but you received the Spirit of adoption by whom we cry out, "Abba, Father." ROMANS 8:15 •

I did not say to the seed of Jacob, "Seek Me in vain." ISAIAH 45:19 • Therefore, brethren, having boldness to enter the Holiest by the blood of Jesus, by a new and living way which He consecrated for us, through the veil, that is, His flesh, and having a High Priest over the house of God, let us draw near with a true heart in full assurance of faith, having our hearts sprinkled from an evil conscience and our bodies washed with pure water. HEBREWS 10:19–22 • So we may boldly say: "The LORD is my helper; I will not fear. What can man do to me?" HEBREWS 13:6 •

Evening Reading

You shall know the truth, and the truth shall make you free.
JOHN 8:32

Where the Spirit of the Lord is, there is liberty. 2 CORINTHIANS 3:17 • The law of the Spirit of life in Christ Jesus has made me free from the law of sin and death. ROMANS 8:2 • If the Son makes you free, you shall be free indeed. JOHN 8:36 •

Brethren, we are not children of the bondwoman but of the free. GALATIANS 4:31 • Knowing that a man is not justified by the works of the law but by faith in Jesus Christ, even we have believed in Christ Jesus, that we might be justified by faith in Christ and not by the works of the law; for by the works of the law no flesh shall be justified. GALATIANS 2:16 •

He who looks into the perfect law of liberty and continues in it, and is not a forgetful hearer but a doer of the work, this one will be blessed in what he does. JAMES 1:25 • Stand fast therefore in the liberty by which Christ has made us free, and do not be entangled again with a yoke of bondage. GALATIANS 5:1 •

December 19

Morning Reading

Unto the upright there arises light in the darkness.
PSALM 112:4

Who among you fears the LORD? Who obeys the voice of His Servant? Who walks in darkness and has no light? Let him trust in the name of the LORD and rely upon his God. ISAIAH 50:10 • Though he fall, he shall not be utterly cast down; for the LORD upholds him with His hand. PSALM 37:24 • The commandment is a lamp, and the law [is] light. PROVERBS 6:23 •

Do not rejoice over me, my enemy; when I fall, I will arise; when I sit in darkness, the LORD will be a light to me. I will bear the indignation of the LORD, because I have sinned against Him, until He pleads my case and executes justice for me. He will bring me forth to the light; I will see His righteousness. MICAH 7:8–9 •

The lamp of the body is the eye. If therefore your eye is good, your whole body will be full of light. But if your eye is bad, your whole body will be full of darkness. If therefore the light that is in you is darkness, how great is that darkness! MATTHEW 6:22–23 •

Evening Reading

He will feed His flock like a shepherd; He will gather the lambs with His arm, and carry them in His bosom, and gently lead those who are with young.
ISAIAH 40:11

Jesus...said, "I have compassion on the multitude, because they have now continued with Me three days and have nothing to eat. And I do not want to send them away hungry, lest they faint on the way." MATTHEW 15:32 • We do not have a High Priest who cannot sympathize with our weaknesses. HEBREWS 4:15 •

They brought little children to Him....And He took them up in His arms, put His hands on them, and blessed them. MARK 10:13, 16 •

I have gone astray like a lost sheep; seek Your servant. PSALM 119:176 • The Son of Man has come to seek and to save that which was lost. LUKE 19:10 • You were like sheep going astray, but have now returned to the Shepherd and Overseer of your souls. 1 PETER 2:25 •

Do not fear, little flock, for it is your Father's good pleasure to give you the kingdom. LUKE 12:32 • "I will feed My flock, and I will make them lie down," says the Lord GOD. EZEKIEL 34:15 •

December 20

Morning Reading

He chose us in Him before the foundation of the world.
EPHESIANS 1:4

That we should be holy and without blame before Him in love. EPHESIANS 1:4 •

God from the beginning chose you for salvation through sanctification by the Spirit and belief in the truth, to which He called you...for the obtaining of the glory of our Lord Jesus Christ. 2 THESSALONIANS 2:13–14 • Whom He foreknew, He also predestined to be conformed to the image of His Son, that He might be the firstborn among many brethren. Moreover whom He predestined, these He also called; whom He called, these He also justified; and whom He justified, these He also glorified. ROMANS 8:29–30 • Elect according to the foreknowledge of God the Father, in sanctification of the Spirit, for obedience and sprinkling of the blood of Jesus Christ. 1 PETER 1:2 •

I will give you a new heart and put a new spirit within you; I will take the heart of stone out of your flesh and give you a heart of flesh. EZEKIEL 36:26 • God did not call us to uncleanness, but in holiness. 1 THESSALONIANS 4:7 •

Evening Reading

If the LORD would make windows in heaven, could this thing be?
2 KINGS 7:2

Have faith in God. MARK 11:22 • Without faith it is impossible to please Him. HEBREWS 11:6 • With God all things are possible. MATTHEW 19:26 •

Is My hand shortened at all that it cannot redeem? Or have I no power to deliver? ISAIAH 50:2 •

"My thoughts are not your thoughts, nor are your ways My ways," says the LORD. "For as the heavens are higher than the earth, so are My ways higher than your ways, and My thoughts than your thoughts." ISAIAH 55:8–9 • "Try Me now in this," says the LORD of hosts, "if I will not open for you the windows of heaven and pour out for you such blessing that there will not be room enough to receive it." MALACHI 3:10 •

Behold, the Lord's hand is not shortened, that it cannot save; nor His ear heavy, that it cannot hear. ISAIAH 59:1 • LORD, it is nothing for You to help, whether with many or with those who have no power. 2 CHRONICLES 14:11 •

We should not trust in ourselves but in God who raises the dead. 2 CORINTHIANS 1:9 •

December 21

Morning Reading

The days of your mourning shall be ended.
Isaiah 60:20

In the world you will have tribulation. John 16:33 • The whole creation groans and labors with birth pangs together until now. Not only that, but we also who have the firstfruits of the Spirit, even we ourselves groan within ourselves, eagerly waiting for the adoption, the redemption of our body. Romans 8:22–23 • We who are in this tent groan, being burdened, not because we want to be unclothed, but further clothed, that mortality may be swallowed up by life. 2 Corinthians 5:4 •

These are the ones who come out of the great tribulation, and washed their robes and made them white in the blood of the Lamb. Therefore they are before the throne of God, and serve Him day and night in His temple. And He who sits on the throne will dwell among them. They shall neither hunger anymore nor thirst anymore; the sun shall not strike them, nor any heat; for the Lamb who is in the midst of the throne will shepherd them and lead them to living fountains of waters. And God will wipe away every tear from their eyes. Revelation 7:14–17 •

Evening Reading

Teacher, do You not care that we are perishing?
Mark 4:38

The Lord is good to all, and His tender mercies are over all His works. Psalm 145:9 •

Every moving thing that lives shall be food for you. I have given you all things, even as the green herbs. Genesis 9:3 • While the earth remains, seedtime and harvest, cold and heat, winter and summer, and day and night shall not cease. Genesis 8:22 •

The Lord is good, a stronghold in the day of trouble; and He knows those who trust in Him. Nahum 1:7 • God heard the voice of the lad [Ishmael]. Then the angel of God called to Hagar out of heaven, and said to her, "What ails you, Hagar? Fear not, for God has heard the voice of the lad where he is...." Then God opened her eyes, and she saw a well of water. And she went and filled the skin with water, and gave the lad a drink. Genesis 21:17, 19 •

Do not worry, saying, "What shall we eat?" or "What shall we drink?"...For your heavenly Father knows that you need all these things. Matthew 6:31–32 • Trust...in the living God, who gives us richly all things to enjoy. 1 Timothy 6:17 •

December 22

Morning Reading

Your work of faith.
1 THESSALONIANS 1:3

This is the work of God, that you believe in Him whom He sent. JOHN 6:29 •

Faith by itself, if it does not have works, is dead. JAMES 2:17 • Faith working through love. GALATIANS 5:6 • He who sows to his flesh will of the flesh reap corruption, but he who sows to the Spirit will of the Spirit reap everlasting life. GALATIANS 6:8 • We are His workmanship, created in Christ Jesus for good works, which God prepared beforehand that we should walk in them. EPHESIANS 2:10 • [Christ] gave Himself for us, that He might redeem us from every lawless deed and purify for Himself His own special people, zealous for good works. TITUS 2:14 •

We are bound to thank God always for you, brethren, as it is fitting, because your faith grows exceedingly, and the love of every one of you all abounds toward each other....Therefore we also pray always for you that our God would count you worthy of this calling, and fulfill all the good pleasure of His goodness and the work of faith with power. 2 THESSALONIANS 1:3, 11 • It is God who works in you both to will and to do for His good pleasure. PHILIPPIANS 2:13 •

Evening Reading

Where is the promise of His coming?
2 PETER 3:4

Enoch, the seventh from Adam, prophesied about these men also, saying, "Behold, the Lord comes with ten thousands of His saints, to execute judgment on all." JUDE 14–15 • Behold, He is coming with clouds, and every eye will see Him, even they who pierced Him. And all the tribes of the earth will mourn because of Him. REVELATION 1:7 •

The Lord Himself will descend from heaven with a shout, with the voice of an archangel, and with the trumpet of God. And the dead in Christ will rise first. Then we who are alive and remain shall be caught up together with them in the clouds to meet the Lord in the air. And thus we shall always be with the Lord. 1 THESSALONIANS 4:16–17 •

The grace of God that brings salvation has appeared to all men, teaching us that, denying ungodliness and worldly lusts, we should live soberly, righteously, and godly in the present age, looking for the blessed hope and glorious appearing of our great God and Savior Jesus Christ. TITUS 2:11–13 •

December 23

Morning Reading

Let him take hold of My strength, that he may make peace with Me;
and he shall make peace with Me.
ISAIAH 27:5

I know the thoughts that I think toward you, says the LORD, thoughts of peace and not of evil, to give you a future and a hope. JEREMIAH 29:11 • "There is no peace," says the LORD, "for the wicked." ISAIAH 48:22 •

In Christ Jesus you who once were far off have been brought near by the blood of Christ. For He Himself is our peace. EPHESIANS 2:13–14 •

It pleased the Father that in Him all the fullness should dwell, and by Him to reconcile all things to Himself,...having made peace through the blood of His cross. COLOSSIANS 1:19–20 • Christ Jesus, whom God set forth as a propitiation by His blood, through faith, to demonstrate His righteousness, because in His forbearance God had passed over the sins that were previously committed,...that He might be just and the justifier of the one who has faith in Jesus. ROMANS 3:24–26 • If we confess our sins, He is faithful and just to forgive us our sins and to cleanse us from all unrighteousness. 1 JOHN 1:9 •

Trust in the LORD forever, for in YAH, the LORD, is everlasting strength. ISAIAH 26:4 •

Evening Reading

God has given us eternal life, and this life is in His Son.
1 JOHN 5:11

As the Father has life in Himself, so He has granted the Son to have life in Himself. JOHN 5:26 • For as the Father raises the dead and gives life to them, even so the Son gives life to whom He will. JOHN 5:21 •

I am the resurrection and the life. He who believes in Me, though he may die, he shall live. And whoever lives and believes in Me shall never die. JOHN 11:25–26 • I am the good shepherd. The good shepherd gives His life for the sheep....I lay down My life that I may take it again. No one takes it from Me, but I lay it down of Myself. I have power to lay it down, and I have power to take it again. This command I have received from My Father. JOHN 10:11, 17–18 • No one comes to the Father except through Me. JOHN 14:6 • He who has the Son has life; he who does not have the Son of God does not have life. 1 JOHN 5:12 • For you died, and your life is hidden with Christ in God. When Christ who is our life appears, then you also will appear with Him in glory. COLOSSIANS 3:3–4 •

December 24

Morning Reading

If you live according to the flesh you will die; but if by the Spirit you put to death the deeds of the body, you will live.
ROMANS 8:13

Now the works of the flesh are evident, which are: adultery, fornication,...and the like; of which I tell you beforehand, just as I also told you in time past, that those who practice such things will not inherit the kingdom of God. But the fruit of the Spirit is love, joy, peace, long-suffering, kindness, goodness, faithfulness, gentleness, self-control. Against such there is no law. And those who are Christ's have crucified the flesh with its passions and desires. If we live in the Spirit, let us also walk in the Spirit. GALATIANS 5:19, 21–25 •

The grace of God that brings salvation has appeared to all men, teaching us that, denying ungodliness and worldly lusts, we should live soberly, righteously, and godly in the present age, looking for the blessed hope and glorious appearing of our great God and Savior Jesus Christ, who gave Himself for us, that He might redeem us from every lawless deed and purify for Himself His own special people, zealous for good works. TITUS 2:11–14 •

Evening Reading

Then the princes of the Philistines said,
"What are these Hebrews doing here?"
1 SAMUEL 29:3

If you are reproached for the name of Christ, blessed are you, for the Spirit of glory and of God rests upon you. On their part He is blasphemed, but on your part He is glorified. But let none of you suffer as a murderer, a thief, an evildoer, or as a busybody in other people's matters. 1 PETER 4:14–15 •

Do not let your good be spoken of as evil. ROMANS 14:16 • Having your conduct honorable among the Gentiles. 1 PETER 2:12 •

Do not be unequally yoked together with unbelievers. For what fellowship has righteousness with lawlessness? And what communion has light with darkness?...You are the temple of the living God....Therefore "Come out from among them and be separate, says the Lord. Do not touch what is unclean." 2 CORINTHIANS 6:14, 16–17 •

You are a chosen generation, a royal priesthood, a holy nation, His own special people, that you may proclaim the praises of Him who called you out of darkness into His marvelous light. 1 PETER 2:9 •

December 25

Morning Reading

*The kindness and the love of God our Savior
toward man appeared.*
TITUS 3:4

I have loved you with an everlasting love. JEREMIAH 31:3 •
In this the love of God was manifested toward us, that God has
sent His only begotten Son into the world, that we might live through
Him. In this is love, not that we loved God, but that He loved us and
sent His Son to be the propitiation for our sins. 1 JOHN 4:9–10 •
When the fullness of the time had come, God sent forth His Son,
born of a woman, born under the law, to redeem those who were under
the law, that we might receive the adoption as sons. GALATIANS 4:4–5 • The
Word became flesh and dwelt among us, and we beheld His glory, the
glory as of the only begotten of the Father, full of grace and truth.
JOHN 1:14 • Great is the mystery of godliness: God was manifested in the
flesh. 1 TIMOTHY 3:16 •
As the children have partaken of flesh and blood, He Himself
likewise shared in the same, that through death He might destroy him
who had the power of death, that is, the devil. HEBREWS 2:14 •

Evening Reading

Thanks be to God for His indescribable gift!
2 CORINTHIANS 9:15

Make a joyful shout to the LORD, all you lands! Serve the LORD with
gladness; come before His presence with singing....Enter into His gates
with thanksgiving, and into His courts with praise. Be thankful to Him,
and bless His name. PSALM 100:1–2, 4 • For unto us a Child is born, unto
us a Son is given; and the government will be upon His shoulder. And
His name will be called Wonderful, Counselor, Mighty God, Everlasting
Father, Prince of Peace. ISAIAH 9:6 •
He...did not spare His own Son, but delivered Him up for us all.
ROMANS 8:32 • Still having one son, his beloved, he also sent him. MARK
12:6 •
Oh, that men would give thanks to the LORD for His goodness,
and for His wonderful works to the children of men! PSALM 107:21 • Bless
the LORD, O my soul; and all that is within me, bless His holy name!
PSALM 103:1 •
My soul magnifies the Lord, and my spirit has rejoiced in God my
Savior. LUKE 1:46–47 •

December 26

Morning Reading

Be steadfast, immovable, always abounding
in the work of the Lord.
1 CORINTHIANS 15:58

Knowing that your labor is not in vain in the Lord. 1 CORINTHIANS 15:58 • As you have therefore received Christ Jesus the Lord, so walk in Him, rooted and built up in Him and established in the faith, as you have been taught, abounding in it with thanksgiving. COLOSSIANS 2:6–7 • He who endures to the end shall be saved. MATTHEW 24:13 • The ones that fell on the good ground are those who, having heard the word with a noble and good heart, keep it and bear fruit with patience. LUKE 8:15 •

By faith you stand. 2 CORINTHIANS 1:24 •

I must work the works of Him who sent Me while it is day; the night is coming when no one can work. JOHN 9:4 •

He who sows to his flesh will of the flesh reap corruption, but he who sows to the Spirit will of the Spirit reap everlasting life. And let us not grow weary while doing good, for in due season we shall reap if we do not lose heart. Therefore, as we have opportunity, let us do good to all, especially to those who are of the household of faith. GALATIANS 6:8–10 •

Evening Reading

He is also able to save to the uttermost those
who come to God through Him.
HEBREWS 7:25

I am the way, the truth, and the life. No one comes to the Father except through Me. JOHN 14:6 • Nor is there salvation in any other, for there is no other name under heaven given among men by which we must be saved. ACTS 4:12 •

My sheep hear My voice, and I know them, and they follow Me. And I give them eternal life, and they shall never perish; neither shall anyone snatch them out of My hand. JOHN 10:27–28 • He who has begun a good work in you will complete it until the day of Jesus Christ. PHILIPPIANS 1:6 • Is anything too hard for the LORD? GENESIS 18:14 •

Now to Him who is able to keep you from stumbling, and to present you faultless before the presence of His glory with exceeding joy, to God our Savior, who alone is wise, be glory and majesty, dominion and power, both now and forever. Amen. JUDE 24–25 •

December 27

Morning Reading

We do not look at the things which are seen, but at the things which are not seen. For the things which are seen are temporary, but the things which are not seen are eternal.
2 CORINTHIANS 4:18

Here we have no continuing city. HEBREWS 13:14 • You have a better and an enduring possession for yourselves in heaven. HEBREWS 10:34 •

Do not fear, little flock, for it is your Father's good pleasure to give you the kingdom. LUKE 12:32 •

Now for a little while, if need be, you have been grieved by various trials. 1 PETER 1:6 • There the wicked cease from troubling, and there the weary are at rest. JOB 3:17 •

We who are in this tent groan, being burdened. 2 CORINTHIANS 5:4 • God will wipe away every tear from their eyes; there shall be no more death, nor sorrow, nor crying. There shall be no more pain, for the former things have passed away. REVELATION 21:4 •

The sufferings of this present time are not worthy to be compared with the glory which shall be revealed in us. ROMANS 8:18 • Our light affliction, which is but for a moment, is working for us a far more exceeding and eternal weight of glory. 2 CORINTHIANS 4:17 •

Evening Reading

He Himself is our peace.
EPHESIANS 2:14

God was in Christ reconciling the world to Himself, not imputing their trespasses to them....For He made Him who knew no sin to be sin for us, that we might become the righteousness of God in Him. 2 CORINTHIANS 5:19, 21 • To reconcile all things to Himself, by Him, whether things on earth or things in heaven, having made peace through the blood of His cross. And you, who once were alienated and enemies in your mind by wicked works, yet now He has reconciled in the body of His flesh through death, to present you holy, and blameless, and above reproach in His sight. COLOSSIANS 1:20–22 • [He has] wiped out the handwriting of requirements that was against us, which was contrary to us. And He has taken it out of the way, having nailed it to the cross. COLOSSIANS 2:14 • Having abolished in His flesh the enmity, that is, the law of commandments contained in ordinances, so as to create in Himself one new man from the two, thus making peace. EPHESIANS 2:15 •

Peace I leave with you, My peace I give to you; not as the world gives do I give to you. Let not your heart be troubled, neither let it be afraid. JOHN 14:27 •

December 28

Morning Reading

Your sins are forgiven you.
MARK 2:5

I will forgive their iniquity, and their sin I will remember no more. JEREMIAH 31:34 • Who can forgive sins but God alone? MARK 2:7 •

I, even I, am He who blots out your transgressions for My own sake; and I will not remember your sins. ISAIAH 43:25 • Blessed is he whose transgression is forgiven, whose sin is covered. Blessed is the man to whom the LORD does not impute iniquity. PSALM 32:1-2 • Who is a God like You, pardoning iniquity? MICAH 7:18 •

God in Christ forgave you. EPHESIANS 4:32 • The blood of Jesus Christ His Son cleanses us from all sin. If we say that we have no sin, we deceive ourselves, and the truth is not in us. If we confess our sins, He is faithful and just to forgive us our sins and to cleanse us from all unrighteousness. 1 JOHN 1:7-9 •

As far as the east is from the west, so far has He removed our transgressions from us. PSALM 103:12 • Sin shall not have dominion over you, for you are not under law but under grace. ROMANS 6:14 • Having been set free from sin, you became slaves of righteousness. ROMANS 6:18 •

Evening Reading

We wish to see Jesus.
JOHN 12:21

O LORD, we have waited for You; the desire of our soul is for Your name and for the remembrance of You. ISAIAH 26:8 •

The LORD is near to all who call upon Him, to all who call upon Him in truth. PSALM 145:18 •

Where two or three are gathered together in My name, I am there in the midst of them. MATTHEW 18:20 • I will not leave you orphans; I will come to you. JOHN 14:18 • Lo, I am with you always, even to the end of the age. MATTHEW 28:20 •

Let us run with endurance the race that is set before us, looking unto Jesus, the author and finisher of our faith. HEBREWS 12:1-2 •

Now we see in a mirror, dimly, but then face to face. 1 CORINTHIANS 13:12 • Having a desire to depart and be with Christ, which is far better. PHILIPPIANS 1:23 •

Beloved, now we are children of God; and it has not yet been revealed what we shall be, but we know that when He is revealed, we shall be like Him, for we shall see Him as He is. And everyone who has this hope in Him purifies himself, just as He is pure. 1 JOHN 3:2-3 •

December 29

Morning Reading

Understand what the will of the Lord is.
EPHESIANS 5:17

This is the will of God, [even] your sanctification. 1 THESSALONIANS 4:3 • Now acquaint yourself with Him, and be at peace; thereby good will come to you. JOB 22:21 • This is eternal life, that they may know You, the only true God, and Jesus Christ whom You have sent. JOHN 17:3 • We know that the Son of God has come and has given us an understanding, that we may know Him who is true; and we are in Him who is true, in His Son Jesus Christ. This is the true God and eternal life. 1 JOHN 5:20 •

We...do not cease to pray for you, and to ask that you may be filled with the knowledge of His will in all wisdom and spiritual understanding. COLOSSIANS 1:9 • That the God of our Lord Jesus Christ, the Father of glory, may give to you the spirit of wisdom and revelation in the knowledge of Him, the eyes of your understanding being enlightened; that you may know what is the hope of His calling, what are the riches of the glory of His inheritance in the saints, and what is the exceeding greatness of His power toward us who believe. EPHESIANS 1:17–19 •

Evening Reading

Draw near to God and He will draw near to you.
JAMES 4:8

Enoch walked with God. GENESIS 5:24 • Can two walk together, unless they are agreed? AMOS 3:3 • It is good for me to draw near to God. PSALM 73:28 •

The LORD is with you while you are with Him. If you seek Him, He will be found by you; but if you forsake Him, He will forsake you....But when in their trouble they turned to the LORD God of Israel, and sought Him, He was found by them. 2 CHRONICLES 15:2, 4 •

For I know the thoughts that I think toward you, says the LORD, thoughts of peace and not of evil, to give you a future and a hope. Then you will call upon Me and go and pray to Me, and I will listen to you. And you will seek Me and find Me, when you search for Me with all your heart. JEREMIAH 29:11–13 •

Therefore, brethren, having boldness to enter the Holiest by the blood of Jesus, by a new and living way,...and having a High Priest over the house of God, let us draw near with a true heart in full assurance of faith. HEBREWS 10:19–22 •

December 30

Morning Reading

Blameless in the day of our Lord Jesus Christ.
1 CORINTHIANS 1:8

You, who once were alienated and enemies in your mind by wicked works, yet now He has reconciled in the body of His flesh through death, to present you holy, and blameless, and above reproach in His sight; if indeed you continue in the faith, grounded and steadfast, and are not moved away from the hope of the gospel. COLOSSIANS 1:21–23 • That you may become blameless and harmless, children of God without fault in the midst of a crooked and perverse generation, among whom you shine as lights in the world. PHILIPPIANS 2:15 •

Therefore, beloved, looking forward to these things, be diligent to be found by Him in peace, without spot and blameless. 2 PETER 3:14 • That you may be sincere and without offense till the day of Christ. PHILIPPIANS 1:10 •

Now to Him who is able to keep you from stumbling, and to present you faultless before the presence of His glory with exceeding joy, to God our Savior, who alone is wise, be glory and majesty, dominion and power, both now and forever. JUDE 24–25 •

Evening Reading

He will guard the feet of His saints.
1 SAMUEL 2:9

If we say that we have fellowship with Him, and walk in darkness, we lie and do not practice the truth. But if we walk in the light as He is in the light, we have fellowship with one another, and the blood of Jesus Christ His Son cleanses us from all sin. 1 JOHN 1:6–7 • He who is bathed needs only to wash his feet, but is completely clean; and you are clean, but not all of you. JOHN 13:10 •

I have taught you in the way of wisdom; I have led you in right paths. When you walk, your steps will not be hindered, and when you run, you will not stumble....Do not enter the path of the wicked, and do not walk in the way of evil. Avoid it, do not travel on it; turn away from it and pass on....Let your eyes look straight ahead, and your eyelids look right before you. Ponder the path of your feet, and let all your ways be established. Do not turn to the right or the left; remove your foot from evil. PROVERBS 4:11–12, 14–15, 25–27 •

The Lord will deliver me from every evil work and preserve me for His heavenly kingdom. To Him be glory forever and ever. Amen! 2 TIMOTHY 4:18 •

December 31

Morning Reading

The LORD your God carried you, as a man carries his son,
in all the way that you went until you came to this place.
DEUTERONOMY 1:31

I bore you on eagles' wings and brought you to Myself. EXODUS 19:4 •
In His love and in His pity He redeemed them; and He bore them and
carried them all the days of old. ISAIAH 63:9 • As an eagle stirs up its nest,
hovers over its young, spreading out its wings, taking them up, carrying them on its wings, so the LORD alone led him. DEUTERONOMY 32:11–12 •

Even to your old age, I am He, and even to gray hairs I will carry
you! I have made, and I will bear; even I will carry, and will deliver you.
ISAIAH 46:4 • This is God, our God forever and ever; He will be our guide
even to death. PSALM 48:14 •

Cast your burden on the LORD, and He shall sustain you; He shall
never permit the righteous to be moved. PSALM 55:22 • Do not worry about
your life, what you will eat or what you will drink; nor about your body,
what you will put on....For your heavenly Father knows that you need all
these things. MATTHEW 6:25, 32 •

Thus far the LORD has helped us. 1 SAMUEL 7:12 •

Evening Reading

There remains very much land yet to be possessed.
JOSHUA 13:1

Not that I have already attained, or am already perfected; but I
press on, that I may lay hold of that for which Christ Jesus has also laid
hold of me. PHILIPPIANS 3:12 •

Therefore you shall be perfect. MATTHEW 5:48 • Giving all diligence,
add to your faith virtue, to virtue knowledge, to knowledge self-control,
to self-control perseverance, to perseverance godliness, to godliness
brotherly kindness, and to brotherly kindness love. 2 PETER 1:5–7 •

This I pray, that your love may abound still more and more in
knowledge and all discernment. PHILIPPIANS 1:9 •

It is written: "Eye has not seen, nor ear heard, nor have entered into
the heart of man the things which God has prepared for those who love
Him." But God has revealed them to us through His Spirit. 1 CORINTHIANS
2:9–10 •

There remains therefore a rest for the people of God. HEBREWS 4:9 •
Your eyes will see the King in His beauty; they will see the land that is
very far off. ISAIAH 33:17 •